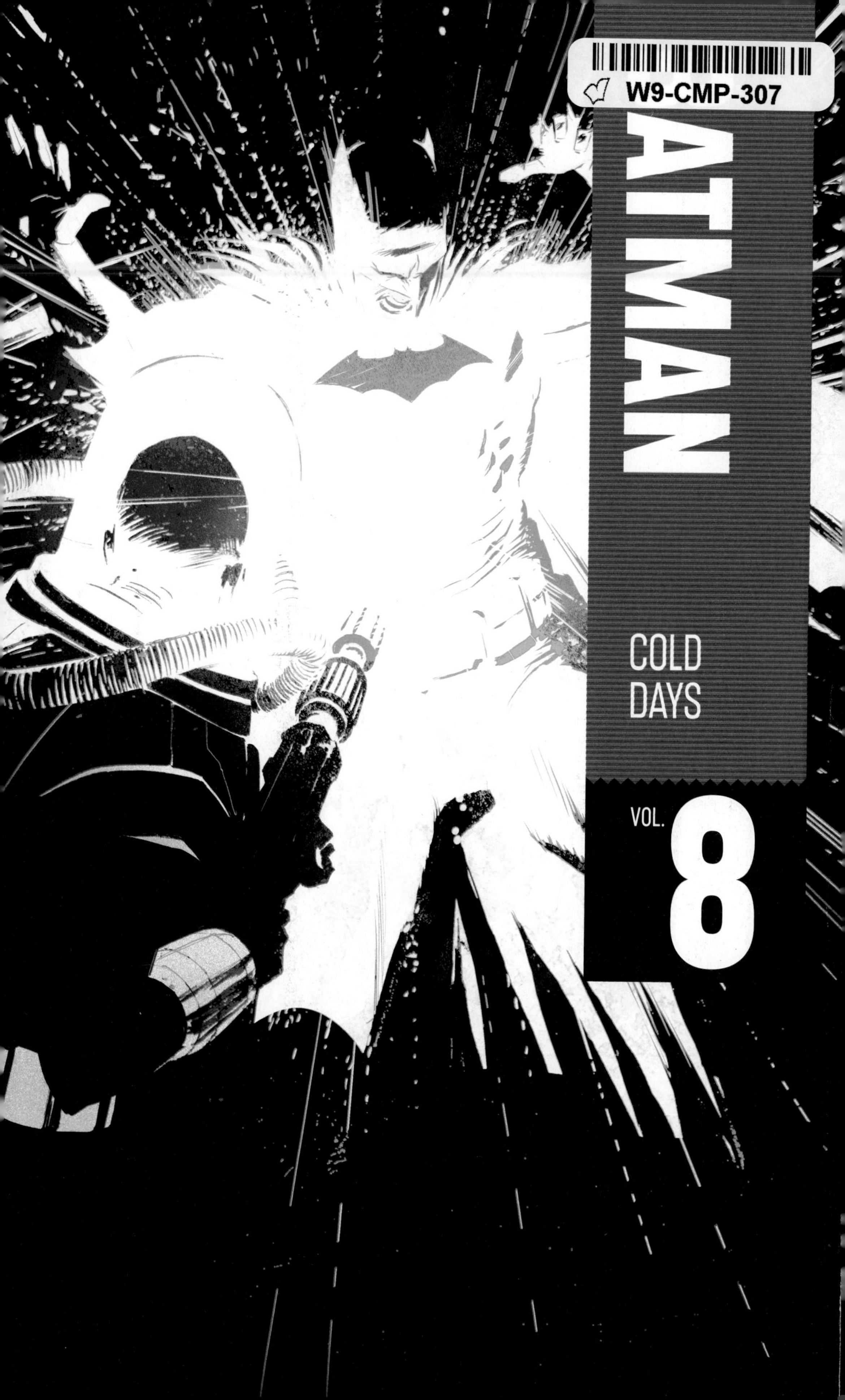
ATMAN
COLD
DAYS
VOL.
8

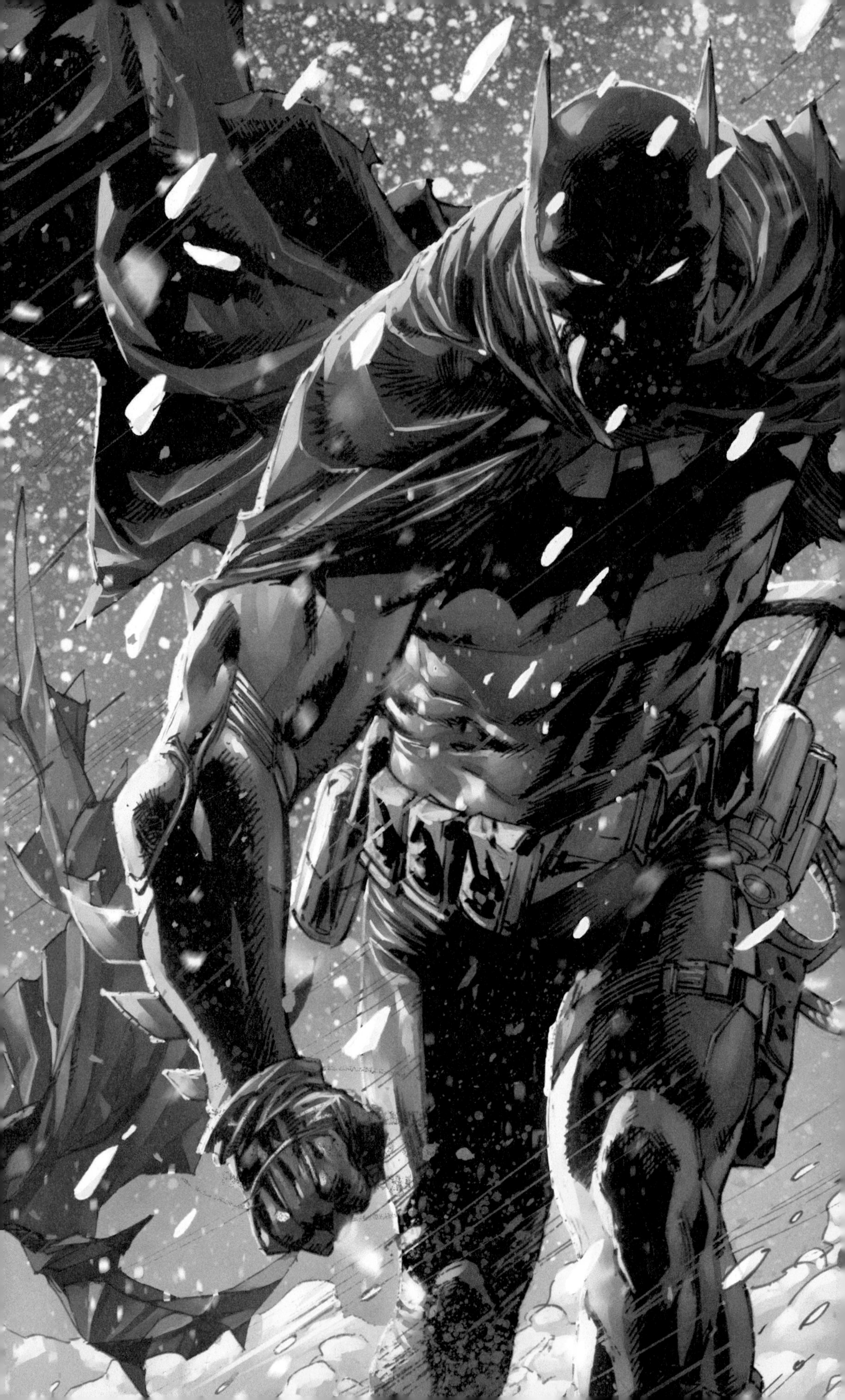

BATMAN
COLD DAYS

writer

TOM KING

artists

LEE WEEKS
TONY S. DANIEL
MATT WAGNER
DANNY MIKI
MARK BUCKINGHAM
ANDREW PEPOY

colorists

TOMEU MOREY
ELIZABETH BREITWEISER

letterer

CLAYTON COWLES

collection cover artists

LEE WEEKS and
ELIZABETH BREITWEISER

BATMAN created by BOB KANE with BILL FINGER

VOL.

8

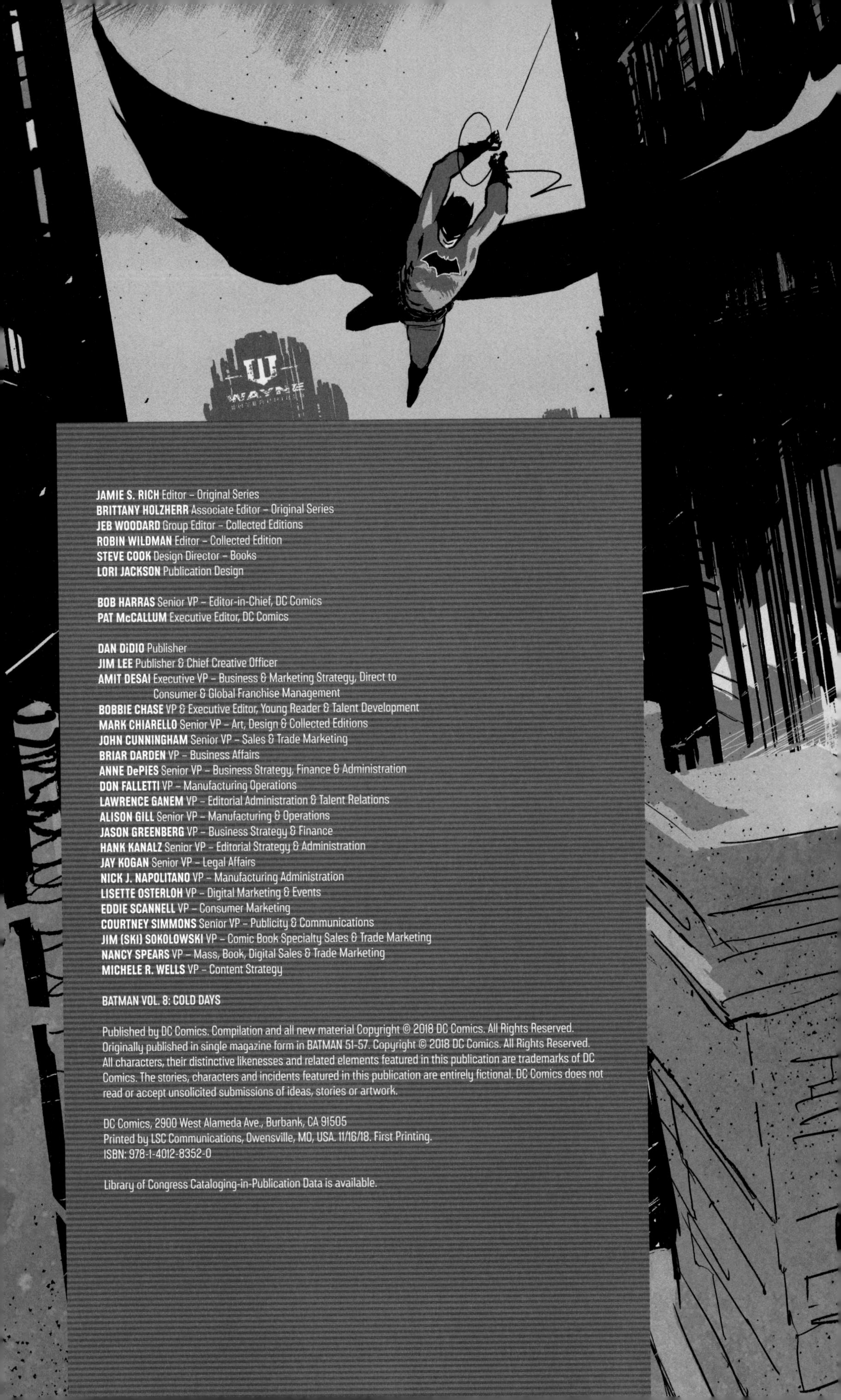
WAYNE

JAMIE S. RICH Editor – Original Series
BRITTANY HOLZHERR Associate Editor – Original Series
JEB WOODARD Group Editor – Collected Editions
ROBIN WILDMAN Editor – Collected Edition
STEVE COOK Design Director – Books
LORI JACKSON Publication Design

BOB HARRAS Senior VP – Editor-in-Chief, DC Comics
PAT McCALLUM Executive Editor, DC Comics

DAN DiDIO Publisher
JIM LEE Publisher & Chief Creative Officer
AMIT DESAI Executive VP – Business & Marketing Strategy, Direct to Consumer & Global Franchise Management
BOBBIE CHASE VP & Executive Editor, Young Reader & Talent Development
MARK CHIARELLO Senior VP – Art, Design & Collected Editions
JOHN CUNNINGHAM Senior VP – Sales & Trade Marketing
BRIAR DARDEN VP – Business Affairs
ANNE DePIES Senior VP – Business Strategy, Finance & Administration
DON FALLETTI VP – Manufacturing Operations
LAWRENCE GANEM VP – Editorial Administration & Talent Relations
ALISON GILL Senior VP – Manufacturing & Operations
JASON GREENBERG VP – Business Strategy & Finance
HANK KANALZ Senior VP – Editorial Strategy & Administration
JAY KOGAN Senior VP – Legal Affairs
NICK J. NAPOLITANO VP – Manufacturing Administration
LISETTE OSTERLOH VP – Digital Marketing & Events
EDDIE SCANNELL VP – Consumer Marketing
COURTNEY SIMMONS Senior VP – Publicity & Communications
JIM (SKI) SOKOLOWSKI VP – Comic Book Specialty Sales & Trade Marketing
NANCY SPEARS VP – Mass, Book, Digital Sales & Trade Marketing
MICHELE R. WELLS VP – Content Strategy

BATMAN VOL. 8: COLD DAYS

DC Comics, 2900 West Alameda Ave., Burbank, CA 91505
Printed by LSC Communications, Owensville, MO, USA. 11/16/18. First Printing.
ISBN: 978-1-4012-8352-0

Library of Congress Cataloging-in-Publication Data is available.

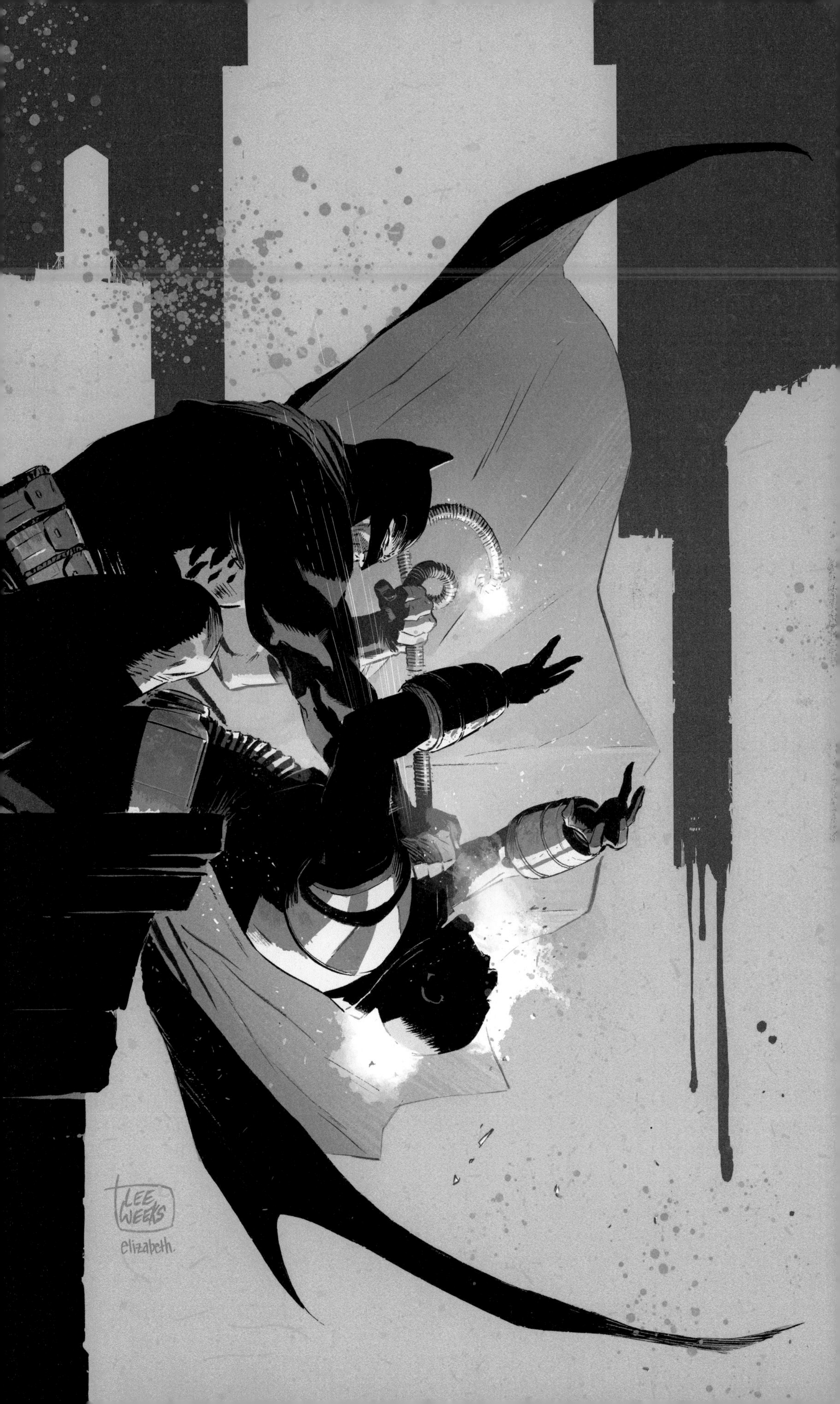
LEE WEEKS
elizabeth.

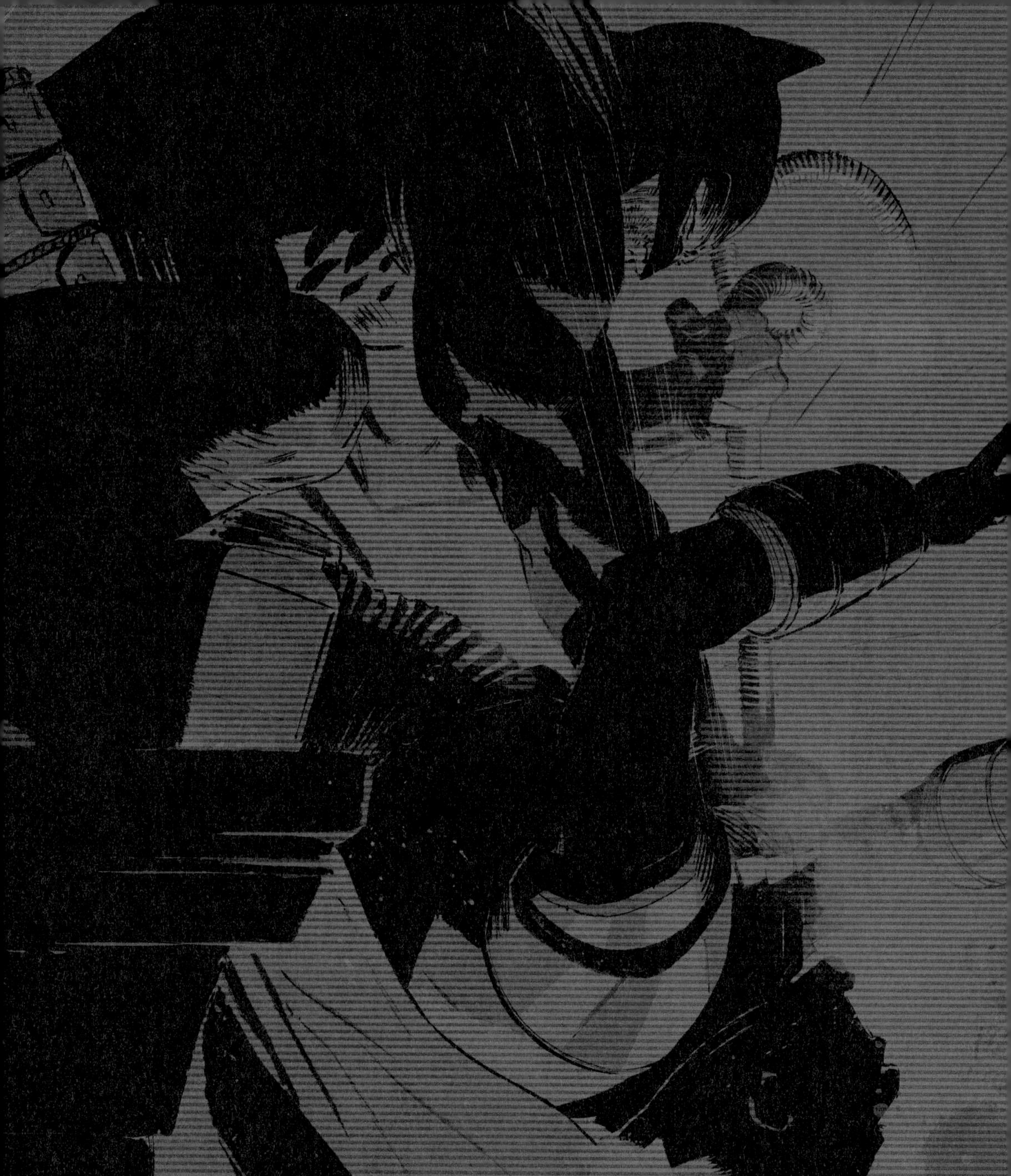

BATMAN
#51

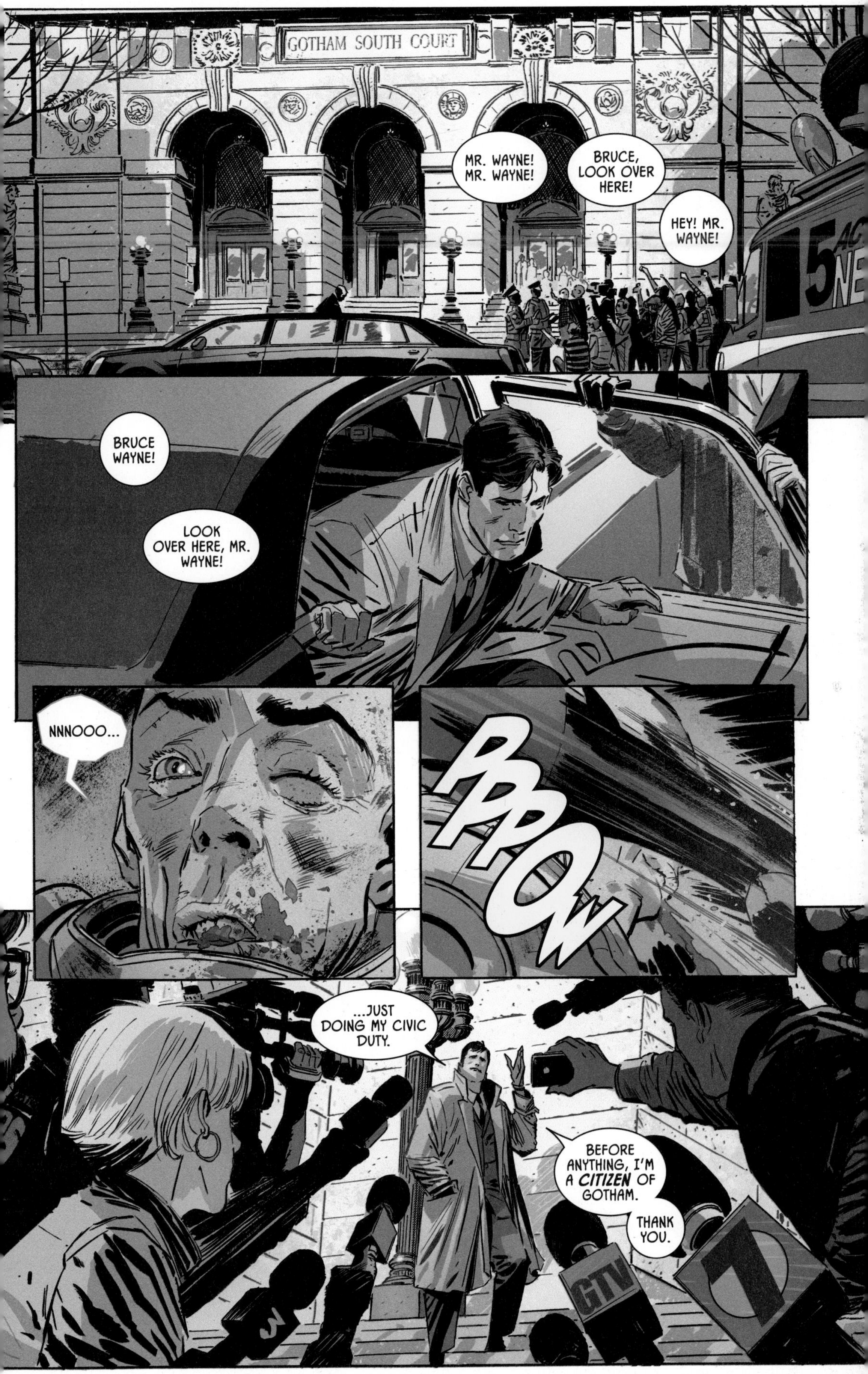
GOTHAM SOUTH COURT
MR. WAYNE! MR. WAYNE!
BRUCE, LOOK OVER HERE!
HEY! MR. WAYNE!
BRUCE WAYNE!
LOOK OVER HERE, MR. WAYNE!
NNNOOO...
PPPOW
...JUST DOING MY CIVIC DUTY.
BEFORE ANYTHING, I'M A *CITIZEN* OF GOTHAM.
THANK YOU.
GTV

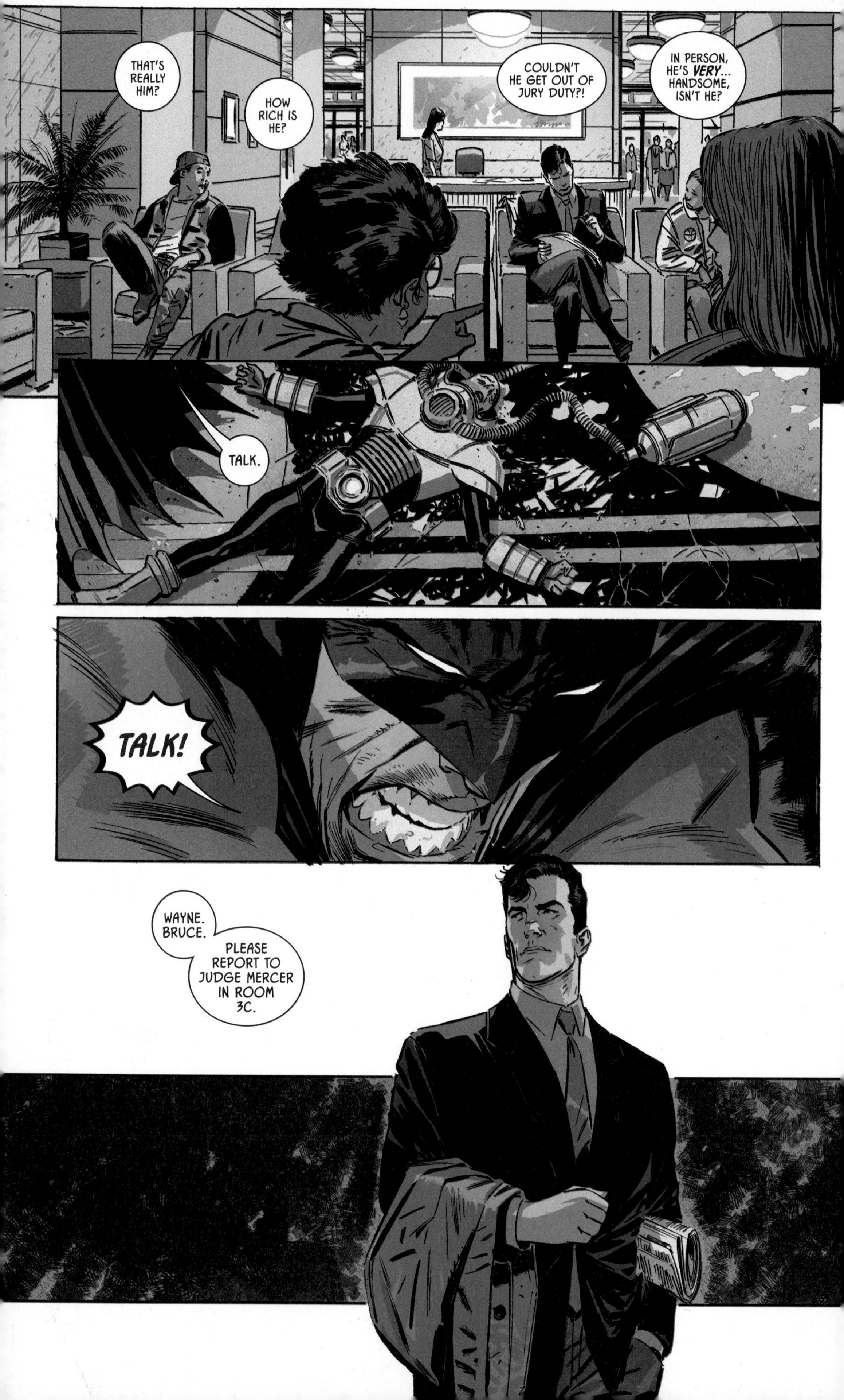
THAT'S REALLY HIM?
HOW RICH IS HE?
COULDN'T HE GET OUT OF JURY DUTY?!
IN PERSON, HE'S VERY... HANDSOME, ISN'T HE?
TALK.
TALK!
WAYNE. BRUCE.
PLEASE REPORT TO JUDGE MERCER IN ROOM 3C.

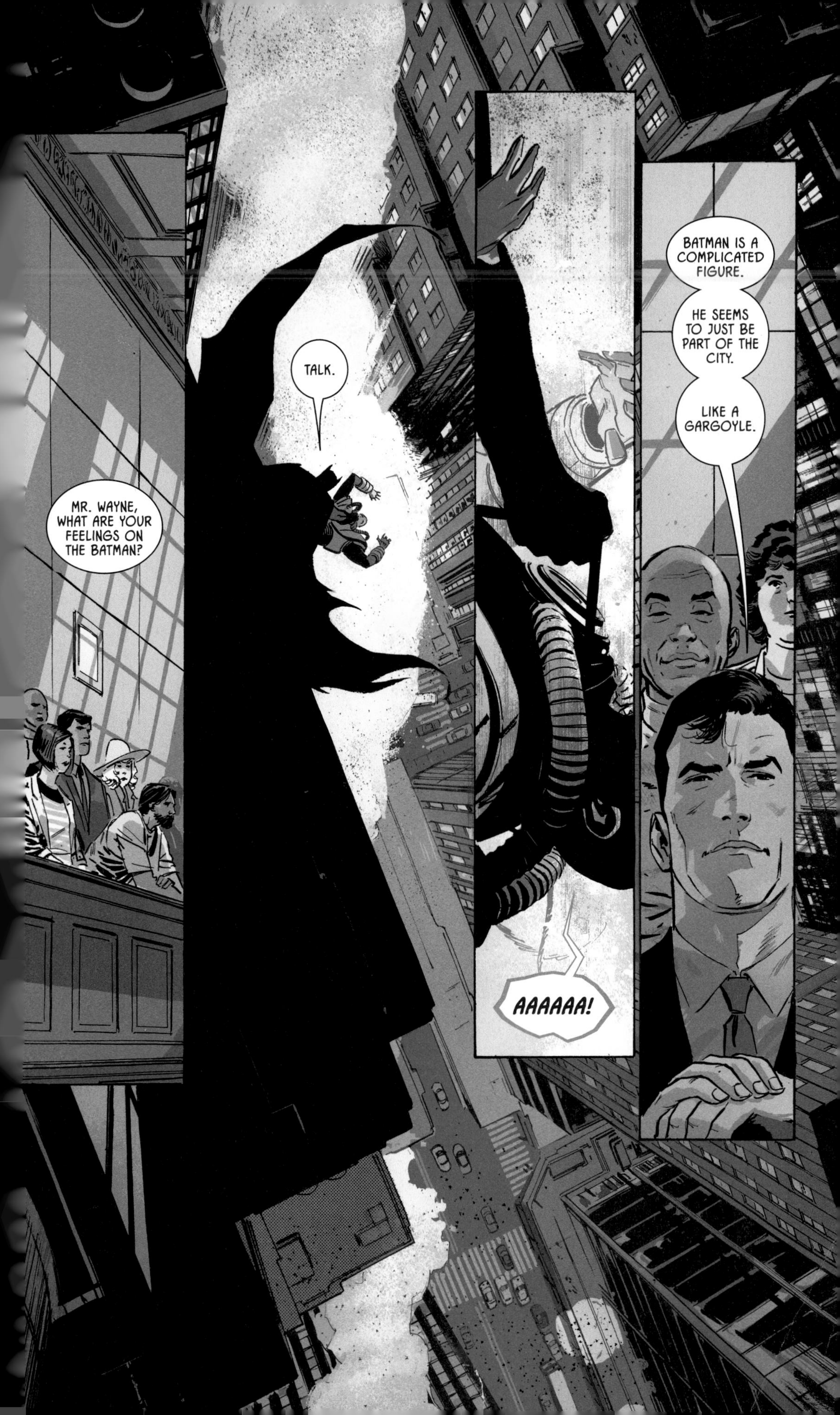
MR. WAYNE, WHAT ARE YOUR FEELINGS ON THE BATMAN?
TALK.
AAAAAA!
BATMAN IS A COMPLICATED FIGURE.
HE SEEMS TO JUST BE PART OF THE CITY.
LIKE A GARGOYLE.

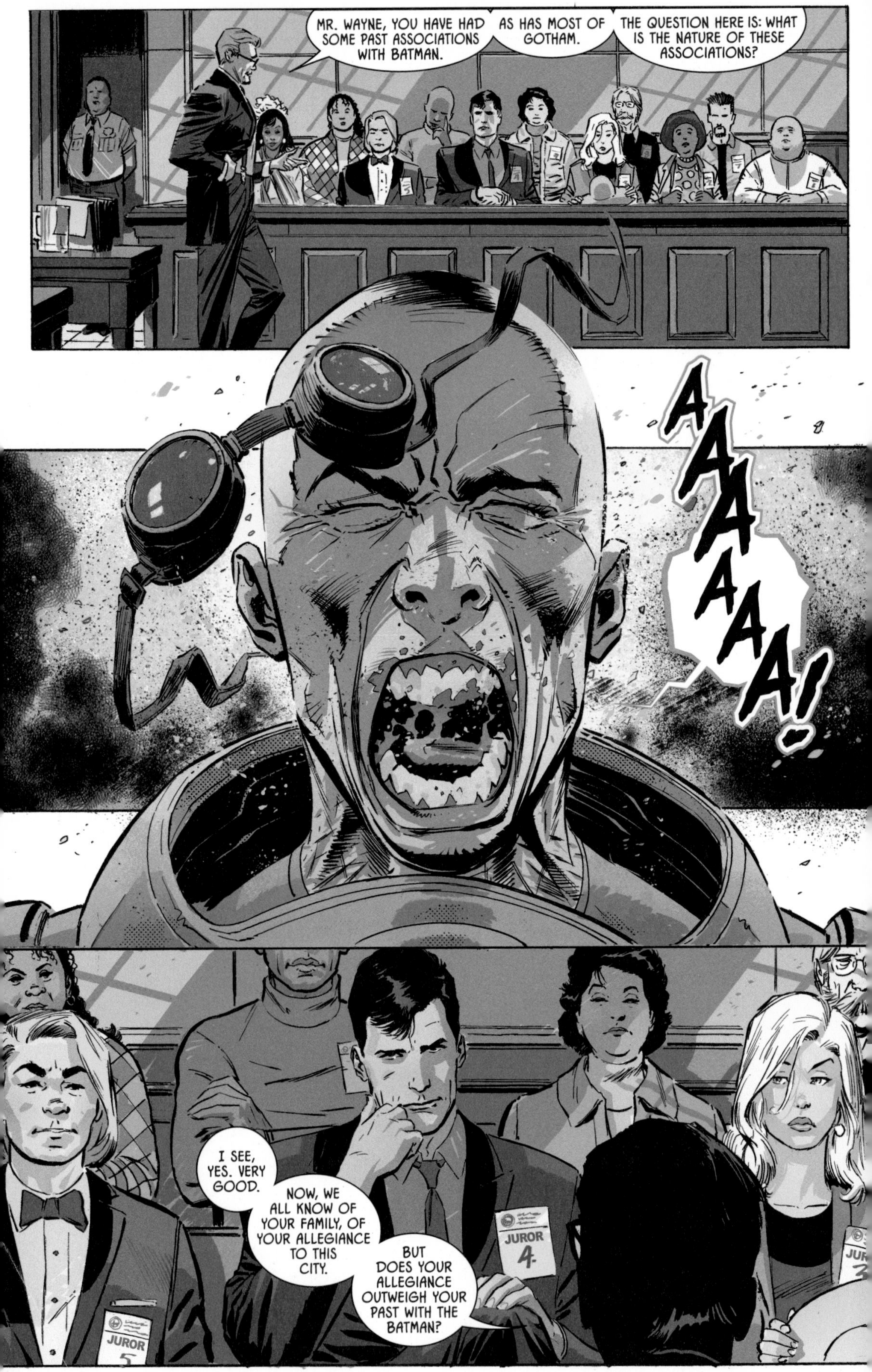
MR. WAYNE, YOU HAVE HAD SOME PAST ASSOCIATIONS WITH BATMAN.
AS HAS MOST OF GOTHAM.
THE QUESTION HERE IS: WHAT IS THE NATURE OF THESE ASSOCIATIONS?
AAAAAA!
I SEE, YES. VERY GOOD.
NOW, WE ALL KNOW OF YOUR FAMILY, OF YOUR ALLEGIANCE TO THIS CITY.
BUT DOES YOUR ALLEGIANCE OUTWEIGH YOUR PAST WITH THE BATMAN?
JUROR 4
JUROR 5

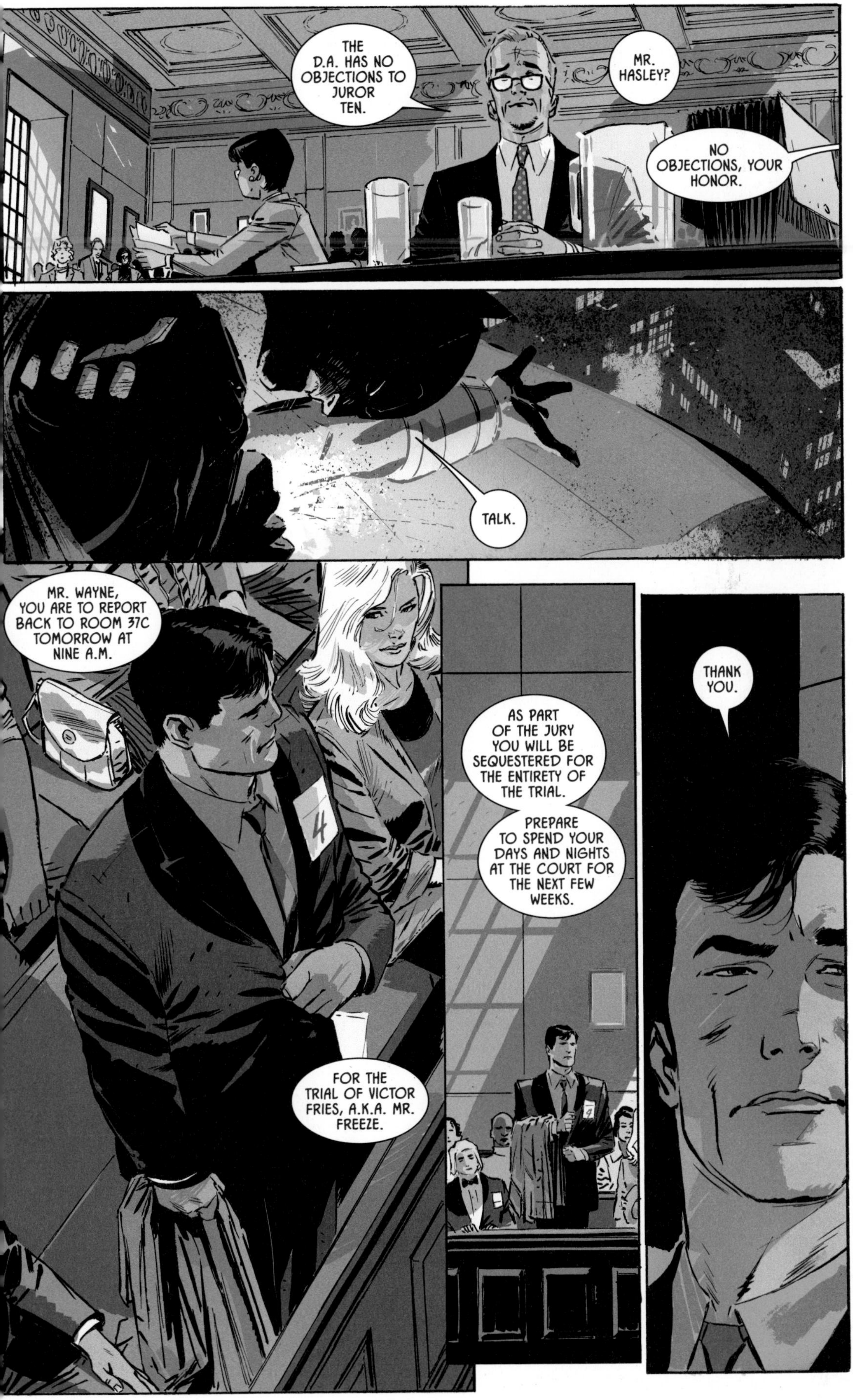
THE D.A. HAS NO OBJECTIONS TO JUROR TEN.
MR. HASLEY?
NO OBJECTIONS, YOUR HONOR.
TALK.
MR. WAYNE, YOU ARE TO REPORT BACK TO ROOM 37C TOMORROW AT NINE A.M.
FOR THE TRIAL OF VICTOR FRIES, A.K.A. MR. FREEZE.
AS PART OF THE JURY YOU WILL BE SEQUESTERED FOR THE ENTIRETY OF THE TRIAL.
PREPARE TO SPEND YOUR DAYS AND NIGHTS AT THE COURT FOR THE NEXT FEW WEEKS.
THANK YOU.

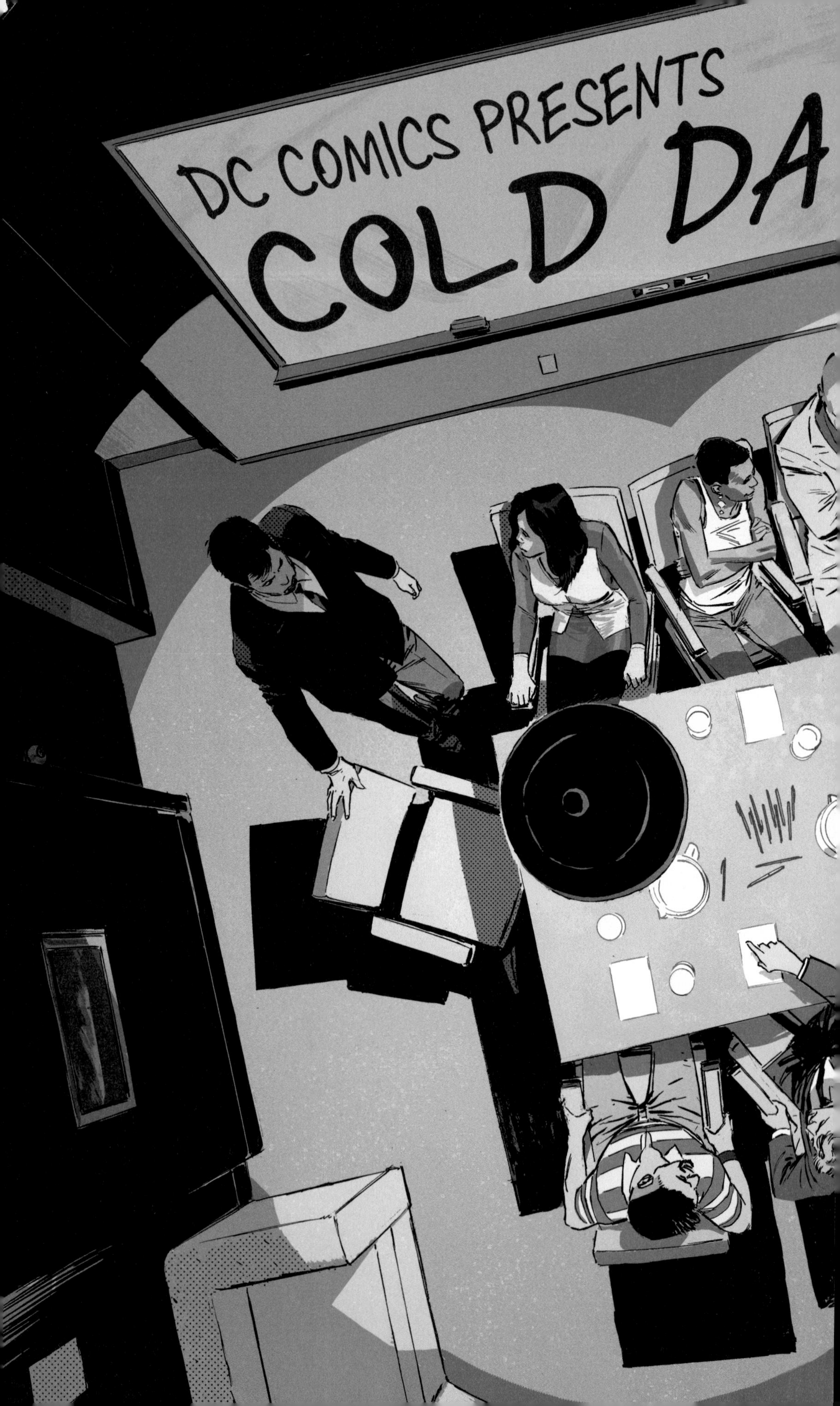
DC COMICS PRESENTS
COLD DA

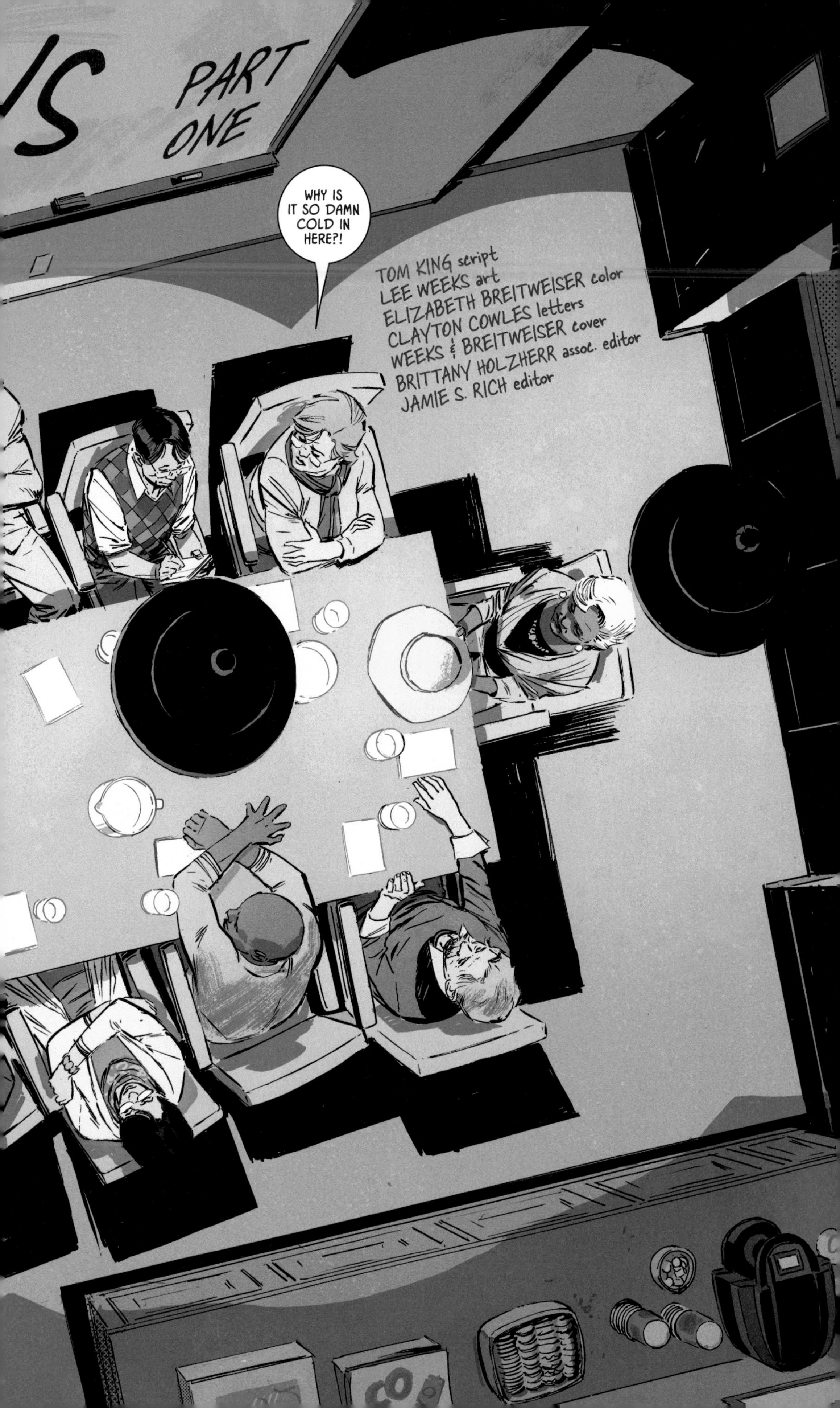

PART ONE
WHY IS IT SO DAMN COLD IN HERE?!
TOM KING script
LEE WEEKS art
ELIZABETH BREITWEISER color
CLAYTON COWLES letters
WEEKS & BREITWEISER cover
BRITTANY HOLZHERR assoc. editor
JAMIE S. RICH editor

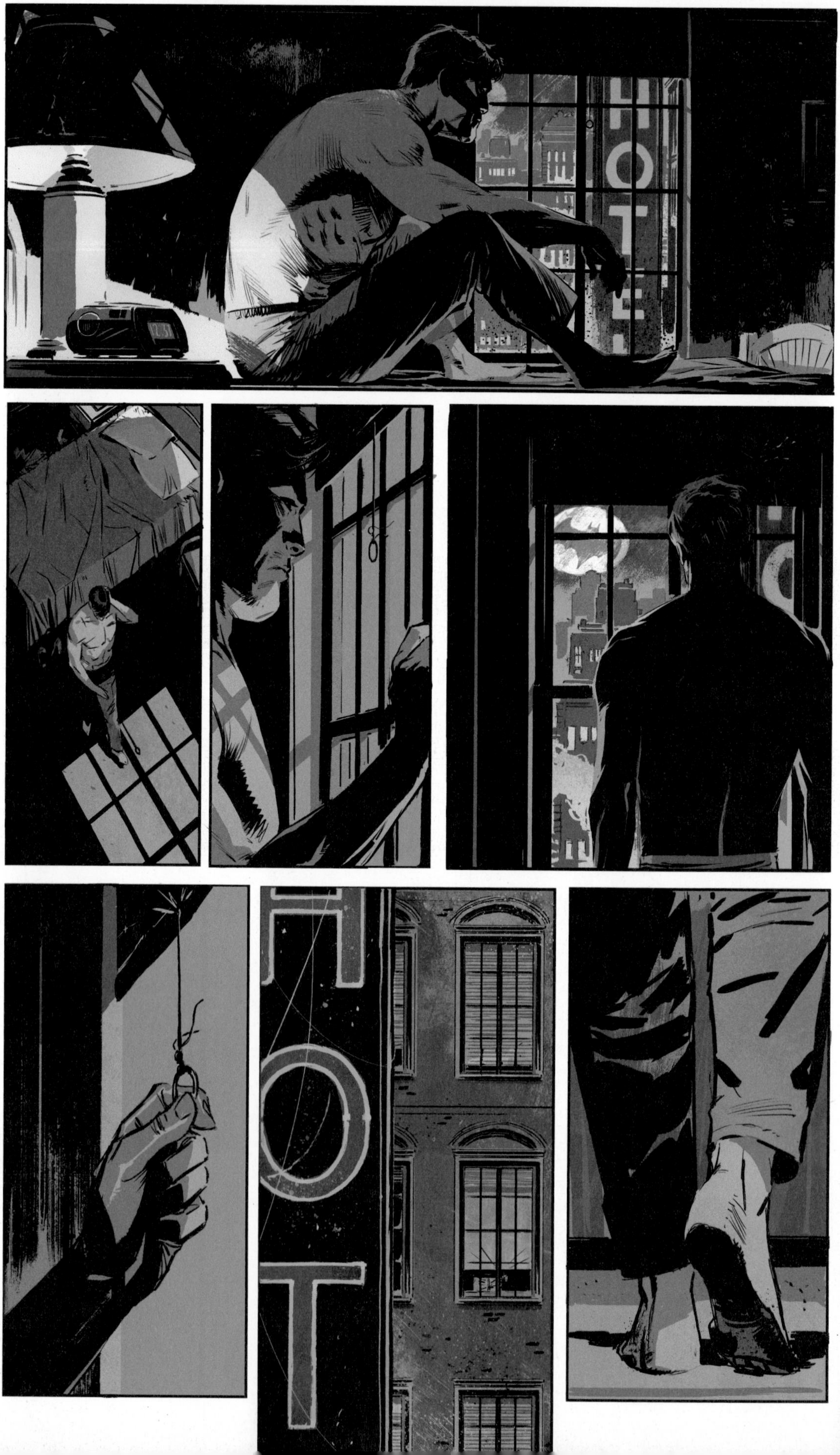

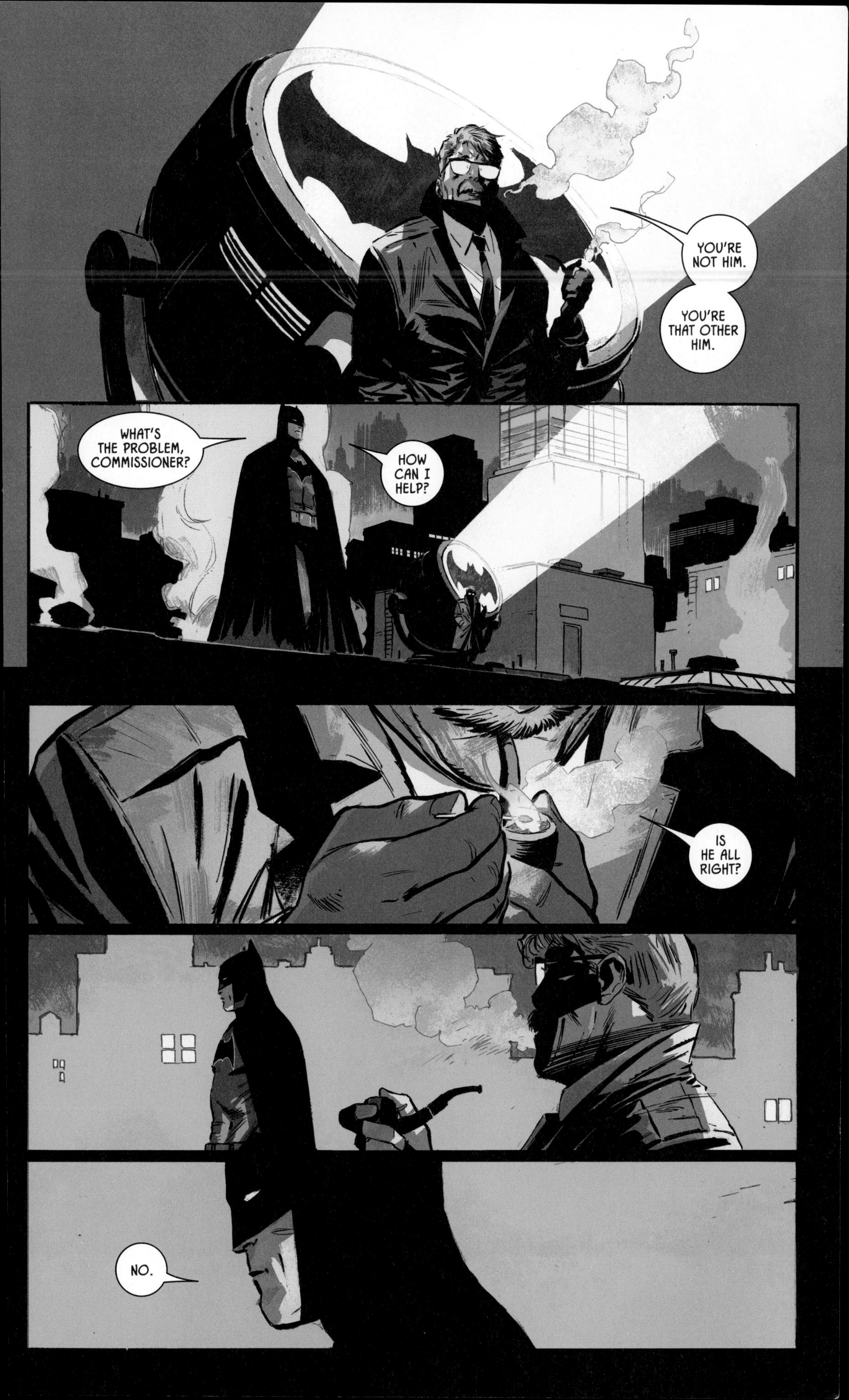
YOU'RE NOT HIM.
YOU'RE THAT OTHER HIM.
WHAT'S THE PROBLEM, COMMISSIONER?
HOW CAN I HELP?
IS HE ALL RIGHT?
NO.

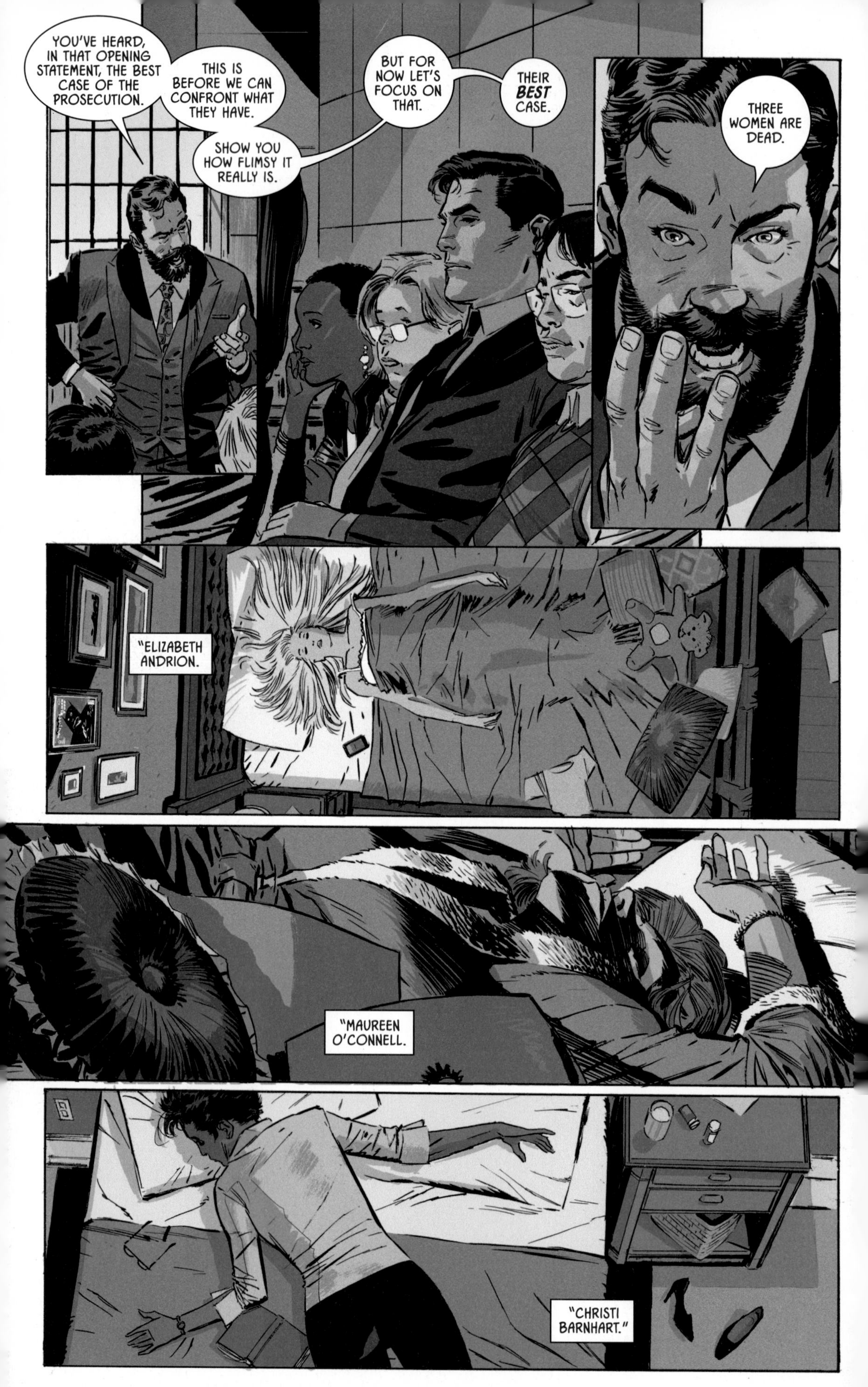
YOU'VE HEARD, IN THAT OPENING STATEMENT, THE BEST CASE OF THE PROSECUTION.
THIS IS BEFORE WE CAN CONFRONT WHAT THEY HAVE.
SHOW YOU HOW FLIMSY IT REALLY IS.
BUT FOR NOW LET'S FOCUS ON THAT.
THEIR BEST CASE.
THREE WOMEN ARE DEAD.
"ELIZABETH ANDRION.
"MAUREEN O'CONNELL.
"CHRISTI BARNHART."

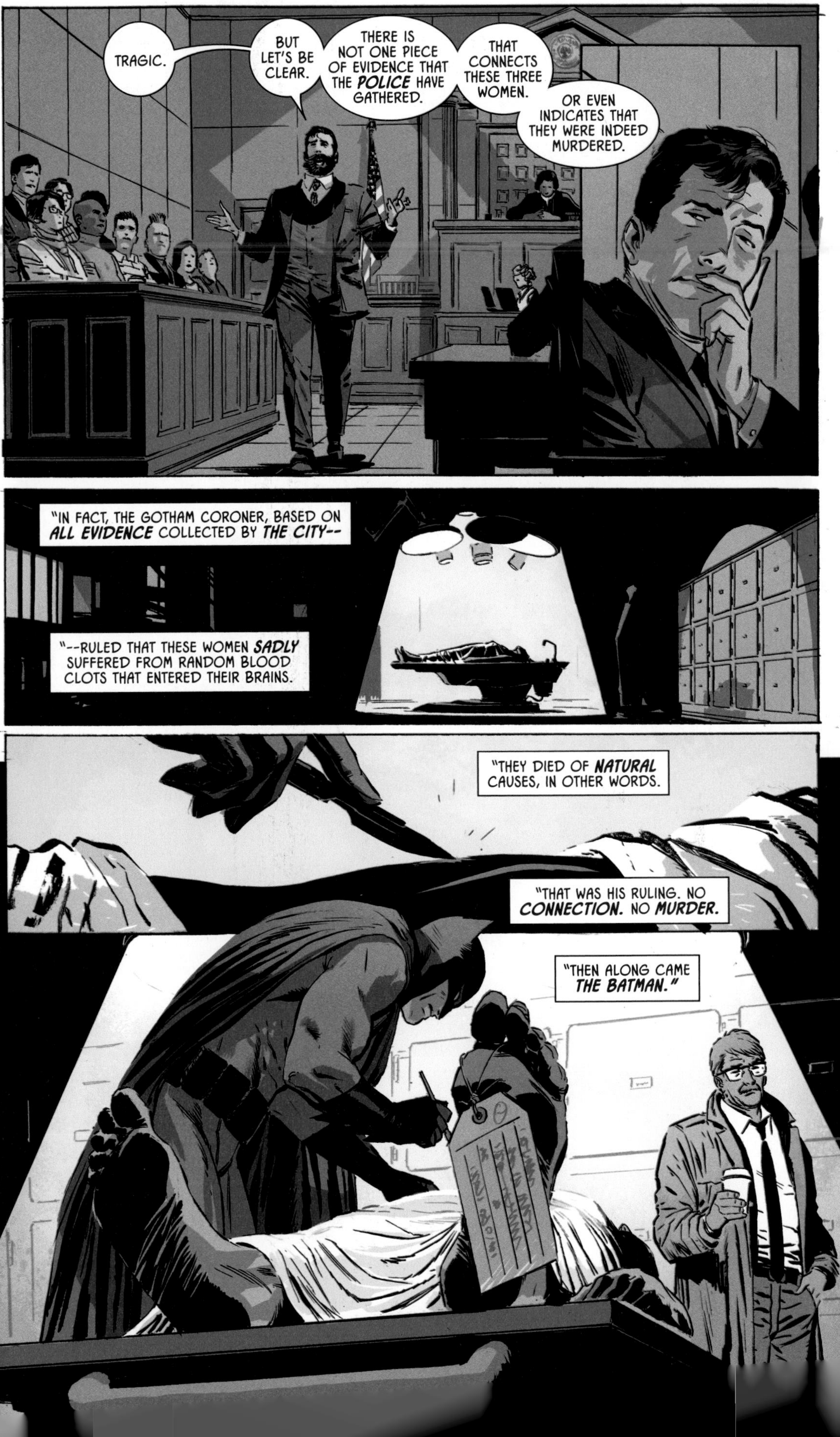

TRAGIC.
BUT LET'S BE CLEAR.
THERE IS NOT ONE PIECE OF EVIDENCE THAT THE POLICE HAVE GATHERED.
THAT CONNECTS THESE THREE WOMEN.
OR EVEN INDICATES THAT THEY WERE INDEED MURDERED.
"IN FACT, THE GOTHAM CORONER, BASED ON ALL EVIDENCE COLLECTED BY THE CITY--
"--RULED THAT THESE WOMEN SADLY SUFFERED FROM RANDOM BLOOD CLOTS THAT ENTERED THEIR BRAINS.
"THEY DIED OF NATURAL CAUSES, IN OTHER WORDS.
"THAT WAS HIS RULING. NO CONNECTION. NO MURDER.
"THEN ALONG CAME THE BATMAN."

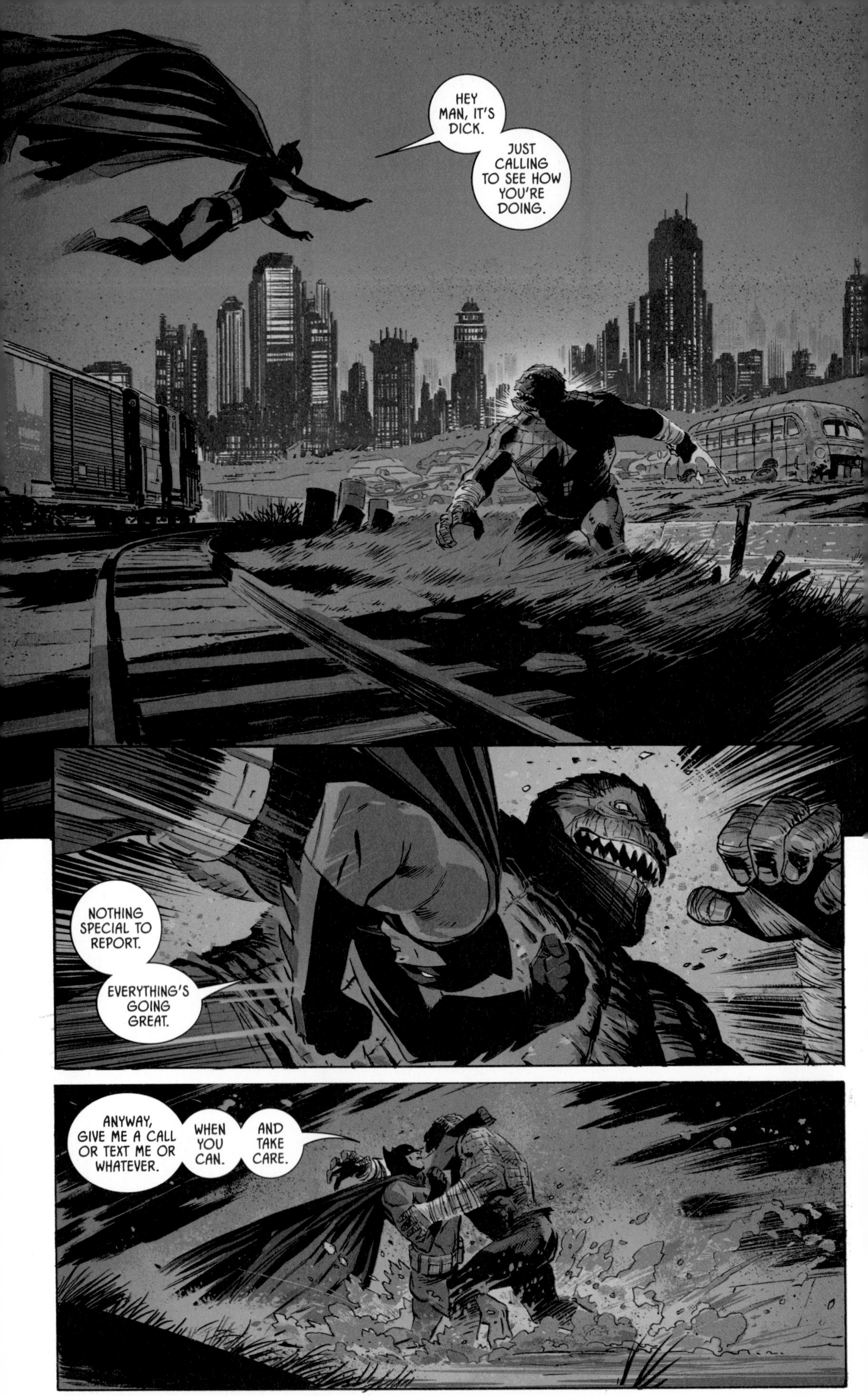
HEY MAN, IT'S DICK.
JUST CALLING TO SEE HOW YOU'RE DOING.
NOTHING SPECIAL TO REPORT.
EVERYTHING'S GOING GREAT.
ANYWAY, GIVE ME A CALL OR TEXT ME OR WHATEVER.
WHEN YOU CAN.
AND TAKE CARE.

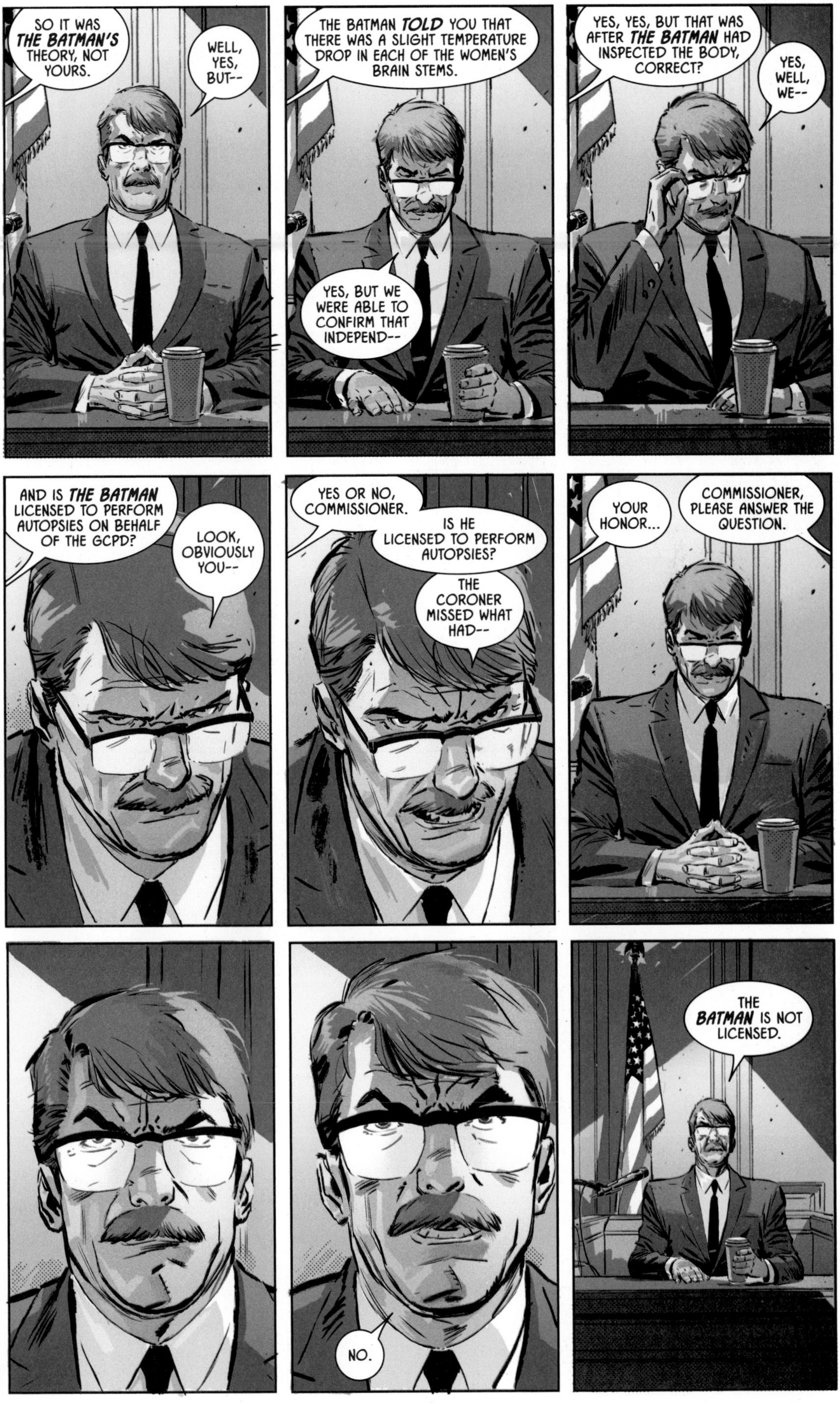

SO IT WAS THE BATMAN'S THEORY, NOT YOURS.
WELL, YES, BUT--
THE BATMAN TOLD YOU THAT THERE WAS A SLIGHT TEMPERATURE DROP IN EACH OF THE WOMEN'S BRAIN STEMS.
YES, BUT WE WERE ABLE TO CONFIRM THAT INDEPEND--
YES, YES, BUT THAT WAS AFTER THE BATMAN HAD INSPECTED THE BODY, CORRECT?
YES, WELL, WE--
AND IS THE BATMAN LICENSED TO PERFORM AUTOPSIES ON BEHALF OF THE GCPD?
LOOK, OBVIOUSLY YOU--
YES OR NO, COMMISSIONER.
IS HE LICENSED TO PERFORM AUTOPSIES?
THE CORONER MISSED WHAT HAD--
YOUR HONOR...
COMMISSIONER, PLEASE ANSWER THE QUESTION.
NO.
THE BATMAN IS NOT LICENSED.

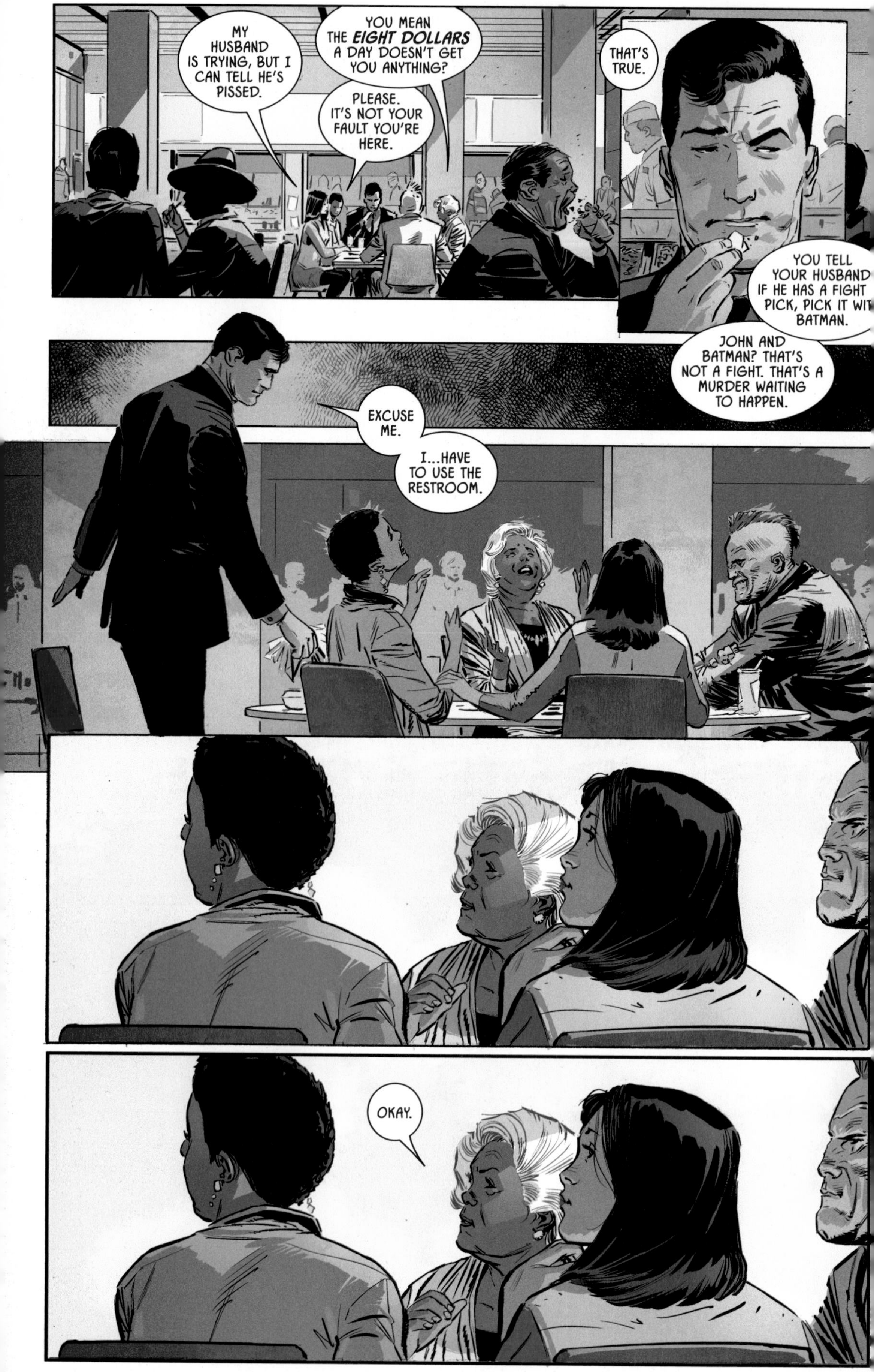
MY HUSBAND IS TRYING, BUT I CAN TELL HE'S PISSED.
YOU MEAN THE EIGHT DOLLARS A DAY DOESN'T GET YOU ANYTHING?
PLEASE. IT'S NOT YOUR FAULT YOU'RE HERE.
THAT'S TRUE.
YOU TELL YOUR HUSBAND IF HE HAS A FIGHT TO PICK, PICK IT WITH BATMAN.
JOHN AND BATMAN? THAT'S NOT A FIGHT. THAT'S A MURDER WAITING TO HAPPEN.
EXCUSE ME.
I...HAVE TO USE THE RESTROOM.
OKAY.

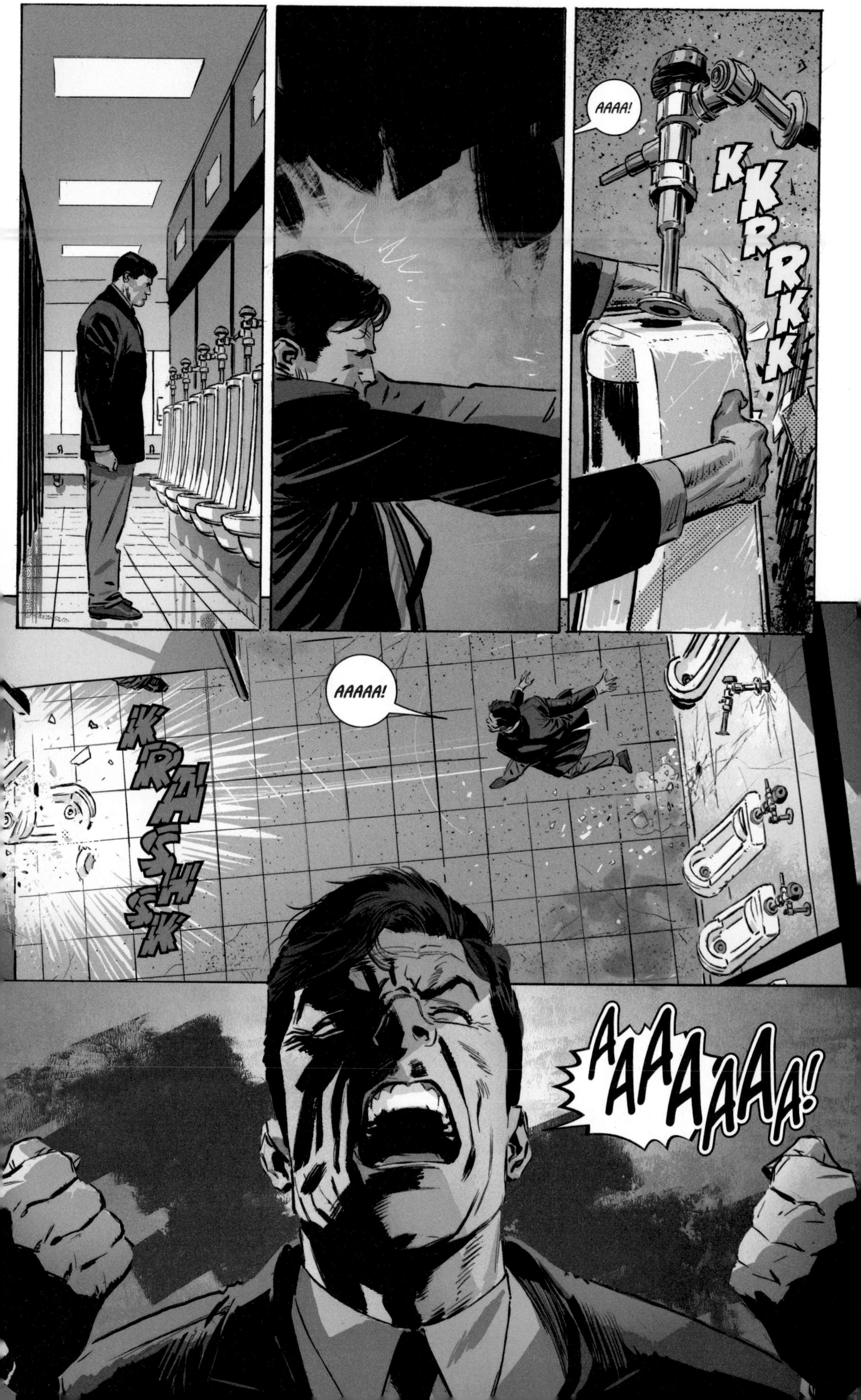
AAAA!
KKRRRKKK
AAAAA!
KRAASHSHSK
AAAAAAAA!

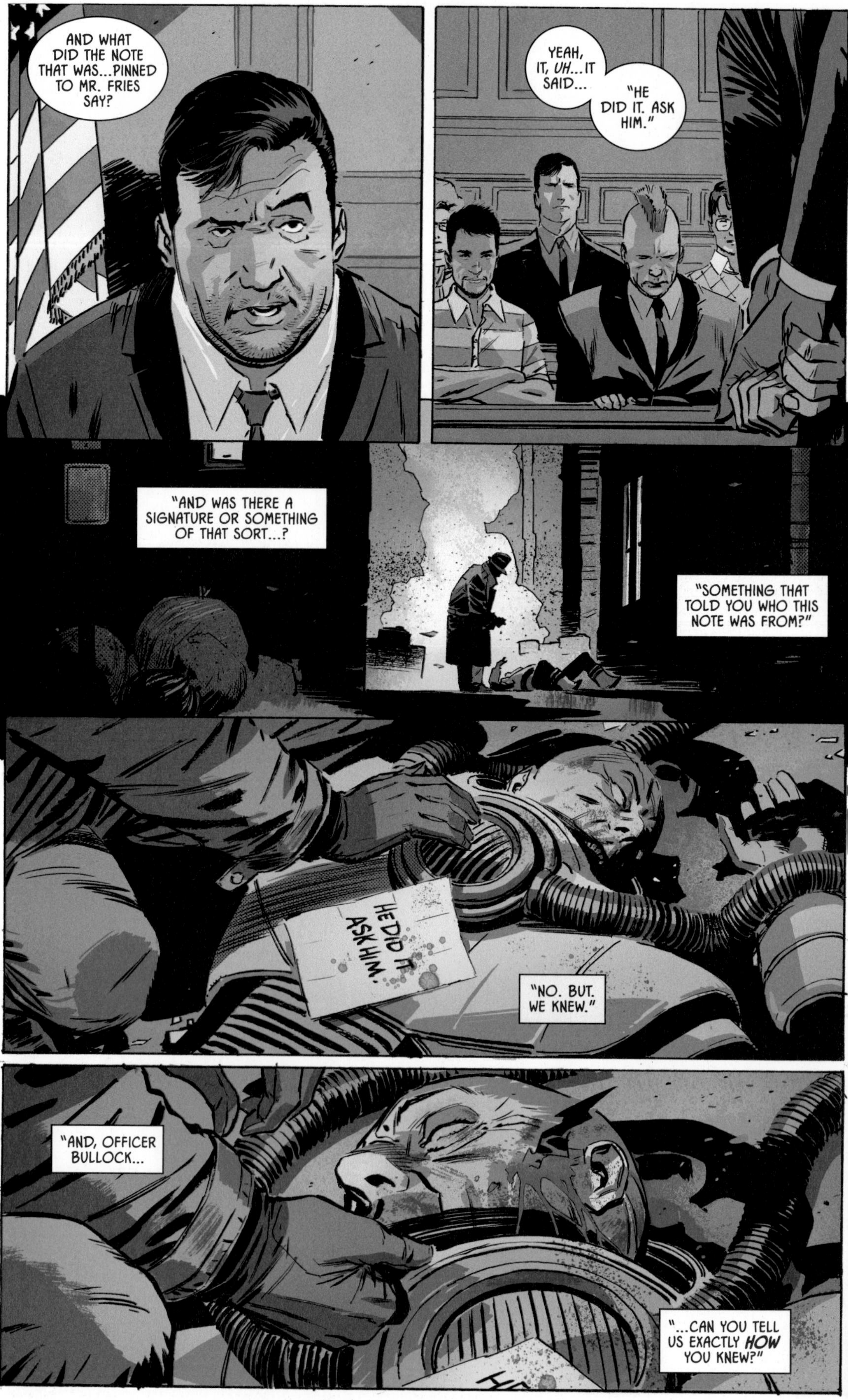
AND WHAT DID THE NOTE THAT WAS...PINNED TO MR. FRIES SAY?
YEAH, IT, UH...IT SAID...
"HE DID IT. ASK HIM."
"AND WAS THERE A SIGNATURE OR SOMETHING OF THAT SORT...?
"SOMETHING THAT TOLD YOU WHO THIS NOTE WAS FROM?"
HE DID IT. ASK HIM.
"NO. BUT. WE KNEW."
"AND, OFFICER BULLOCK...
"...CAN YOU TELL US EXACTLY HOW YOU KNEW?"

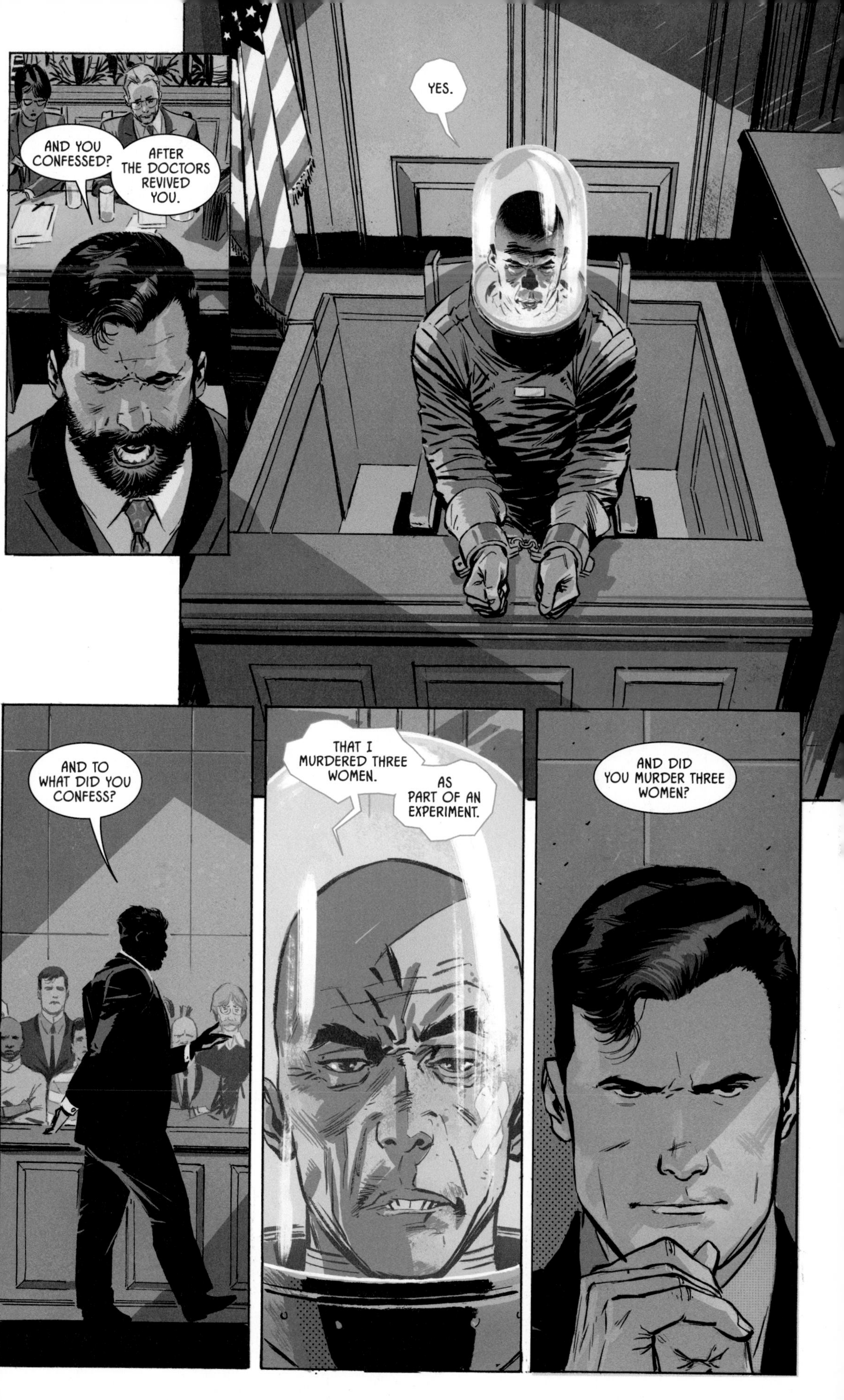
AND YOU CONFESSED?
AFTER THE DOCTORS REVIVED YOU.
YES.
AND TO WHAT DID YOU CONFESS?
THAT I MURDERED THREE WOMEN.
AS PART OF AN EXPERIMENT.
AND DID YOU MURDER THREE WOMEN?

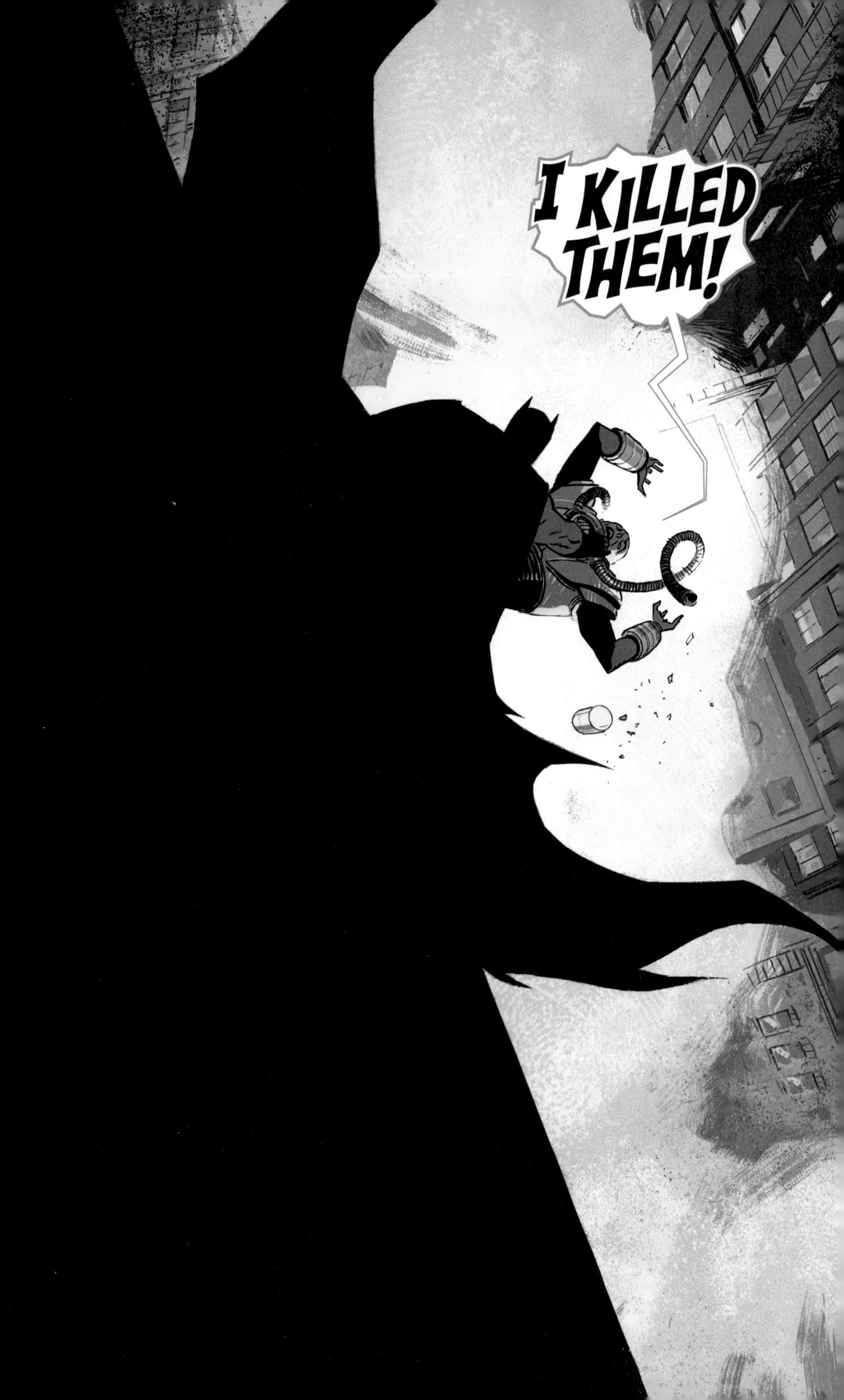
I KILLED THEM!

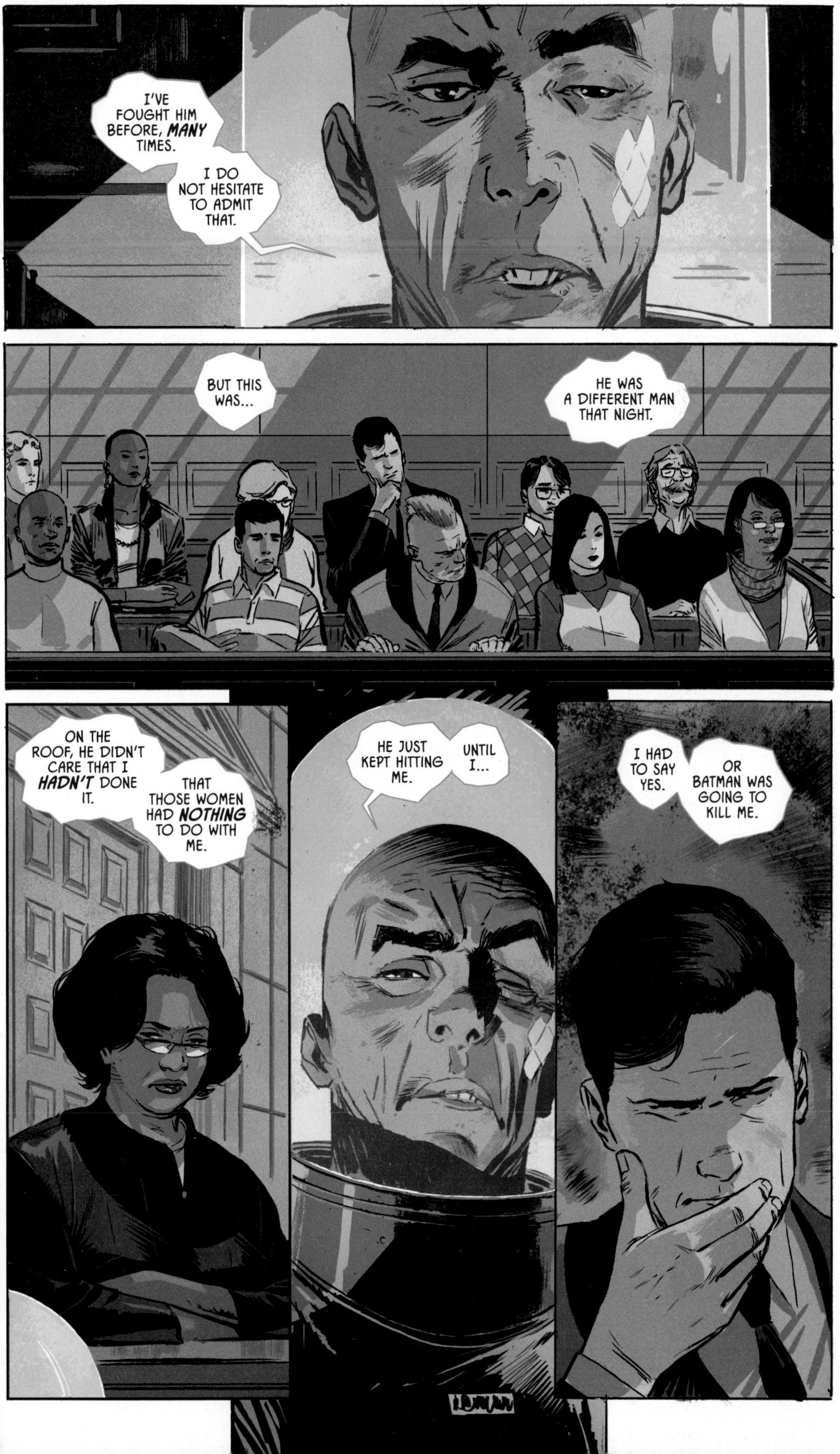
I'VE FOUGHT HIM BEFORE, *MANY* TIMES.
I DO NOT HESITATE TO ADMIT THAT.
BUT THIS WAS...
HE WAS A DIFFERENT MAN THAT NIGHT.
ON THE ROOF, HE DIDN'T CARE THAT I *HADN'T* DONE IT.
THAT THOSE WOMEN HAD *NOTHING* TO DO WITH ME.
HE JUST KEPT HITTING ME.
UNTIL I...
I HAD TO SAY YES.
OR BATMAN WAS GOING TO KILL ME.

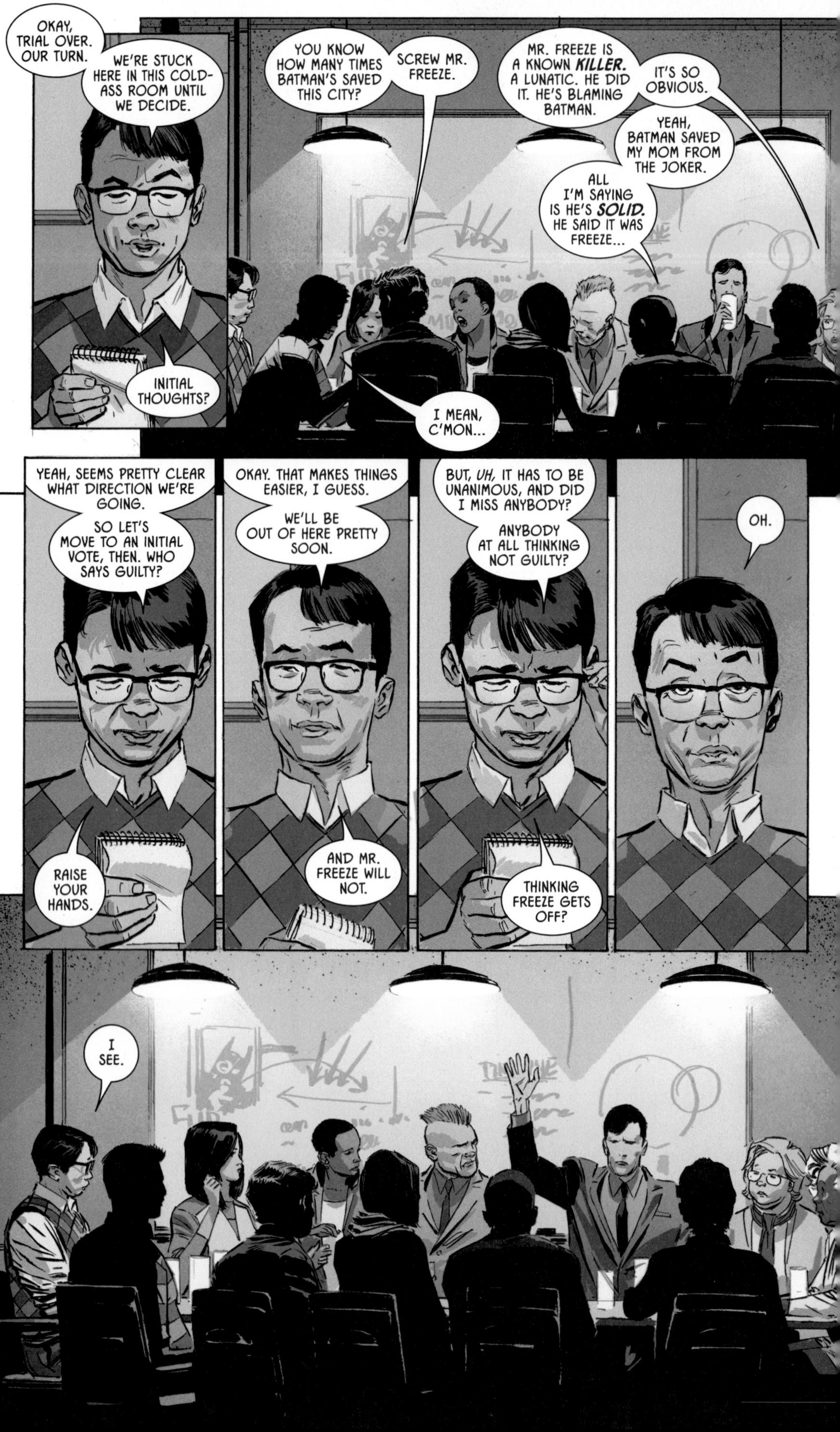
OKAY, TRIAL OVER. OUR TURN.
WE'RE STUCK HERE IN THIS COLD-ASS ROOM UNTIL WE DECIDE.
INITIAL THOUGHTS?
YOU KNOW HOW MANY TIMES BATMAN'S SAVED THIS CITY?
SCREW MR. FREEZE.
MR. FREEZE IS A KNOWN **KILLER.** A LUNATIC. HE DID IT. HE'S BLAMING BATMAN.
IT'S SO OBVIOUS.
YEAH, BATMAN SAVED MY MOM FROM THE JOKER.
ALL I'M SAYING IS HE'S ***SOLID.*** HE SAID IT WAS FREEZE...
I MEAN, C'MON...
YEAH, SEEMS PRETTY CLEAR WHAT DIRECTION WE'RE GOING.
SO LET'S MOVE TO AN INITIAL VOTE, THEN. WHO SAYS GUILTY?
RAISE YOUR HANDS.
OKAY. THAT MAKES THINGS EASIER, I GUESS.
WE'LL BE OUT OF HERE PRETTY SOON.
AND MR. FREEZE WILL NOT.
BUT, *UH,* IT HAS TO BE UNANIMOUS, AND DID I MISS ANYBODY?
ANYBODY AT ALL THINKING NOT GUILTY?
THINKING FREEZE GETS OFF?
OH.
I SEE.

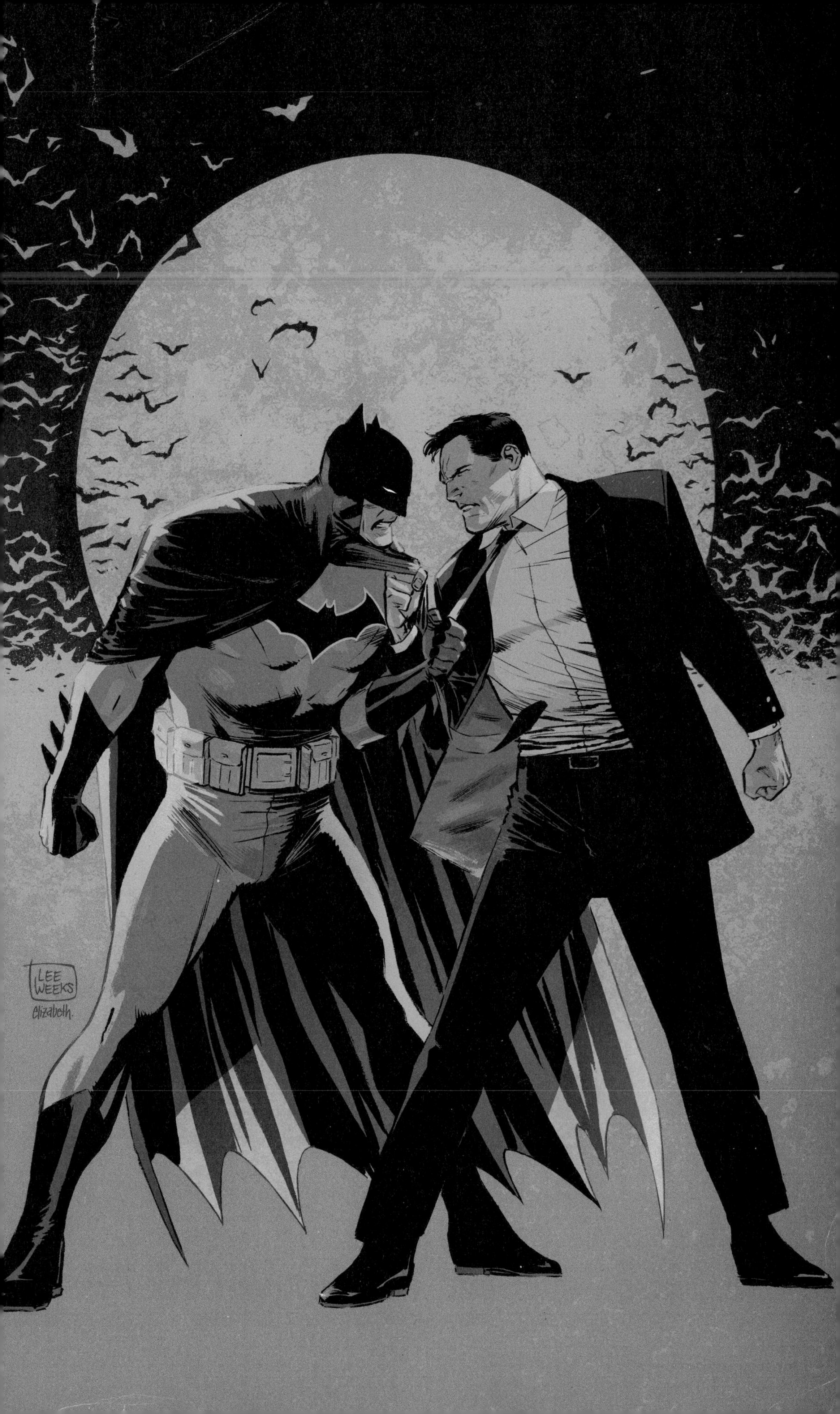
LEE WEEKS
Elizabeth.

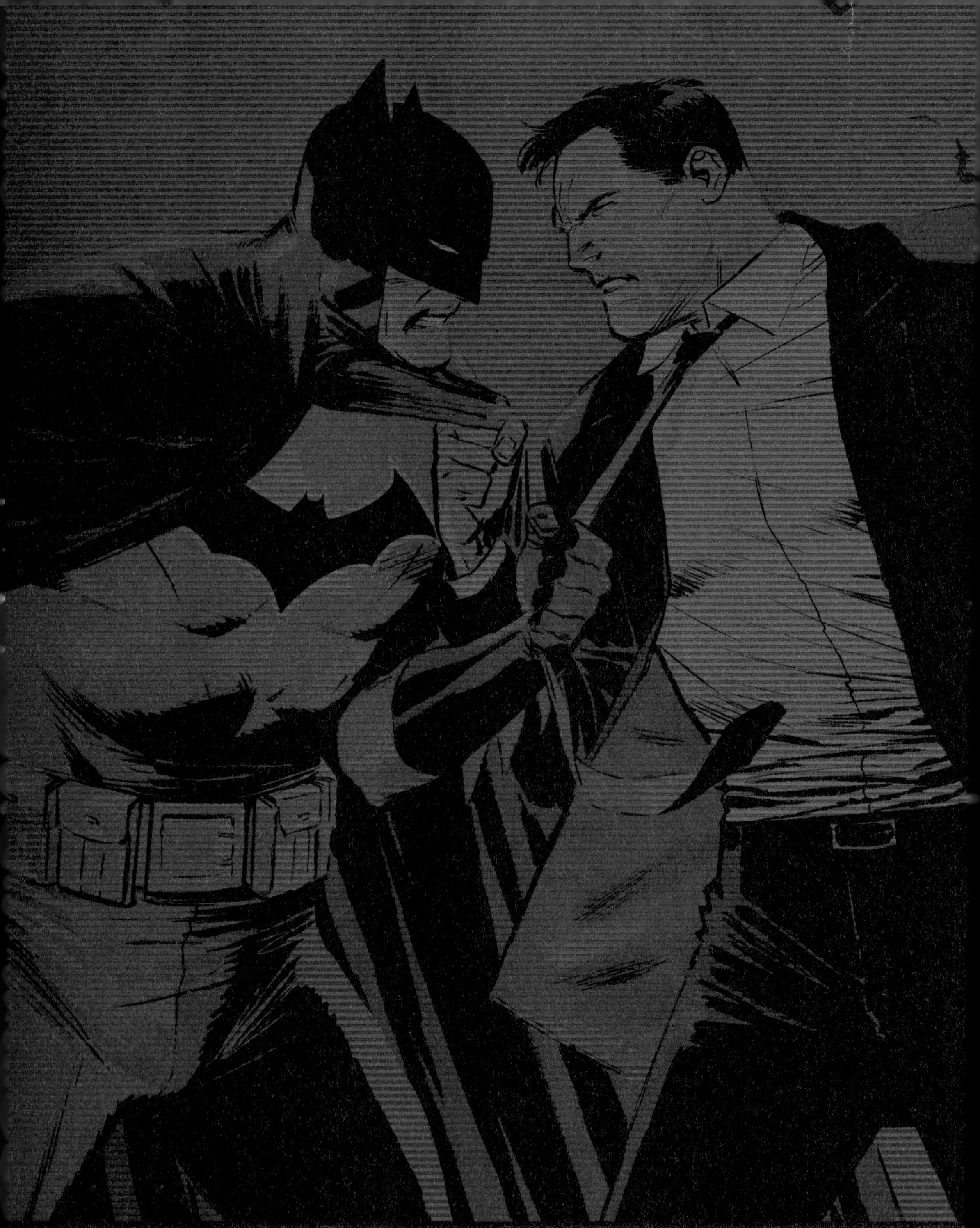

BATMAN
#52

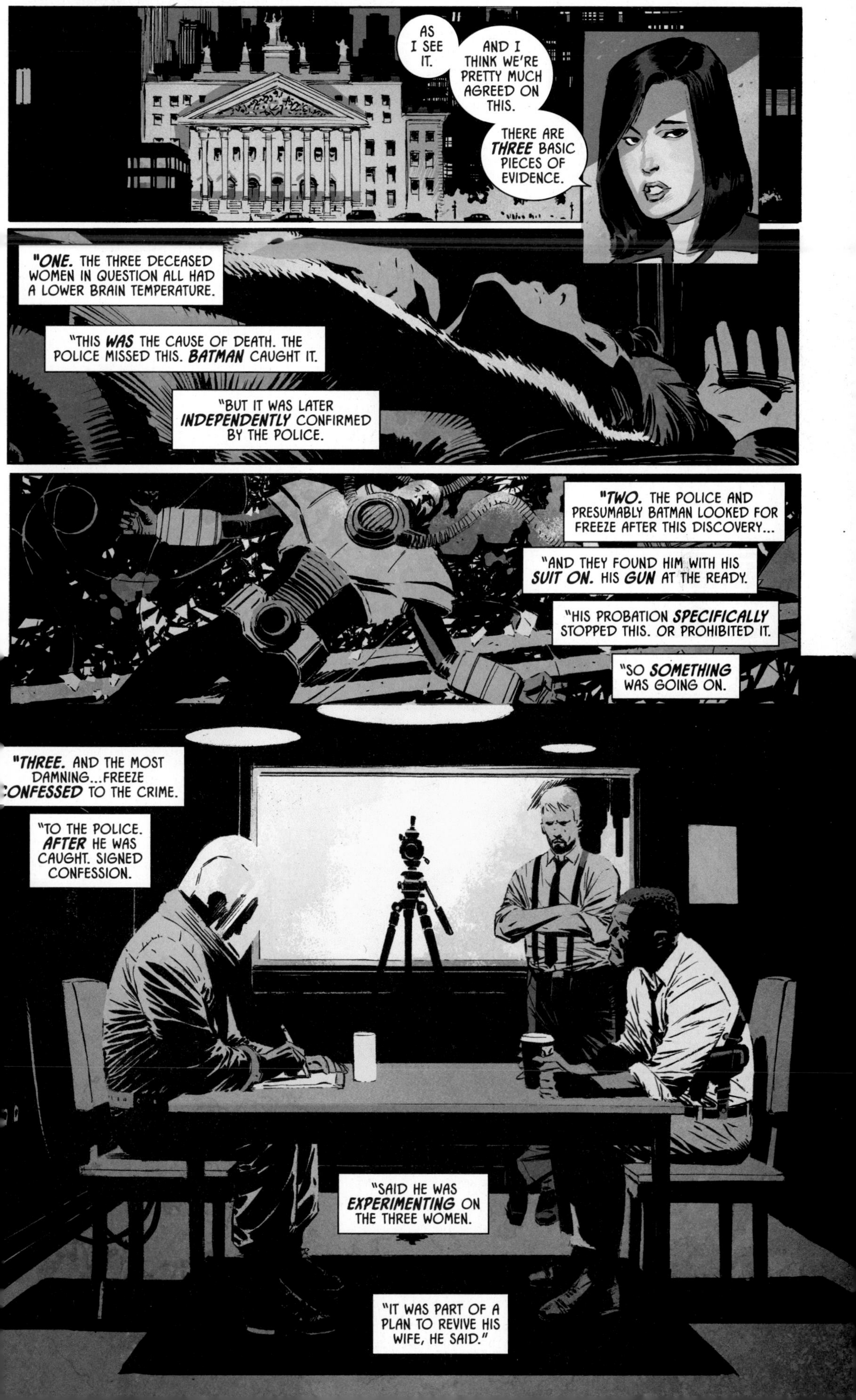
AS I SEE IT.
AND I THINK WE'RE PRETTY MUCH AGREED ON THIS.
THERE ARE THREE BASIC PIECES OF EVIDENCE.
"ONE. THE THREE DECEASED WOMEN IN QUESTION ALL HAD A LOWER BRAIN TEMPERATURE.
"THIS WAS THE CAUSE OF DEATH. THE POLICE MISSED THIS. BATMAN CAUGHT IT.
"BUT IT WAS LATER INDEPENDENTLY CONFIRMED BY THE POLICE.
"TWO. THE POLICE AND PRESUMABLY BATMAN LOOKED FOR FREEZE AFTER THIS DISCOVERY...
"AND THEY FOUND HIM WITH HIS SUIT ON. HIS GUN AT THE READY.
"HIS PROBATION SPECIFICALLY STOPPED THIS. OR PROHIBITED IT.
"SO SOMETHING WAS GOING ON.
"THREE. AND THE MOST DAMNING...FREEZE CONFESSED TO THE CRIME.
"TO THE POLICE. AFTER HE WAS CAUGHT. SIGNED CONFESSION.
"SAID HE WAS EXPERIMENTING ON THE THREE WOMEN.
"IT WAS PART OF A PLAN TO REVIVE HIS WIFE, HE SAID."

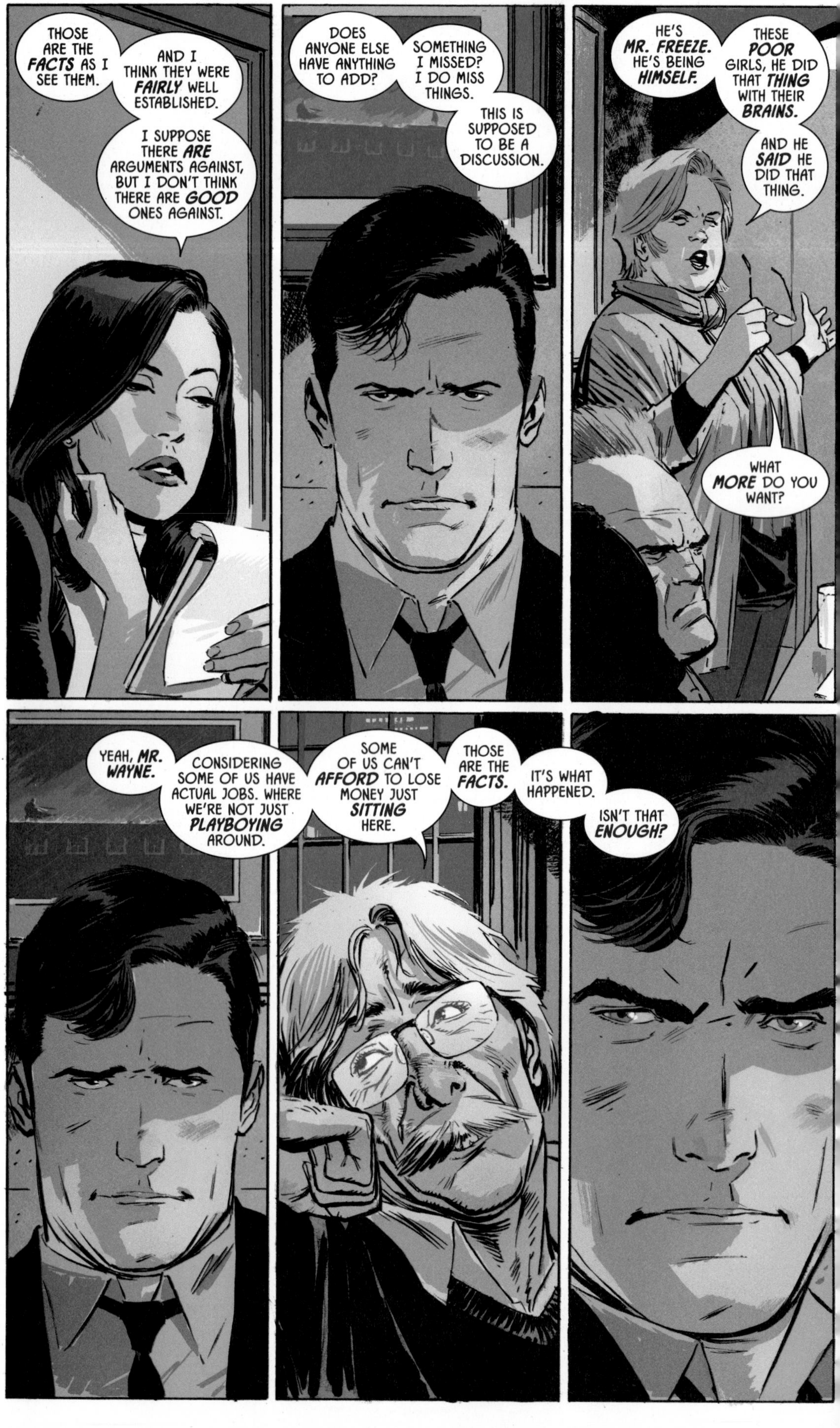
THOSE ARE THE FACTS AS I SEE THEM.
AND I THINK THEY WERE FAIRLY WELL ESTABLISHED.
I SUPPOSE THERE ARE ARGUMENTS AGAINST, BUT I DON'T THINK THERE ARE GOOD ONES AGAINST.
DOES ANYONE ELSE HAVE ANYTHING TO ADD?
SOMETHING I MISSED? I DO MISS THINGS.
THIS IS SUPPOSED TO BE A DISCUSSION.
HE'S MR. FREEZE. HE'S BEING HIMSELF.
THESE POOR GIRLS, HE DID THAT THING WITH THEIR BRAINS.
AND HE SAID HE DID THAT THING.
WHAT MORE DO YOU WANT?
YEAH, MR. WAYNE.
CONSIDERING SOME OF US HAVE ACTUAL JOBS. WHERE WE'RE NOT JUST PLAYBOYING AROUND.
SOME OF US CAN'T AFFORD TO LOSE MONEY JUST SITTING HERE.
THOSE ARE THE FACTS.
IT'S WHAT HAPPENED.
ISN'T THAT ENOUGH?

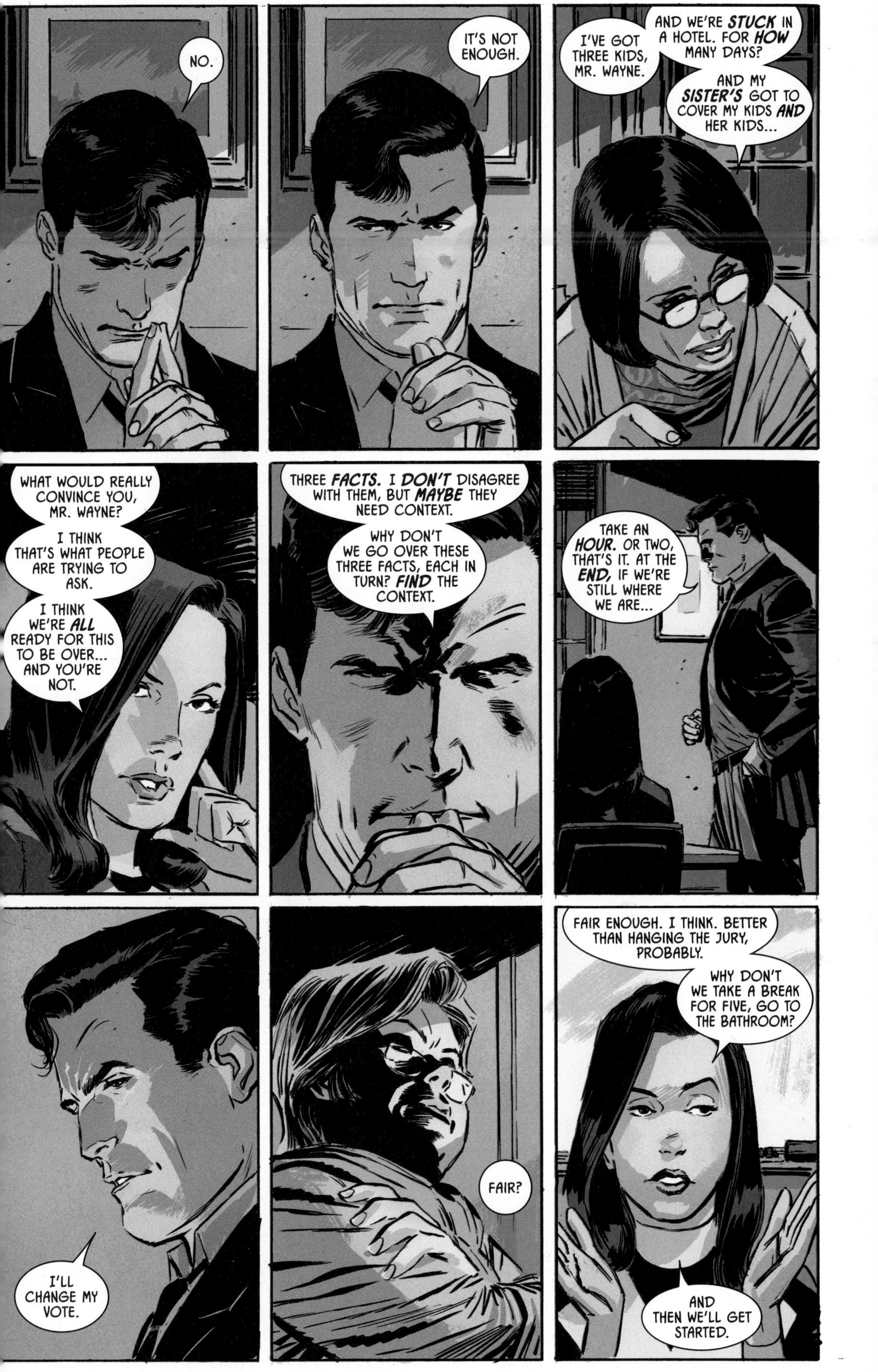

NO.
IT'S NOT ENOUGH.
I'VE GOT THREE KIDS, MR. WAYNE.
AND WE'RE STUCK IN A HOTEL. FOR HOW MANY DAYS?
AND MY SISTER'S GOT TO COVER MY KIDS AND HER KIDS...
WHAT WOULD REALLY CONVINCE YOU, MR. WAYNE?
I THINK THAT'S WHAT PEOPLE ARE TRYING TO ASK.
I THINK WE'RE ALL READY FOR THIS TO BE OVER... AND YOU'RE NOT.
THREE FACTS. I DON'T DISAGREE WITH THEM, BUT MAYBE THEY NEED CONTEXT.
WHY DON'T WE GO OVER THESE THREE FACTS, EACH IN TURN? FIND THE CONTEXT.
TAKE AN HOUR. OR TWO, THAT'S IT. AT THE END, IF WE'RE STILL WHERE WE ARE...
I'LL CHANGE MY VOTE.
FAIR?
FAIR ENOUGH. I THINK. BETTER THAN HANGING THE JURY, PROBABLY.
WHY DON'T WE TAKE A BREAK FOR FIVE, GO TO THE BATHROOM?
AND THEN WE'LL GET STARTED.

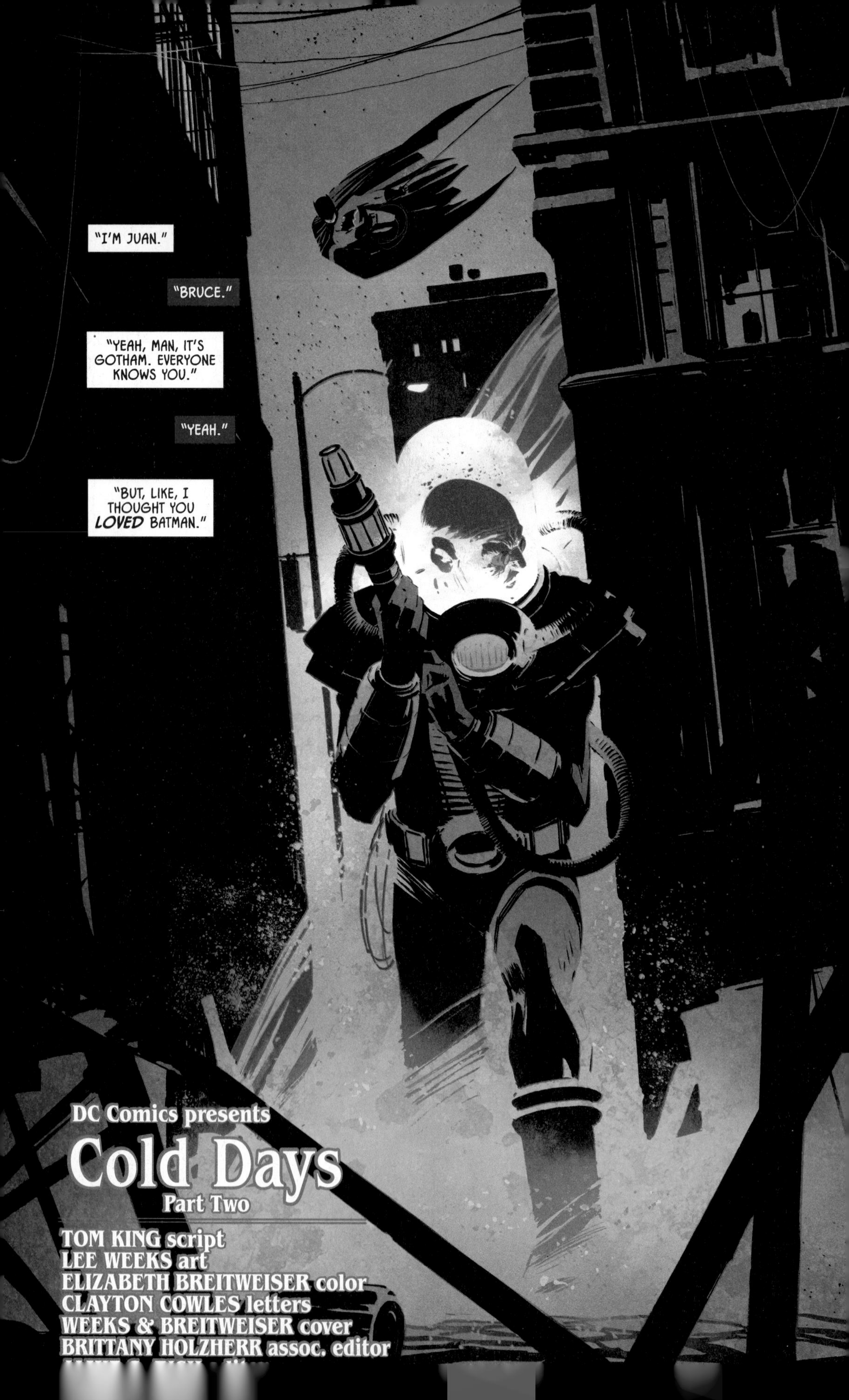
"I'M JUAN."
"BRUCE."
"YEAH, MAN, IT'S GOTHAM. EVERYONE KNOWS YOU."
"YEAH."
"BUT, LIKE, I THOUGHT YOU LOVED BATMAN."
DC Comics presents
Cold Days
Part Two
TOM KING script
LEE WEEKS art
ELIZABETH BREITWEISER color
CLAYTON COWLES letters
WEEKS & BREITWEISER cover
BRITTANY HOLZHERR assoc. editor

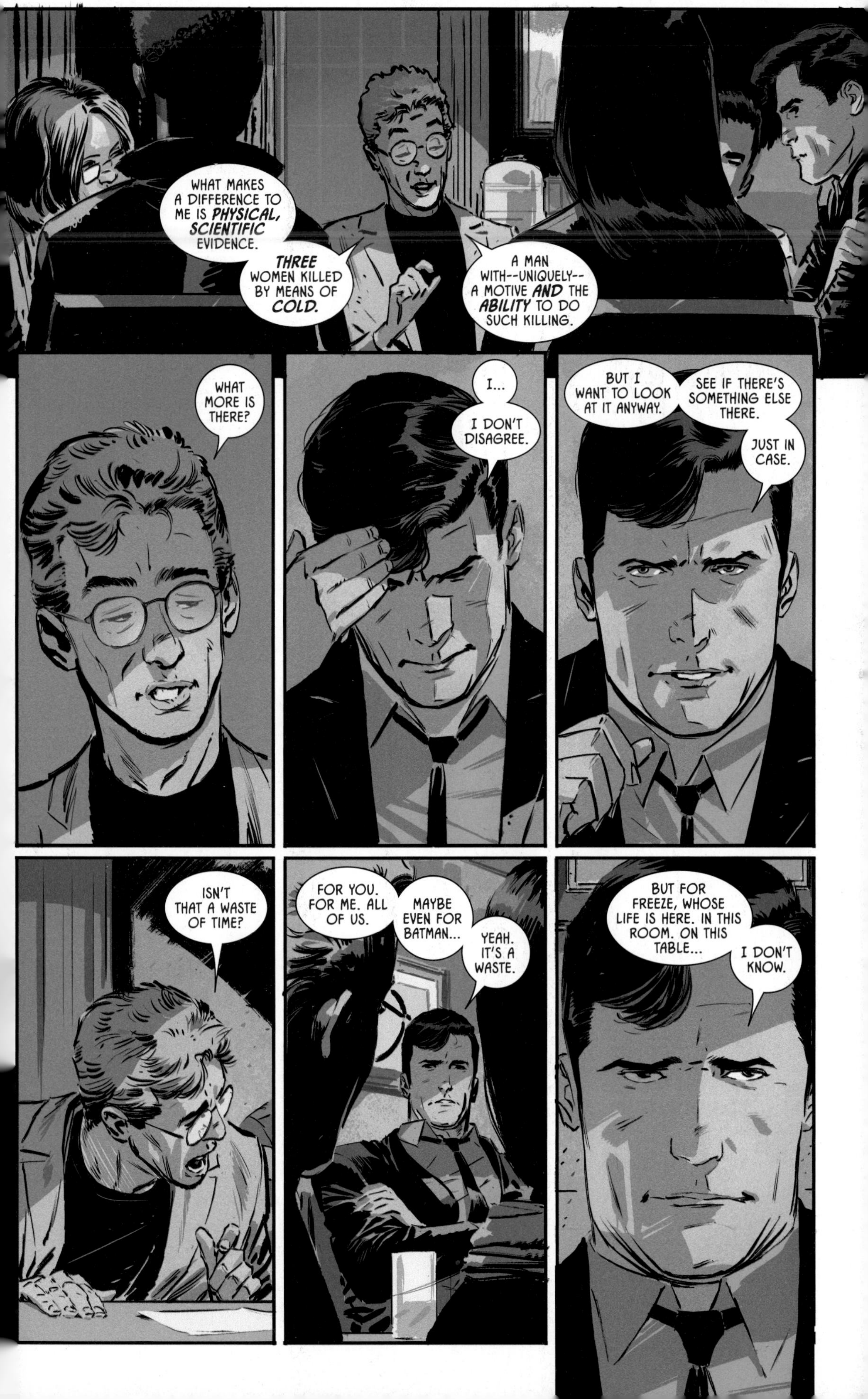
WHAT MAKES A DIFFERENCE TO ME IS PHYSICAL, SCIENTIFIC EVIDENCE.
THREE WOMEN KILLED BY MEANS OF COLD.
A MAN WITH--UNIQUELY--A MOTIVE AND THE ABILITY TO DO SUCH KILLING.
WHAT MORE IS THERE?
I...
I DON'T DISAGREE.
BUT I WANT TO LOOK AT IT ANYWAY.
SEE IF THERE'S SOMETHING ELSE THERE.
JUST IN CASE.
ISN'T THAT A WASTE OF TIME?
FOR YOU. FOR ME. ALL OF US.
MAYBE EVEN FOR BATMAN...
YEAH. IT'S A WASTE.
BUT FOR FREEZE, WHOSE LIFE IS HERE. IN THIS ROOM. ON THIS TABLE...
I DON'T KNOW.

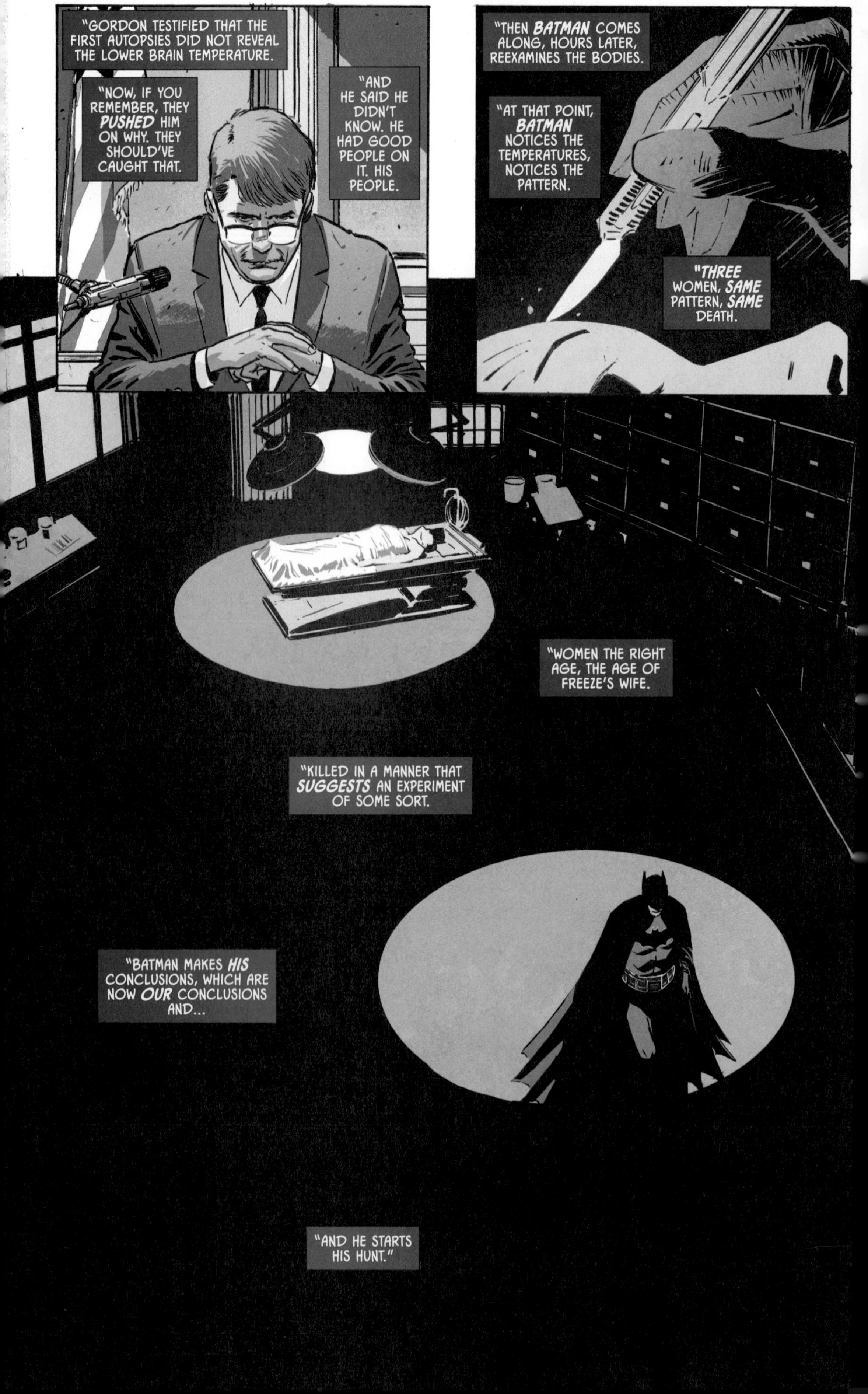
"GORDON TESTIFIED THAT THE FIRST AUTOPSIES DID NOT REVEAL THE LOWER BRAIN TEMPERATURE.
"NOW, IF YOU REMEMBER, THEY PUSHED HIM ON WHY. THEY SHOULD'VE CAUGHT THAT.
"AND HE SAID HE DIDN'T KNOW. HE HAD GOOD PEOPLE ON IT. HIS PEOPLE.
"THEN BATMAN COMES ALONG, HOURS LATER, REEXAMINES THE BODIES.
"AT THAT POINT, BATMAN NOTICES THE TEMPERATURES, NOTICES THE PATTERN.
"THREE WOMEN, SAME PATTERN, SAME DEATH.
"WOMEN THE RIGHT AGE, THE AGE OF FREEZE'S WIFE.
"KILLED IN A MANNER THAT SUGGESTS AN EXPERIMENT OF SOME SORT.
"BATMAN MAKES HIS CONCLUSIONS, WHICH ARE NOW OUR CONCLUSIONS AND...
"AND HE STARTS HIS HUNT."

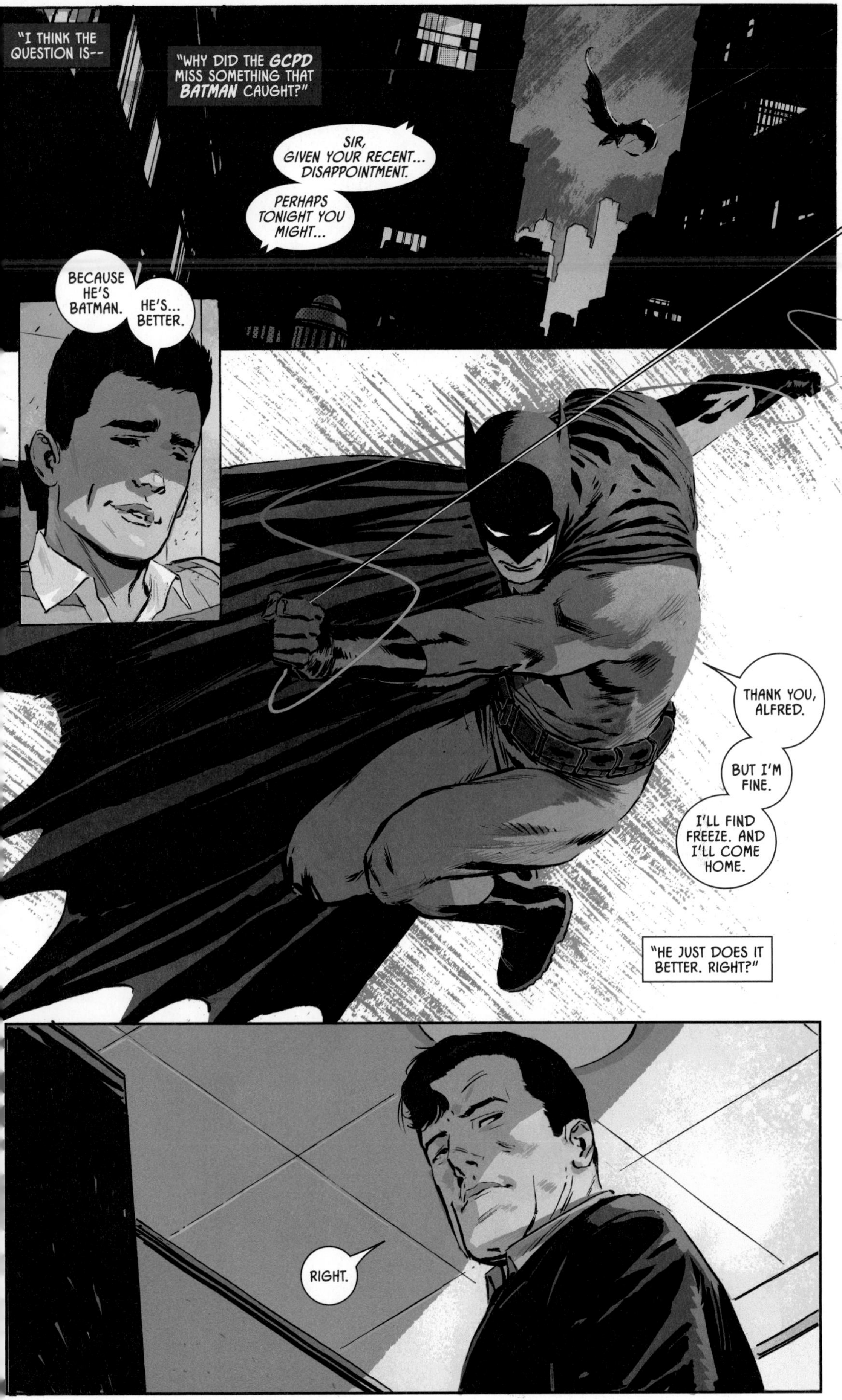
"I THINK THE QUESTION IS--
"WHY DID THE GCPD MISS SOMETHING THAT BATMAN CAUGHT?"
SIR, GIVEN YOUR RECENT... DISAPPOINTMENT.
PERHAPS TONIGHT YOU MIGHT...
BECAUSE HE'S BATMAN.
HE'S... BETTER.
THANK YOU, ALFRED.
BUT I'M FINE.
I'LL FIND FREEZE. AND I'LL COME HOME.
"HE JUST DOES IT BETTER. RIGHT?"
RIGHT.

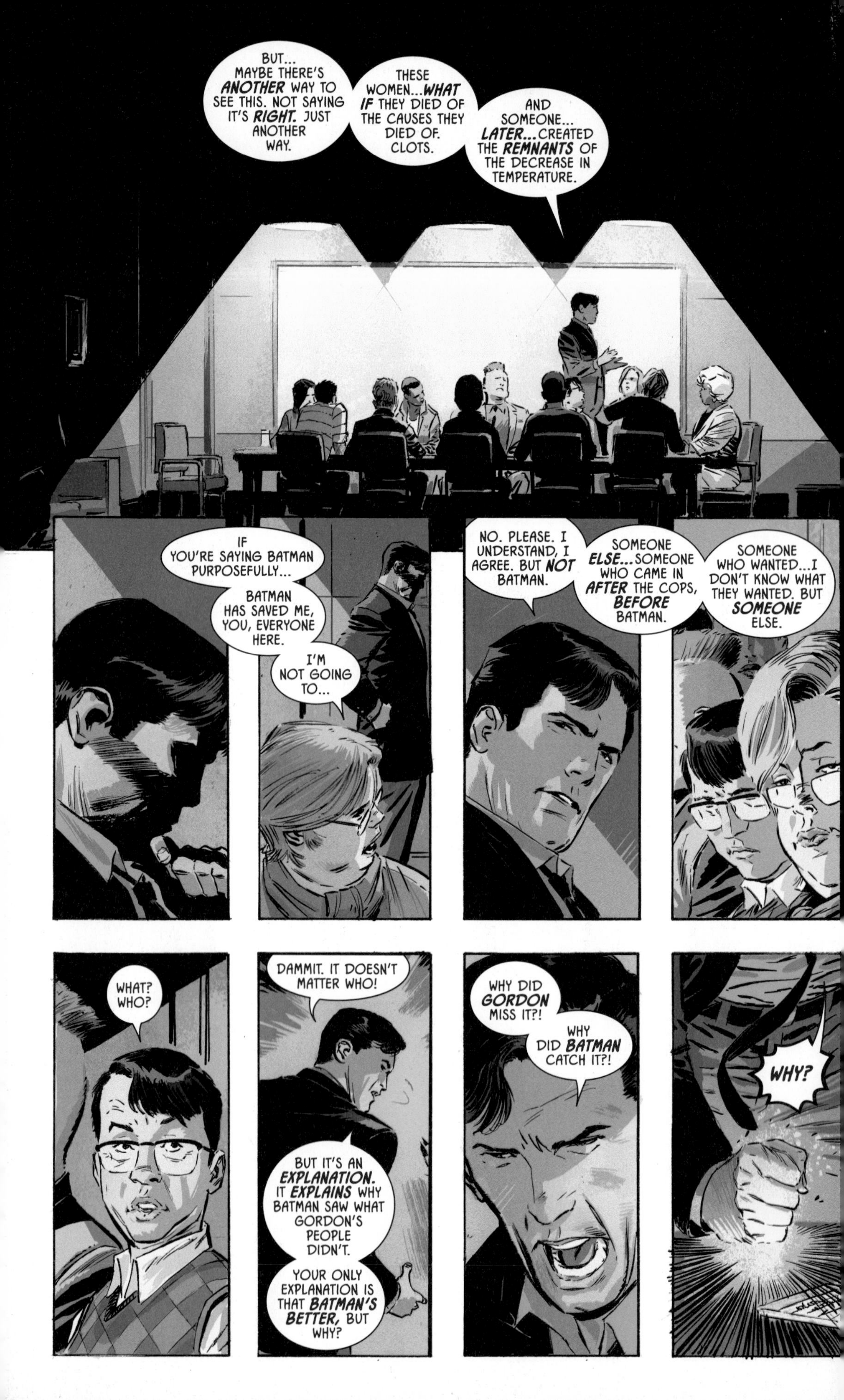

BUT... MAYBE THERE'S ANOTHER WAY TO SEE THIS. NOT SAYING IT'S RIGHT. JUST ANOTHER WAY.
THESE WOMEN...WHAT IF THEY DIED OF THE CAUSES THEY DIED OF. CLOTS.
AND SOMEONE... LATER...CREATED THE REMNANTS OF THE DECREASE IN TEMPERATURE.
IF YOU'RE SAYING BATMAN PURPOSEFULLY...
BATMAN HAS SAVED ME, YOU, EVERYONE HERE.
I'M NOT GOING TO...
NO. PLEASE. I UNDERSTAND, I AGREE. BUT NOT BATMAN.
SOMEONE ELSE...SOMEONE WHO CAME IN AFTER THE COPS, BEFORE BATMAN.
SOMEONE WHO WANTED...I DON'T KNOW WHAT THEY WANTED. BUT SOMEONE ELSE.
WHAT? WHO?
DAMMIT. IT DOESN'T MATTER WHO!
BUT IT'S AN EXPLANATION. IT EXPLAINS WHY BATMAN SAW WHAT GORDON'S PEOPLE DIDN'T.
YOUR ONLY EXPLANATION IS THAT BATMAN'S BETTER, BUT WHY?
WHY DID GORDON MISS IT?!
WHY DID BATMAN CATCH IT?!
WHY?

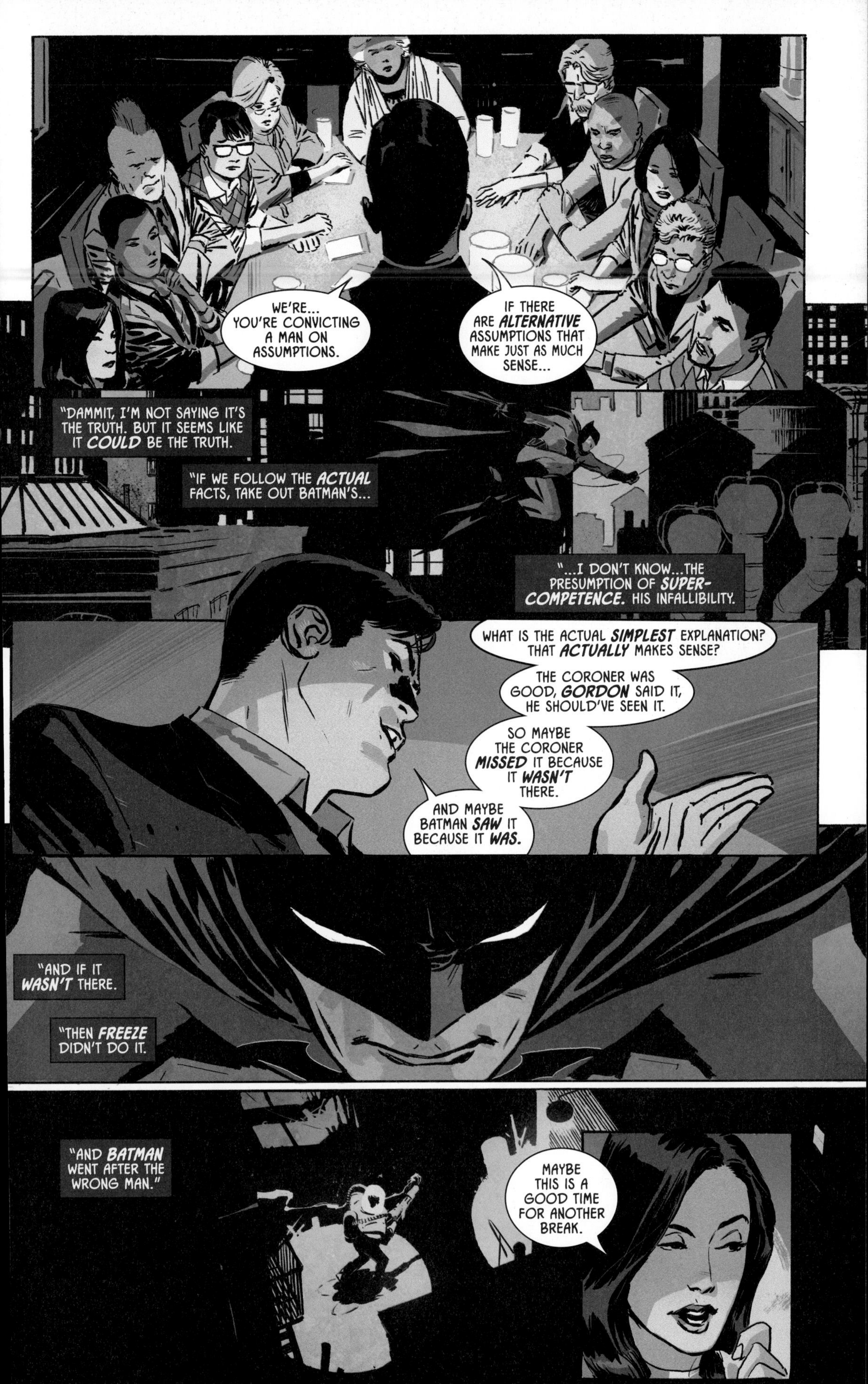
WE'RE... YOU'RE CONVICTING A MAN ON ASSUMPTIONS.
IF THERE ARE ALTERNATIVE ASSUMPTIONS THAT MAKE JUST AS MUCH SENSE...
"DAMMIT, I'M NOT SAYING IT'S THE TRUTH. BUT IT SEEMS LIKE IT COULD BE THE TRUTH.
"IF WE FOLLOW THE ACTUAL FACTS, TAKE OUT BATMAN'S...
"...I DON'T KNOW...THE PRESUMPTION OF SUPER-COMPETENCE. HIS INFALLIBILITY.
WHAT IS THE ACTUAL SIMPLEST EXPLANATION? THAT ACTUALLY MAKES SENSE?
THE CORONER WAS GOOD, GORDON SAID IT, HE SHOULD'VE SEEN IT.
SO MAYBE THE CORONER MISSED IT BECAUSE IT WASN'T THERE.
AND MAYBE BATMAN SAW IT BECAUSE IT WAS.
"AND IF IT WASN'T THERE.
"THEN FREEZE DIDN'T DO IT.
"AND BATMAN WENT AFTER THE WRONG MAN."
MAYBE THIS IS A GOOD TIME FOR ANOTHER BREAK.

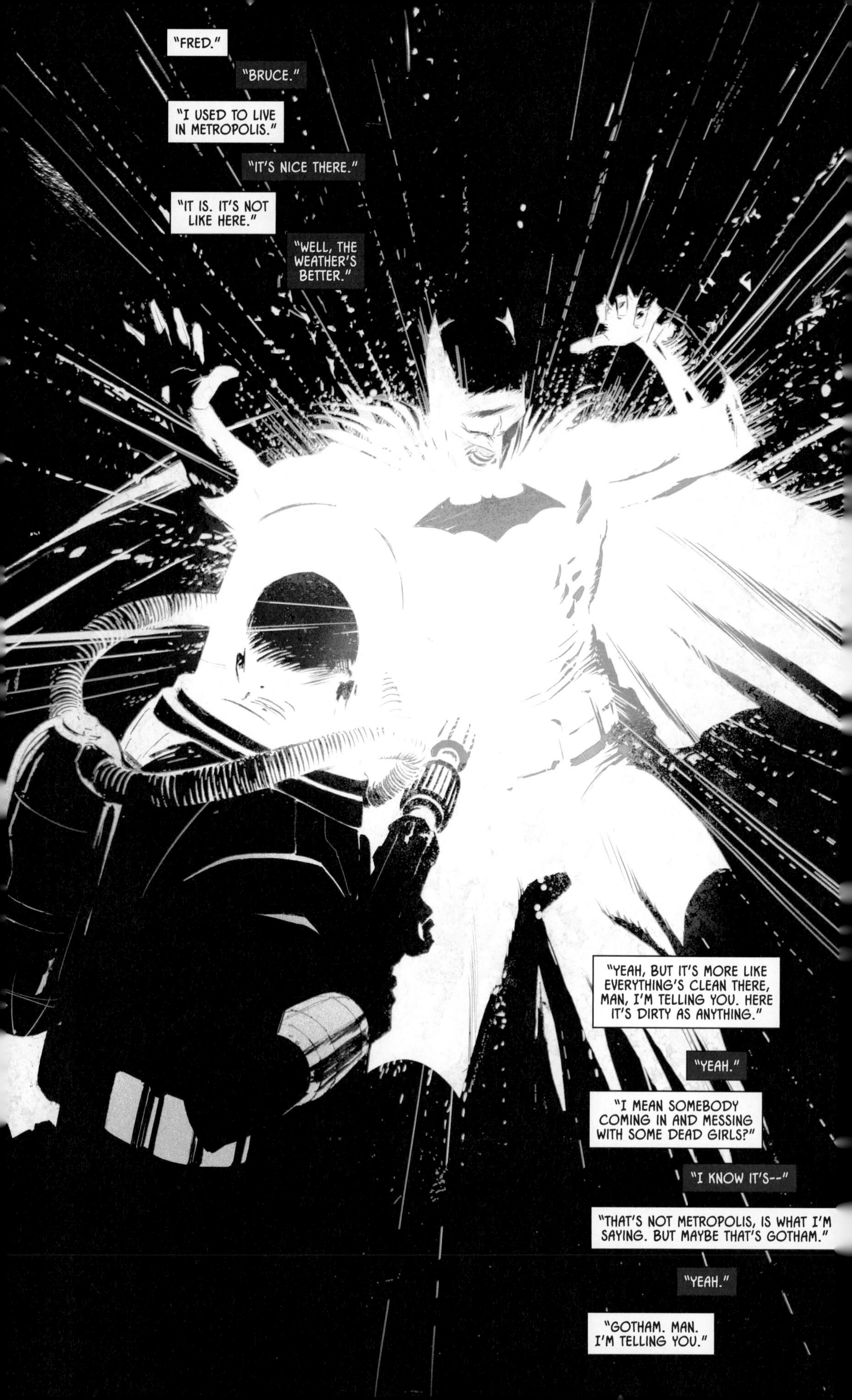
"FRED."
"BRUCE."
"I USED TO LIVE IN METROPOLIS."
"IT'S NICE THERE."
"IT IS. IT'S NOT LIKE HERE."
"WELL, THE WEATHER'S BETTER."
"YEAH, BUT IT'S MORE LIKE EVERYTHING'S CLEAN THERE, MAN, I'M TELLING YOU. HERE IT'S DIRTY AS ANYTHING."
"YEAH."
"I MEAN SOMEBODY COMING IN AND MESSING WITH SOME DEAD GIRLS?"
"I KNOW IT'S--"
"THAT'S NOT METROPOLIS, IS WHAT I'M SAYING. BUT MAYBE THAT'S GOTHAM."
"YEAH."
"GOTHAM. MAN. I'M TELLING YOU."

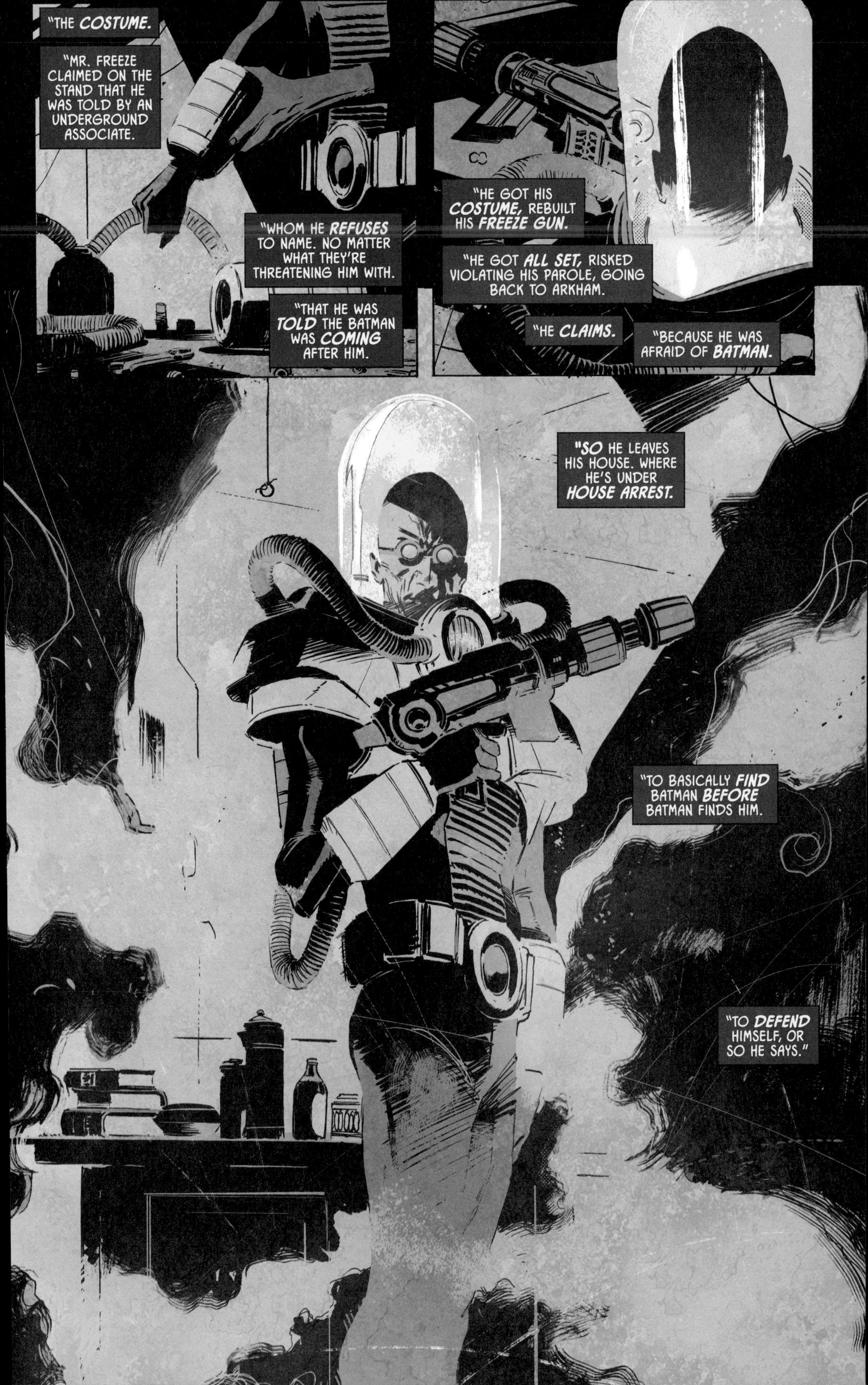
"THE COSTUME.
"MR. FREEZE CLAIMED ON THE STAND THAT HE WAS TOLD BY AN UNDERGROUND ASSOCIATE.
"WHOM HE REFUSES TO NAME. NO MATTER WHAT THEY'RE THREATENING HIM WITH.
"THAT HE WAS TOLD THE BATMAN WAS COMING AFTER HIM.
"HE GOT HIS COSTUME, REBUILT HIS FREEZE GUN.
"HE GOT ALL SET, RISKED VIOLATING HIS PAROLE, GOING BACK TO ARKHAM.
"HE CLAIMS.
"BECAUSE HE WAS AFRAID OF BATMAN.
"SO HE LEAVES HIS HOUSE. WHERE HE'S UNDER HOUSE ARREST.
"TO BASICALLY FIND BATMAN BEFORE BATMAN FINDS HIM.
"TO DEFEND HIMSELF, OR SO HE SAYS."

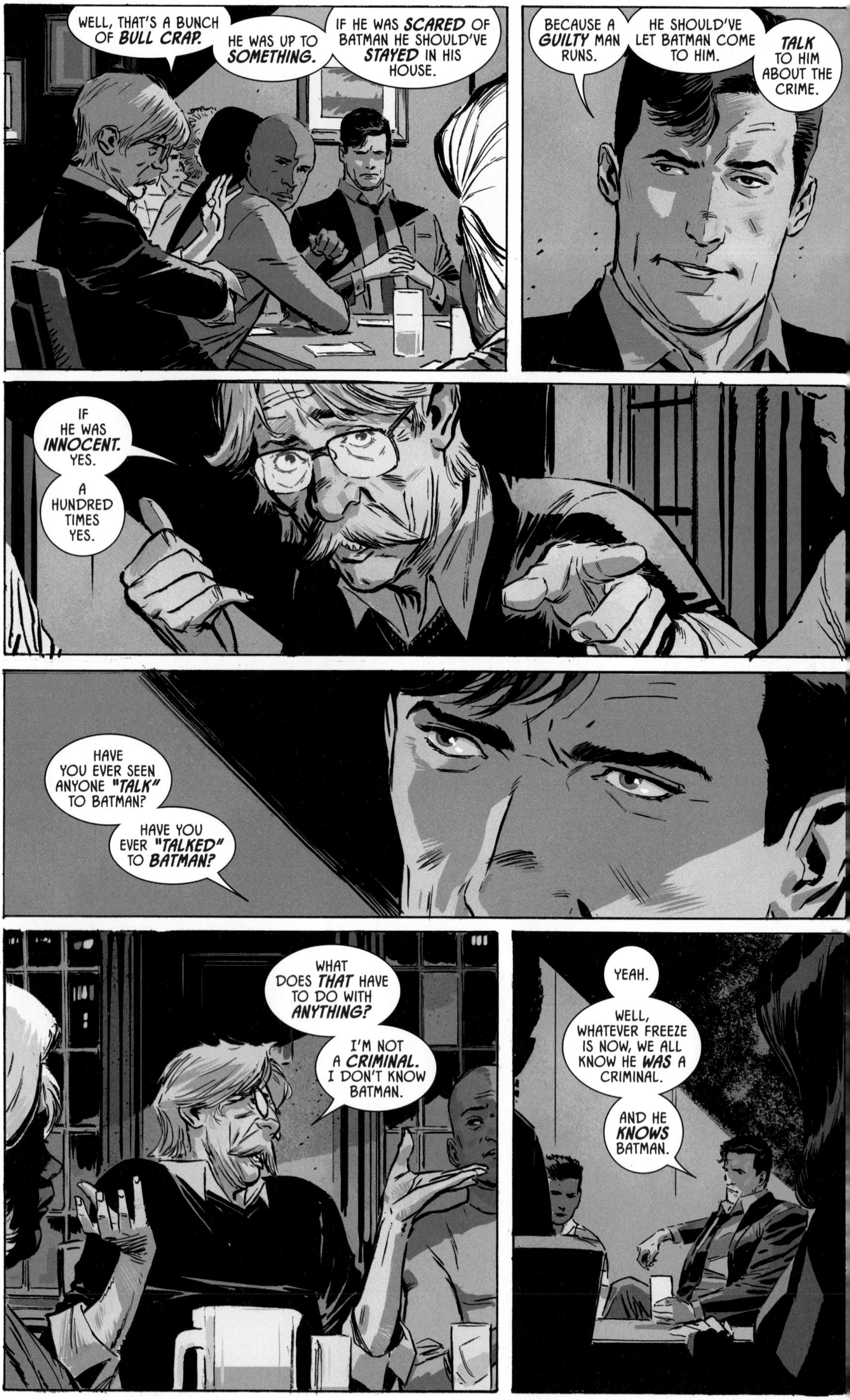
WELL, THAT'S A BUNCH OF BULL CRAP.
HE WAS UP TO SOMETHING.
IF HE WAS SCARED OF BATMAN HE SHOULD'VE STAYED IN HIS HOUSE.
BECAUSE A GUILTY MAN RUNS.
HE SHOULD'VE LET BATMAN COME TO HIM.
TALK TO HIM ABOUT THE CRIME.
IF HE WAS INNOCENT. YES.
A HUNDRED TIMES YES.
HAVE YOU EVER SEEN ANYONE "TALK" TO BATMAN?
HAVE YOU EVER "TALKED" TO BATMAN?
WHAT DOES THAT HAVE TO DO WITH ANYTHING?
I'M NOT A CRIMINAL. I DON'T KNOW BATMAN.
YEAH.
WELL, WHATEVER FREEZE IS NOW, WE ALL KNOW HE WAS A CRIMINAL.
AND HE KNOWS BATMAN.

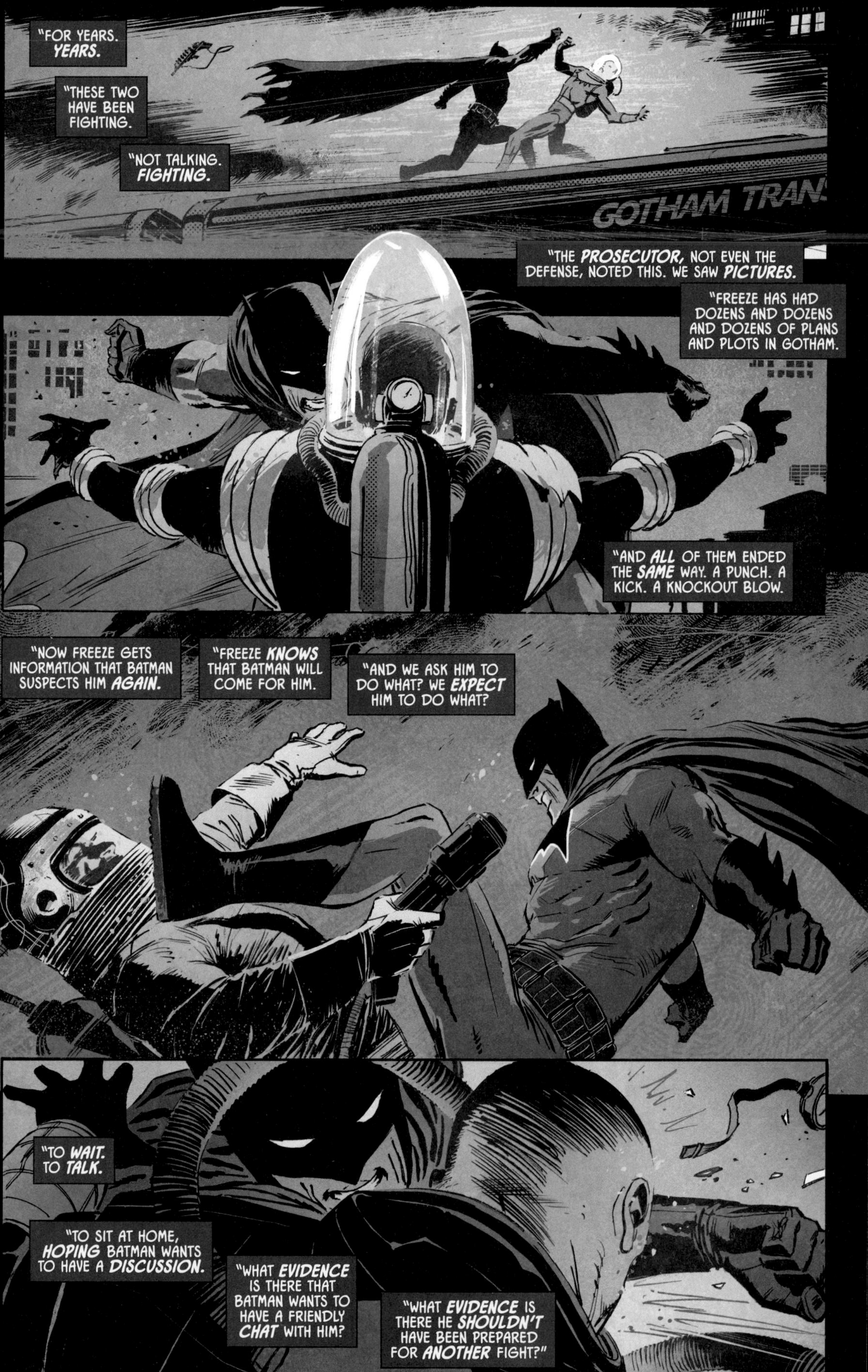
"FOR YEARS. YEARS.
"THESE TWO HAVE BEEN FIGHTING.
"NOT TALKING. FIGHTING.
GOTHAM TRANS
"THE PROSECUTOR, NOT EVEN THE DEFENSE, NOTED THIS. WE SAW PICTURES.
"FREEZE HAS HAD DOZENS AND DOZENS AND DOZENS OF PLANS AND PLOTS IN GOTHAM.
"AND ALL OF THEM ENDED THE SAME WAY. A PUNCH. A KICK. A KNOCKOUT BLOW.
"NOW FREEZE GETS INFORMATION THAT BATMAN SUSPECTS HIM AGAIN.
"FREEZE KNOWS THAT BATMAN WILL COME FOR HIM.
"AND WE ASK HIM TO DO WHAT? WE EXPECT HIM TO DO WHAT?
"TO WAIT. TO TALK.
"TO SIT AT HOME, HOPING BATMAN WANTS TO HAVE A DISCUSSION.
"WHAT EVIDENCE IS THERE THAT BATMAN WANTS TO HAVE A FRIENDLY CHAT WITH HIM?
"WHAT EVIDENCE IS THERE HE SHOULDN'T HAVE BEEN PREPARED FOR ANOTHER FIGHT?"

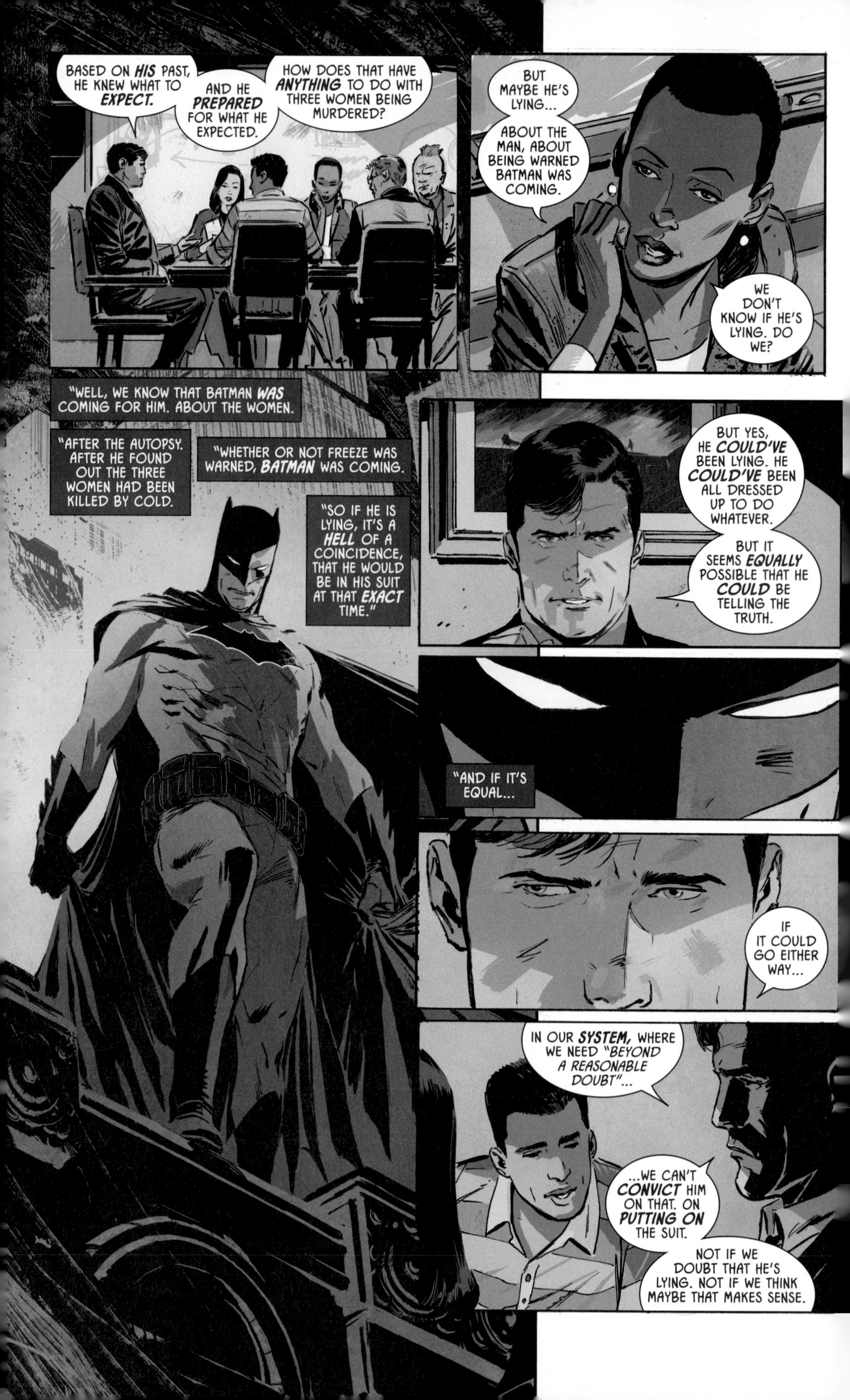
BASED ON HIS PAST, HE KNEW WHAT TO EXPECT.
AND HE PREPARED FOR WHAT HE EXPECTED.
HOW DOES THAT HAVE ANYTHING TO DO WITH THREE WOMEN BEING MURDERED?
BUT MAYBE HE'S LYING...
ABOUT THE MAN, ABOUT BEING WARNED BATMAN WAS COMING.
WE DON'T KNOW IF HE'S LYING. DO WE?
"WELL, WE KNOW THAT BATMAN WAS COMING FOR HIM. ABOUT THE WOMEN.
"AFTER THE AUTOPSY. AFTER HE FOUND OUT THE THREE WOMEN HAD BEEN KILLED BY COLD.
"WHETHER OR NOT FREEZE WAS WARNED, BATMAN WAS COMING.
"SO IF HE IS LYING, IT'S A HELL OF A COINCIDENCE, THAT HE WOULD BE IN HIS SUIT AT THAT EXACT TIME."
BUT YES, HE COULD'VE BEEN LYING. HE COULD'VE BEEN ALL DRESSED UP TO DO WHATEVER.
BUT IT SEEMS EQUALLY POSSIBLE THAT HE COULD BE TELLING THE TRUTH.
"AND IF IT'S EQUAL...
IF IT COULD GO EITHER WAY...
IN OUR SYSTEM, WHERE WE NEED "BEYOND A REASONABLE DOUBT"...
...WE CAN'T CONVICT HIM ON THAT. ON PUTTING ON THE SUIT.
NOT IF WE DOUBT THAT HE'S LYING. NOT IF WE THINK MAYBE THAT MAKES SENSE.

"MR. WAYNE, I'M TAY."

"HELLO."

"MY BOY USED TO GET INTO FIGHTS WITH THIS OTHER BOY. HARD FIGHTS."

"I'M SORRY."

"MY BOY IS A GOOD BOY AND THIS BOY WASN'T. IT HAPPENS. WHEN YOU'RE A PARENT."

"IT DOES."

"WELL, ONE TIME THIS BOY WAS COMING OVER, AND WAS COMING HARD, AND MY BOY KNEW HE WAS COMING."

"I SEE."

"MY BOY, HE GOT A GUN, LEGALLY, BUT HE GOT ONE. I WAS MAD...BUT..."

"YEAH."

"I TOOK THAT GUN AWAY FROM HIM, MADE HIM GO TO THE COPS. AND YOU KNOW WHAT THE COPS SAID? I SWEAR. TO MY FACE."

"NO."

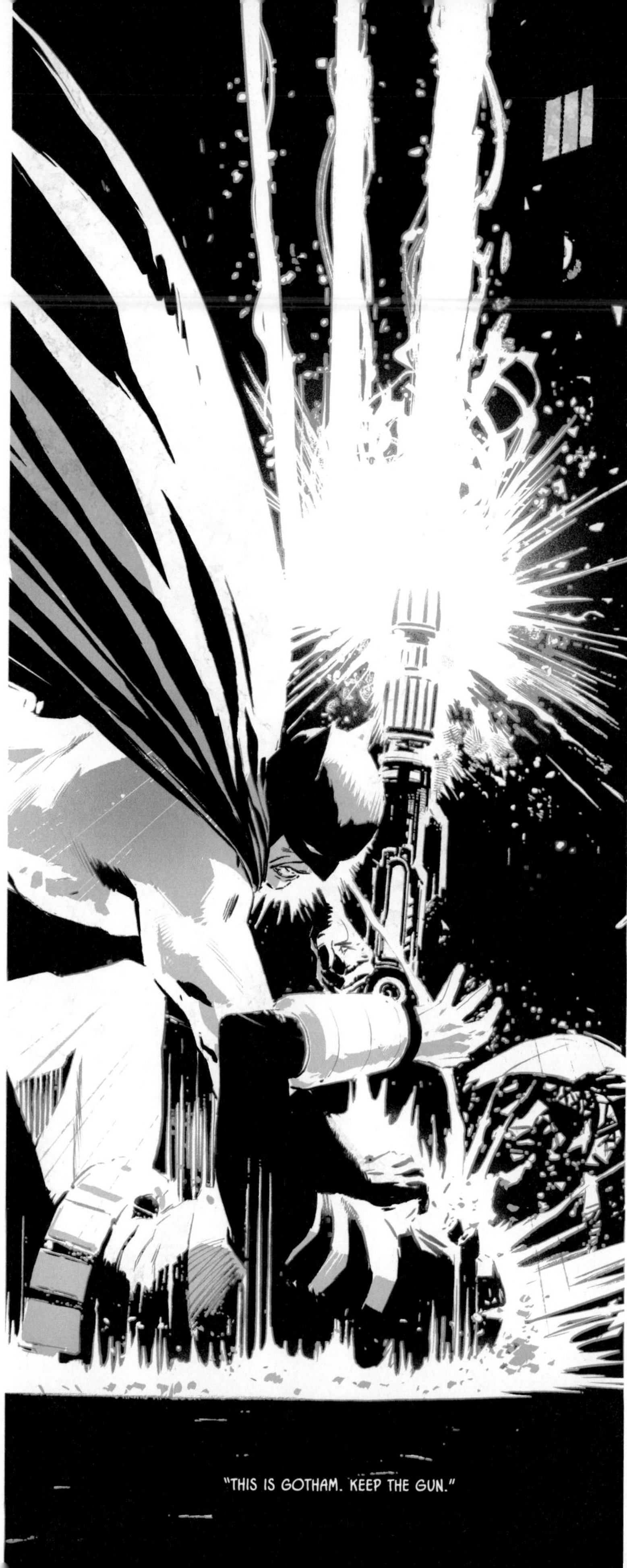
"THIS IS GOTHAM. KEEP THE GUN."

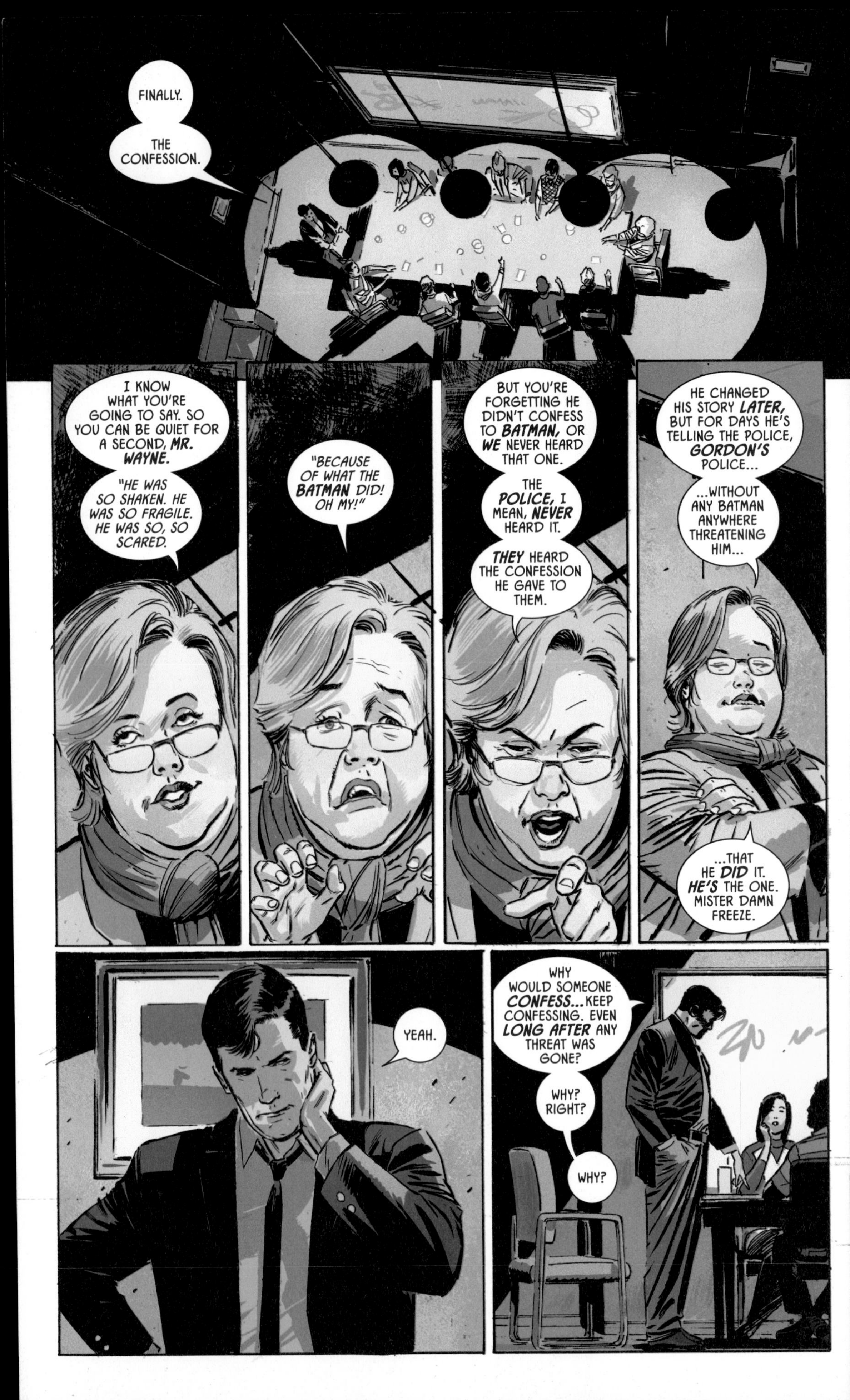
FINALLY.
THE CONFESSION.
I KNOW WHAT YOU'RE GOING TO SAY. SO YOU CAN BE QUIET FOR A SECOND, MR. WAYNE.
"HE WAS SO SHAKEN. HE WAS SO FRAGILE. HE WAS SO, SO SCARED.
"BECAUSE OF WHAT THE BATMAN DID! OH MY!"
BUT YOU'RE FORGETTING HE DIDN'T CONFESS TO BATMAN, OR WE NEVER HEARD THAT ONE.
THE POLICE, I MEAN, NEVER HEARD IT.
THEY HEARD THE CONFESSION HE GAVE TO THEM.
HE CHANGED HIS STORY LATER, BUT FOR DAYS HE'S TELLING THE POLICE, GORDON'S POLICE...
...WITHOUT ANY BATMAN ANYWHERE THREATENING HIM...
...THAT HE DID IT. HE'S THE ONE. MISTER DAMN FREEZE.
YEAH.
WHY WOULD SOMEONE CONFESS...KEEP CONFESSING. EVEN LONG AFTER ANY THREAT WAS GONE?
WHY? RIGHT?
WHY?

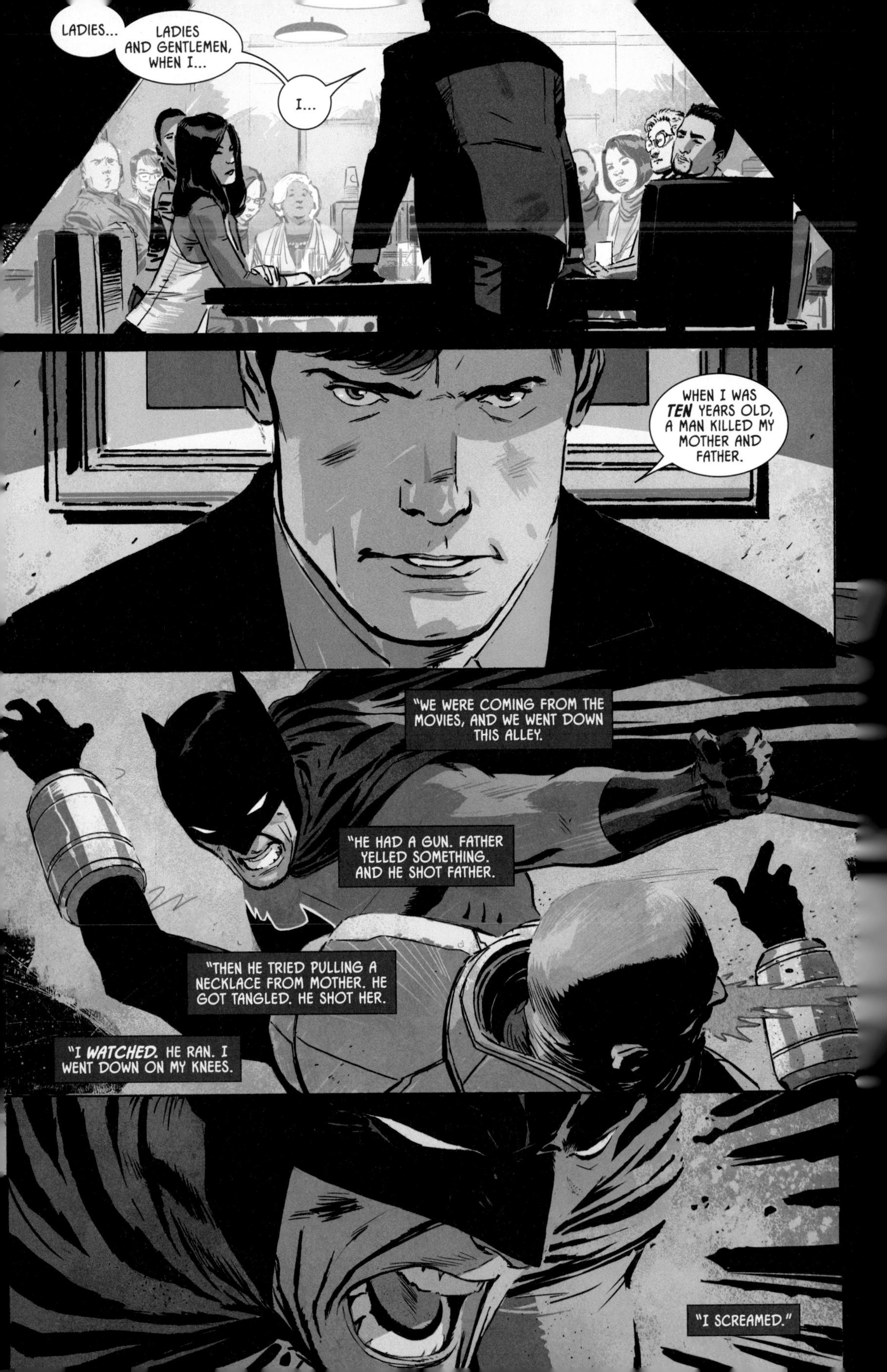

LADIES...
LADIES AND GENTLEMEN, WHEN I...
I...
WHEN I WAS TEN YEARS OLD, A MAN KILLED MY MOTHER AND FATHER.
"WE WERE COMING FROM THE MOVIES, AND WE WENT DOWN THIS ALLEY.
"HE HAD A GUN. FATHER YELLED SOMETHING. AND HE SHOT FATHER.
"THEN HE TRIED PULLING A NECKLACE FROM MOTHER. HE GOT TANGLED. HE SHOT HER.
"I WATCHED. HE RAN. I WENT DOWN ON MY KNEES.
"I SCREAMED."

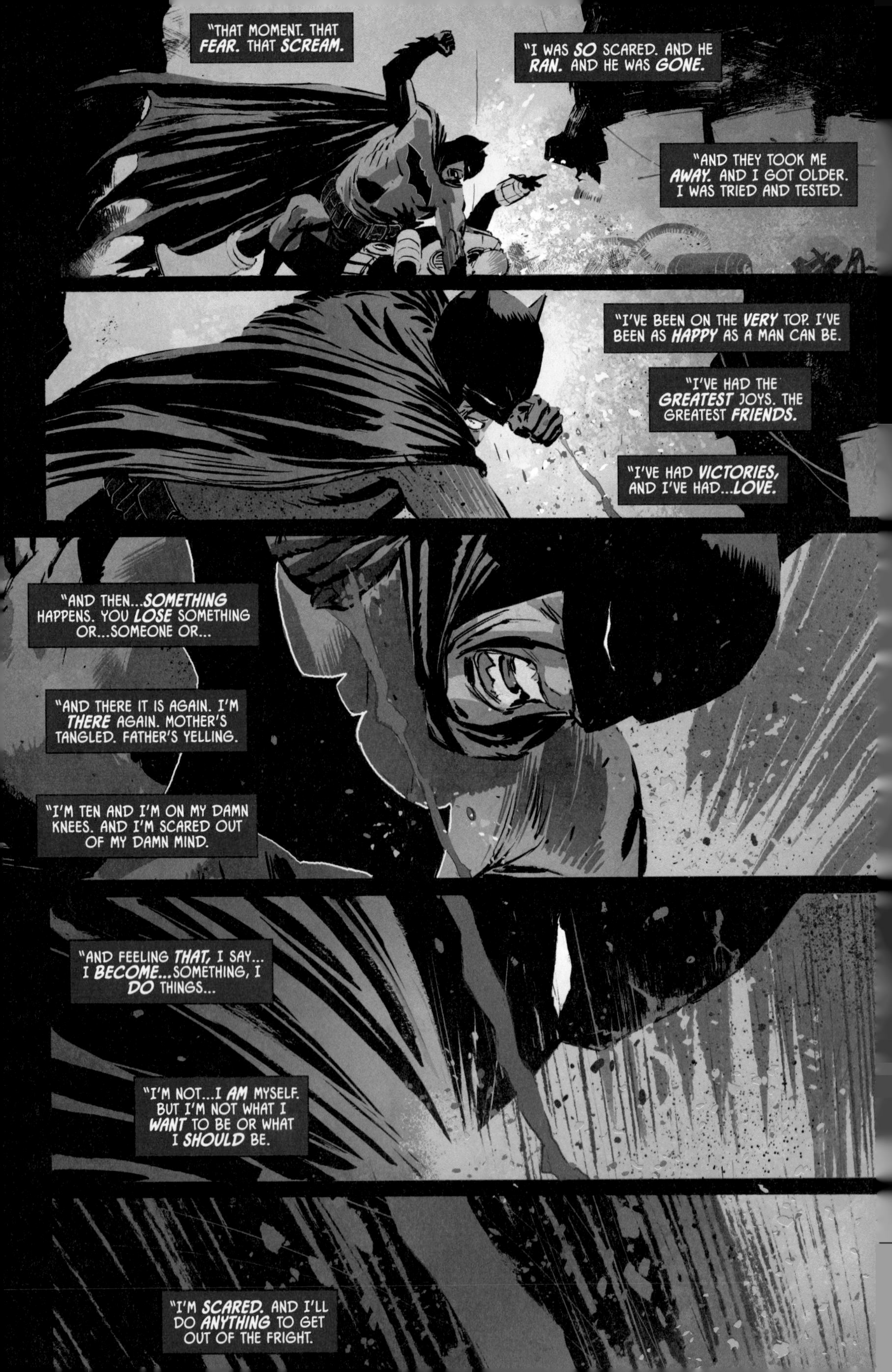
"THAT MOMENT. THAT FEAR. THAT SCREAM.
"I WAS SO SCARED. AND HE RAN. AND HE WAS GONE.
"AND THEY TOOK ME AWAY. AND I GOT OLDER. I WAS TRIED AND TESTED.
"I'VE BEEN ON THE VERY TOP. I'VE BEEN AS HAPPY AS A MAN CAN BE.
"I'VE HAD THE GREATEST JOYS. THE GREATEST FRIENDS.
"I'VE HAD VICTORIES, AND I'VE HAD...LOVE.
"AND THEN...SOMETHING HAPPENS. YOU LOSE SOMETHING OR...SOMEONE OR...
"AND THERE IT IS AGAIN. I'M THERE AGAIN. MOTHER'S TANGLED. FATHER'S YELLING.
"I'M TEN AND I'M ON MY DAMN KNEES. AND I'M SCARED OUT OF MY DAMN MIND.
"AND FEELING THAT, I SAY... I BECOME...SOMETHING, I DO THINGS...
"I'M NOT...I AM MYSELF. BUT I'M NOT WHAT I WANT TO BE OR WHAT I SHOULD BE.
"I'M SCARED. AND I'LL DO ANYTHING TO GET OUT OF THE FRIGHT.

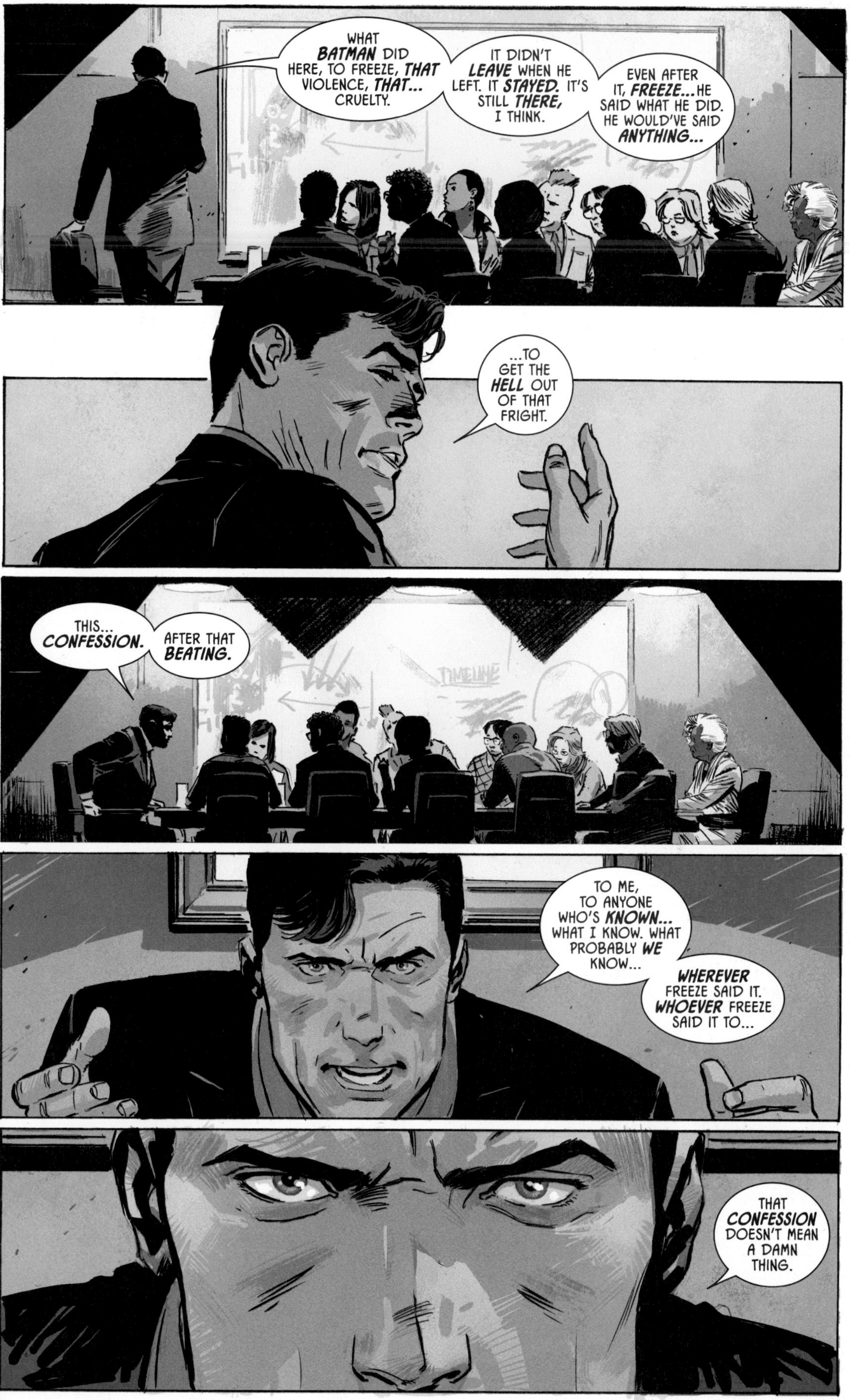
WHAT BATMAN DID HERE, TO FREEZE, THAT VIOLENCE, THAT... CRUELTY.
IT DIDN'T LEAVE WHEN HE LEFT. IT STAYED. IT'S STILL THERE, I THINK.
EVEN AFTER IT, FREEZE... HE SAID WHAT HE DID. HE WOULD'VE SAID ANYTHING...
...TO GET THE HELL OUT OF THAT FRIGHT.
THIS... CONFESSION.
AFTER THAT BEATING.
TIMELINE
TO ME, TO ANYONE WHO'S KNOWN... WHAT I KNOW. WHAT PROBABLY WE KNOW...
WHEREVER FREEZE SAID IT. WHOEVER FREEZE SAID IT TO...
THAT CONFESSION DOESN'T MEAN A DAMN THING.

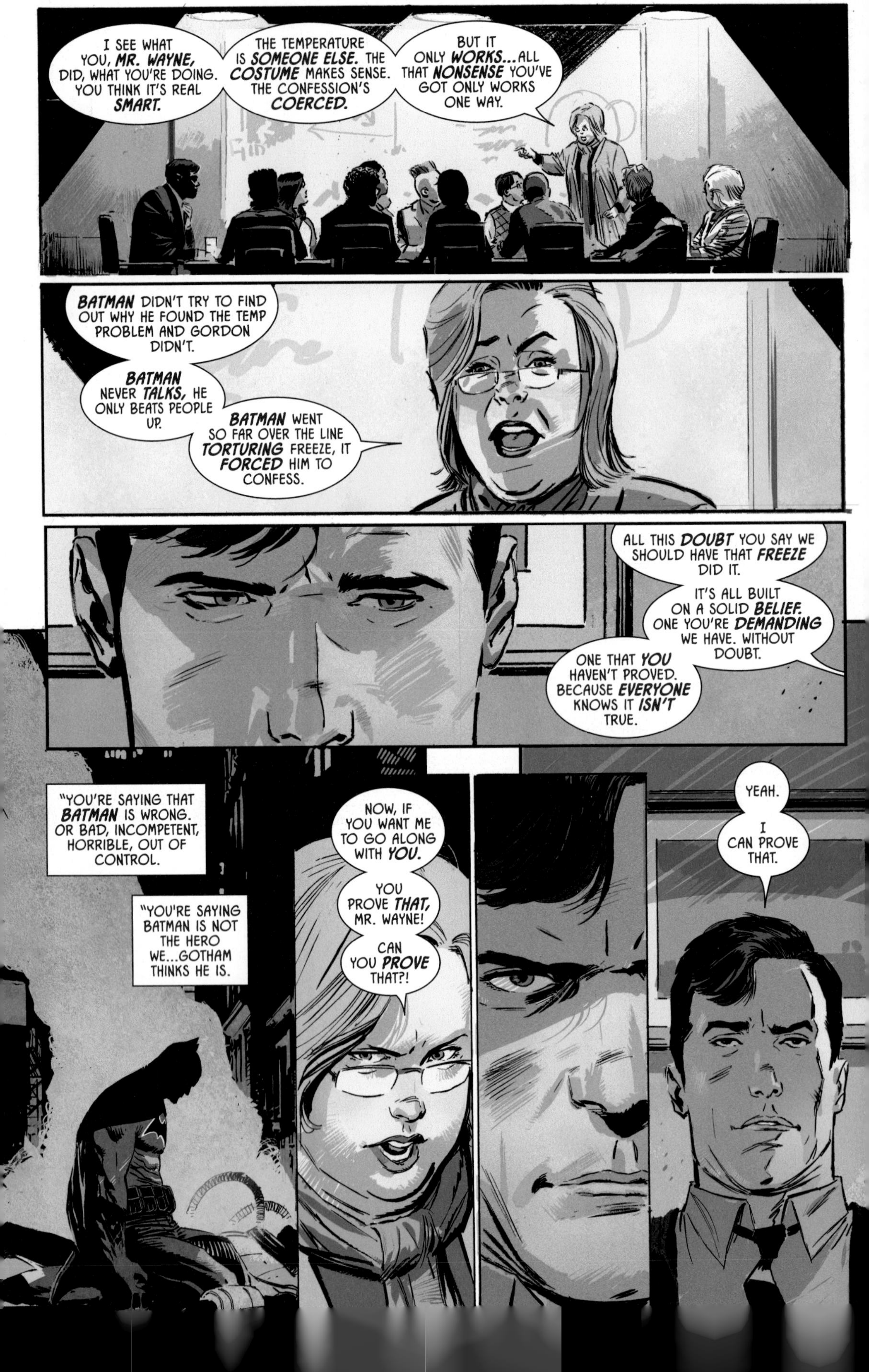

I SEE WHAT YOU, MR. WAYNE, DID, WHAT YOU'RE DOING. YOU THINK IT'S REAL SMART.
THE TEMPERATURE IS SOMEONE ELSE. THE COSTUME MAKES SENSE. THE CONFESSION'S COERCED.
BUT IT ONLY WORKS...ALL THAT NONSENSE YOU'VE GOT ONLY WORKS ONE WAY.
BATMAN DIDN'T TRY TO FIND OUT WHY HE FOUND THE TEMP PROBLEM AND GORDON DIDN'T.
BATMAN NEVER TALKS, HE ONLY BEATS PEOPLE UP.
BATMAN WENT SO FAR OVER THE LINE TORTURING FREEZE, IT FORCED HIM TO CONFESS.
ALL THIS DOUBT YOU SAY WE SHOULD HAVE THAT FREEZE DID IT.
IT'S ALL BUILT ON A SOLID BELIEF. ONE YOU'RE DEMANDING WE HAVE. WITHOUT DOUBT.
ONE THAT YOU HAVEN'T PROVED. BECAUSE EVERYONE KNOWS IT ISN'T TRUE.
"YOU'RE SAYING THAT BATMAN IS WRONG. OR BAD, INCOMPETENT, HORRIBLE, OUT OF CONTROL.
"YOU'RE SAYING BATMAN IS NOT THE HERO WE...GOTHAM THINKS HE IS.
NOW, IF YOU WANT ME TO GO ALONG WITH YOU.
YOU PROVE THAT, MR. WAYNE!
CAN YOU PROVE THAT?!
YEAH.
I CAN PROVE THAT.

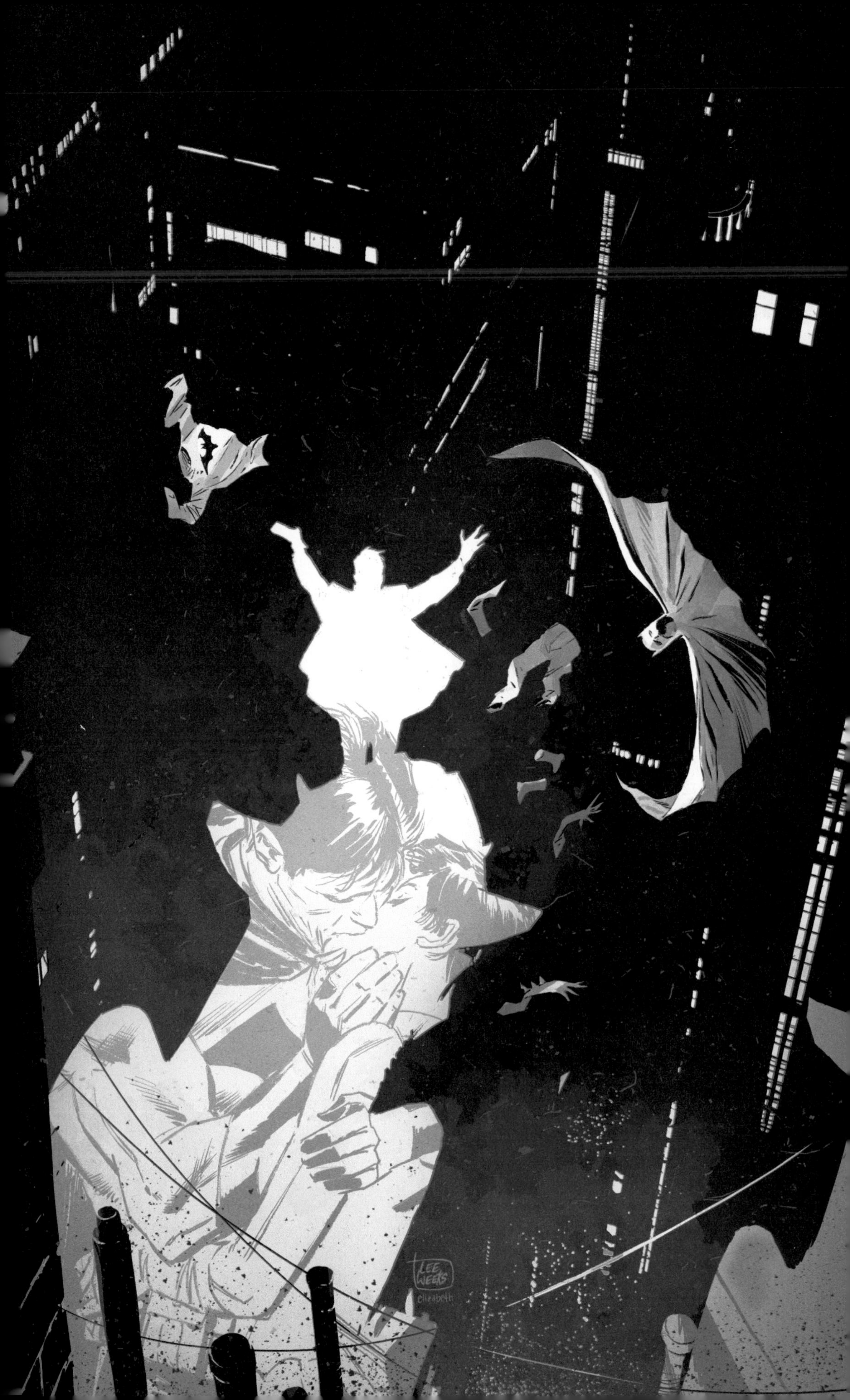
LEE WEEKS
elizabeth

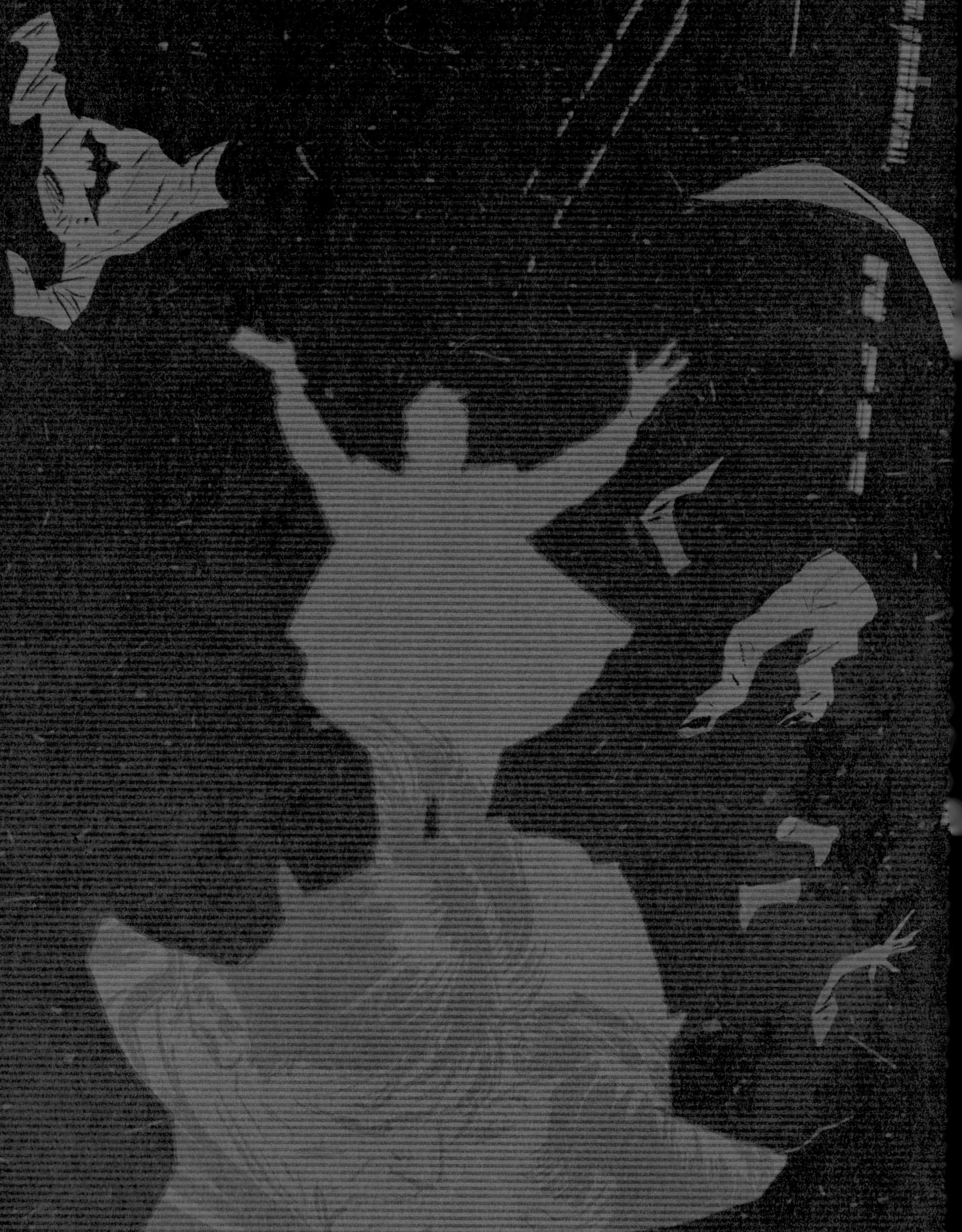

BATMAN
#53

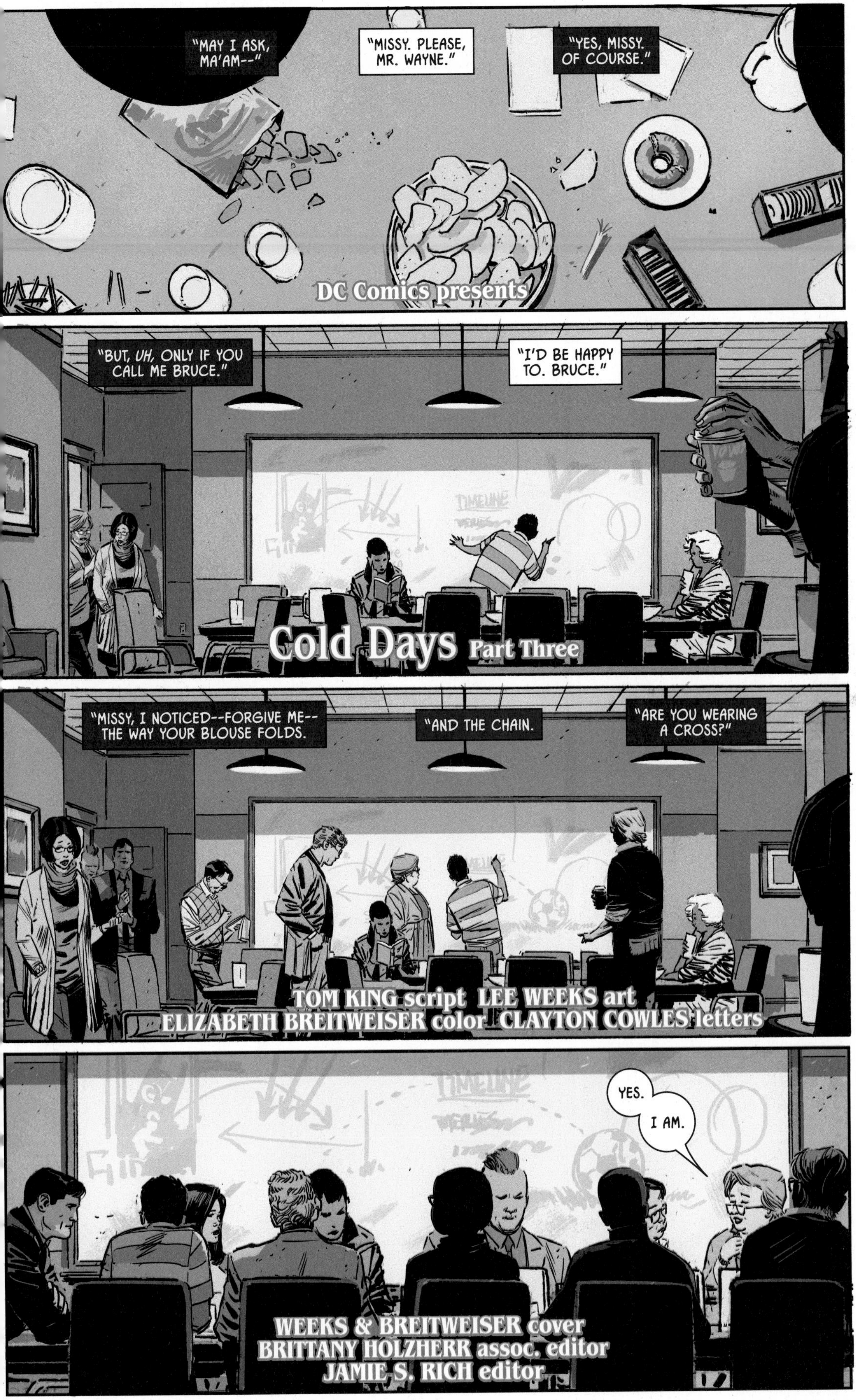
"MAY I ASK, MA'AM--"
"MISSY. PLEASE, MR. WAYNE."
"YES, MISSY. OF COURSE."
DC Comics presents
"BUT, UH, ONLY IF YOU CALL ME BRUCE."
"I'D BE HAPPY TO. BRUCE."
Cold Days Part Three
"MISSY, I NOTICED--FORGIVE ME-- THE WAY YOUR BLOUSE FOLDS.
"AND THE CHAIN.
"ARE YOU WEARING A CROSS?"
TOM KING script LEE WEEKS art
ELIZABETH BREITWEISER color CLAYTON COWLES letters
YES.
I AM.
WEEKS & BREITWEISER cover
BRITTANY HOLZHERR assoc. editor
JAMIE S. RICH editor

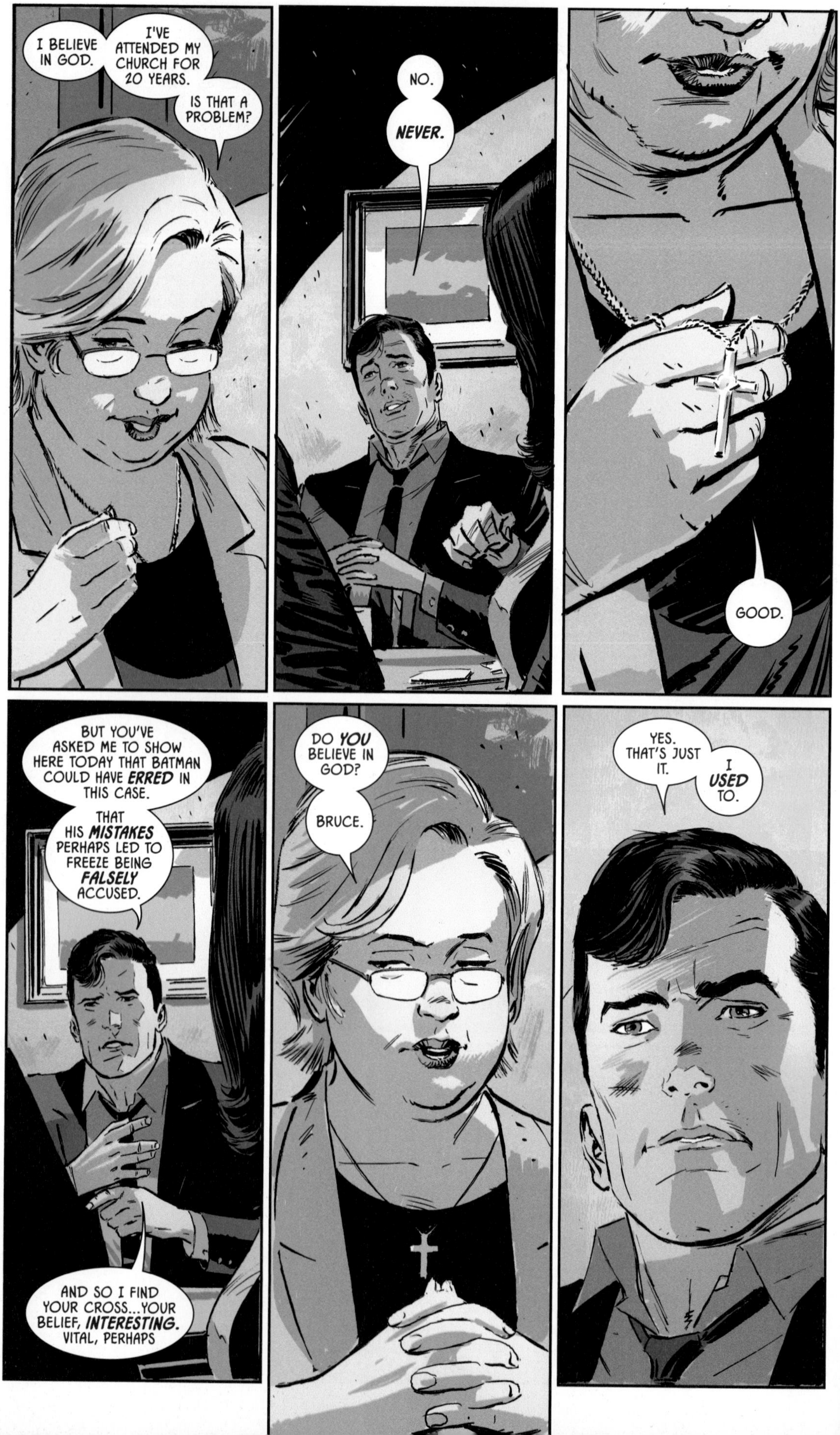

I BELIEVE IN GOD.
I'VE ATTENDED MY CHURCH FOR 20 YEARS.
IS THAT A PROBLEM?
NO.
NEVER.
GOOD.
BUT YOU'VE ASKED ME TO SHOW HERE TODAY THAT BATMAN COULD HAVE ERRED IN THIS CASE.
THAT HIS MISTAKES PERHAPS LED TO FREEZE BEING FALSELY ACCUSED.
AND SO I FIND YOUR CROSS...YOUR BELIEF, INTERESTING. VITAL, PERHAPS
DO YOU BELIEVE IN GOD?
BRUCE.
YES. THAT'S JUST IT.
I USED TO.

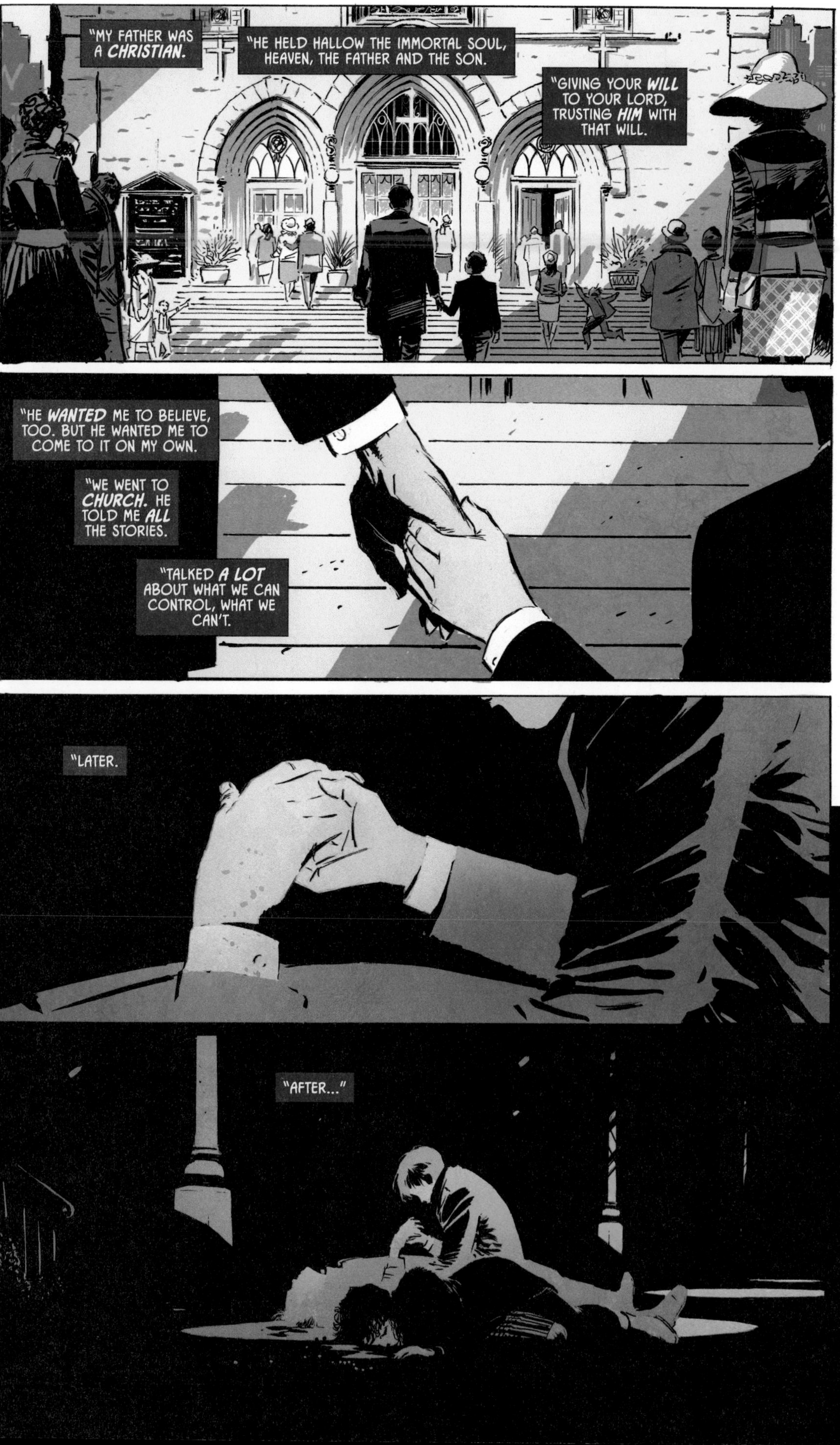
"MY FATHER WAS A CHRISTIAN.
"HE HELD HALLOW THE IMMORTAL SOUL, HEAVEN, THE FATHER AND THE SON.
"GIVING YOUR WILL TO YOUR LORD, TRUSTING HIM WITH THAT WILL.
"HE WANTED ME TO BELIEVE, TOO. BUT HE WANTED ME TO COME TO IT ON MY OWN.
"WE WENT TO CHURCH. HE TOLD ME ALL THE STORIES.
"TALKED A LOT ABOUT WHAT WE CAN CONTROL, WHAT WE CAN'T.
"LATER.
"AFTER..."

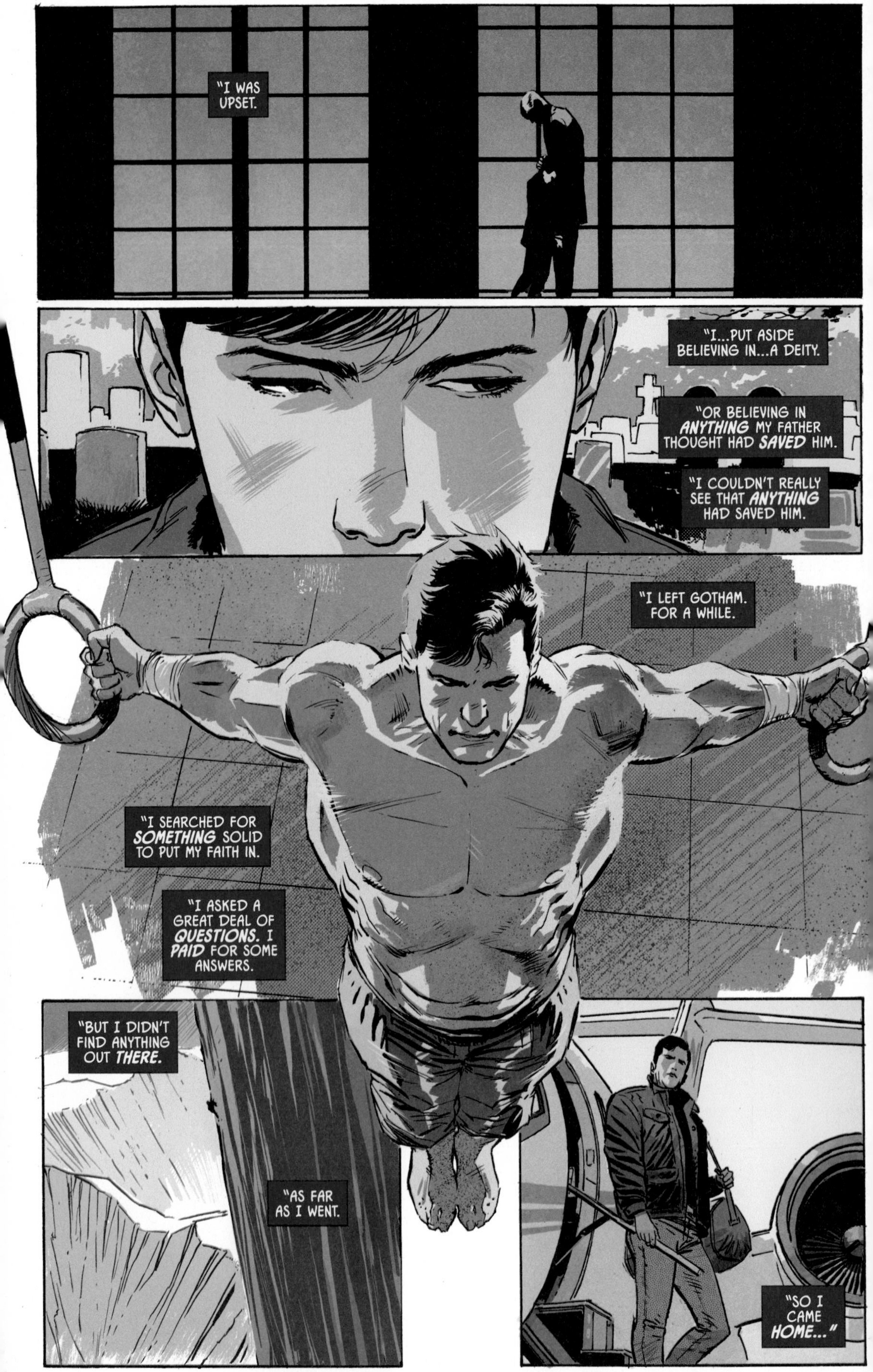
"I WAS UPSET.
"I...PUT ASIDE BELIEVING IN...A DEITY.
"OR BELIEVING IN ANYTHING MY FATHER THOUGHT HAD SAVED HIM.
"I COULDN'T REALLY SEE THAT ANYTHING HAD SAVED HIM.
"I LEFT GOTHAM. FOR A WHILE.
"I SEARCHED FOR SOMETHING SOLID TO PUT MY FAITH IN.
"I ASKED A GREAT DEAL OF QUESTIONS. I PAID FOR SOME ANSWERS.
"BUT I DIDN'T FIND ANYTHING OUT THERE.
"AS FAR AS I WENT.
"SO I CAME HOME..."

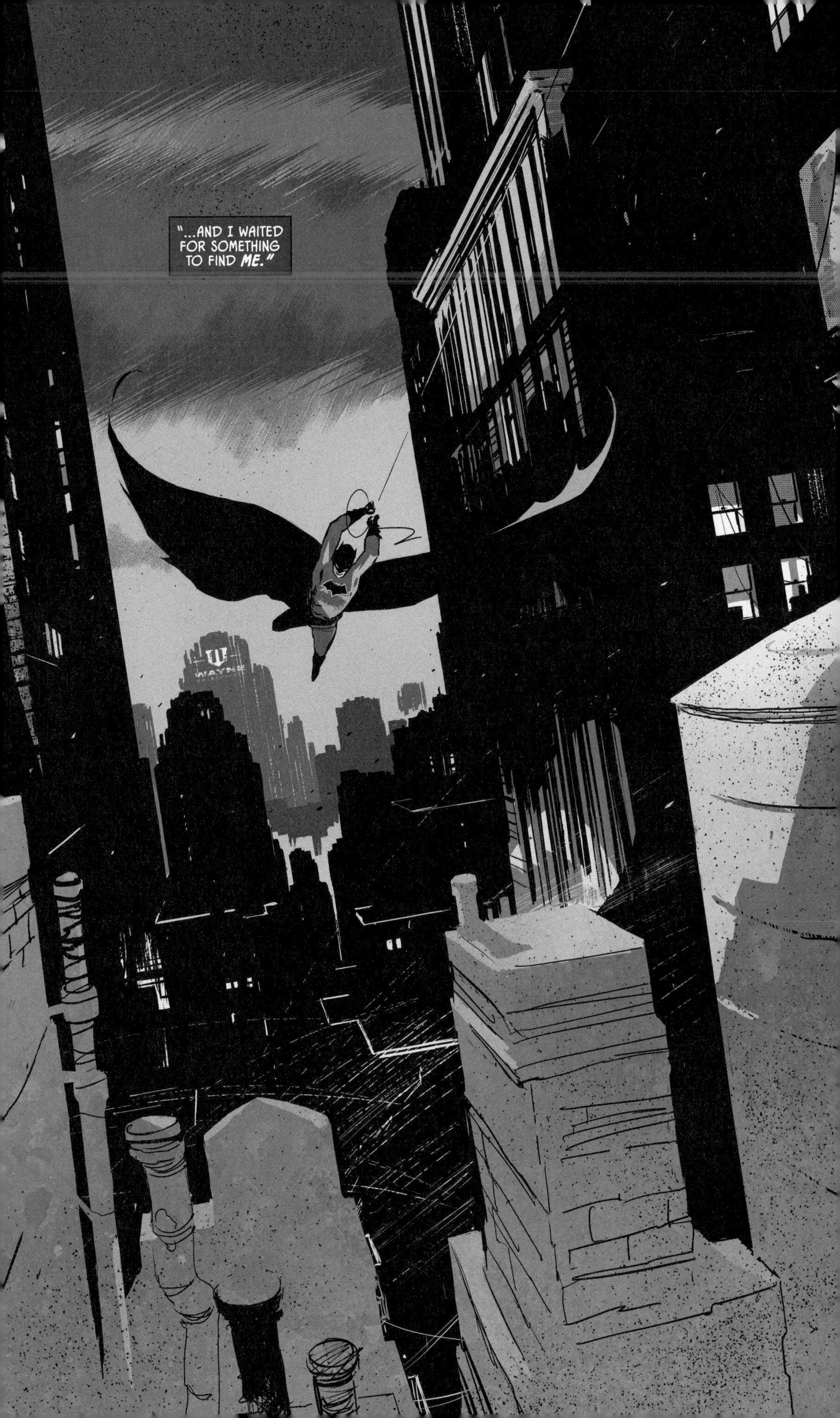
"...AND I WAITED FOR SOMETHING TO FIND ME."

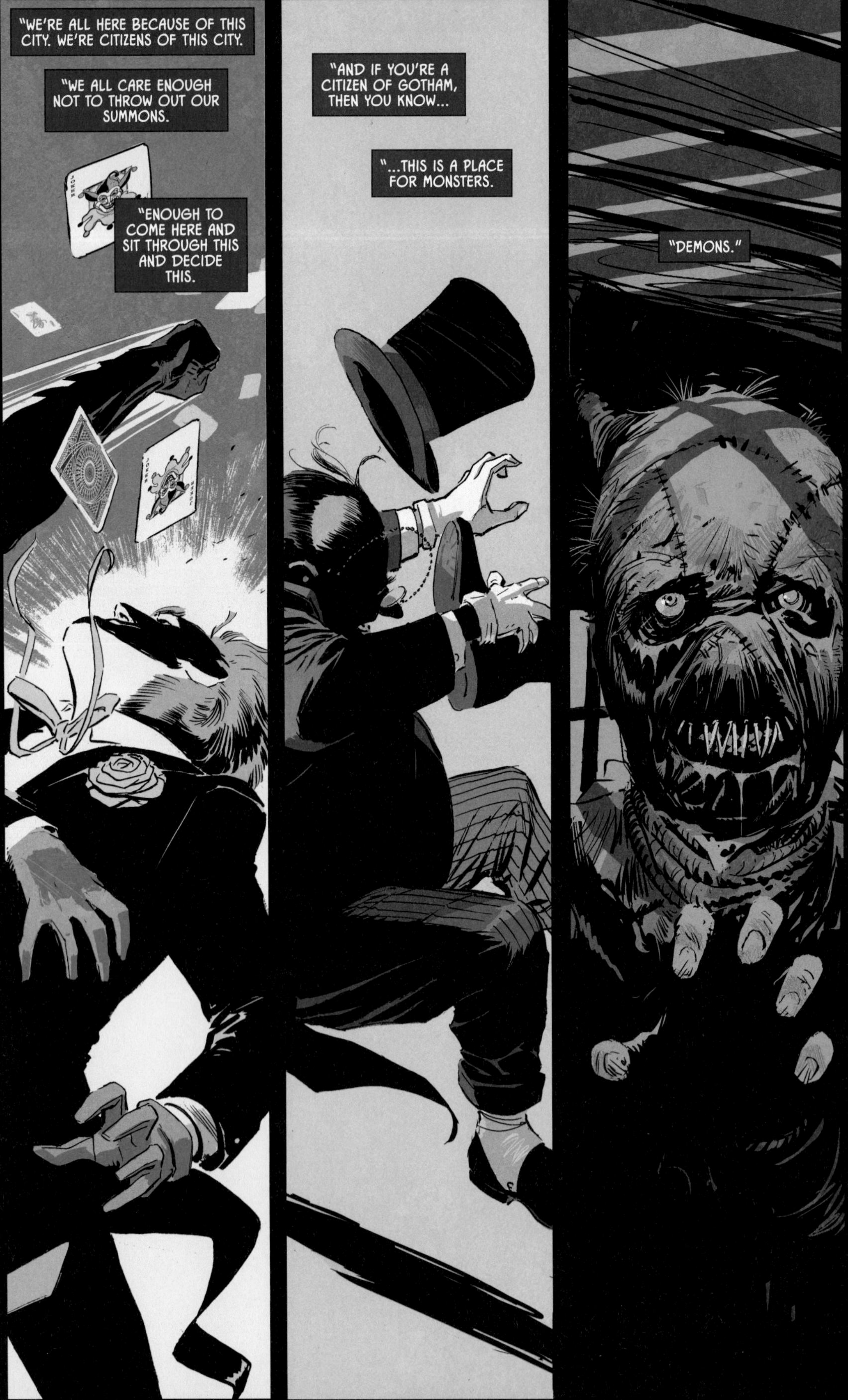
"WE'RE ALL HERE BECAUSE OF THIS CITY. WE'RE CITIZENS OF THIS CITY.
"WE ALL CARE ENOUGH NOT TO THROW OUT OUR SUMMONS.
"ENOUGH TO COME HERE AND SIT THROUGH THIS AND DECIDE THIS.
"AND IF YOU'RE A CITIZEN OF GOTHAM, THEN YOU KNOW...
"...THIS IS A PLACE FOR MONSTERS.
"DEMONS."

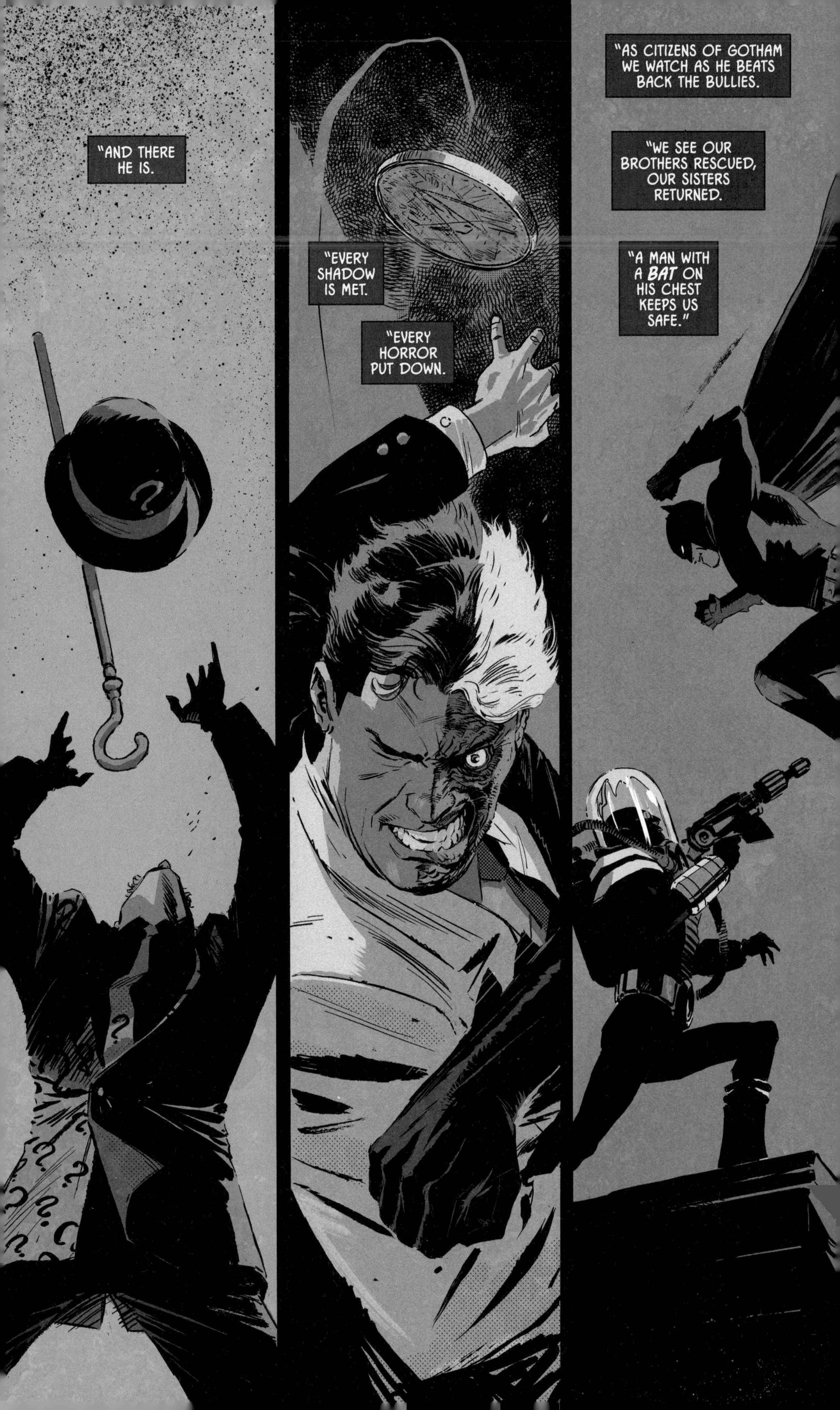
"AND THERE HE IS.
"EVERY SHADOW IS MET.
"EVERY HORROR PUT DOWN.
"AS CITIZENS OF GOTHAM WE WATCH AS HE BEATS BACK THE BULLIES.
"WE SEE OUR BROTHERS RESCUED, OUR SISTERS RETURNED.
"A MAN WITH A BAT ON HIS CHEST KEEPS US SAFE."

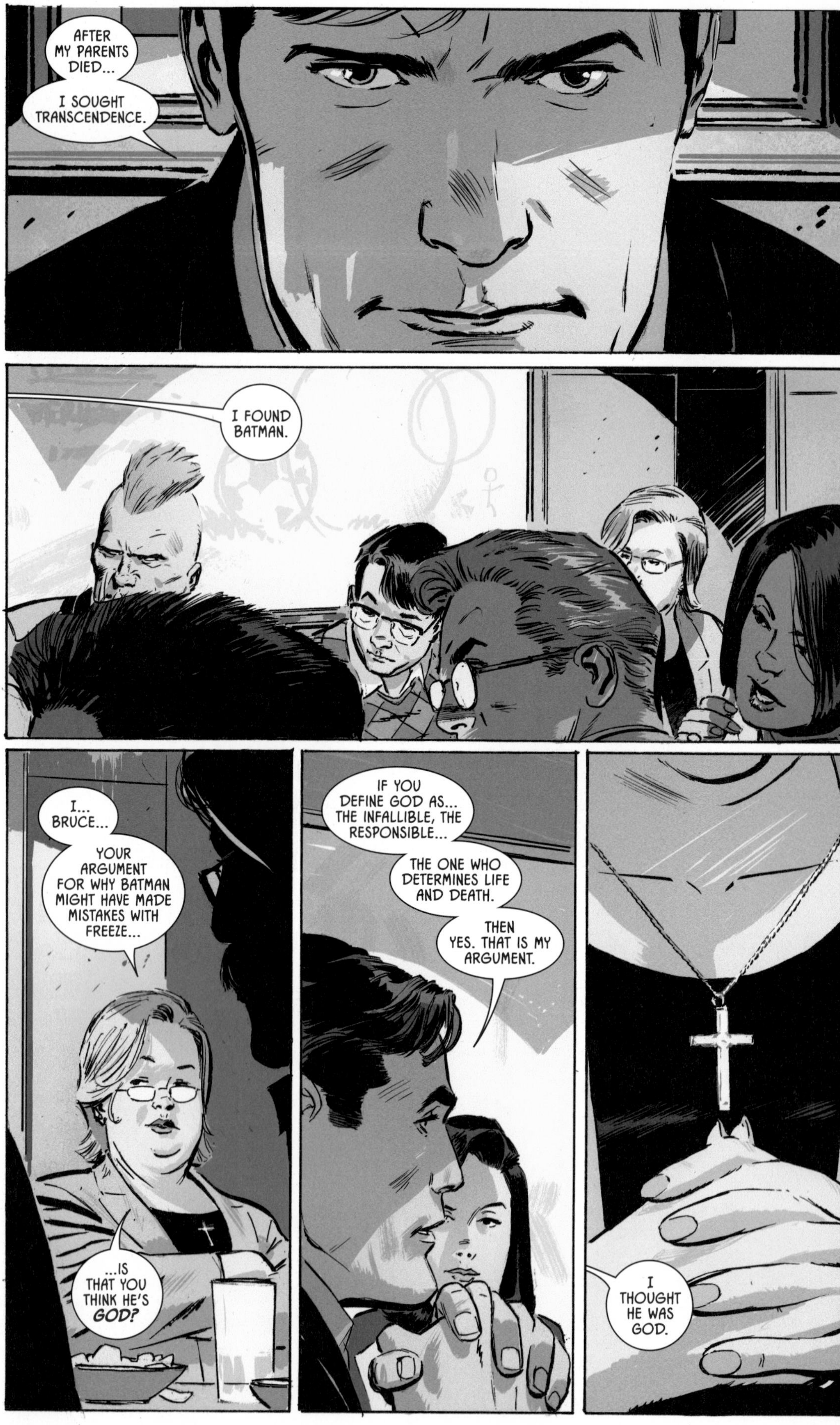
AFTER MY PARENTS DIED...
I SOUGHT TRANSCENDENCE.
I FOUND BATMAN.
I... BRUCE...
YOUR ARGUMENT FOR WHY BATMAN MIGHT HAVE MADE MISTAKES WITH FREEZE...
...IS THAT YOU THINK HE'S *GOD?*
IF YOU DEFINE GOD AS... THE INFALLIBLE, THE RESPONSIBLE...
THE ONE WHO DETERMINES LIFE AND DEATH.
THEN YES. THAT IS MY ARGUMENT.
I THOUGHT HE WAS GOD.

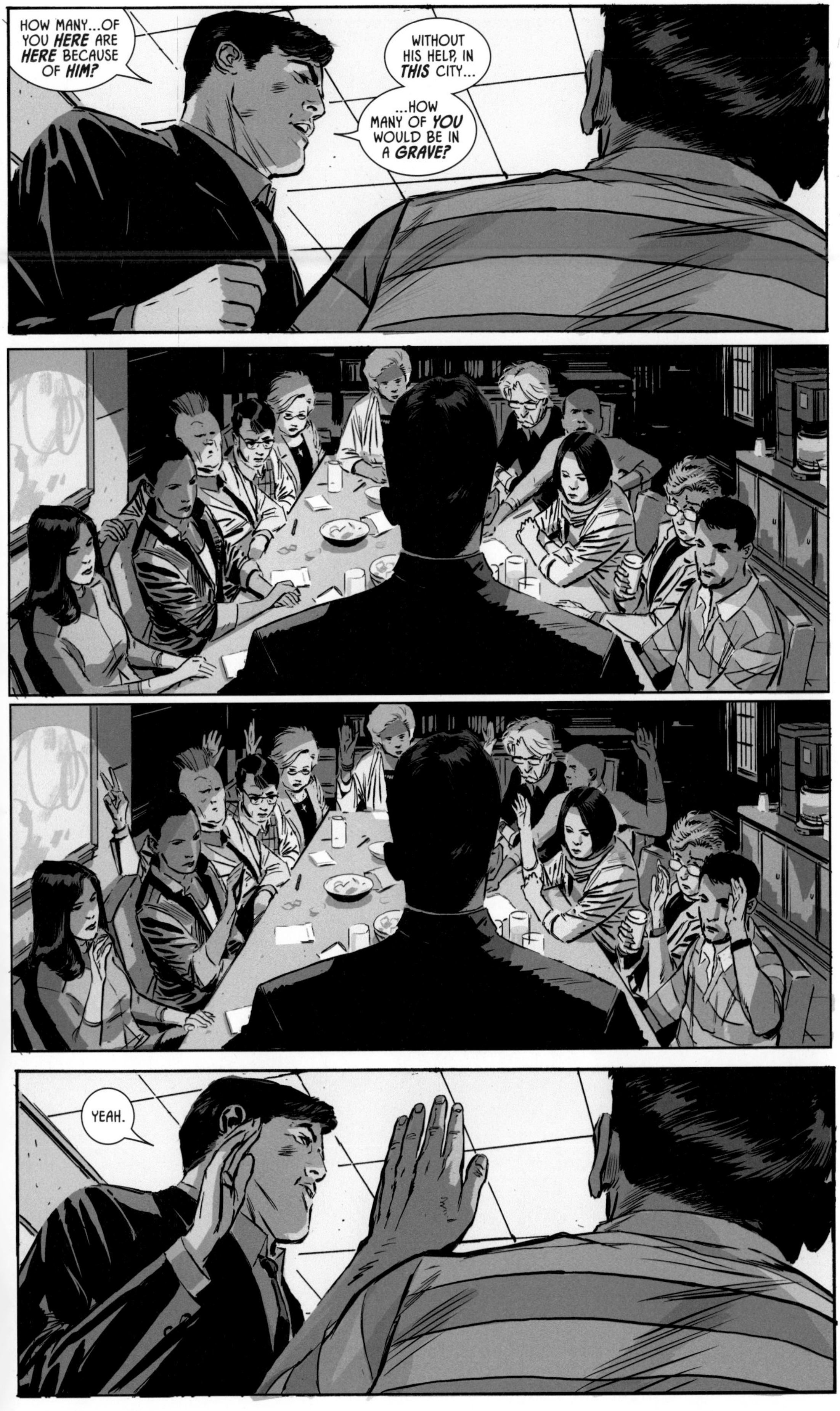
HOW MANY...OF YOU HERE ARE HERE BECAUSE OF HIM?
WITHOUT HIS HELP, IN THIS CITY...
...HOW MANY OF YOU WOULD BE IN A GRAVE?
YEAH.

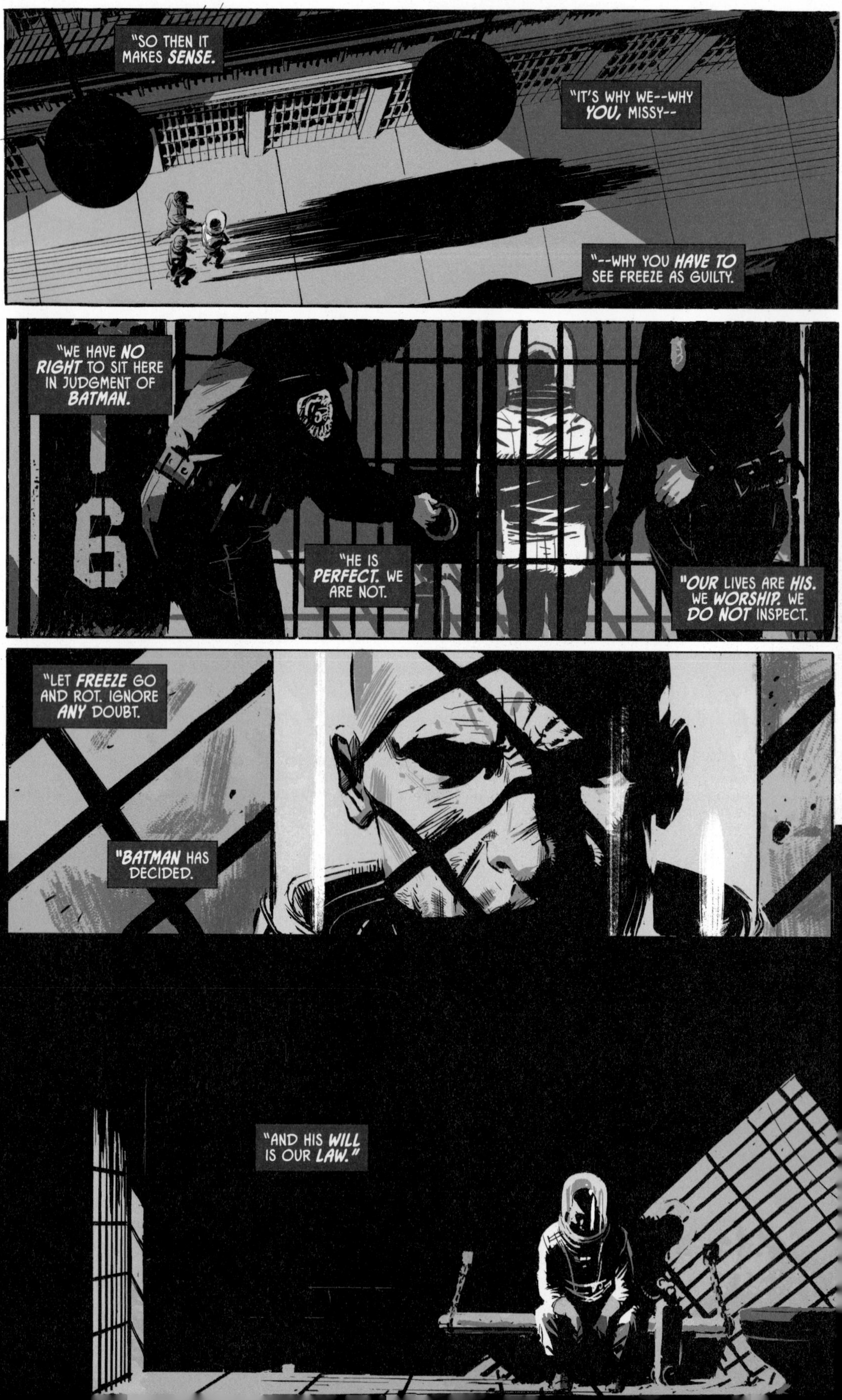
"SO THEN IT MAKES SENSE.
"IT'S WHY WE--WHY YOU, MISSY--
"--WHY YOU HAVE TO SEE FREEZE AS GUILTY.
"WE HAVE NO RIGHT TO SIT HERE IN JUDGMENT OF BATMAN.
6
"HE IS PERFECT. WE ARE NOT.
"OUR LIVES ARE HIS. WE WORSHIP. WE DO NOT INSPECT.
"LET FREEZE GO AND ROT. IGNORE ANY DOUBT.
"BATMAN HAS DECIDED.
"AND HIS WILL IS OUR LAW."

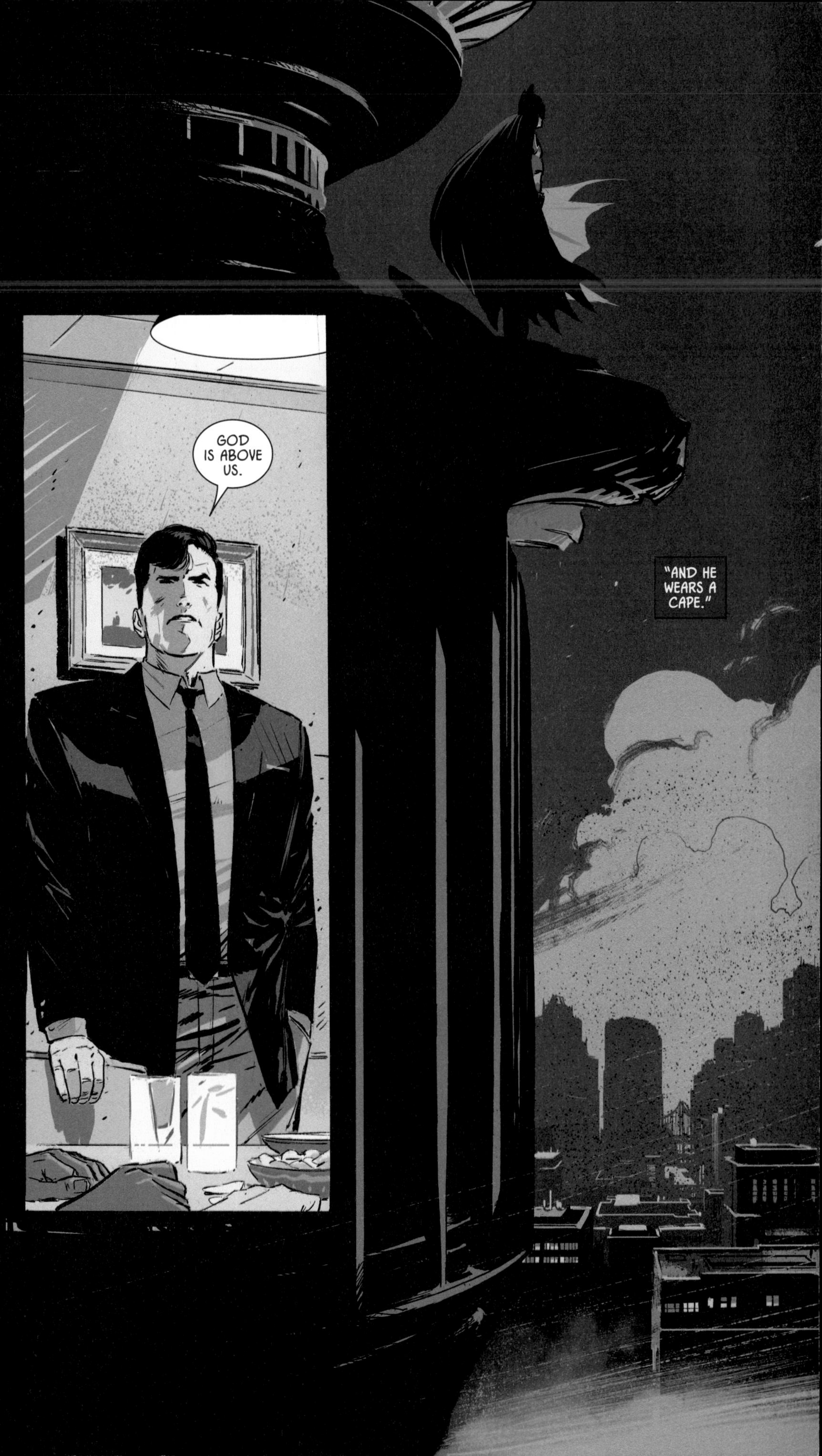
GOD IS ABOVE US.
"AND HE WEARS A CAPE."

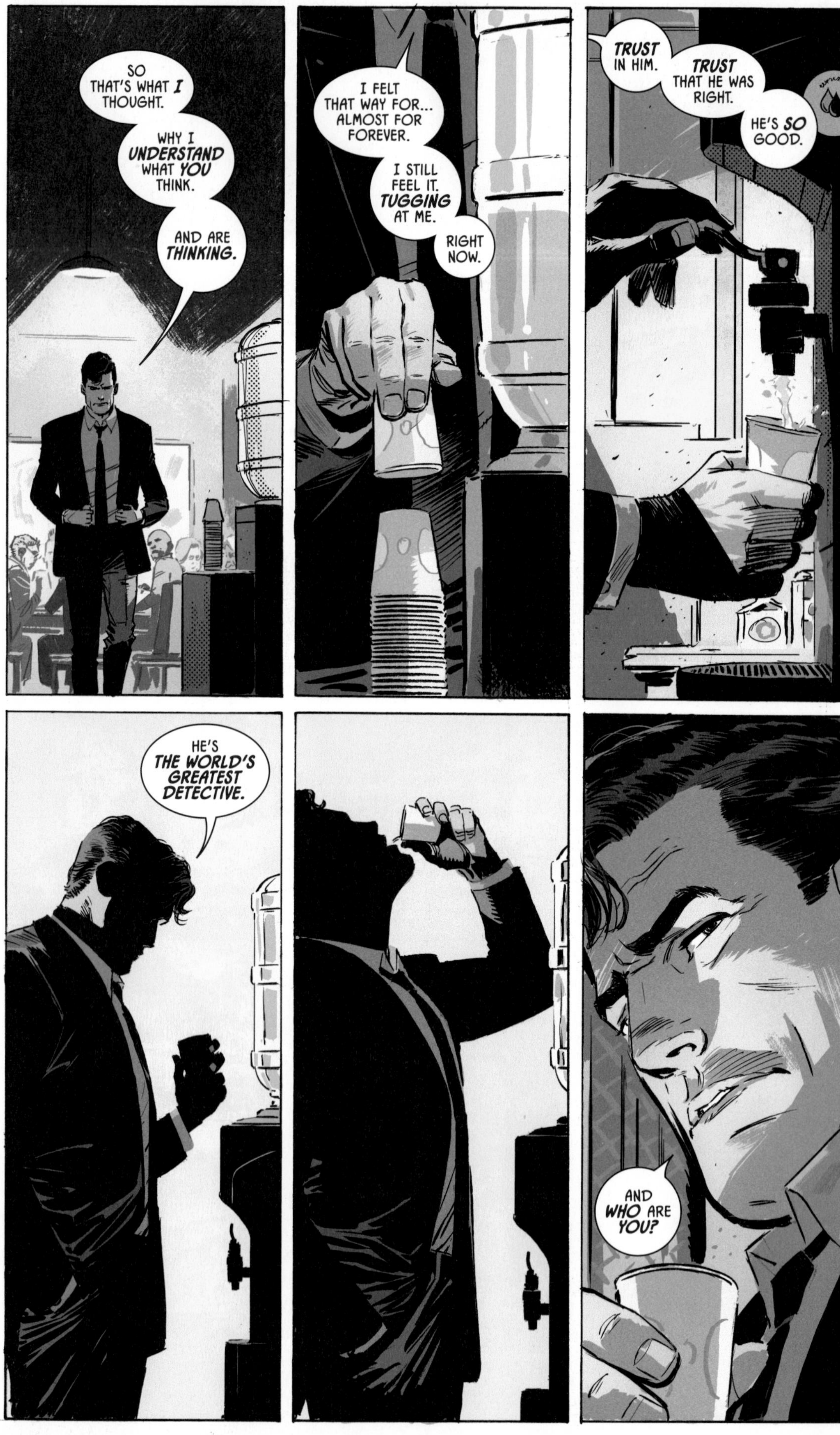
SO THAT'S WHAT I THOUGHT.
WHY I UNDERSTAND WHAT YOU THINK.
AND ARE THINKING.
I FELT THAT WAY FOR... ALMOST FOR FOREVER.
I STILL FEEL IT. TUGGING AT ME.
RIGHT NOW.
TRUST IN HIM.
TRUST THAT HE WAS RIGHT.
HE'S SO GOOD.
HE'S THE WORLD'S GREATEST DETECTIVE.
AND WHO ARE YOU?

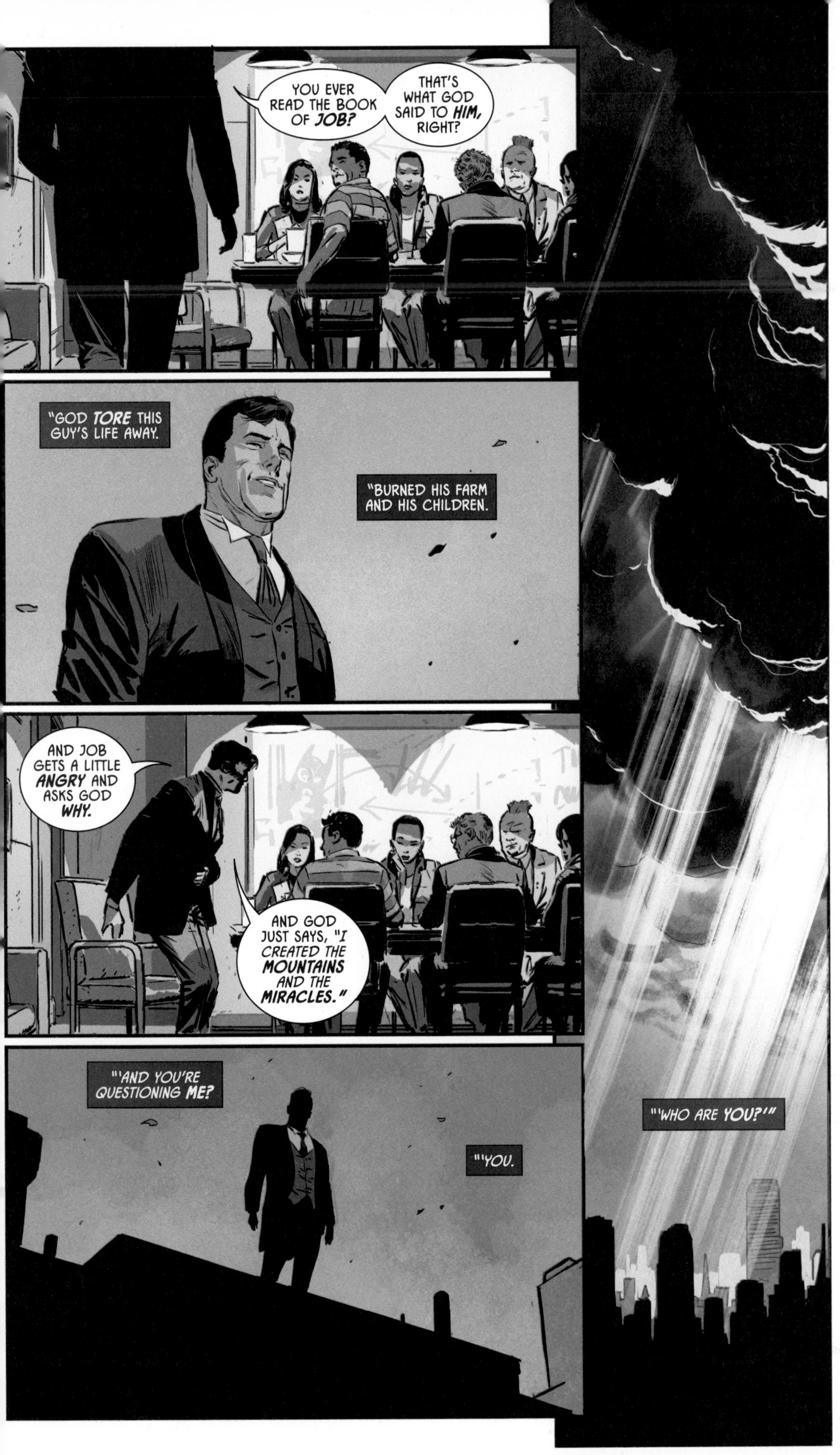
YOU EVER READ THE BOOK OF JOB?
THAT'S WHAT GOD SAID TO HIM, RIGHT?
"GOD TORE THIS GUY'S LIFE AWAY.
"BURNED HIS FARM AND HIS CHILDREN.
AND JOB GETS A LITTLE ANGRY AND ASKS GOD WHY.
AND GOD JUST SAYS, "I CREATED THE MOUNTAINS AND THE MIRACLES."
"'AND YOU'RE QUESTIONING ME?
"'YOU.
"'WHO ARE YOU?'"

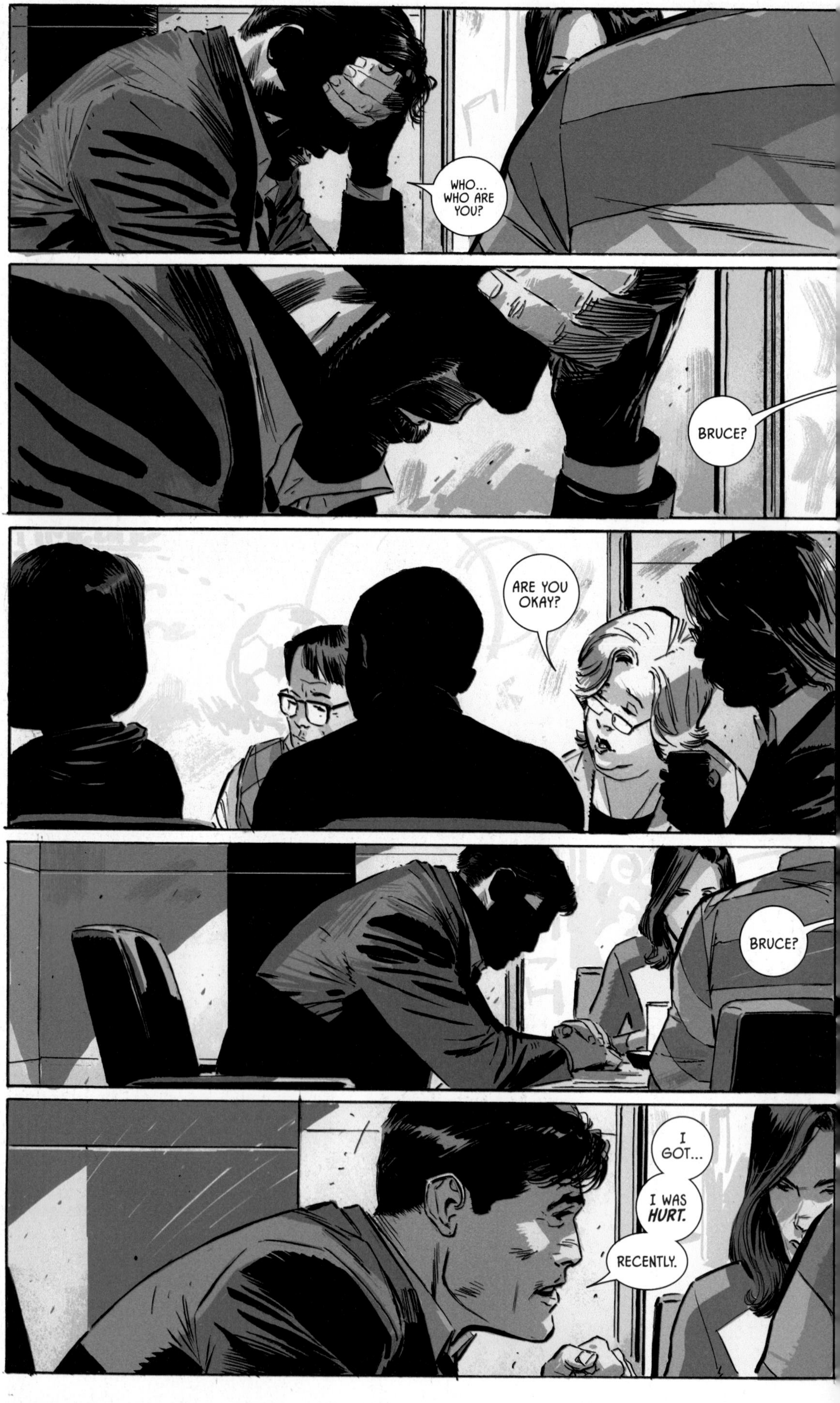
WHO... WHO ARE YOU?
BRUCE?
ARE YOU OKAY?
BRUCE?
I GOT...
I WAS *HURT.*
RECENTLY.

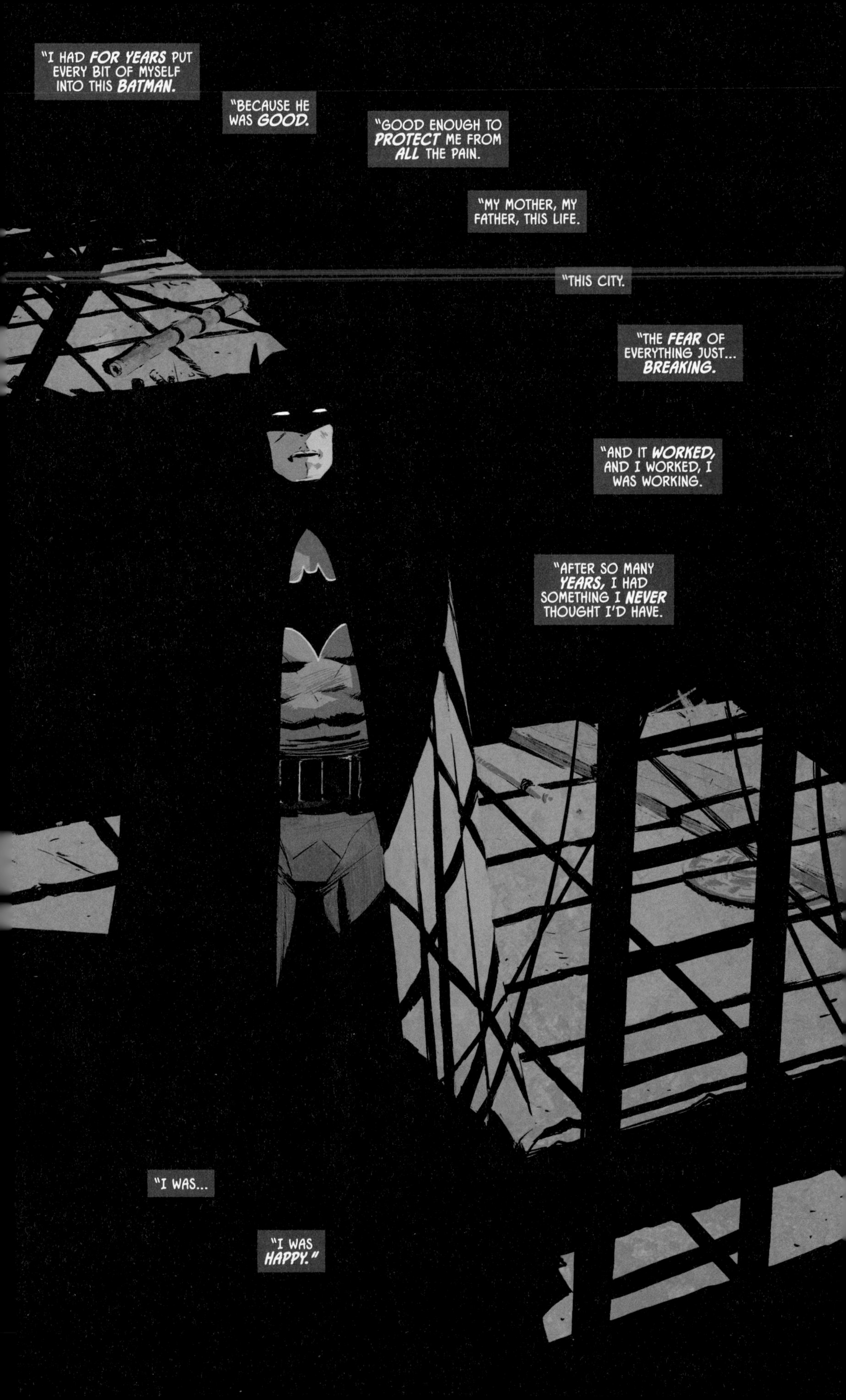
"I HAD FOR YEARS PUT EVERY BIT OF MYSELF INTO THIS BATMAN.
"BECAUSE HE WAS GOOD.
"GOOD ENOUGH TO PROTECT ME FROM ALL THE PAIN.
"MY MOTHER, MY FATHER, THIS LIFE.
"THIS CITY.
"THE FEAR OF EVERYTHING JUST... BREAKING.
"AND IT WORKED, AND I WORKED, I WAS WORKING.
"AFTER SO MANY YEARS, I HAD SOMETHING I NEVER THOUGHT I'D HAVE.
"I WAS...
"I WAS HAPPY."

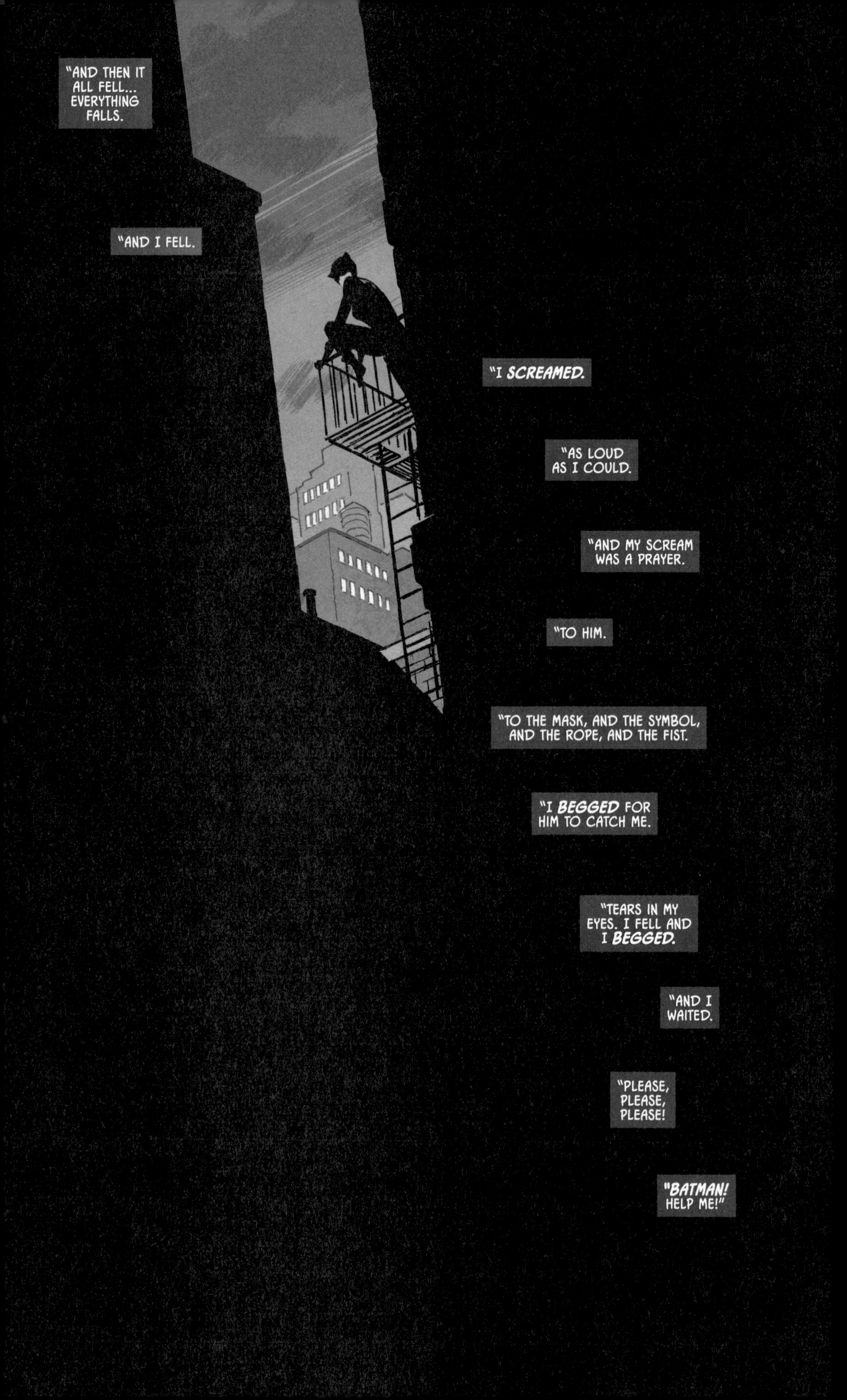
"AND THEN IT ALL FELL... EVERYTHING FALLS.
"AND I FELL.
"I *SCREAMED.*
"AS LOUD AS I COULD.
"AND MY SCREAM WAS A PRAYER.
"TO HIM.
"TO THE MASK, AND THE SYMBOL, AND THE ROPE, AND THE FIST.
"I *BEGGED* FOR HIM TO CATCH ME.
"TEARS IN MY EYES. I FELL AND I *BEGGED.*
"AND I WAITED.
"PLEASE, PLEASE, PLEASE!
"*BATMAN!* HELP ME!"

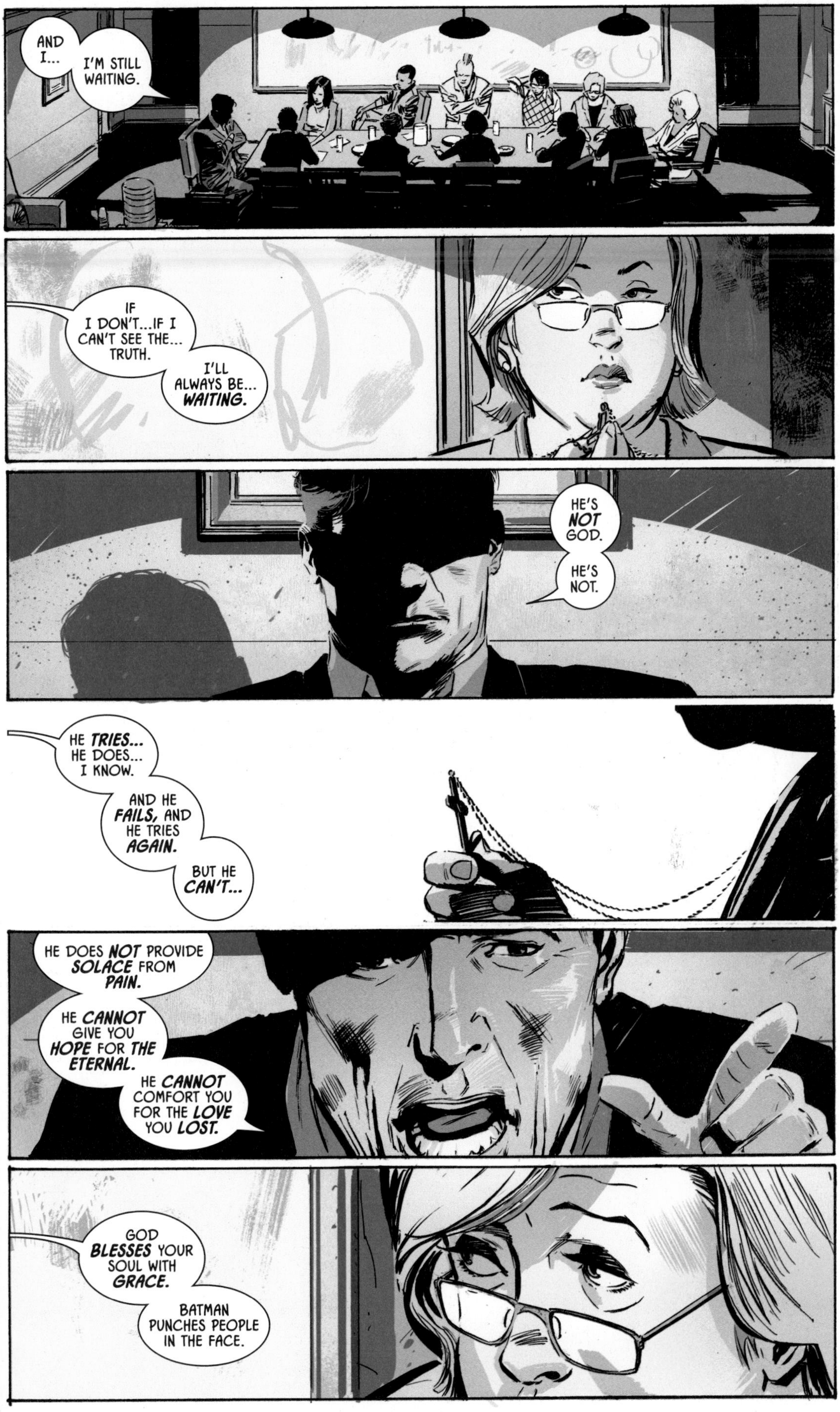
AND I...
I'M STILL WAITING.
IF I DON'T...IF I CAN'T SEE THE... TRUTH.
I'LL ALWAYS BE... WAITING.
HE'S NOT GOD.
HE'S NOT.
HE TRIES... HE DOES... I KNOW.
AND HE FAILS, AND HE TRIES AGAIN.
BUT HE CAN'T...
HE DOES NOT PROVIDE SOLACE FROM PAIN.
HE CANNOT GIVE YOU HOPE FOR THE ETERNAL.
HE CANNOT COMFORT YOU FOR THE LOVE YOU LOST.
GOD BLESSES YOUR SOUL WITH GRACE.
BATMAN PUNCHES PEOPLE IN THE FACE.

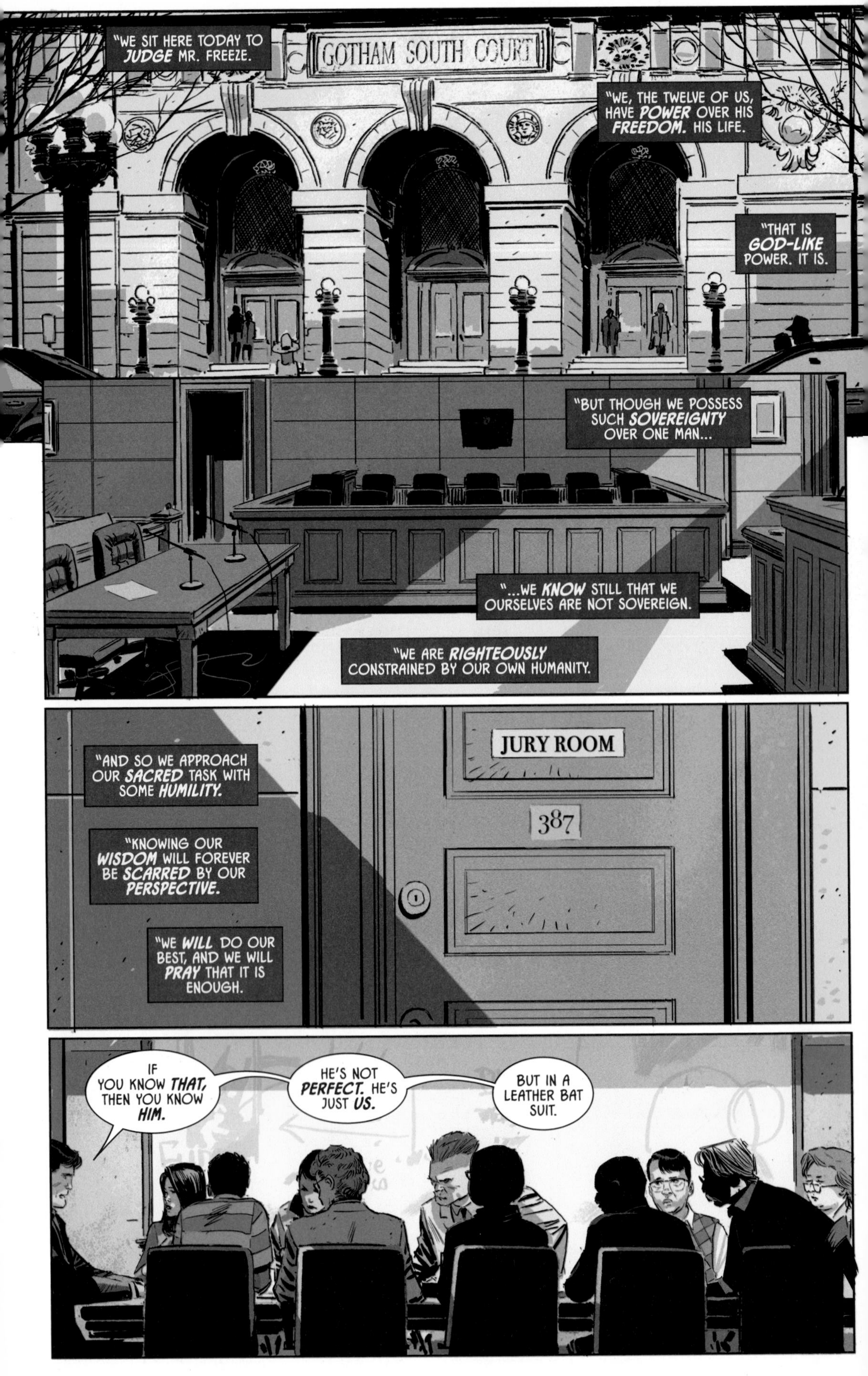
"WE SIT HERE TODAY TO JUDGE MR. FREEZE.
GOTHAM SOUTH COURT
"WE, THE TWELVE OF US, HAVE POWER OVER HIS FREEDOM. HIS LIFE.
"THAT IS GOD-LIKE POWER. IT IS.
"BUT THOUGH WE POSSESS SUCH SOVEREIGNTY OVER ONE MAN...
"...WE KNOW STILL THAT WE OURSELVES ARE NOT SOVEREIGN.
"WE ARE RIGHTEOUSLY CONSTRAINED BY OUR OWN HUMANITY.
JURY ROOM
387
"AND SO WE APPROACH OUR SACRED TASK WITH SOME HUMILITY.
"KNOWING OUR WISDOM WILL FOREVER BE SCARRED BY OUR PERSPECTIVE.
"WE WILL DO OUR BEST, AND WE WILL PRAY THAT IT IS ENOUGH.
IF YOU KNOW THAT, THEN YOU KNOW HIM.
HE'S NOT PERFECT. HE'S JUST US.
BUT IN A LEATHER BAT SUIT.

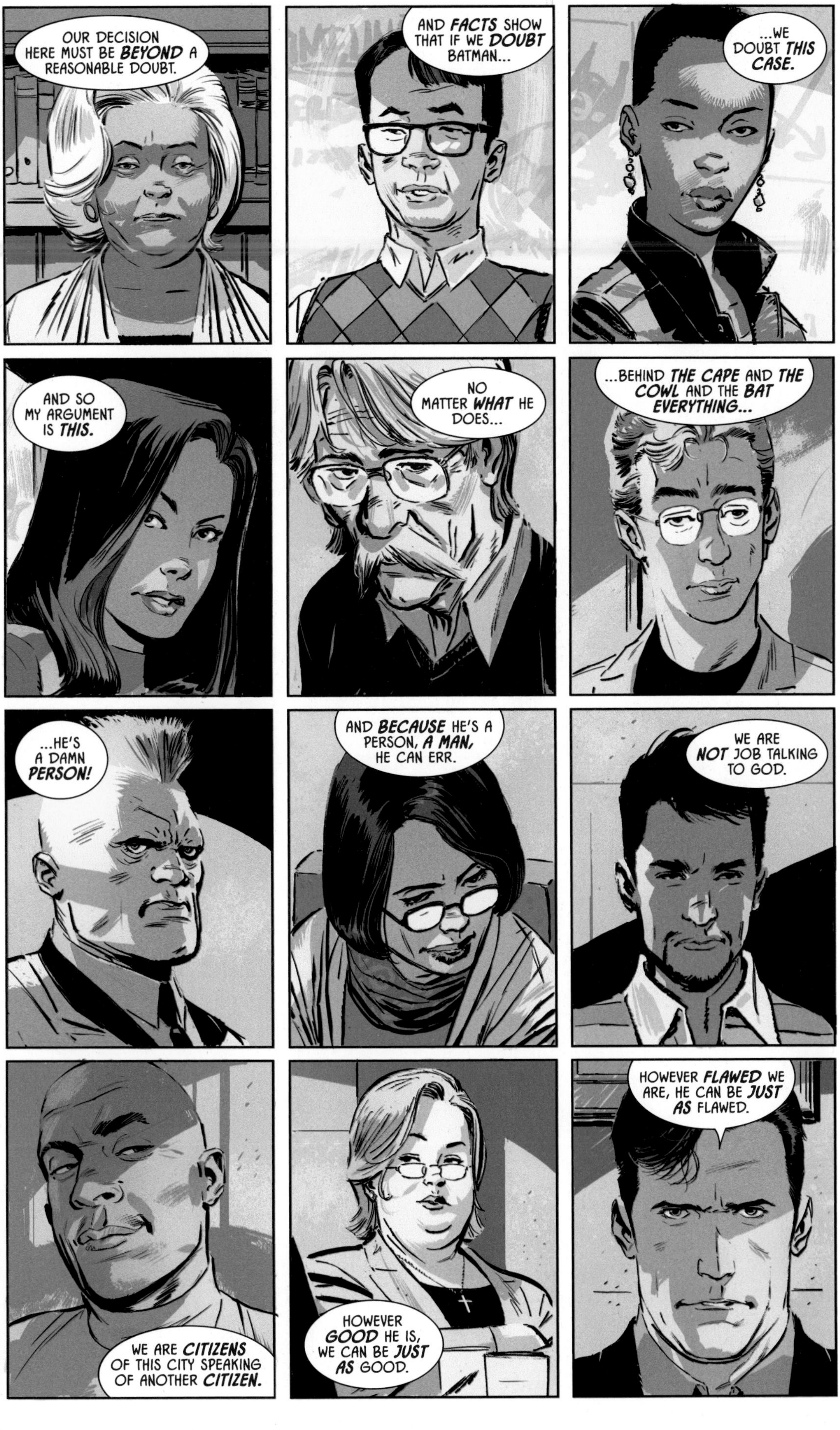
OUR DECISION HERE MUST BE BEYOND A REASONABLE DOUBT.
AND FACTS SHOW THAT IF WE DOUBT BATMAN...
...WE DOUBT THIS CASE.
AND SO MY ARGUMENT IS THIS.
NO MATTER WHAT HE DOES...
...BEHIND THE CAPE AND THE COWL AND THE BAT EVERYTHING...
...HE'S A DAMN PERSON!
AND BECAUSE HE'S A PERSON, A MAN, HE CAN ERR.
WE ARE NOT JOB TALKING TO GOD.
WE ARE CITIZENS OF THIS CITY SPEAKING OF ANOTHER CITIZEN.
HOWEVER GOOD HE IS, WE CAN BE JUST AS GOOD.
HOWEVER FLAWED WE ARE, HE CAN BE JUST AS FLAWED.

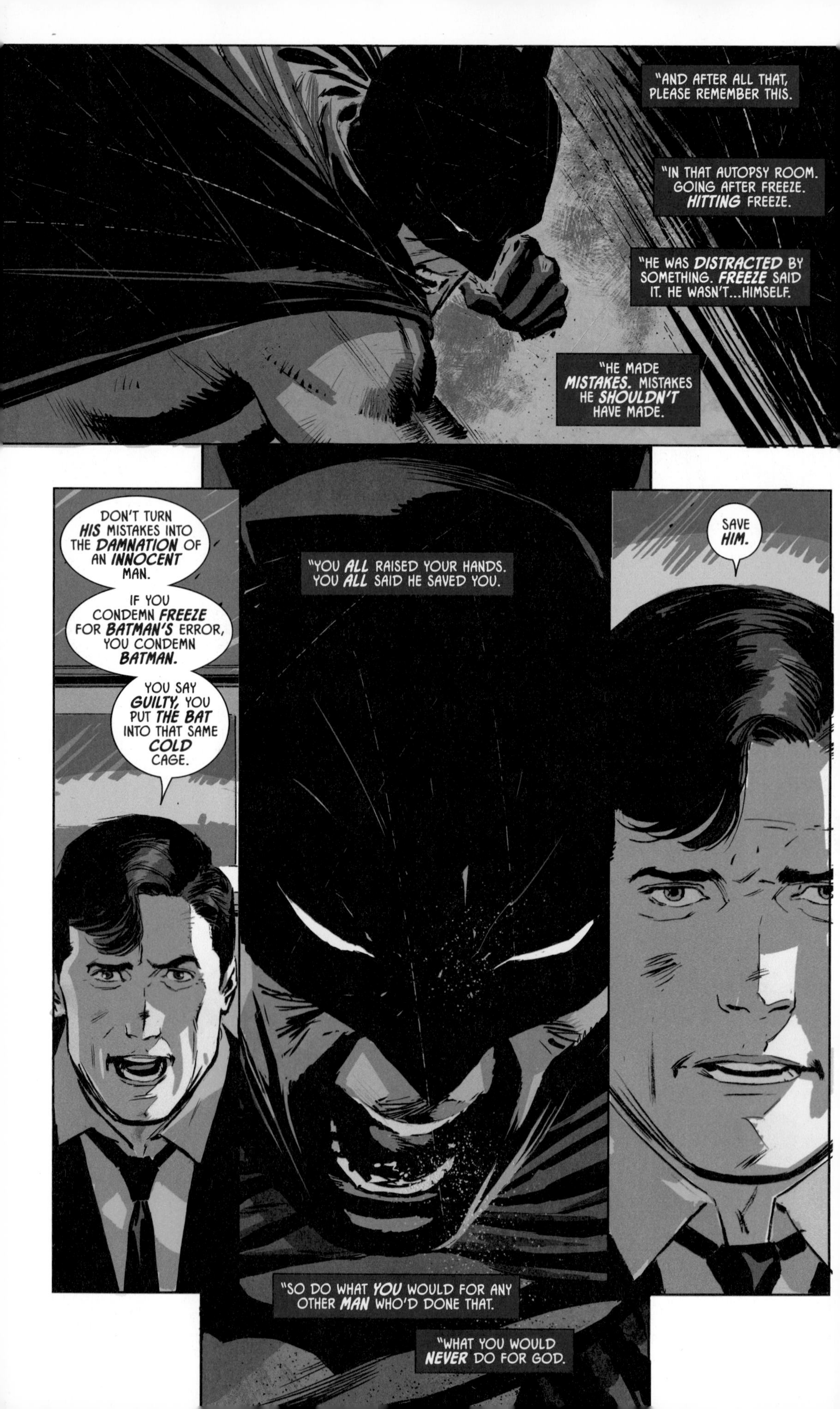
"AND AFTER ALL THAT, PLEASE REMEMBER THIS.
"IN THAT AUTOPSY ROOM. GOING AFTER FREEZE. HITTING FREEZE.
"HE WAS DISTRACTED BY SOMETHING. FREEZE SAID IT. HE WASN'T...HIMSELF.
"HE MADE MISTAKES. MISTAKES HE SHOULDN'T HAVE MADE.
DON'T TURN HIS MISTAKES INTO THE DAMNATION OF AN INNOCENT MAN.
IF YOU CONDEMN FREEZE FOR BATMAN'S ERROR, YOU CONDEMN BATMAN.
YOU SAY GUILTY, YOU PUT THE BAT INTO THAT SAME COLD CAGE.
"YOU ALL RAISED YOUR HANDS. YOU ALL SAID HE SAVED YOU.
SAVE HIM.
"SO DO WHAT YOU WOULD FOR ANY OTHER MAN WHO'D DONE THAT.
"WHAT YOU WOULD NEVER DO FOR GOD.

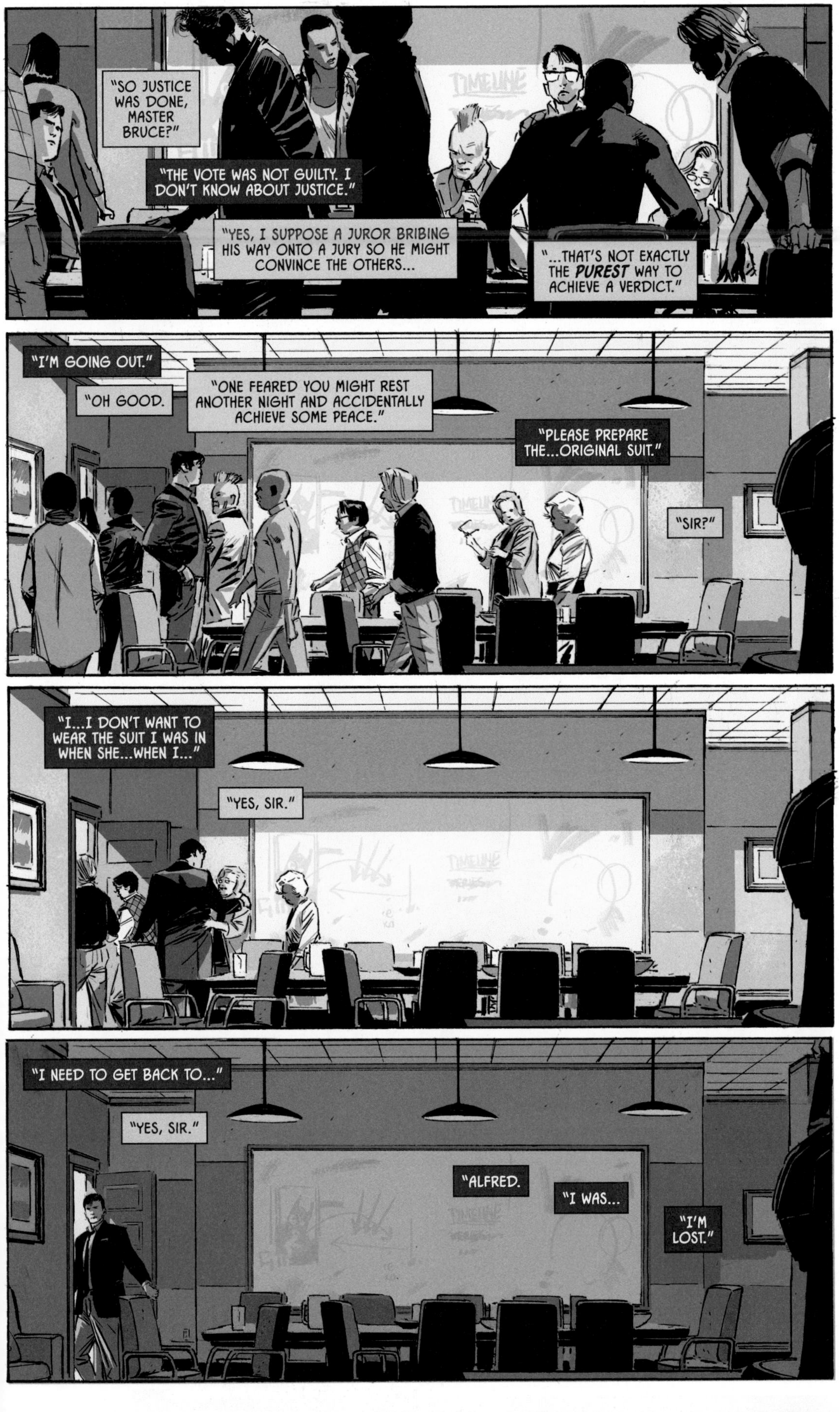
"SO JUSTICE WAS DONE, MASTER BRUCE?"
"THE VOTE WAS NOT GUILTY. I DON'T KNOW ABOUT JUSTICE."
"YES, I SUPPOSE A JUROR BRIBING HIS WAY ONTO A JURY SO HE MIGHT CONVINCE THE OTHERS...
"...THAT'S NOT EXACTLY THE PUREST WAY TO ACHIEVE A VERDICT."
"I'M GOING OUT."
"OH GOOD.
"ONE FEARED YOU MIGHT REST ANOTHER NIGHT AND ACCIDENTALLY ACHIEVE SOME PEACE."
"PLEASE PREPARE THE...ORIGINAL SUIT."
"SIR?"
"I...I DON'T WANT TO WEAR THE SUIT I WAS IN WHEN SHE...WHEN I..."
"YES, SIR."
"I NEED TO GET BACK TO..."
"YES, SIR."
"ALFRED.
"I WAS...
"I'M LOST."

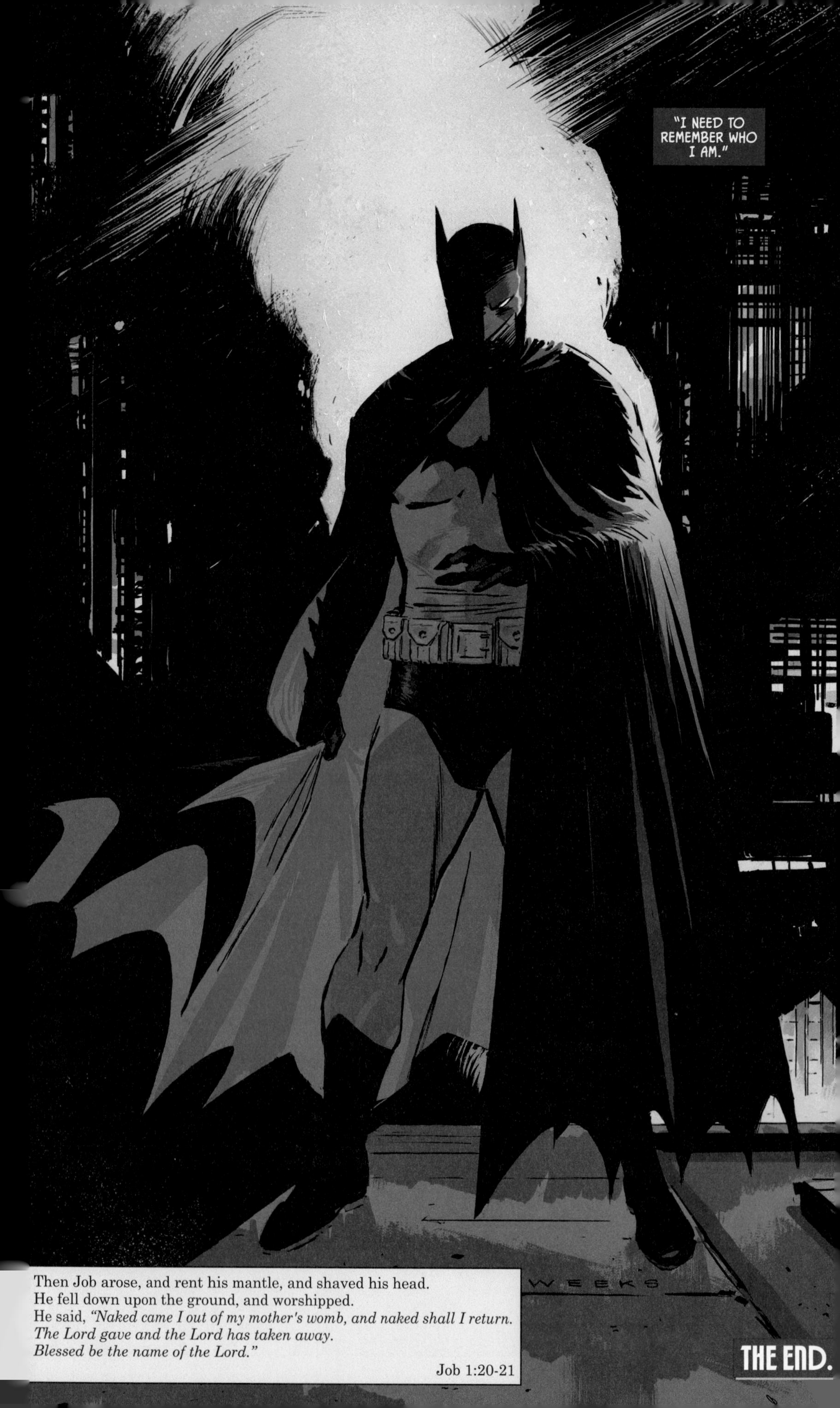
"I NEED TO REMEMBER WHO I AM."
Then Job arose, and rent his mantle, and shaved his head.
He fell down upon the ground, and worshipped.
He said, *"Naked came I out of my mother's womb, and naked shall I return.*
The Lord gave and the Lord has taken away.
Blessed be the name of the Lord."
Job 1:20-21
WEEKS
THE END.

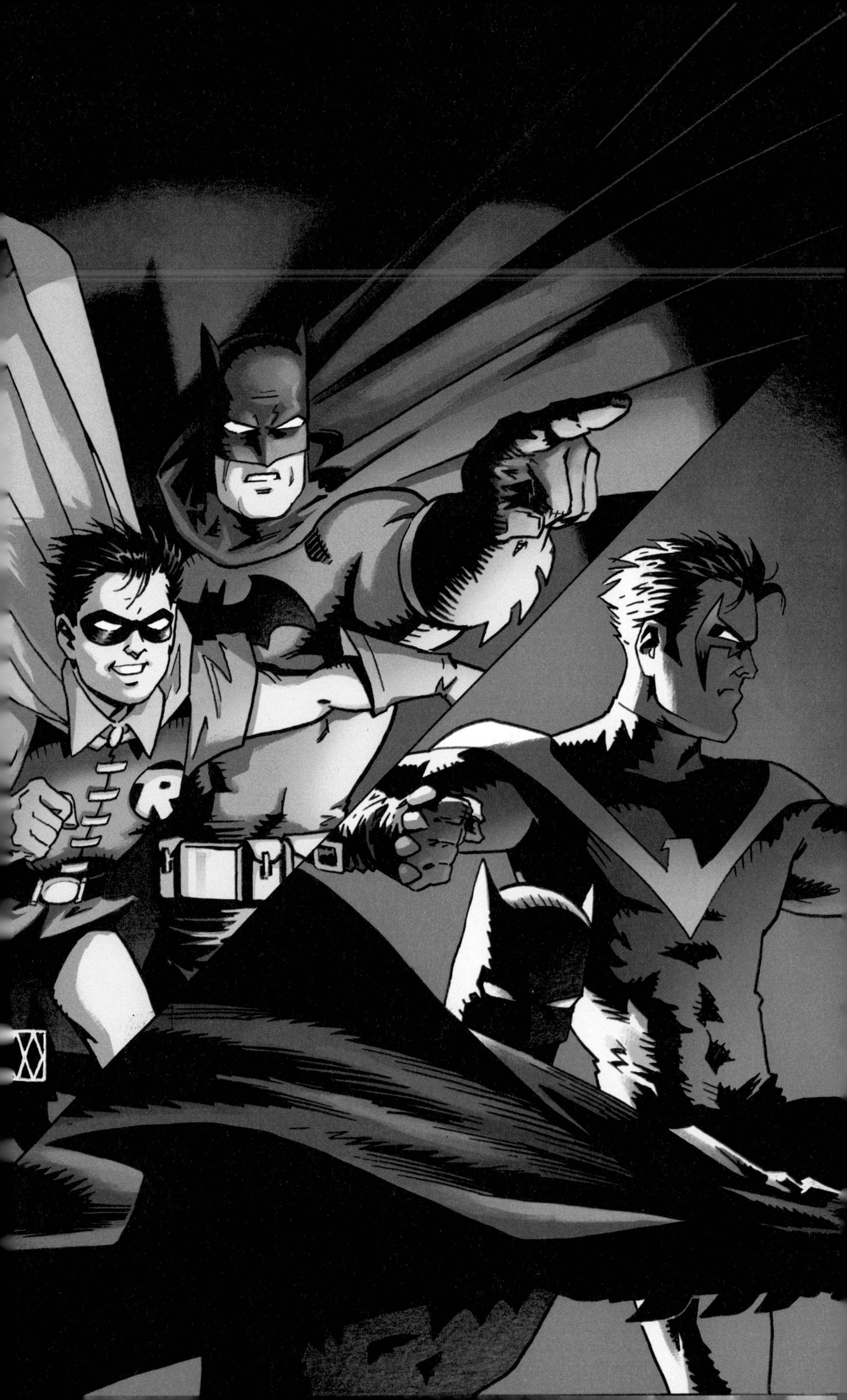

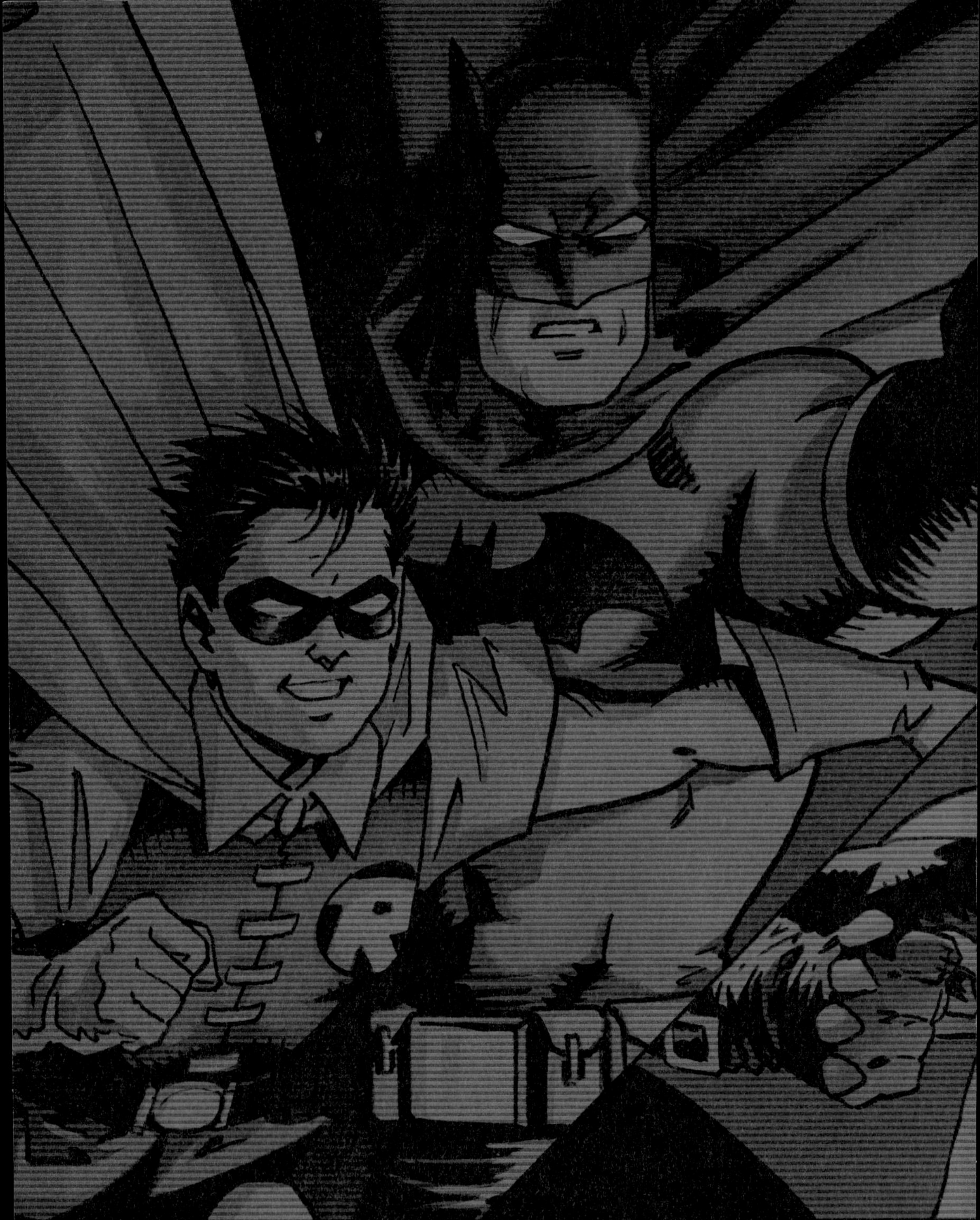

BATMAN
#54

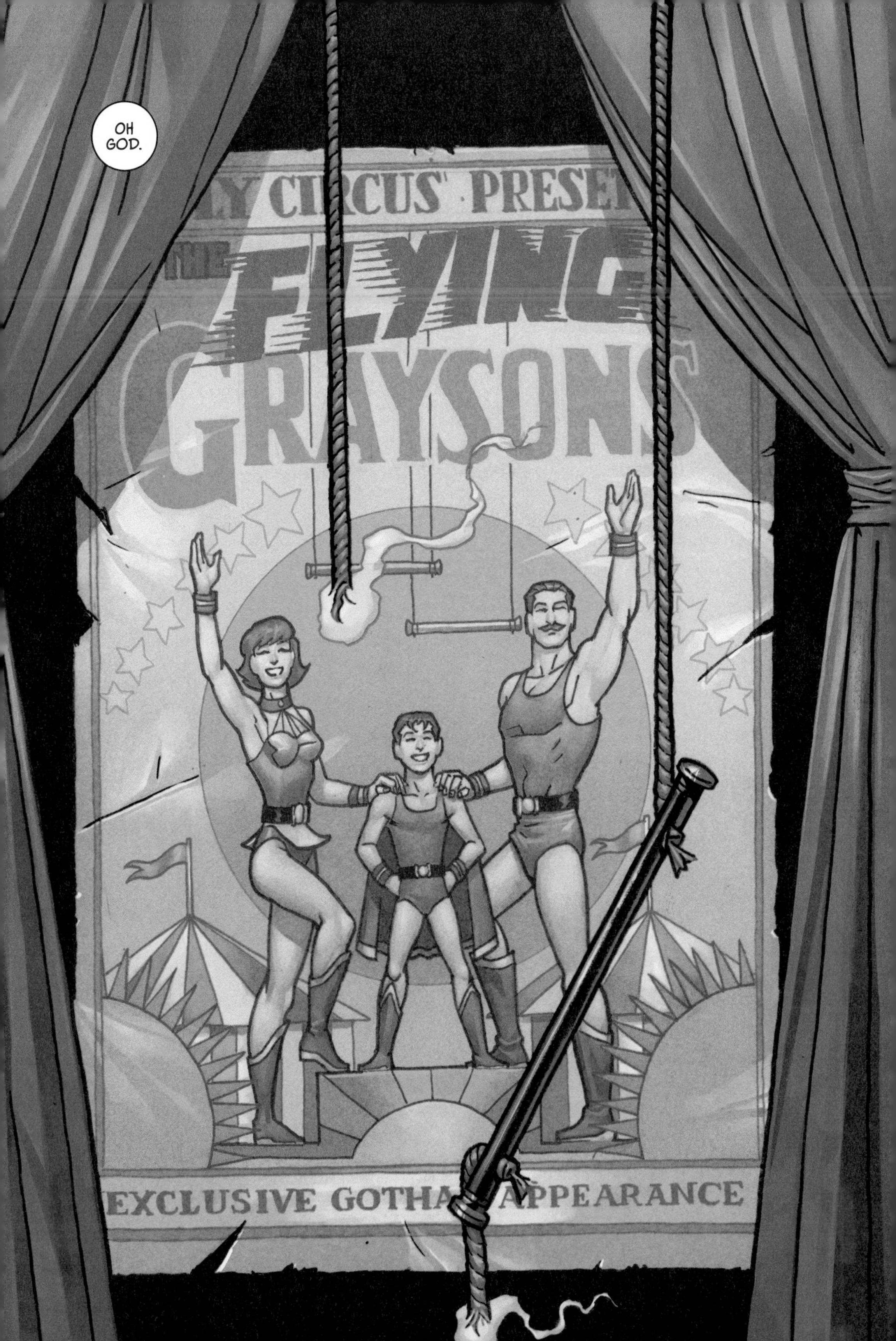
OH GOD.
CIRCUS' PRESE
FLYING
GRAYSONS
EXCLUSIVE GOTHA APPEARANCE

THE BETTER MAN

Tom King Writer Matt Wagner Artist Tomeu Morey Colorist
Clayton Cowles Letterer Matt and Brennan Wagner Cover
Brittany Holzherr Assoc. Editor Jamie S. Rich Editor

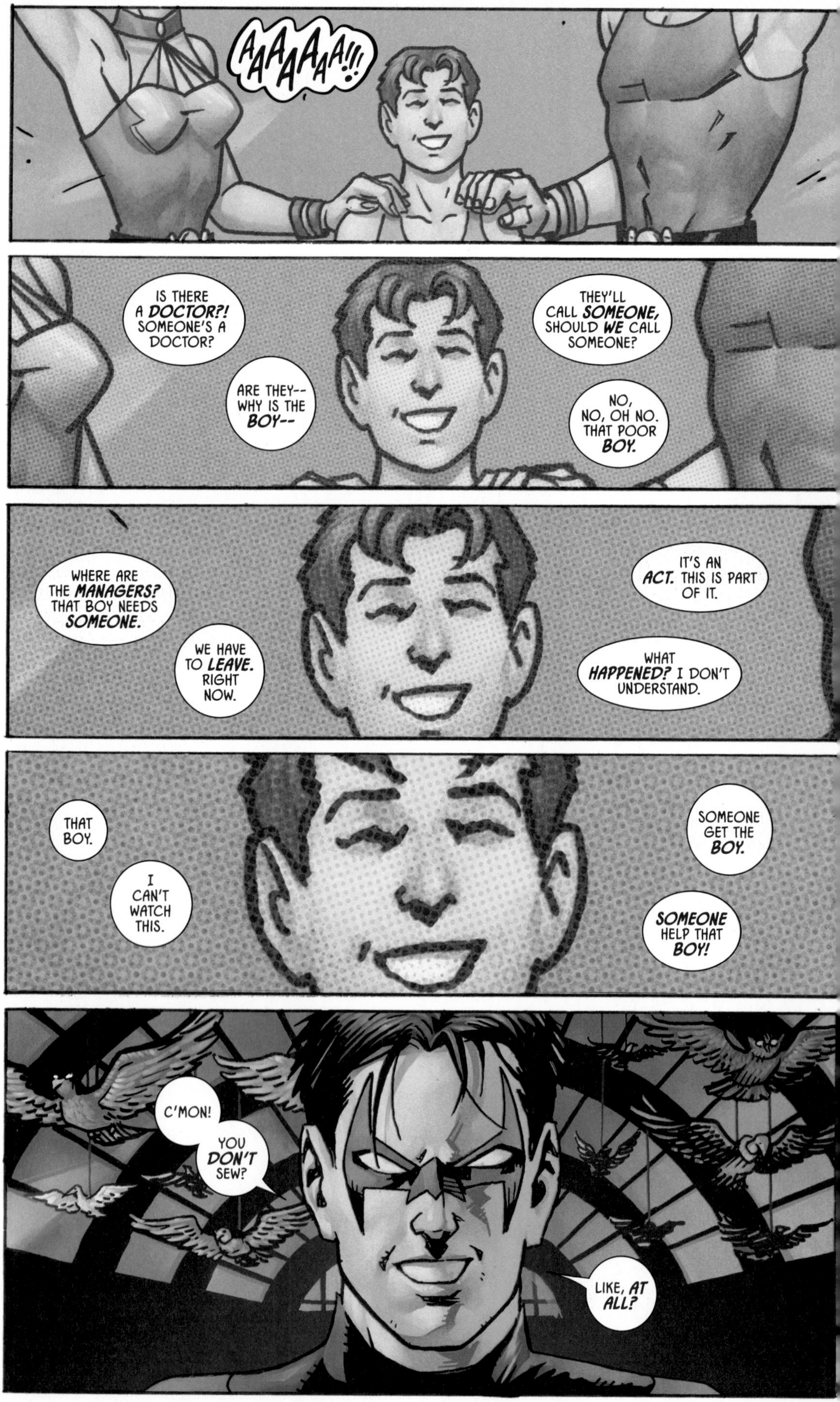
AAAAAAA!!!
IS THERE A DOCTOR?! SOMEONE'S A DOCTOR?
ARE THEY-- WHY IS THE BOY--
THEY'LL CALL SOMEONE, SHOULD WE CALL SOMEONE?
NO, NO, OH NO. THAT POOR BOY.
WHERE ARE THE MANAGERS? THAT BOY NEEDS SOMEONE.
WE HAVE TO LEAVE. RIGHT NOW.
IT'S AN ACT. THIS IS PART OF IT.
WHAT HAPPENED? I DON'T UNDERSTAND.
THAT BOY.
I CAN'T WATCH THIS.
SOMEONE GET THE BOY.
SOMEONE HELP THAT BOY!
C'MON!
YOU DON'T SEW?
LIKE, AT ALL?

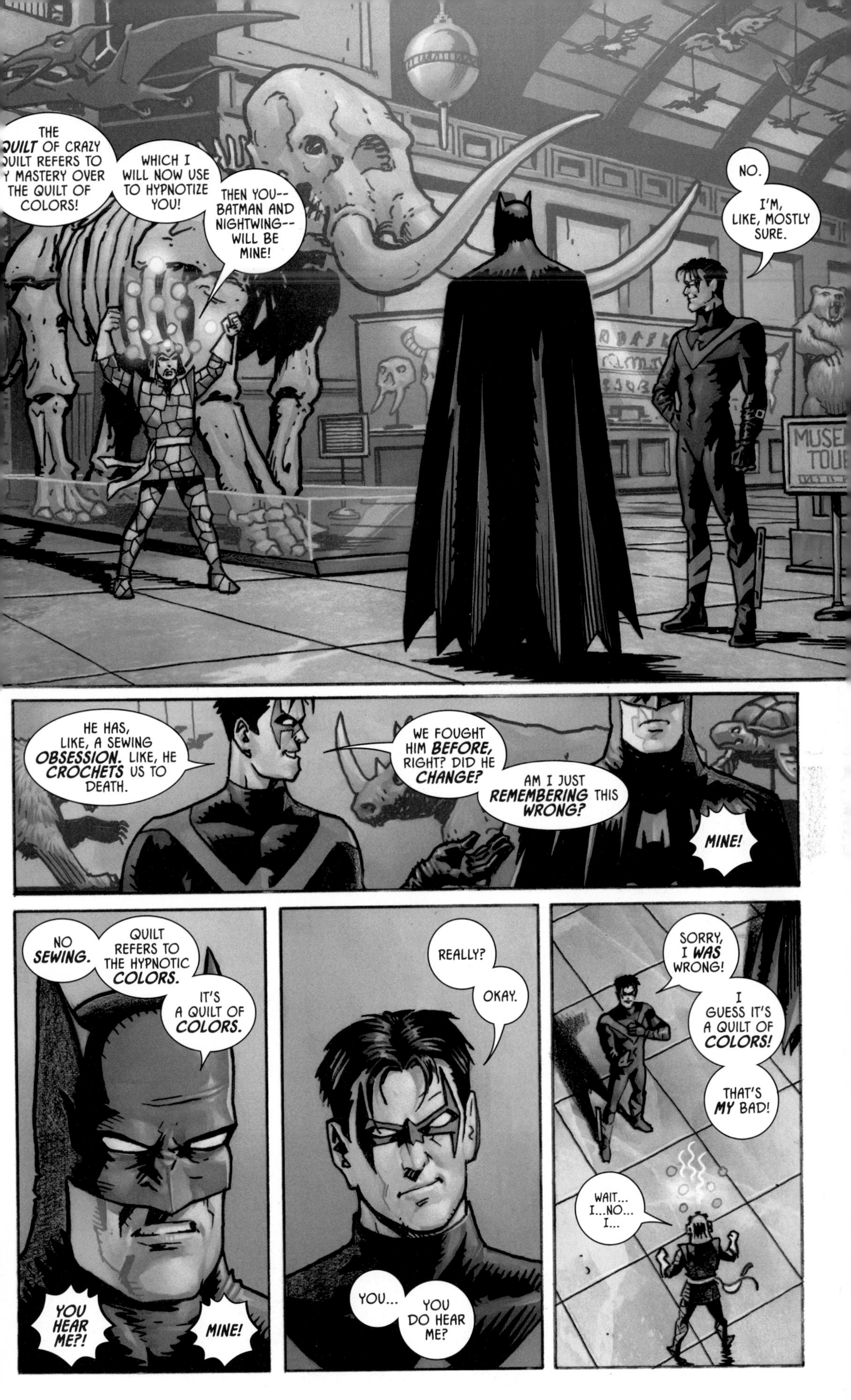

THE QUILT OF CRAZY QUILT REFERS TO Y MASTERY OVER THE QUILT OF COLORS!
WHICH I WILL NOW USE TO HYPNOTIZE YOU!
THEN YOU-- BATMAN AND NIGHTWING-- WILL BE MINE!
NO.
I'M, LIKE, MOSTLY SURE.
MUSE TOU
HE HAS, LIKE, A SEWING OBSESSION. LIKE, HE CROCHETS US TO DEATH.
WE FOUGHT HIM BEFORE, RIGHT? DID HE CHANGE?
AM I JUST REMEMBERING THIS WRONG?
MINE!
NO SEWING.
QUILT REFERS TO THE HYPNOTIC COLORS.
IT'S A QUILT OF COLORS.
YOU HEAR ME?!
MINE!
REALLY?
OKAY.
YOU...
YOU DO HEAR ME?
SORRY, I WAS WRONG!
I GUESS IT'S A QUILT OF COLORS!
THAT'S MY BAD!
WAIT... I...NO... I...

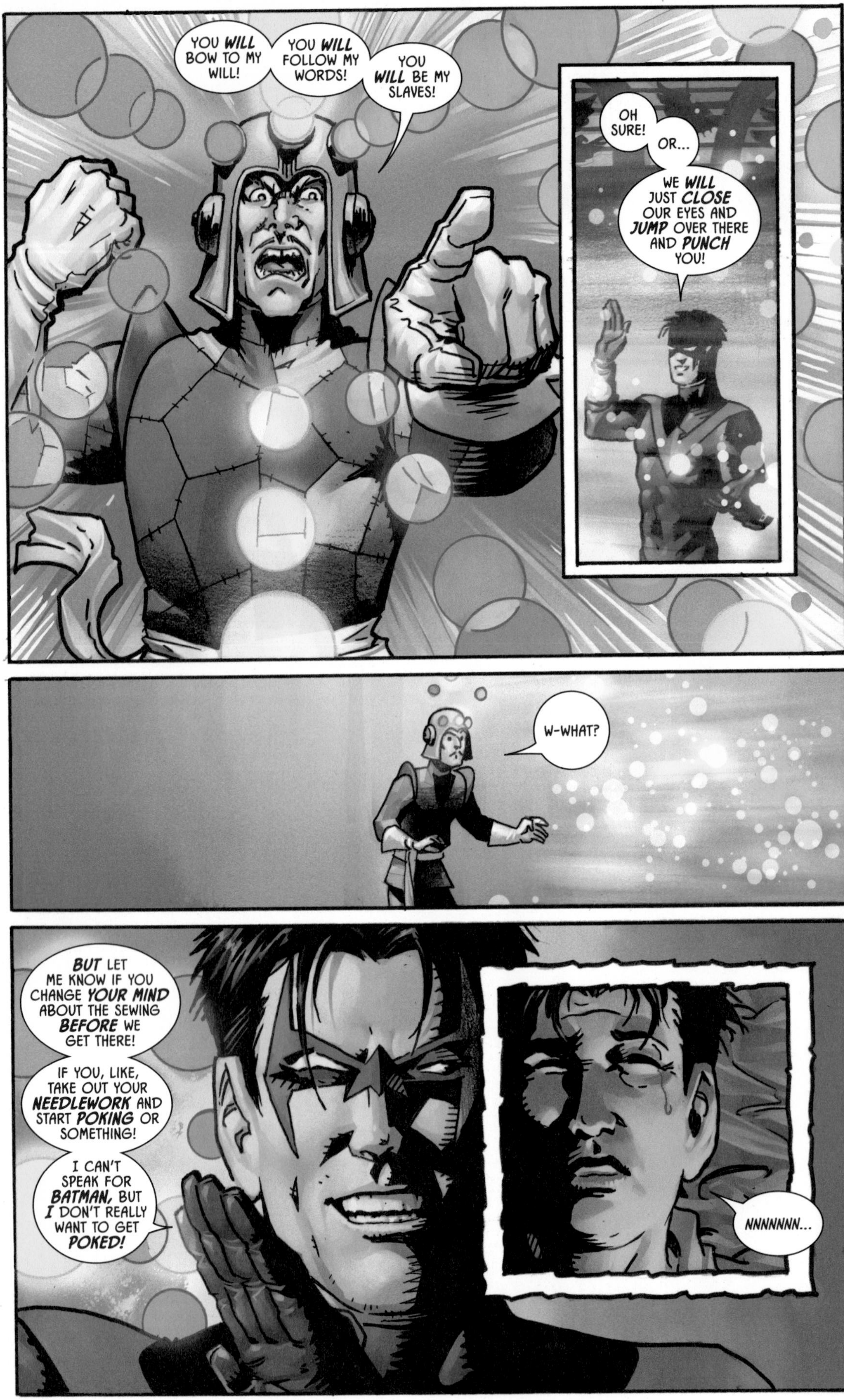
YOU WILL BOW TO MY WILL!
YOU WILL FOLLOW MY WORDS!
YOU WILL BE MY SLAVES!
OH SURE!
OR...
WE WILL JUST CLOSE OUR EYES AND JUMP OVER THERE AND PUNCH YOU!
W-WHAT?
BUT LET ME KNOW IF YOU CHANGE YOUR MIND ABOUT THE SEWING BEFORE WE GET THERE!
IF YOU, LIKE, TAKE OUT YOUR NEEDLEWORK AND START POKING OR SOMETHING!
I CAN'T SPEAK FOR BATMAN, BUT I DON'T REALLY WANT TO GET POKED!
NNNNNNN...

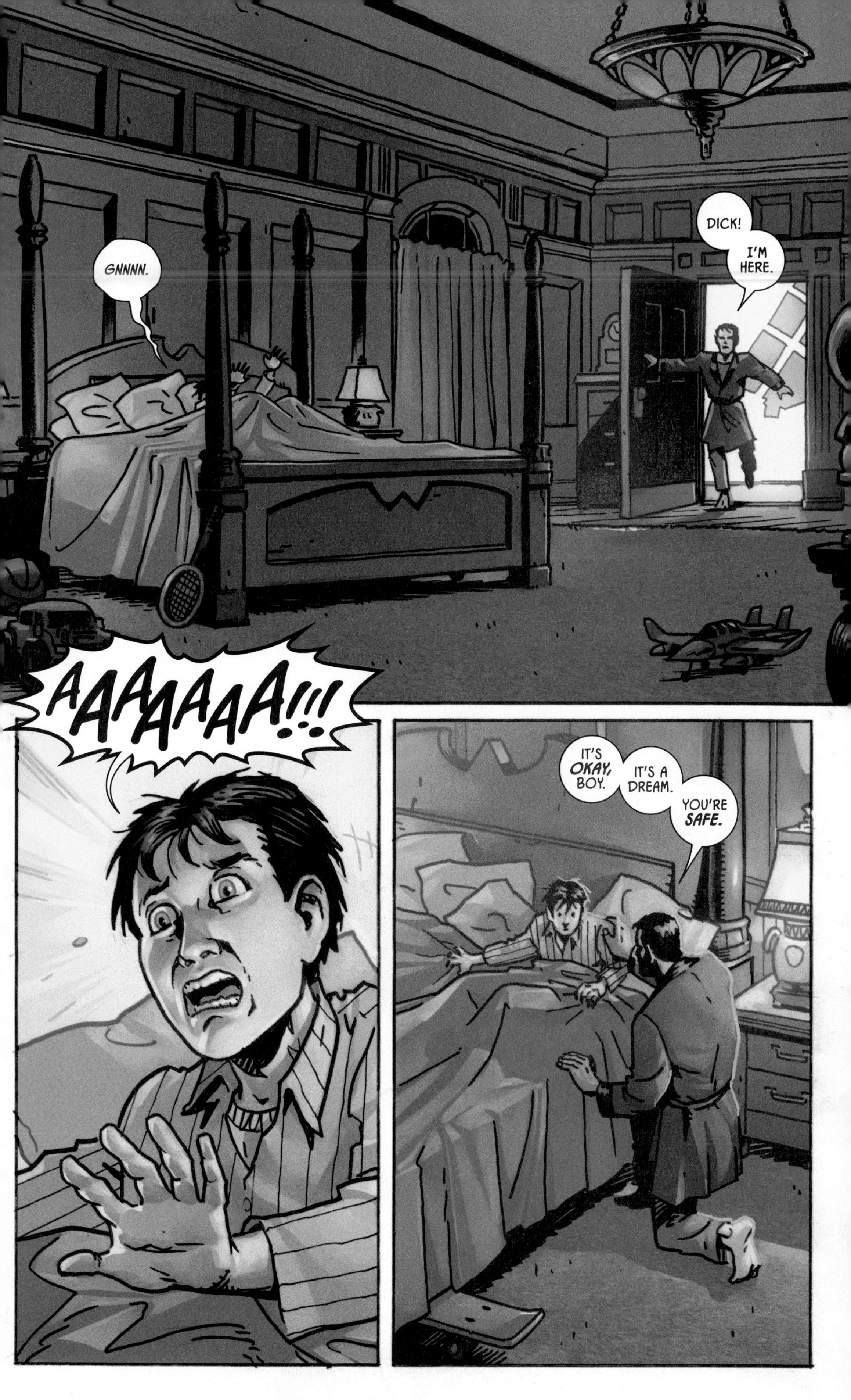
GNNNN.
DICK!
I'M HERE.
AAAAAAA!!!
IT'S OKAY, BOY.
IT'S A DREAM.
YOU'RE SAFE.

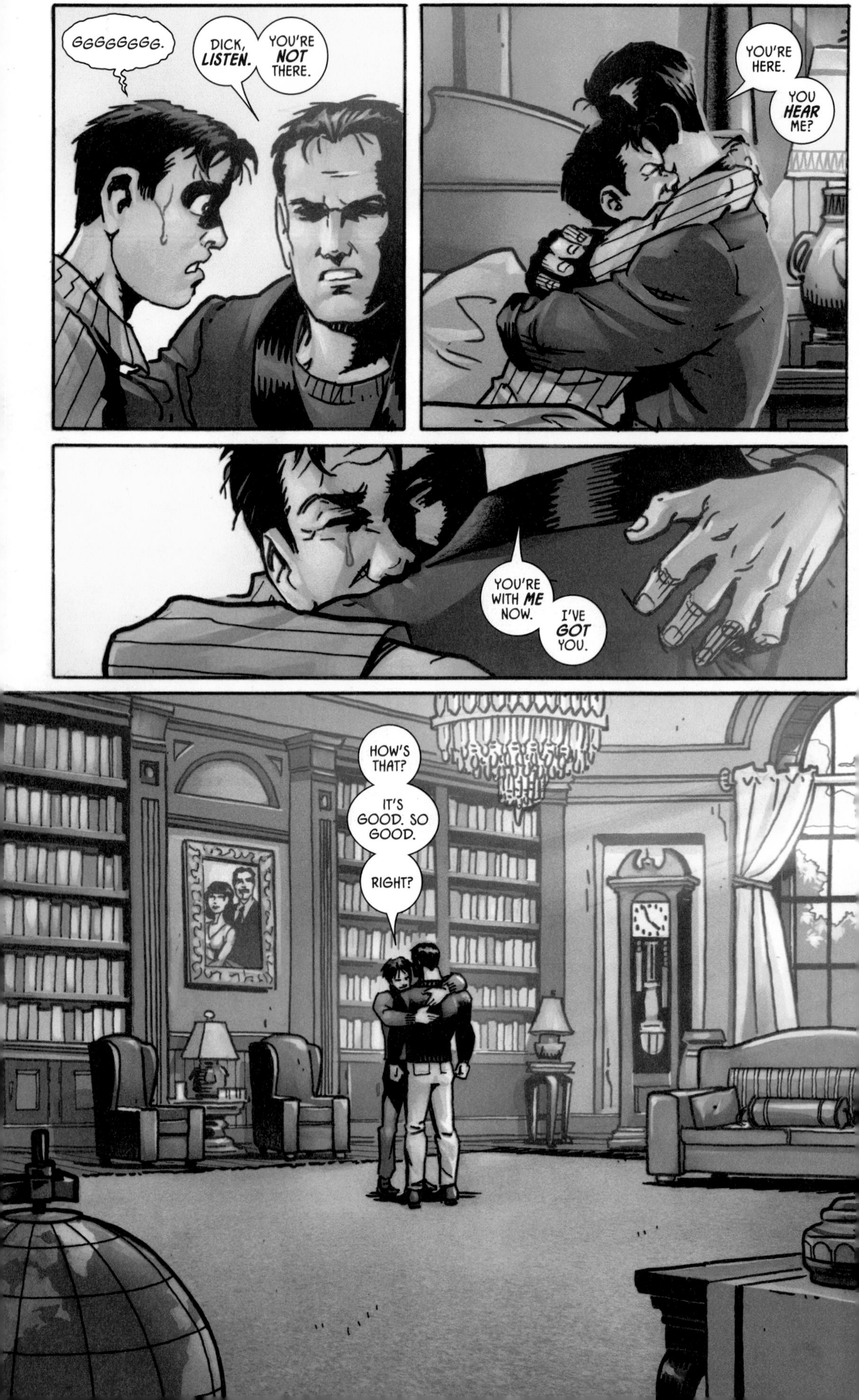
GGGGGGGG.
DICK, LISTEN.
YOU'RE NOT THERE.
YOU'RE HERE.
YOU HEAR ME?
YOU'RE WITH ME NOW.
I'VE GOT YOU.
HOW'S THAT?
IT'S GOOD. SO GOOD.
RIGHT?

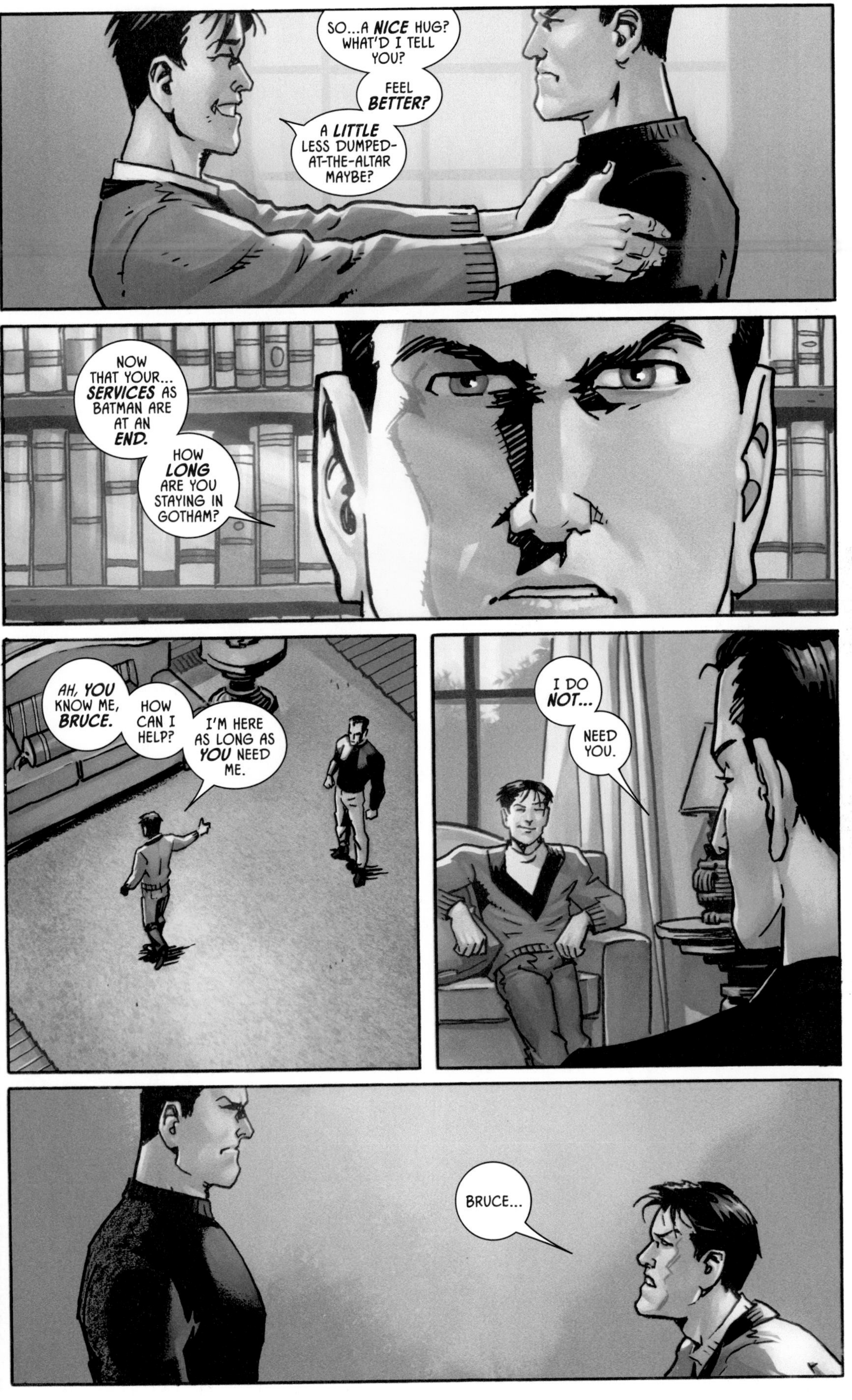
SO...A NICE HUG? WHAT'D I TELL YOU?
FEEL BETTER?
A LITTLE LESS DUMPED-AT-THE-ALTAR MAYBE?
NOW THAT YOUR... SERVICES AS BATMAN ARE AT AN END.
HOW LONG ARE YOU STAYING IN GOTHAM?
AH, YOU KNOW ME, BRUCE.
HOW CAN I HELP?
I'M HERE AS LONG AS YOU NEED ME.
I DO NOT...
NEED YOU.
BRUCE...

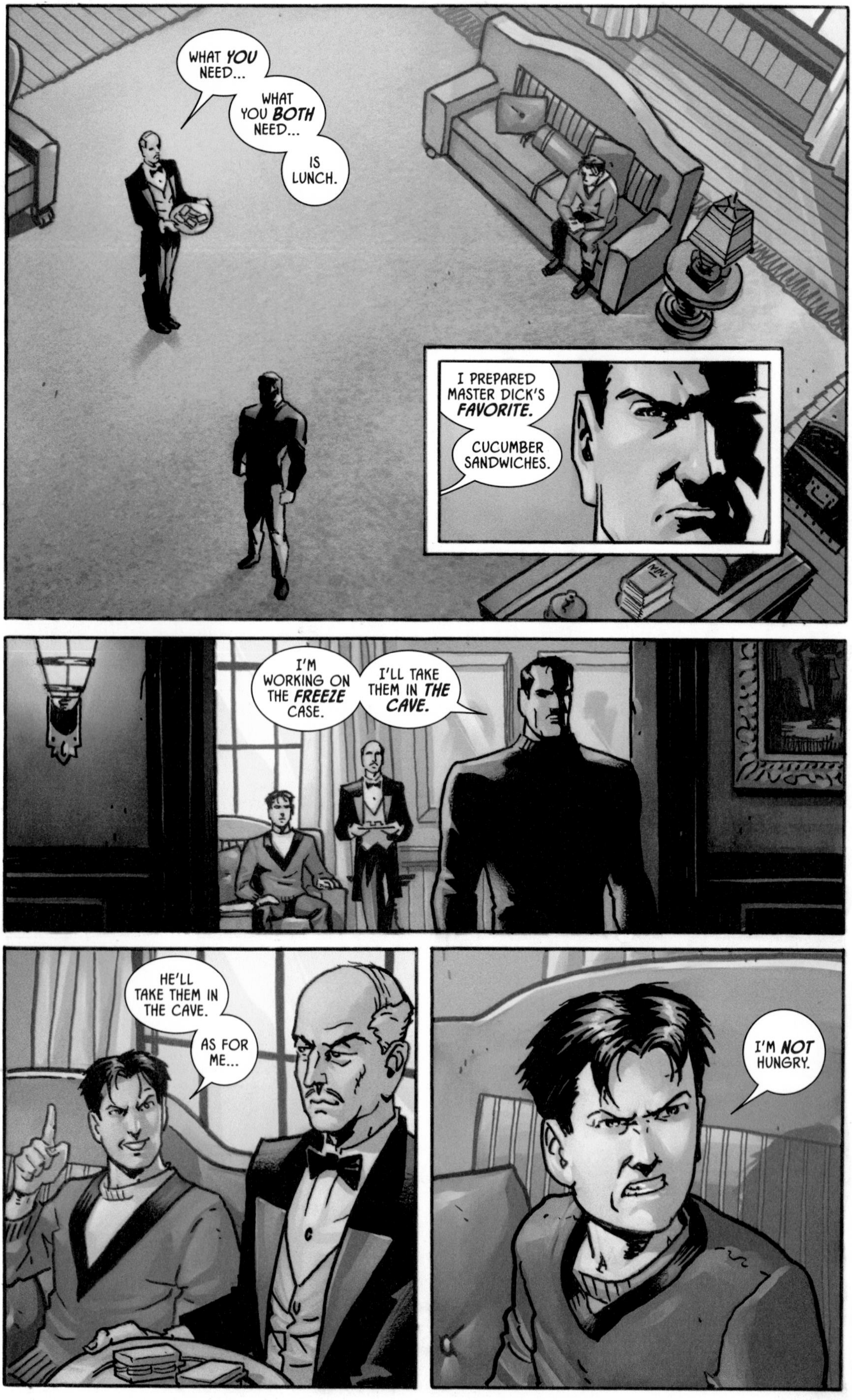
WHAT *YOU* NEED...
WHAT YOU *BOTH* NEED...
IS LUNCH.
I PREPARED MASTER DICK'S *FAVORITE.*
CUCUMBER SANDWICHES.
I'M WORKING ON THE *FREEZE* CASE.
I'LL TAKE THEM IN *THE CAVE.*
HE'LL TAKE THEM IN THE CAVE.
AS FOR ME...
I'M *NOT* HUNGRY.

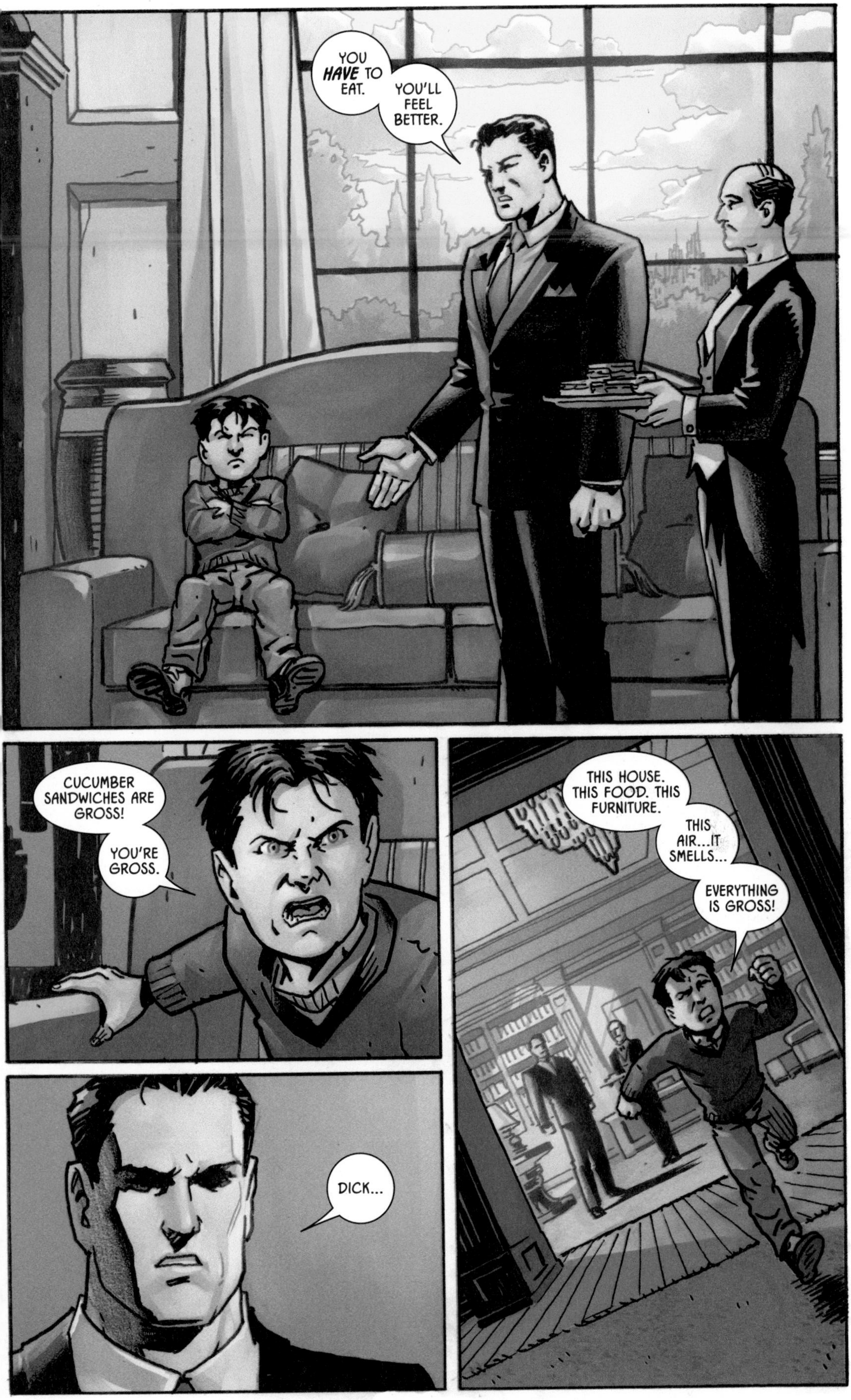
YOU HAVE TO EAT.
YOU'LL FEEL BETTER.
CUCUMBER SANDWICHES ARE GROSS!
YOU'RE GROSS.
THIS HOUSE. THIS FOOD. THIS FURNITURE.
THIS AIR...IT SMELLS...
EVERYTHING IS GROSS!
DICK...

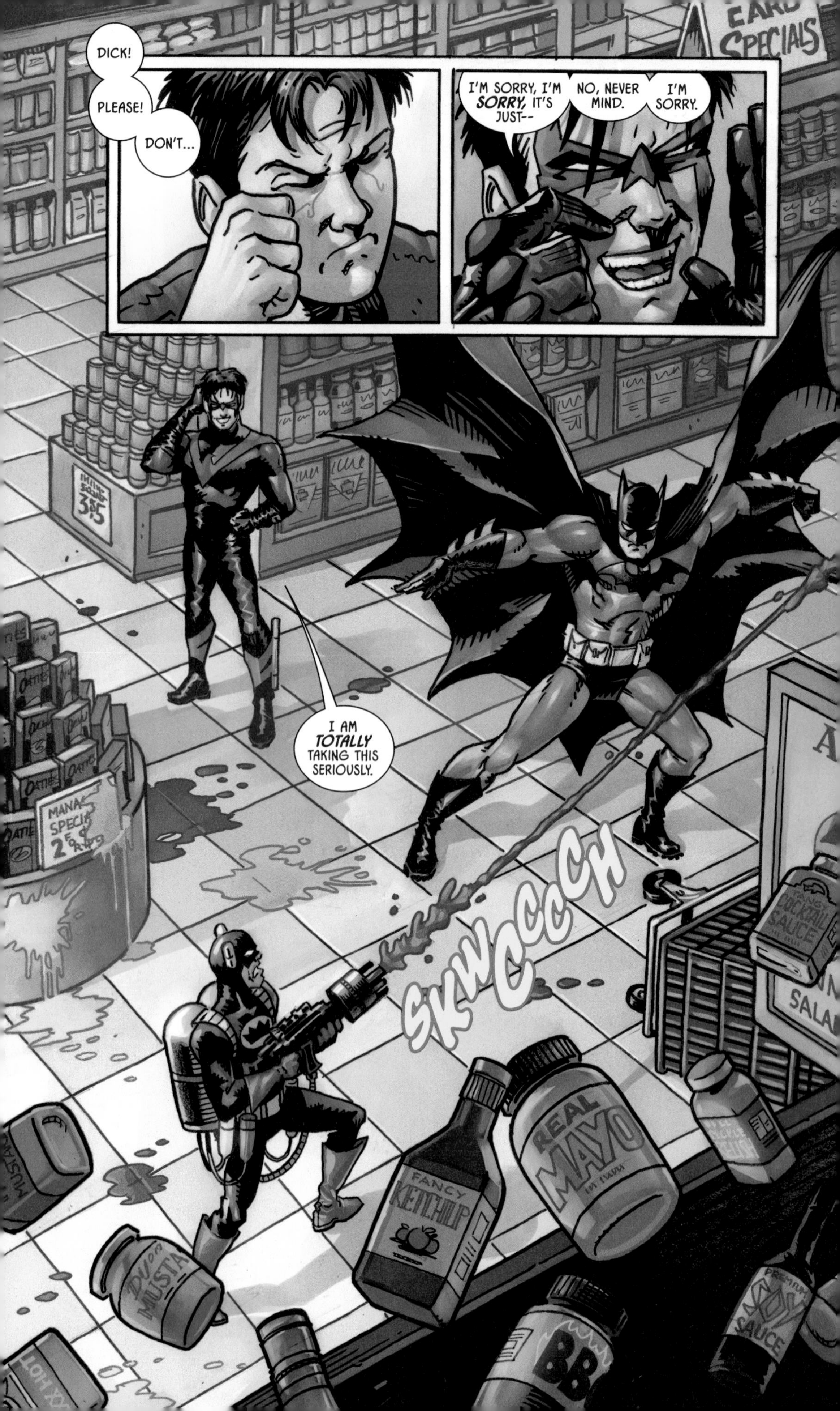

SPECIALS
DICK!
PLEASE!
DON'T...
I'M SORRY, I'M SORRY, IT'S JUST--
NO, NEVER MIND.
I'M SORRY.
I AM TOTALLY TAKING THIS SERIOUSLY.
SKWCCCCH
FANCY KETCHUP
REAL MAYO
COCKTAIL SAUCE
SAUCE

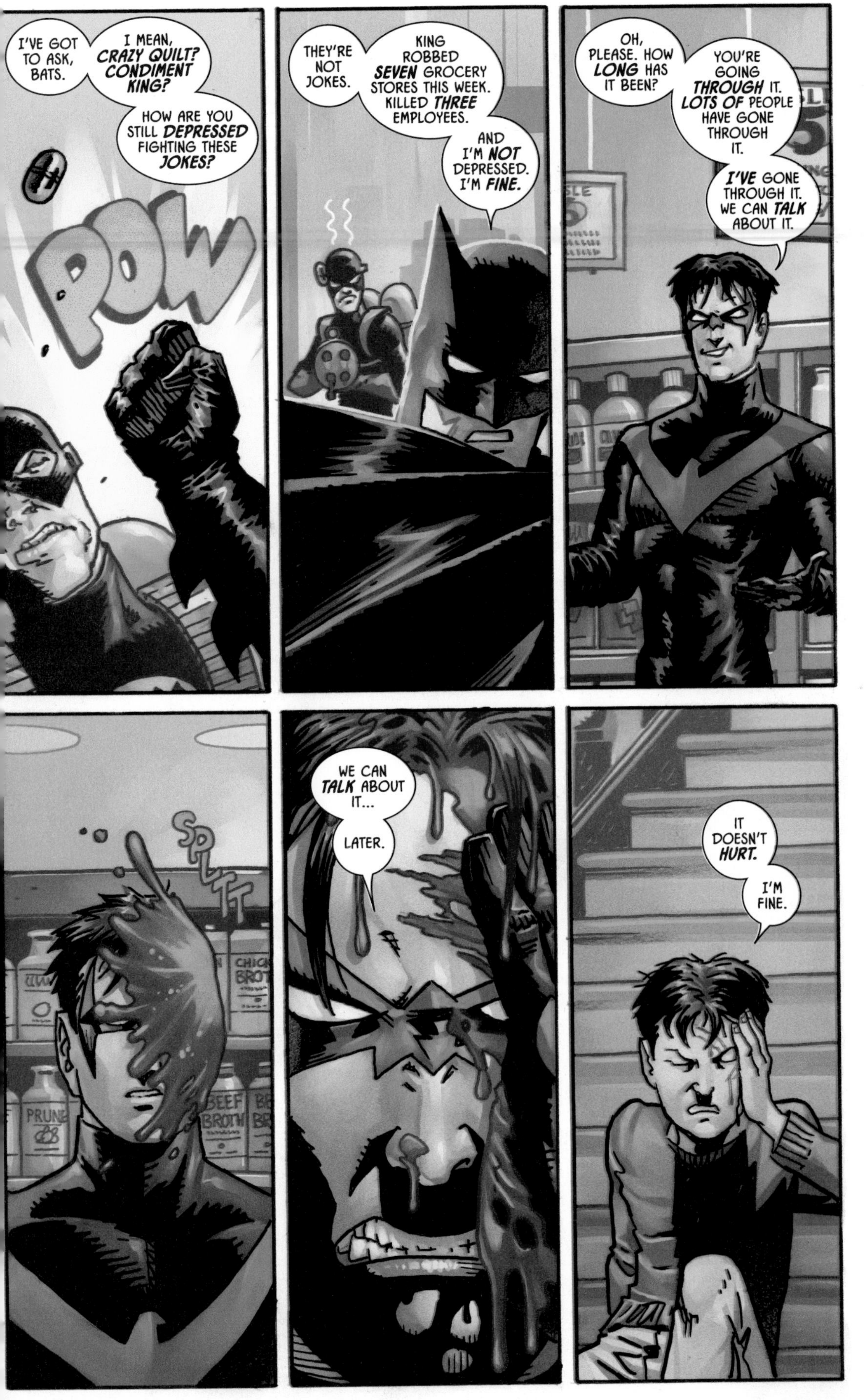
I'VE GOT TO ASK, BATS.
I MEAN, CRAZY QUILT? CONDIMENT KING?
HOW ARE YOU STILL DEPRESSED FIGHTING THESE JOKES?
POW
THEY'RE NOT JOKES.
KING ROBBED SEVEN GROCERY STORES THIS WEEK. KILLED THREE EMPLOYEES.
AND I'M NOT DEPRESSED. I'M FINE.
OH, PLEASE. HOW LONG HAS IT BEEN?
YOU'RE GOING THROUGH IT. LOTS OF PEOPLE HAVE GONE THROUGH IT.
I'VE GONE THROUGH IT. WE CAN TALK ABOUT IT.
SPLTT
PRUNE
BEEF BROTH
WE CAN TALK ABOUT IT...
LATER.
IT DOESN'T HURT.
I'M FINE.

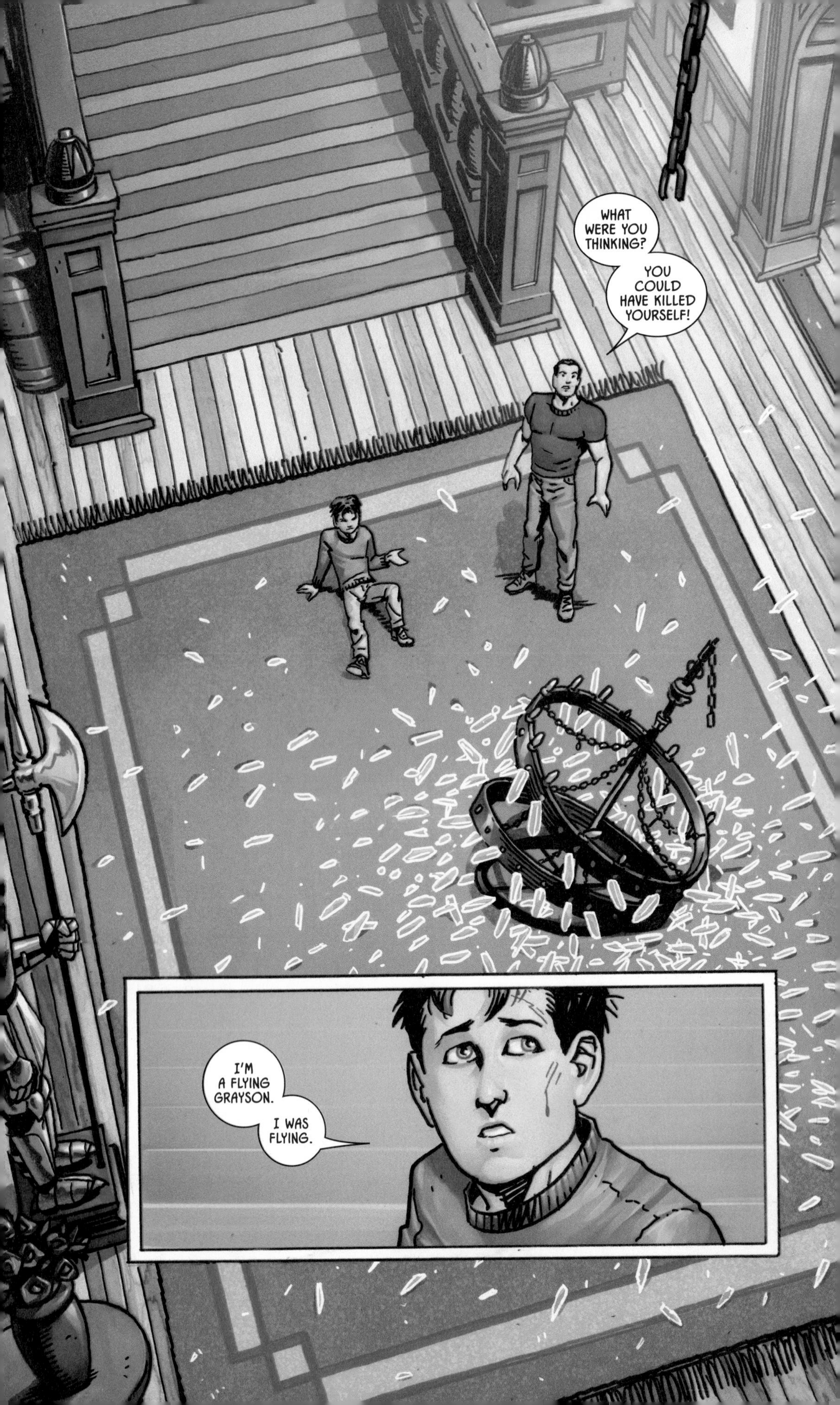

WHAT WERE YOU THINKING?
YOU COULD HAVE KILLED YOURSELF!
I'M A FLYING GRAYSON.
I WAS FLYING.

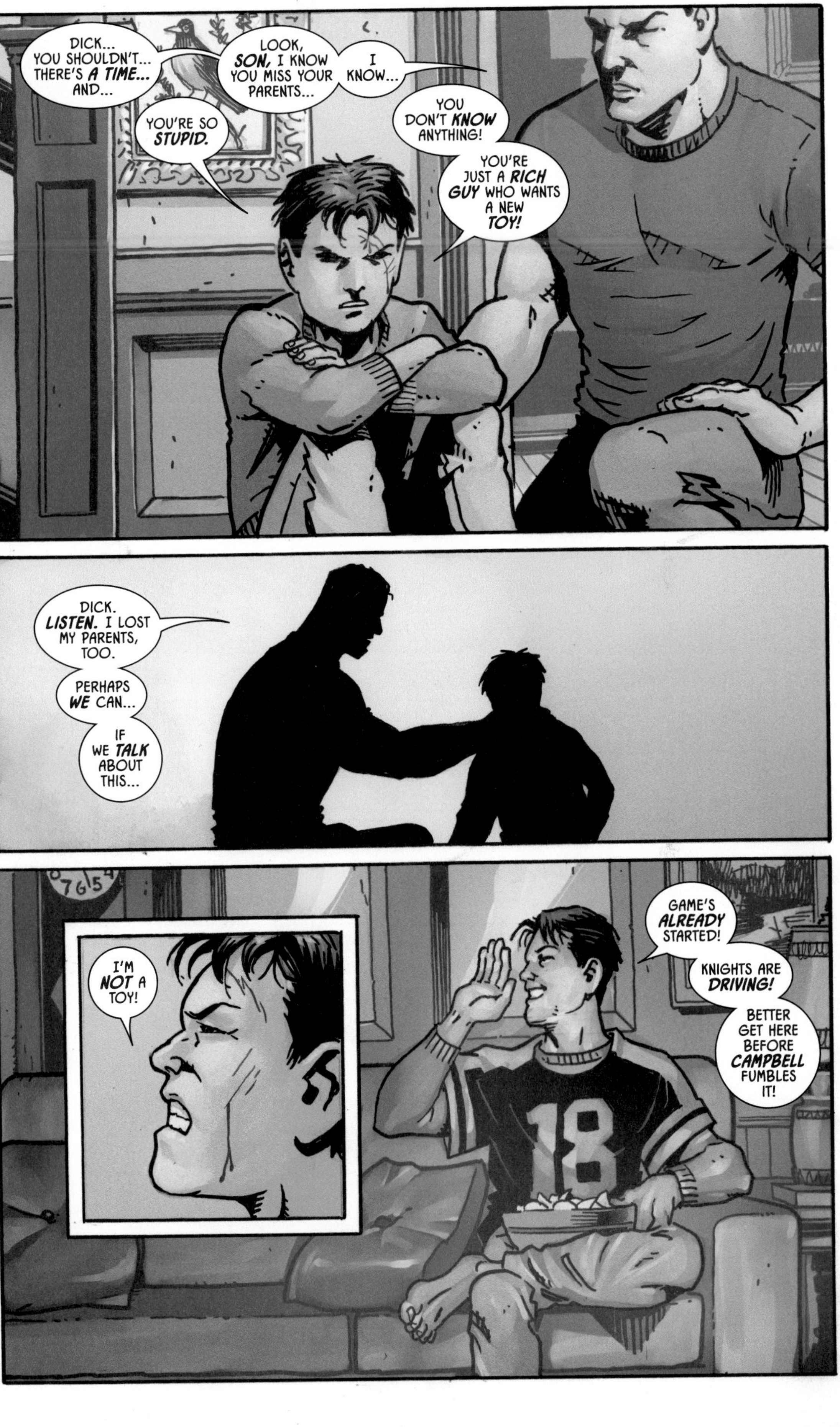

DICK... YOU SHOULDN'T... THERE'S A TIME... AND...
LOOK, SON, I KNOW YOU MISS YOUR PARENTS...
I KNOW...
YOU'RE SO STUPID.
YOU DON'T KNOW ANYTHING!
YOU'RE JUST A RICH GUY WHO WANTS A NEW TOY!
DICK. LISTEN. I LOST MY PARENTS, TOO.
PERHAPS WE CAN...
IF WE TALK ABOUT THIS...
I'M NOT A TOY!
GAME'S ALREADY STARTED!
KNIGHTS ARE DRIVING!
BETTER GET HERE BEFORE CAMPBELL FUMBLES IT!

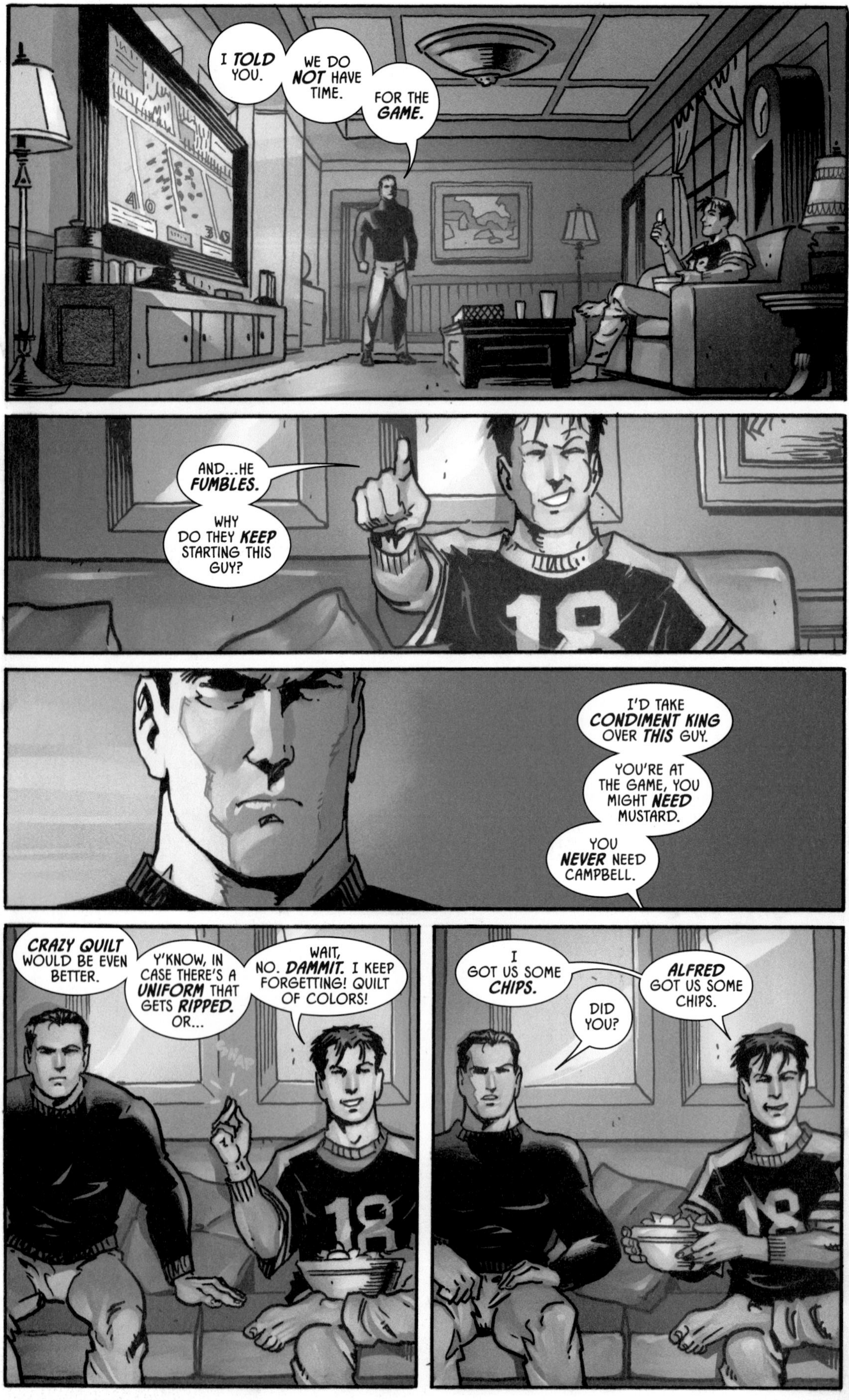

I TOLD YOU.
WE DO NOT HAVE TIME.
FOR THE GAME.
AND...HE FUMBLES.
WHY DO THEY KEEP STARTING THIS GUY?
I'D TAKE CONDIMENT KING OVER THIS GUY.
YOU'RE AT THE GAME, YOU MIGHT NEED MUSTARD.
YOU NEVER NEED CAMPBELL.
CRAZY QUILT WOULD BE EVEN BETTER.
Y'KNOW, IN CASE THERE'S A UNIFORM THAT GETS RIPPED. OR...
WAIT, NO. DAMMIT. I KEEP FORGETTING! QUILT OF COLORS!
I GOT US SOME CHIPS.
ALFRED GOT US SOME CHIPS.
DID YOU?

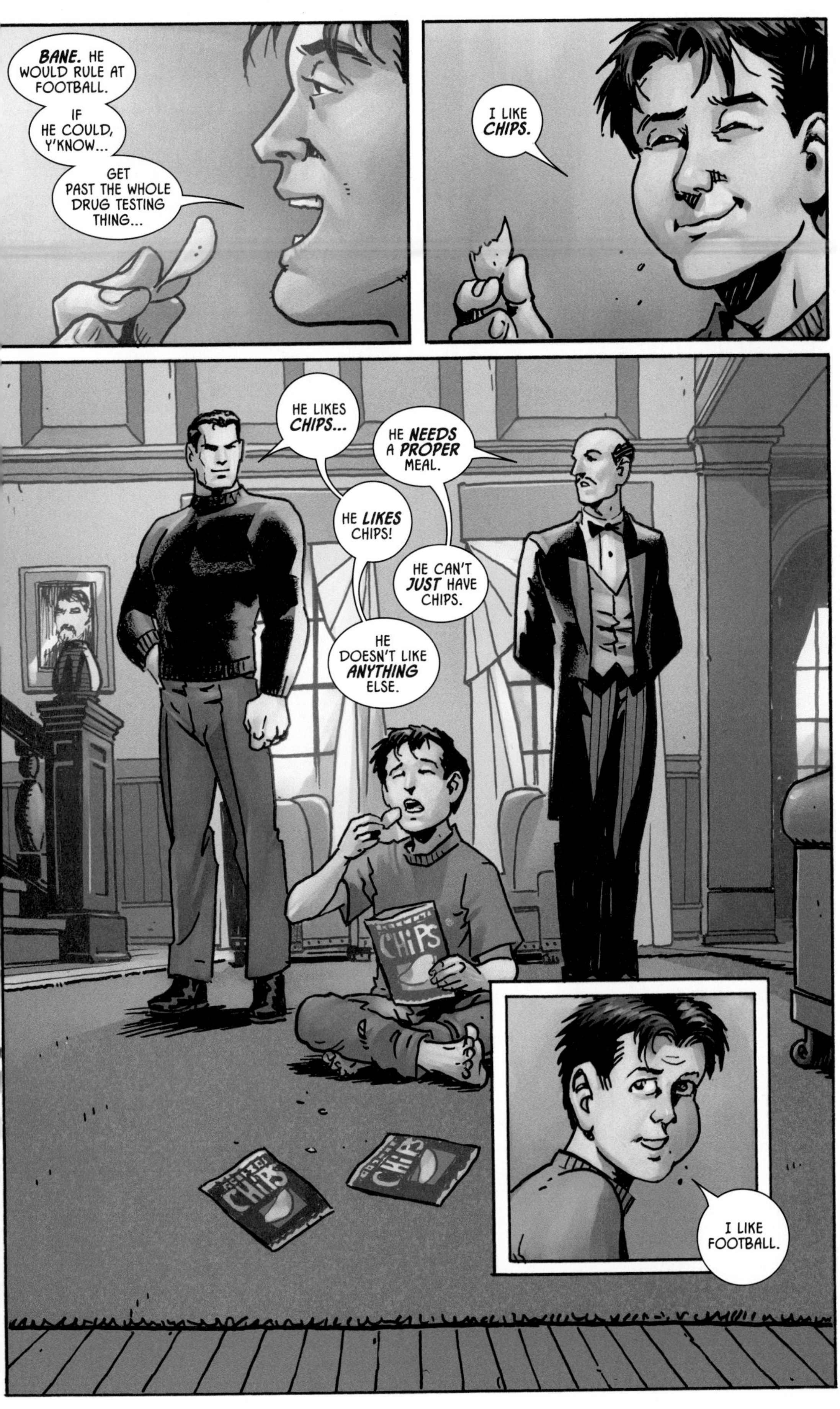
BANE. HE WOULD RULE AT FOOTBALL.
IF HE COULD, Y'KNOW...
GET PAST THE WHOLE DRUG TESTING THING...
I LIKE CHIPS.
HE LIKES CHIPS...
HE NEEDS A PROPER MEAL.
HE LIKES CHIPS!
HE CAN'T JUST HAVE CHIPS.
HE DOESN'T LIKE ANYTHING ELSE.
CHIPS
CHIPS
CHIPS
I LIKE FOOTBALL.

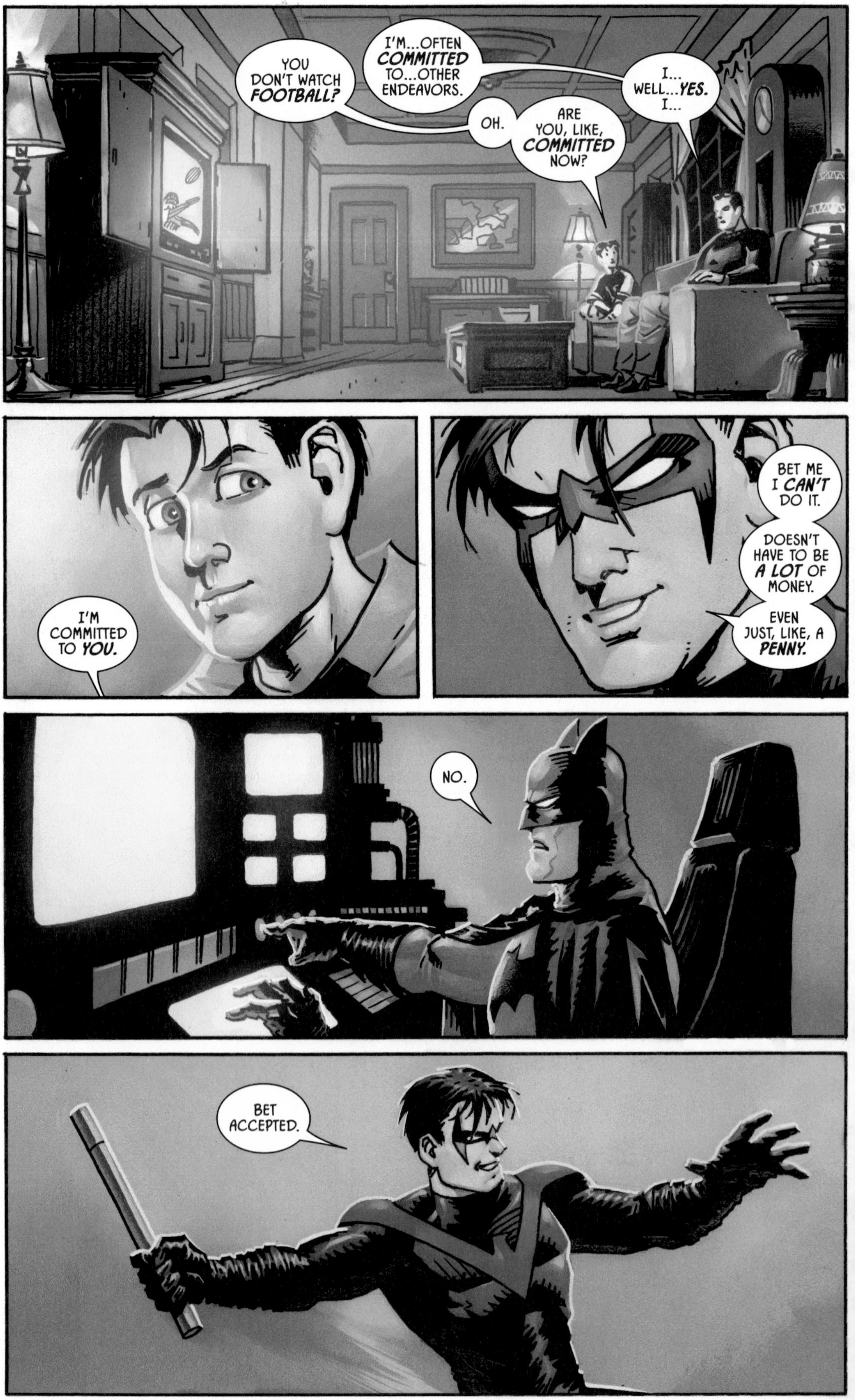
YOU DON'T WATCH FOOTBALL?
I'M...OFTEN COMMITTED TO...OTHER ENDEAVORS.
OH.
ARE YOU, LIKE, COMMITTED NOW?
I... WELL...YES. I...
I'M COMMITTED TO YOU.
BET ME I CAN'T DO IT.
DOESN'T HAVE TO BE A LOT OF MONEY.
EVEN JUST, LIKE, A PENNY.
NO.
BET ACCEPTED.

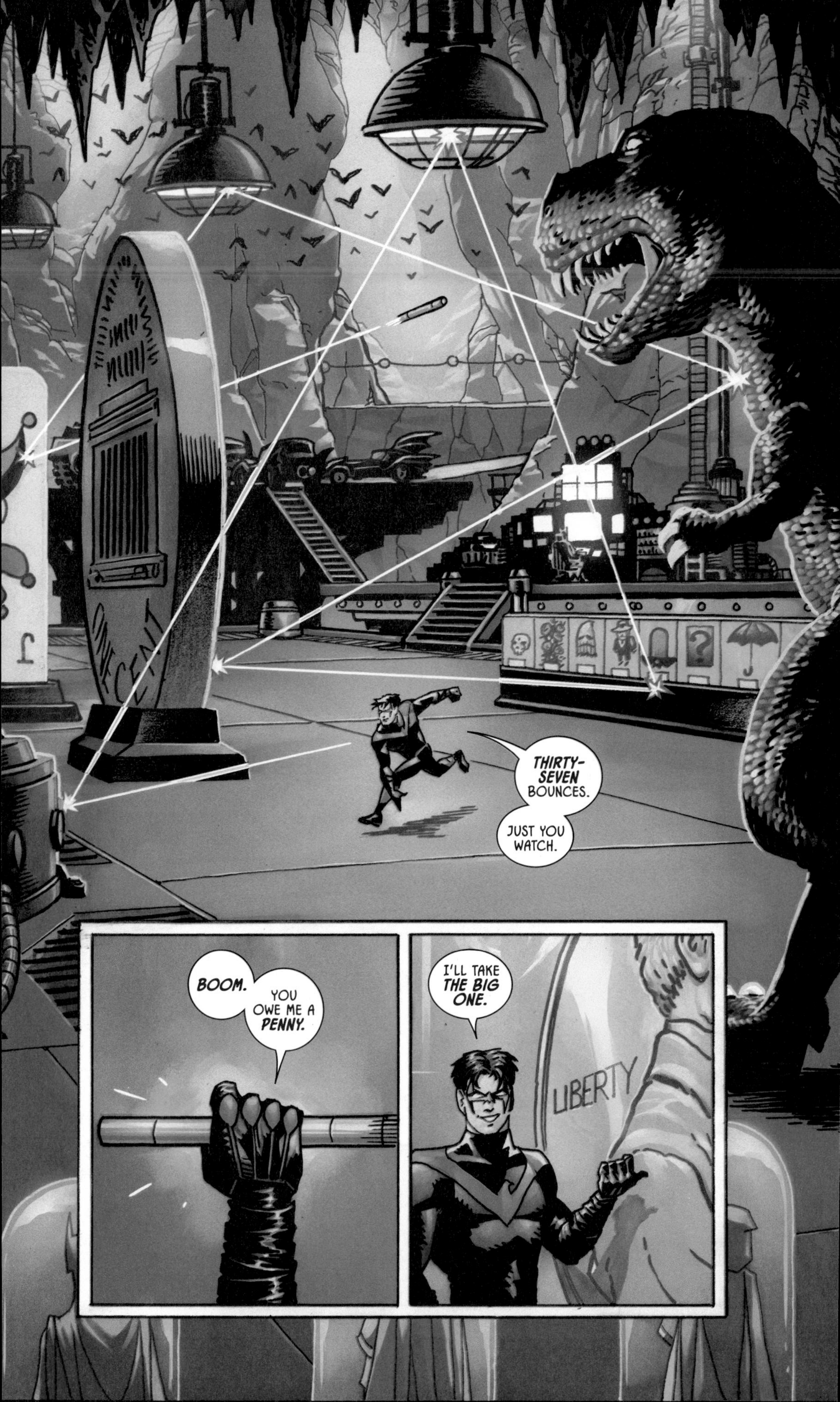

ONE CENT
THIRTY-SEVEN BOUNCES.
JUST YOU WATCH.
BOOM.
YOU OWE ME A PENNY.
I'LL TAKE THE BIG ONE.
LIBERTY

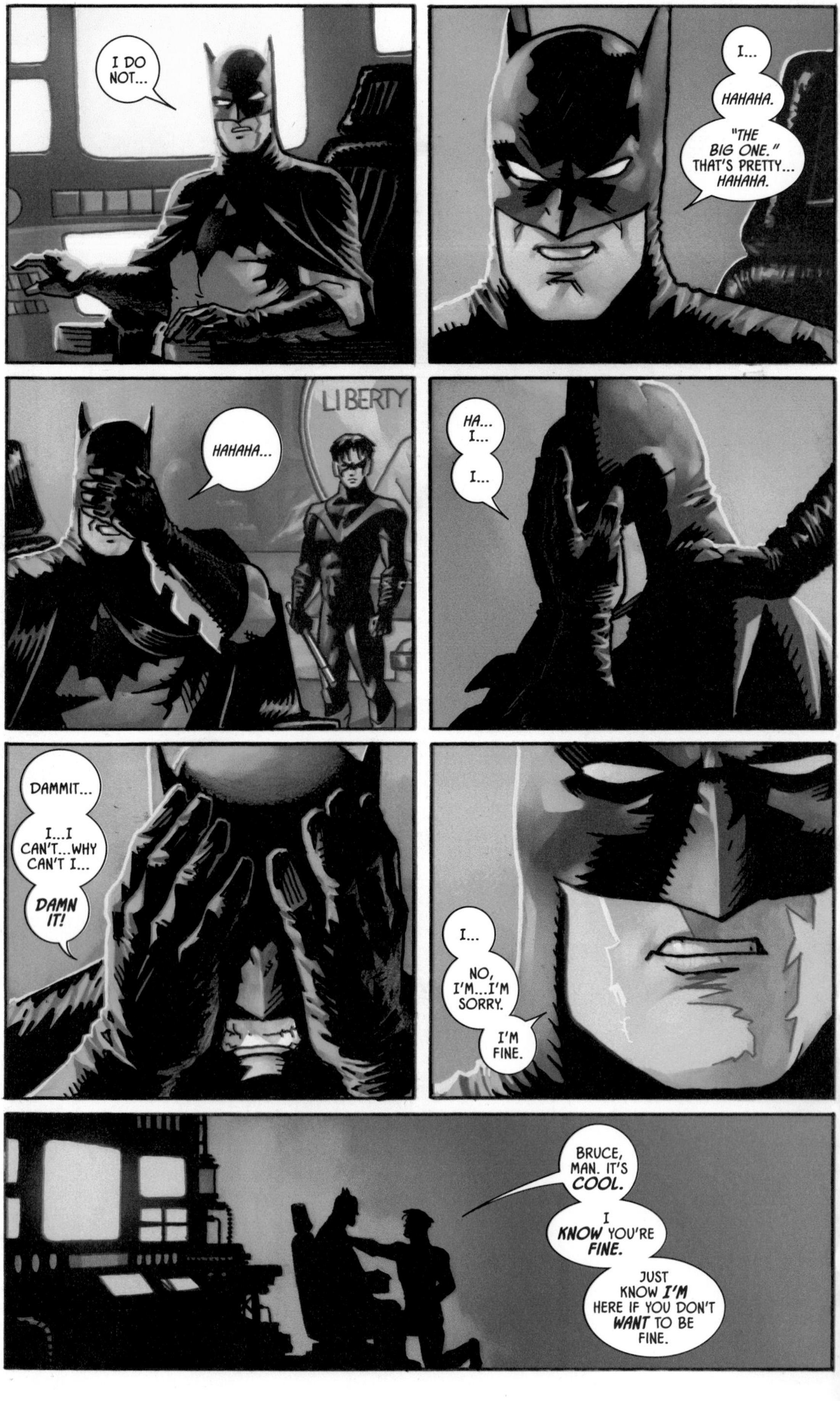
I DO NOT...
I...
HAHAHA.
"THE BIG ONE." THAT'S PRETTY... HAHAHA.
HAHAHA...
HA... I...
I...
DAMMIT...
I...I CAN'T...WHY CAN'T I...
DAMN IT!
I...
NO, I'M...I'M SORRY.
I'M FINE.
LIBERTY
BRUCE, MAN. IT'S COOL.
I KNOW YOU'RE FINE.
JUST KNOW I'M HERE IF YOU DON'T WANT TO BE FINE.

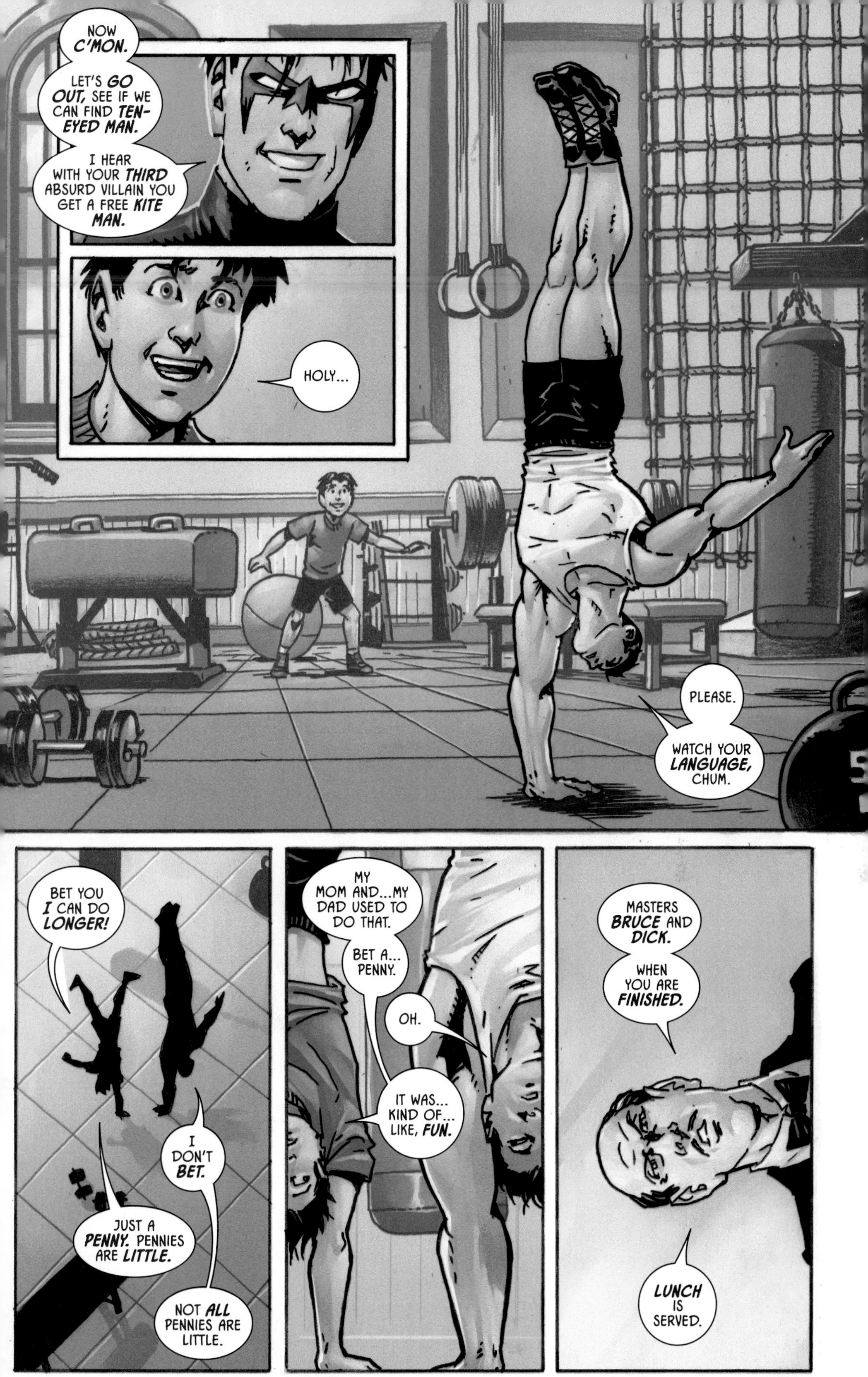
NOW C'MON.
LET'S GO OUT, SEE IF WE CAN FIND TEN-EYED MAN.
I HEAR WITH YOUR THIRD ABSURD VILLAIN YOU GET A FREE KITE MAN.
HOLY...
PLEASE.
WATCH YOUR LANGUAGE, CHUM.
BET YOU I CAN DO LONGER!
I DON'T BET.
JUST A PENNY. PENNIES ARE LITTLE.
NOT ALL PENNIES ARE LITTLE.
MY MOM AND...MY DAD USED TO DO THAT.
BET A... PENNY.
OH.
IT WAS... KIND OF... LIKE, FUN.
MASTERS BRUCE AND DICK.
WHEN YOU ARE FINISHED.
LUNCH IS SERVED.

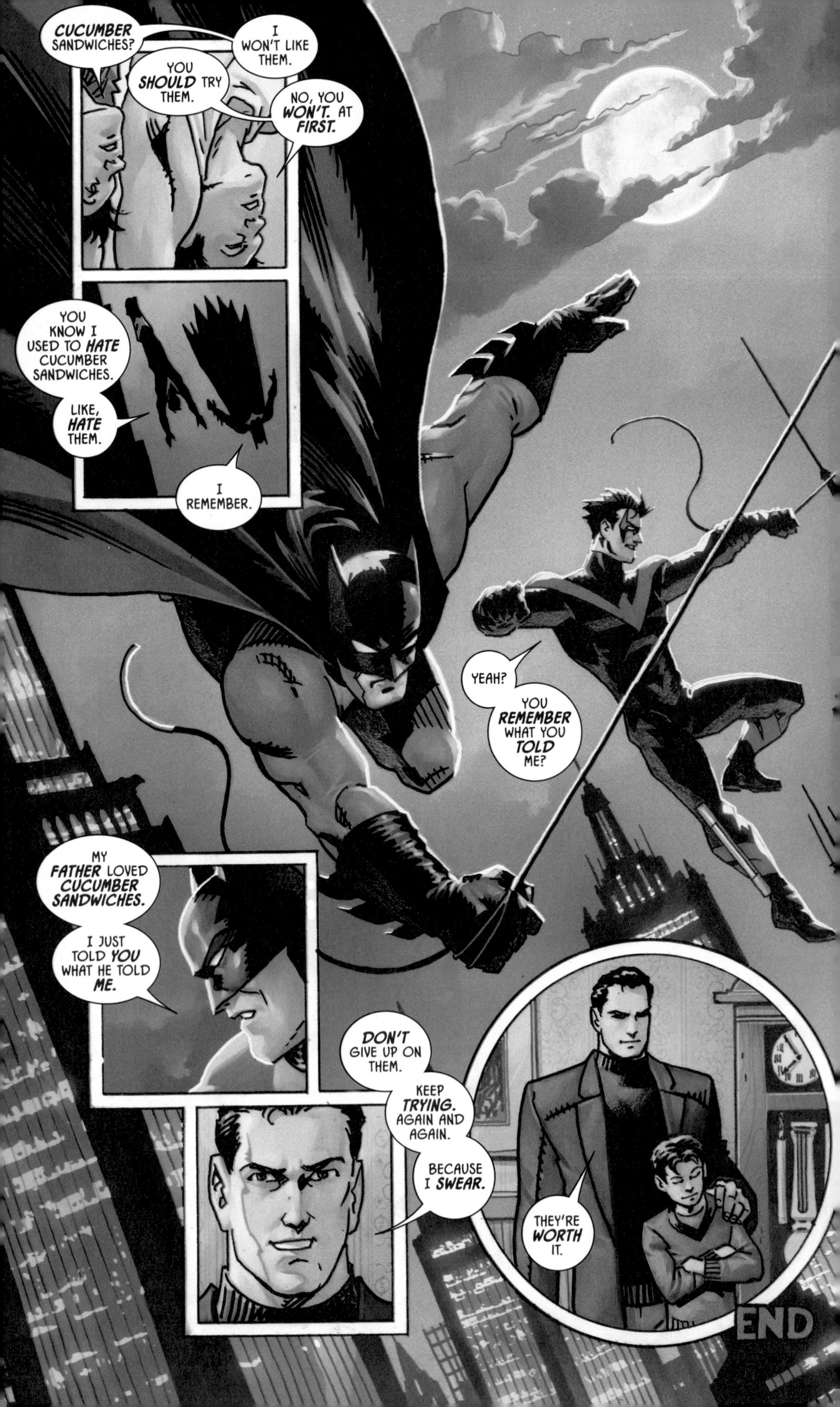

CUCUMBER SANDWICHES?
I WON'T LIKE THEM.
YOU SHOULD TRY THEM.
NO, YOU WON'T. AT FIRST.
YOU KNOW I USED TO HATE CUCUMBER SANDWICHES.
LIKE, HATE THEM.
I REMEMBER.
YEAH?
YOU REMEMBER WHAT YOU TOLD ME?
MY FATHER LOVED CUCUMBER SANDWICHES.
I JUST TOLD YOU WHAT HE TOLD ME.
DON'T GIVE UP ON THEM.
KEEP TRYING. AGAIN AND AGAIN.
BECAUSE I SWEAR.
THEY'RE WORTH IT.
END

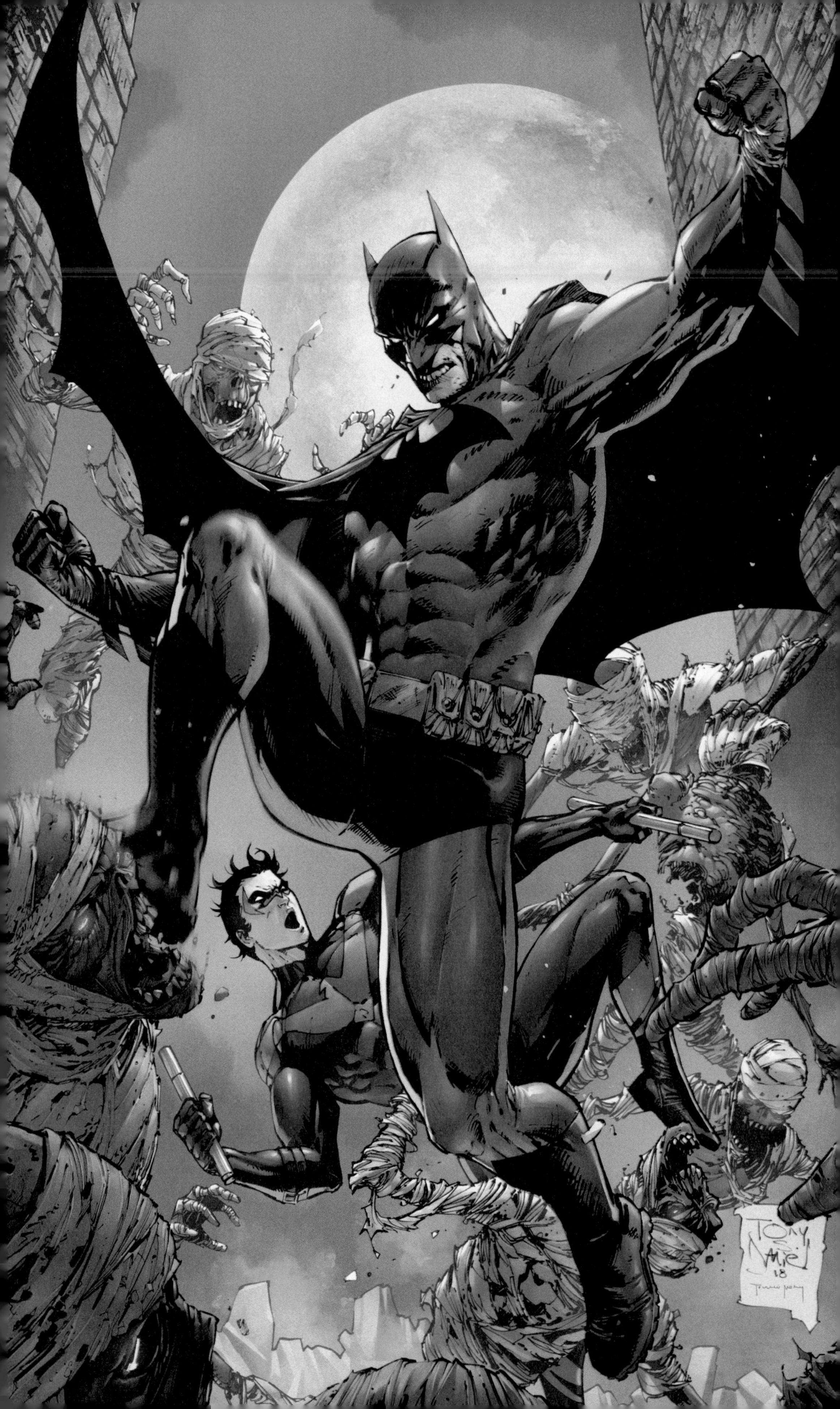

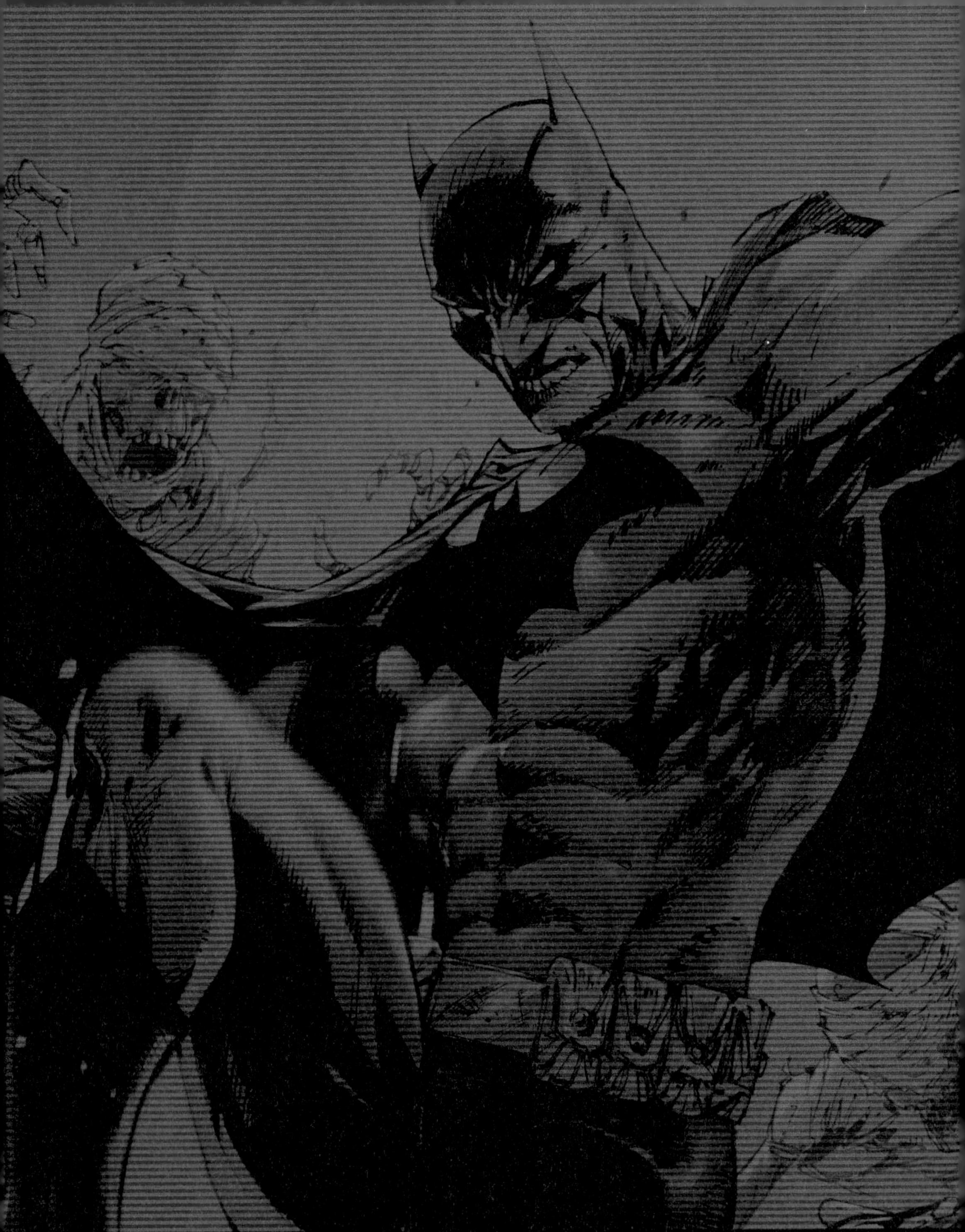

BATMAN
#55

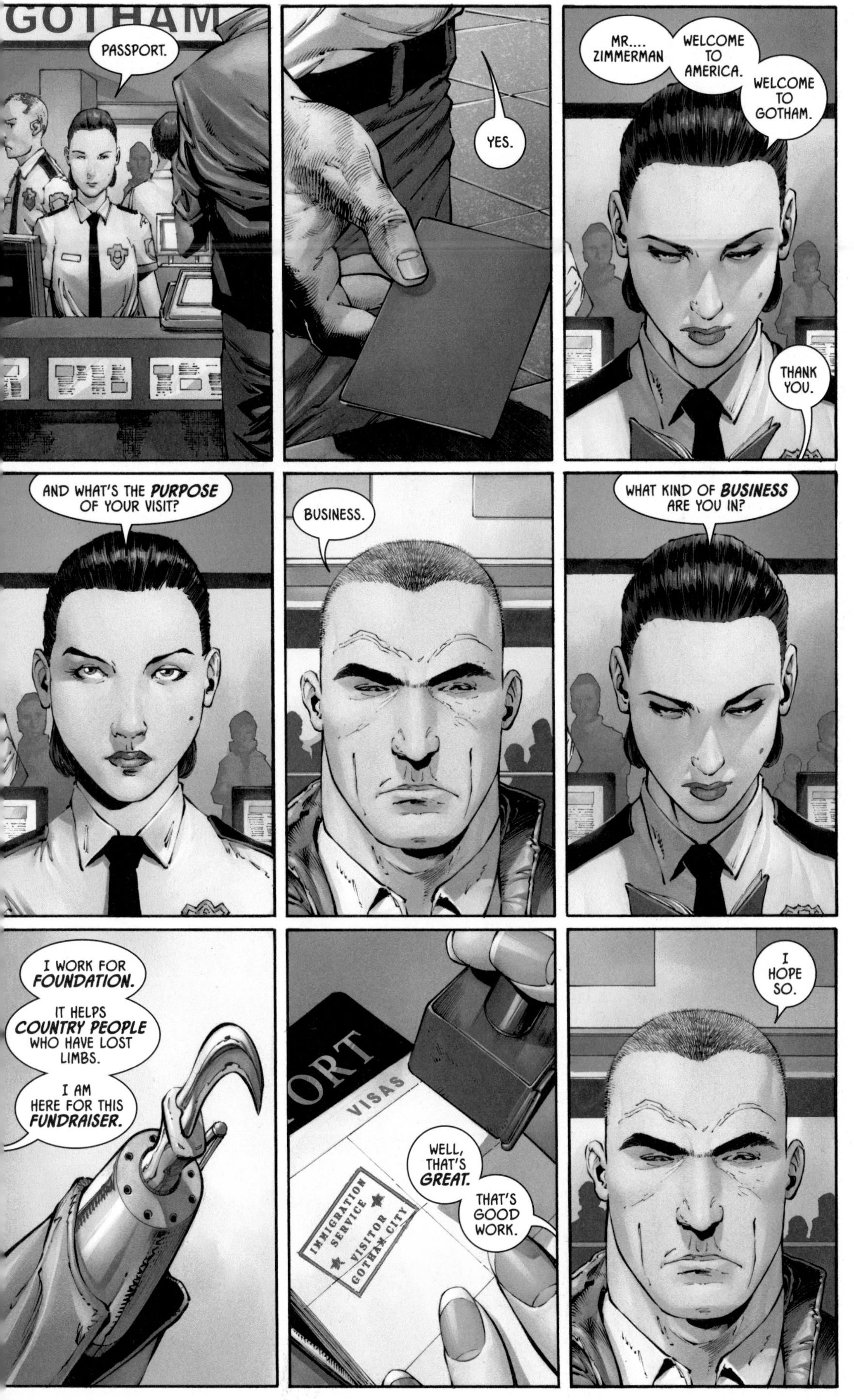
GOTHAM
PASSPORT.
YES.
MR.... ZIMMERMAN
WELCOME TO AMERICA.
WELCOME TO GOTHAM.
THANK YOU.
AND WHAT'S THE PURPOSE OF YOUR VISIT?
BUSINESS.
WHAT KIND OF BUSINESS ARE YOU IN?
I WORK FOR FOUNDATION.
IT HELPS COUNTRY PEOPLE WHO HAVE LOST LIMBS.
I AM HERE FOR THIS FUNDRAISER.
ORT
VISAS
IMMIGRATION SERVICE
VISITOR GOTHAM CITY
WELL, THAT'S GREAT.
THAT'S GOOD WORK.
I HOPE SO.

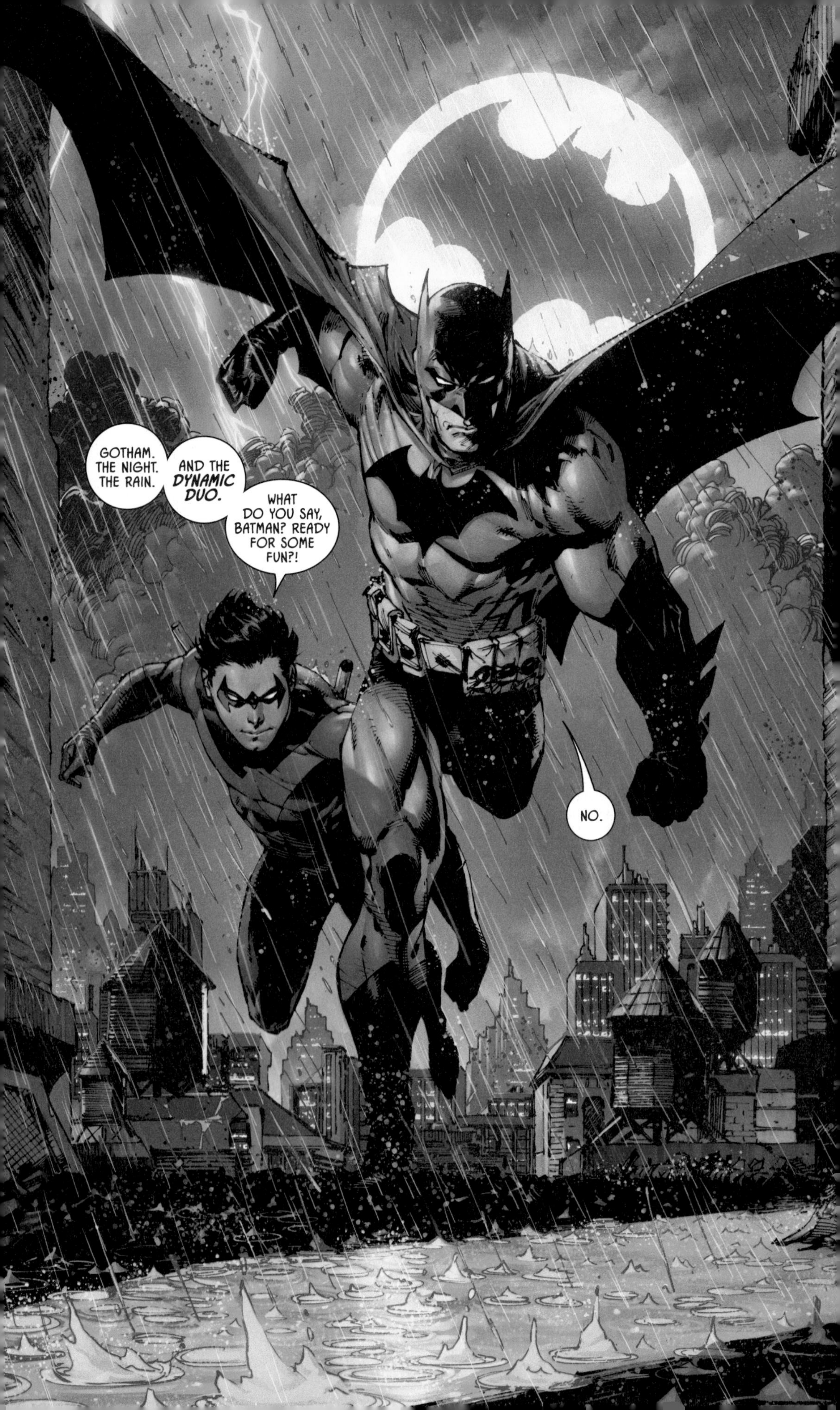
GOTHAM. THE NIGHT. THE RAIN.
AND THE DYNAMIC DUO.
WHAT DO YOU SAY, BATMAN? READY FOR SOME FUN?!
NO.

WE HAVE YOU STAYING FOR...THREE NIGHTS. IS THAT CORRECT?

YES.

HEY!

WHAT HAPPENED TO YOUR ARM?

Ghhchch

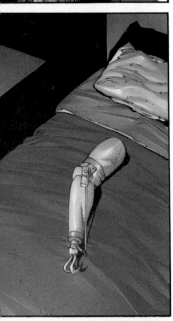

PSHHHHHH

JUST ANSWER ME THIS, ONE...ONE QUESTION!

IS CHRIS CAMPBELL STILL THE GOTHAM KNIGHTS' STARTING QUARTERBACK?

BECAUSE IF YOU SAY YES, THEN WHY ARE WE EVEN TALKING ABOUT THE PLAYOFFS?

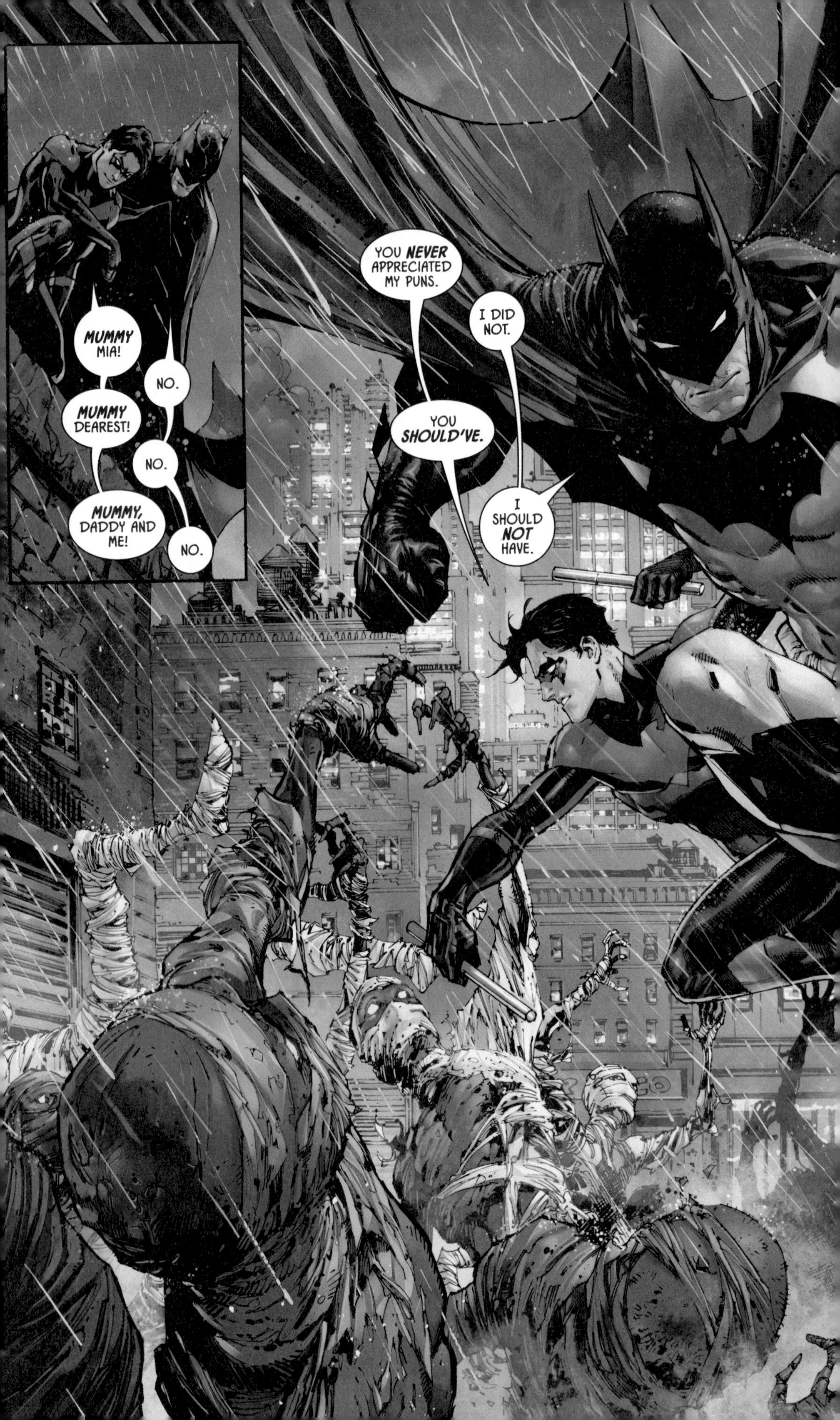
MUMMY MIA!
NO.
MUMMY DEAREST!
NO.
MUMMY, DADDY AND ME!
NO.
YOU NEVER APPRECIATED MY PUNS.
I DID NOT.
YOU SHOULD'VE.
I SHOULD NOT HAVE.

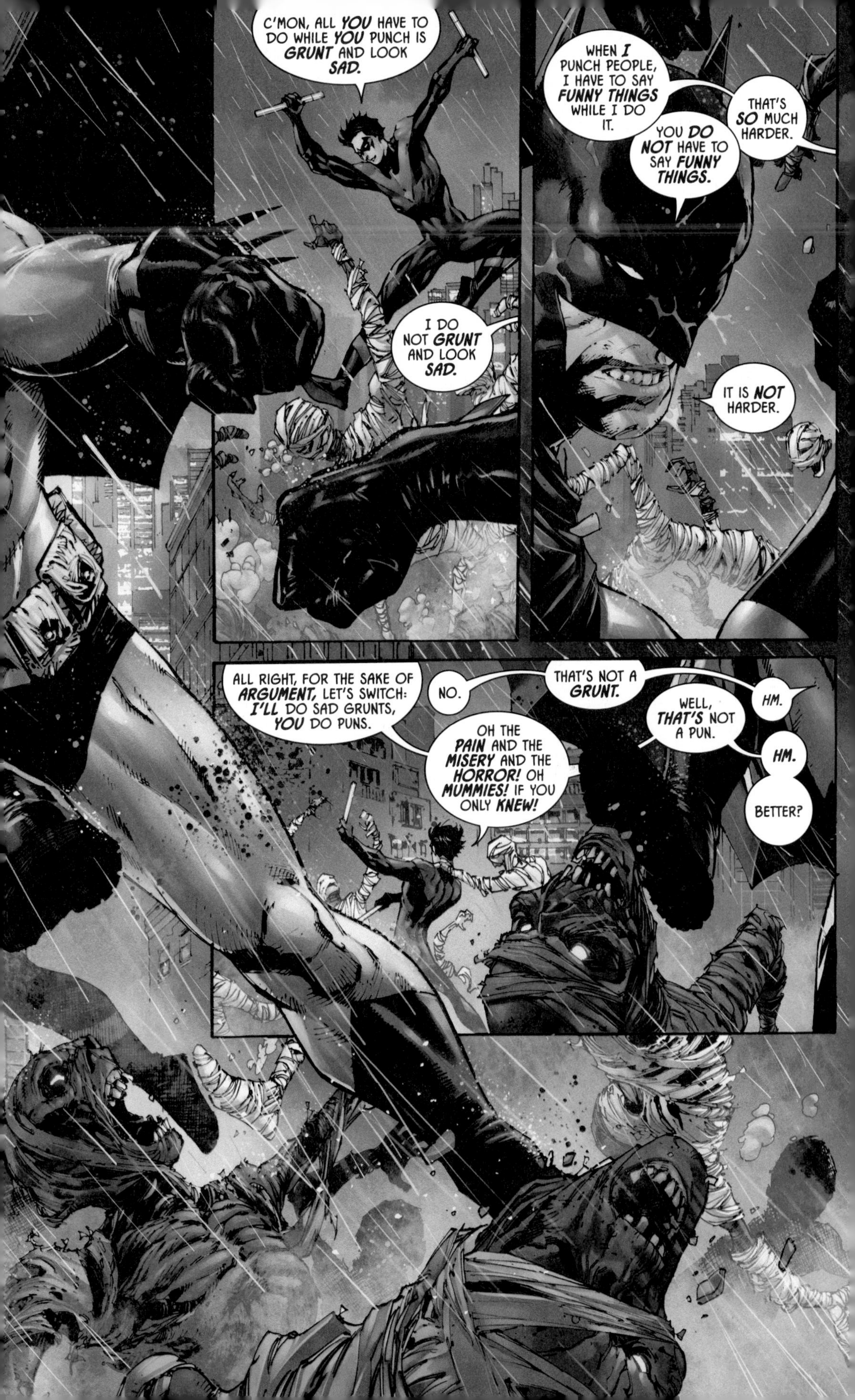
C'MON, ALL YOU HAVE TO DO WHILE YOU PUNCH IS GRUNT AND LOOK SAD.
I DO NOT GRUNT AND LOOK SAD.
WHEN I PUNCH PEOPLE, I HAVE TO SAY FUNNY THINGS WHILE I DO IT.
THAT'S SO MUCH HARDER.
YOU DO NOT HAVE TO SAY FUNNY THINGS.
IT IS NOT HARDER.
ALL RIGHT, FOR THE SAKE OF ARGUMENT, LET'S SWITCH: I'LL DO SAD GRUNTS, YOU DO PUNS.
OH THE PAIN AND THE MISERY AND THE HORROR! OH MUMMIES! IF YOU ONLY KNEW!
NO.
THAT'S NOT A GRUNT.
HM.
WELL, THAT'S NOT A PUN.
HM.
BETTER?

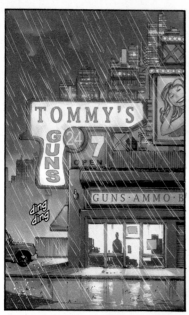

TOMMY'S
GUNS
24 7
OPEN
GUNS·AMMO·B
ding ding
I WOULD LIKE TO BUY RIFLE.
PLEASE.
GOT A LOT OF RIFLES, BUDDY.
GONNA NEED A LITTLE MORE *SPECIFICITY.*
OF COURSE.
HERE.
YEAH, THAT'S...*UH...* ***SPECIFIC.***
NOT SAYING I ***CAN'T*** DO IT, BUT GETTING IT ***ALL*** HERE, NOW...
NOT GOING TO EXACTLY BE ***CHEAP.***
THANK YOU, I UNDERSTAND.
I HAVE MONEY.
HIP. HIP. HOORAY.
SO.
YOU WANT TO ***WAIT*** FOR ALL THE GOVERNMENT CHECKS?
OR YOU WANT TO ***PAY*** FOR THE LATE-NIGHT ***EXPEDITED*** SPECIAL?
EXPEDITED.
PLEASE.

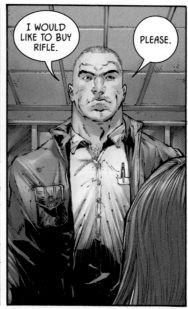

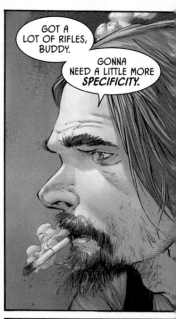

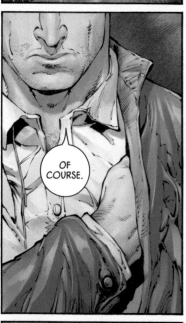

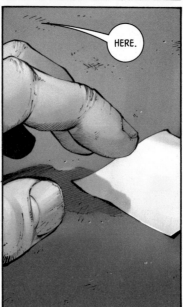

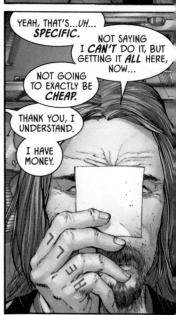

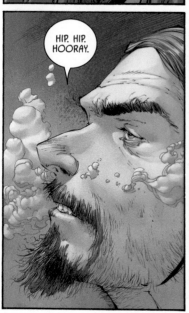

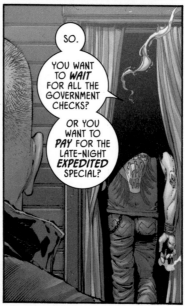

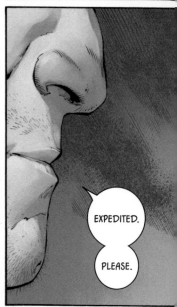

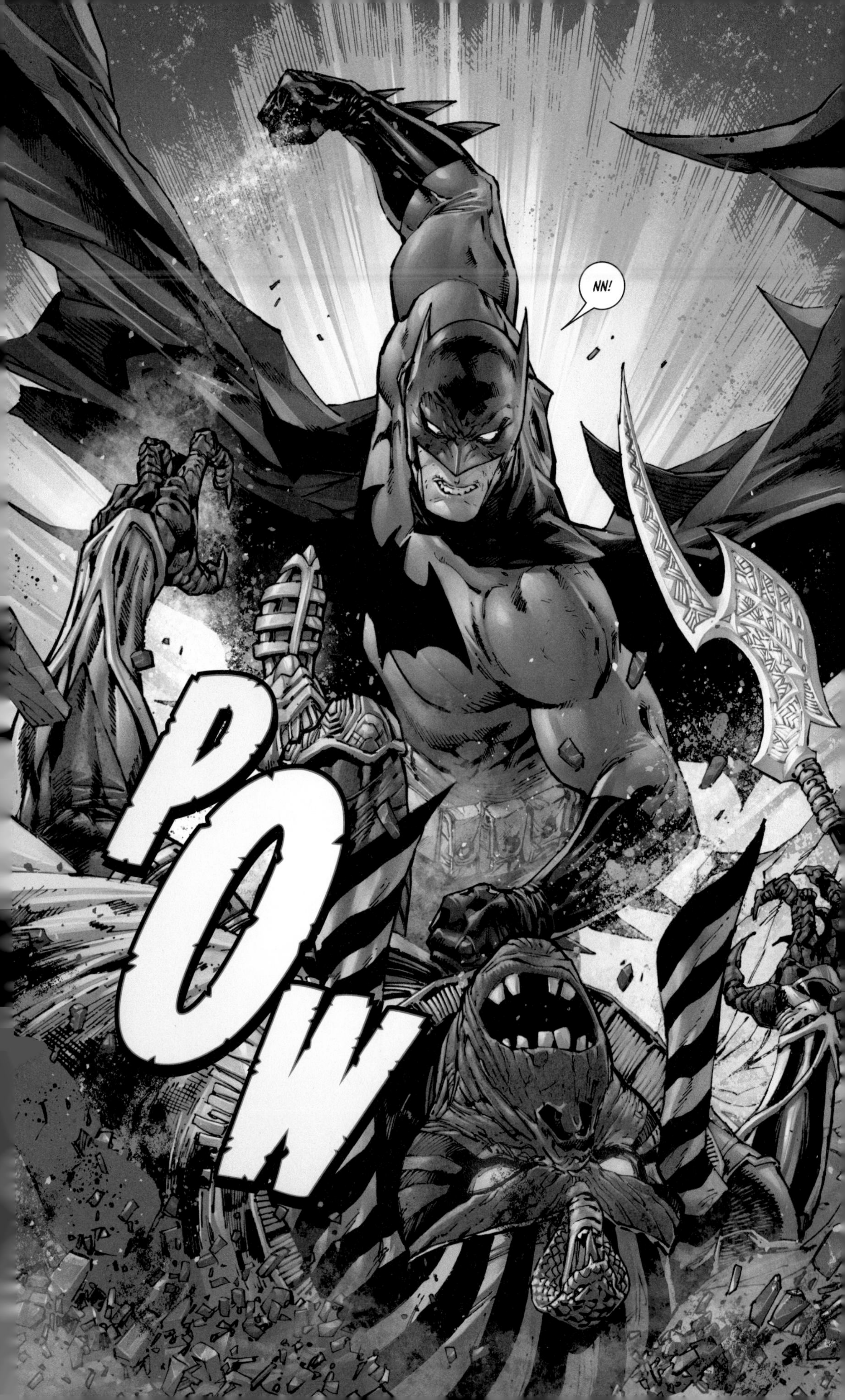

NN!
POW

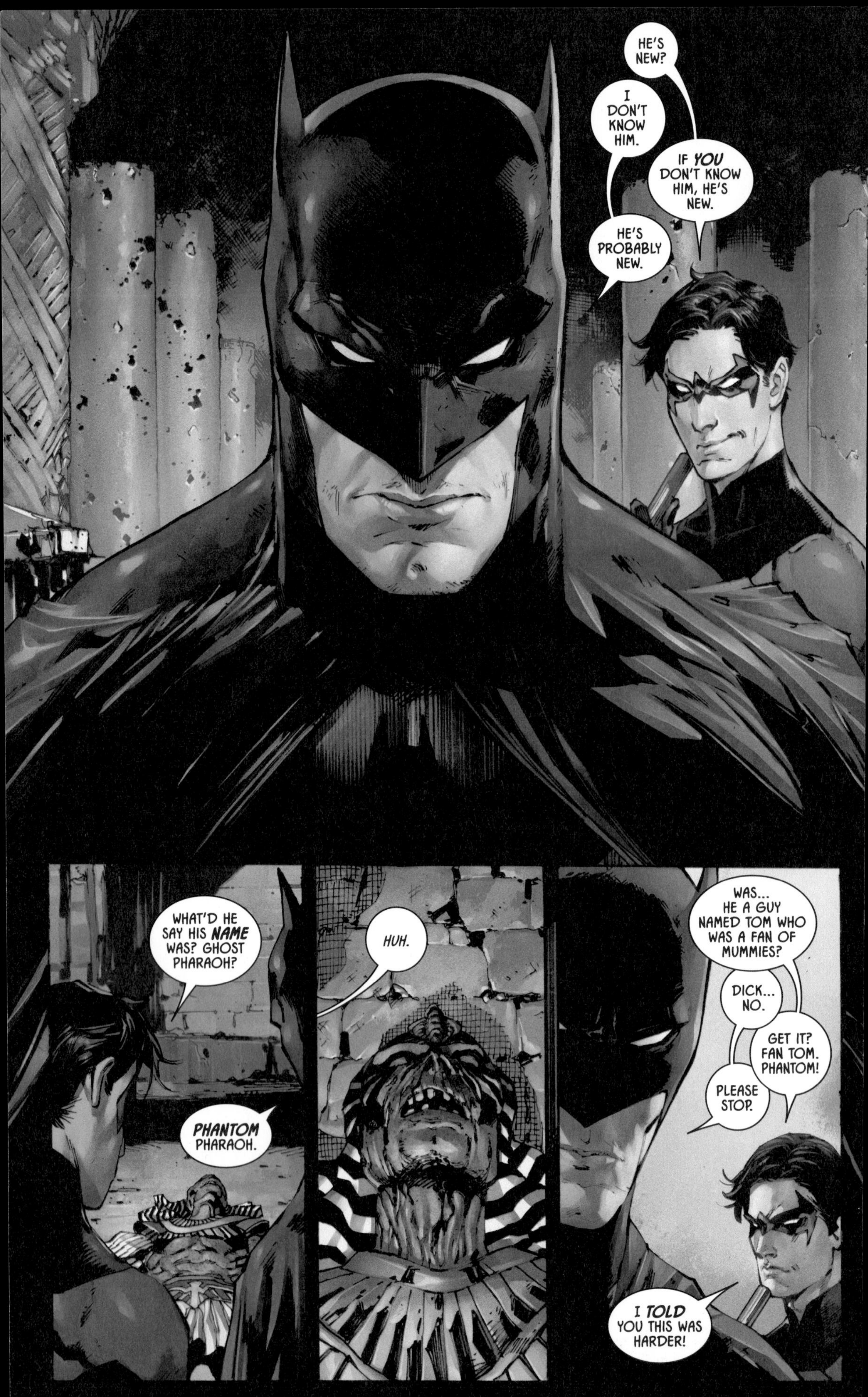
HE'S NEW?
I DON'T KNOW HIM.
IF *YOU* DON'T KNOW HIM, HE'S NEW.
HE'S PROBABLY NEW.
WHAT'D HE SAY HIS *NAME* WAS? GHOST PHARAOH?
PHANTOM PHARAOH.
HUH.
WAS... HE A GUY NAMED TOM WHO WAS A FAN OF MUMMIES?
DICK... NO.
GET IT? FAN TOM. PHANTOM!
PLEASE STOP.
I *TOLD* YOU THIS WAS HARDER!

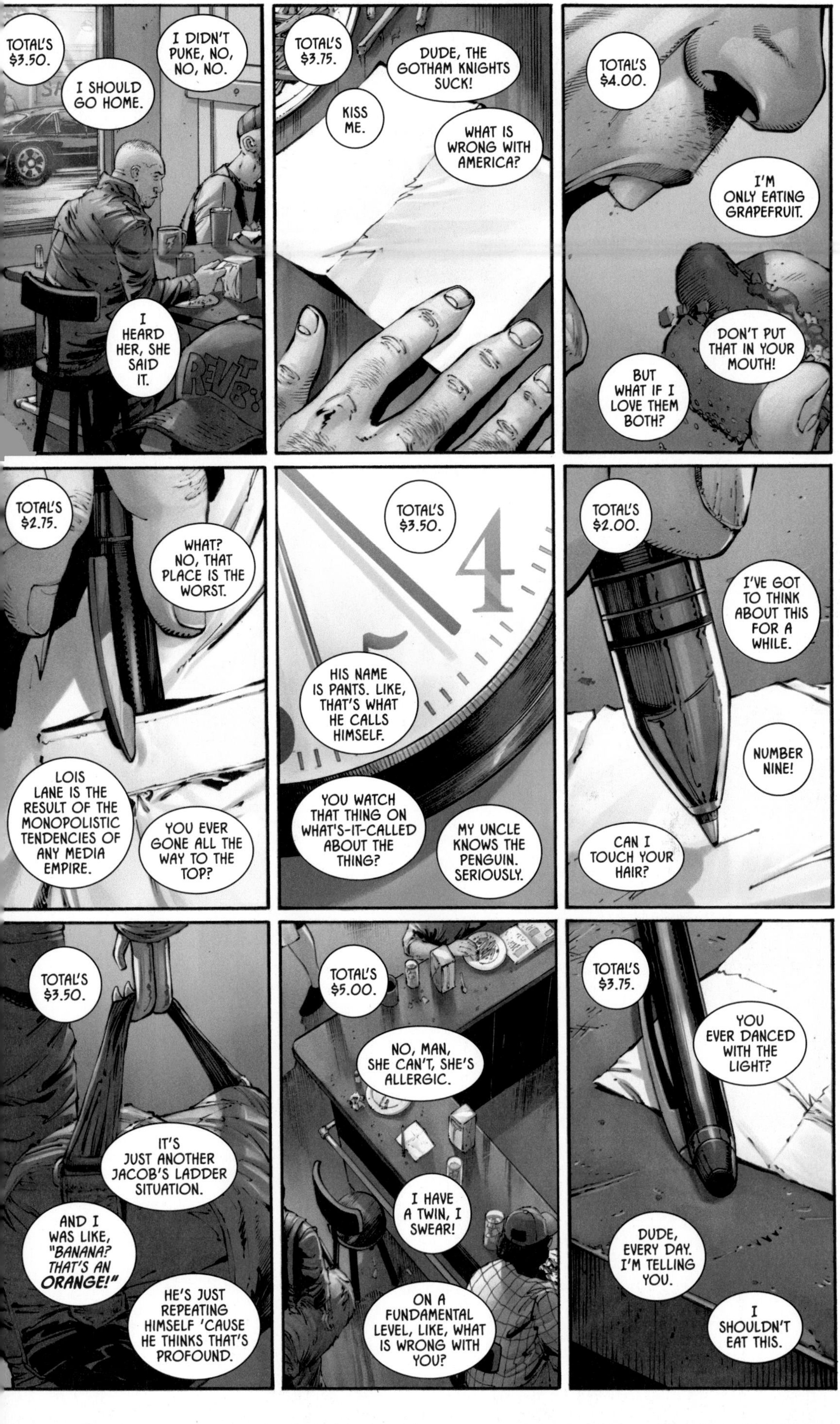
TOTAL'S $3.50.
I DIDN'T PUKE, NO, NO, NO.
I SHOULD GO HOME.
I HEARD HER, SHE SAID IT.
REVT
TOTAL'S $3.75.
DUDE, THE GOTHAM KNIGHTS SUCK!
KISS ME.
WHAT IS WRONG WITH AMERICA?
TOTAL'S $4.00.
I'M ONLY EATING GRAPEFRUIT.
DON'T PUT THAT IN YOUR MOUTH!
BUT WHAT IF I LOVE THEM BOTH?
TOTAL'S $2.75.
WHAT? NO, THAT PLACE IS THE WORST.
LOIS LANE IS THE RESULT OF THE MONOPOLISTIC TENDENCIES OF ANY MEDIA EMPIRE.
YOU EVER GONE ALL THE WAY TO THE TOP?
TOTAL'S $3.50.
4
HIS NAME IS PANTS. LIKE, THAT'S WHAT HE CALLS HIMSELF.
YOU WATCH THAT THING ON WHAT'S-IT-CALLED ABOUT THE THING?
MY UNCLE KNOWS THE PENGUIN. SERIOUSLY.
TOTAL'S $2.00.
I'VE GOT TO THINK ABOUT THIS FOR A WHILE.
NUMBER NINE!
CAN I TOUCH YOUR HAIR?
TOTAL'S $3.50.
IT'S JUST ANOTHER JACOB'S LADDER SITUATION.
AND I WAS LIKE, *"BANANA? THAT'S AN **ORANGE!**"*
HE'S JUST REPEATING HIMSELF 'CAUSE HE THINKS THAT'S PROFOUND.
TOTAL'S $5.00.
NO, MAN, SHE CAN'T, SHE'S ALLERGIC.
I HAVE A TWIN, I SWEAR!
ON A FUNDAMENTAL LEVEL, LIKE, WHAT IS WRONG WITH YOU?
TOTAL'S $3.75.
YOU EVER DANCED WITH THE LIGHT?
DUDE, EVERY DAY. I'M TELLING YOU.
I SHOULDN'T EAT THIS.

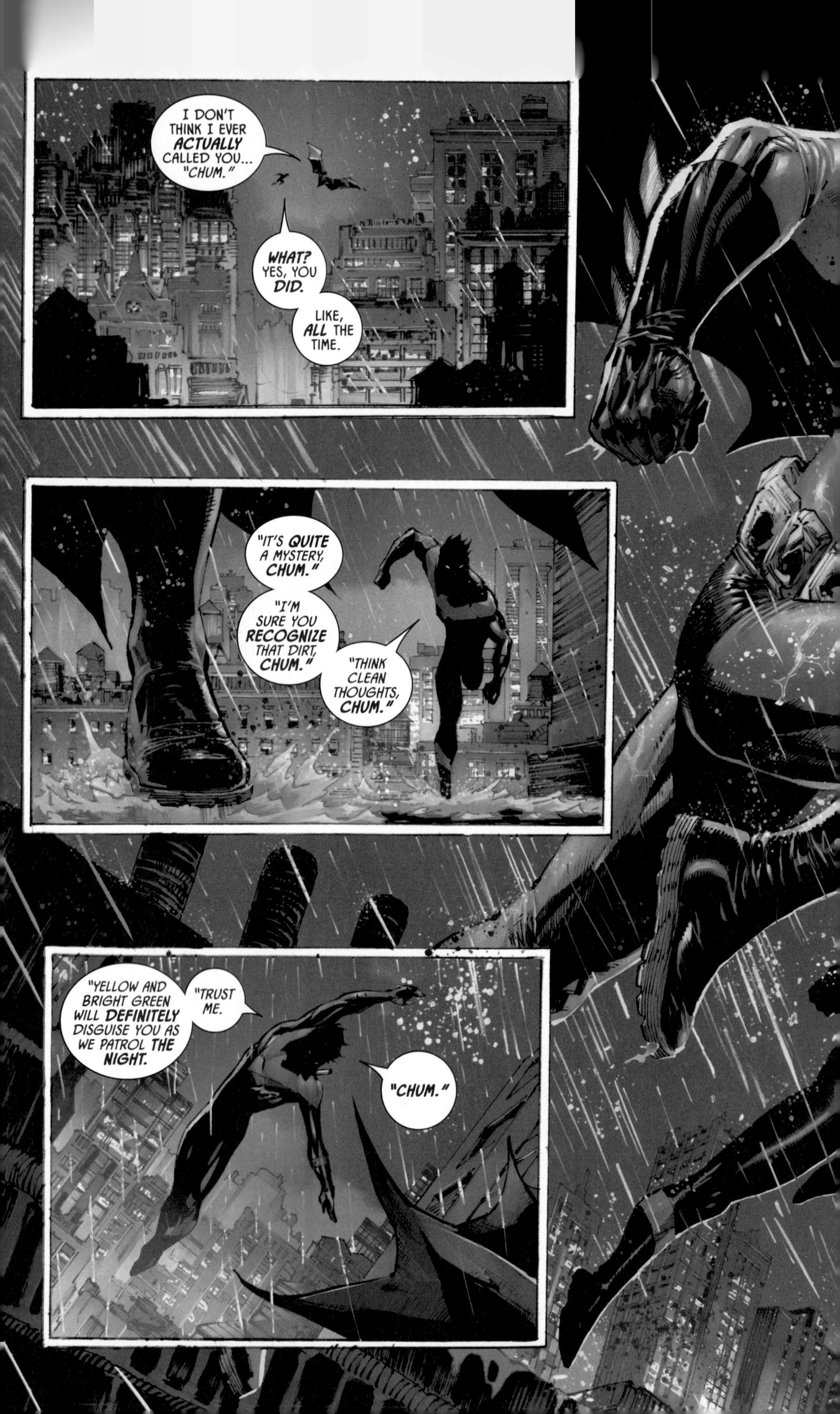
I DON'T THINK I EVER ACTUALLY CALLED YOU... "CHUM."
WHAT? YES, YOU DID.
LIKE, ALL THE TIME.
"IT'S QUITE A MYSTERY, CHUM."
"I'M SURE YOU RECOGNIZE THAT DIRT, CHUM."
"THINK CLEAN THOUGHTS, CHUM."
"YELLOW AND BRIGHT GREEN WILL DEFINITELY DISGUISE YOU AS WE PATROL THE NIGHT.
"TRUST ME.
"CHUM."

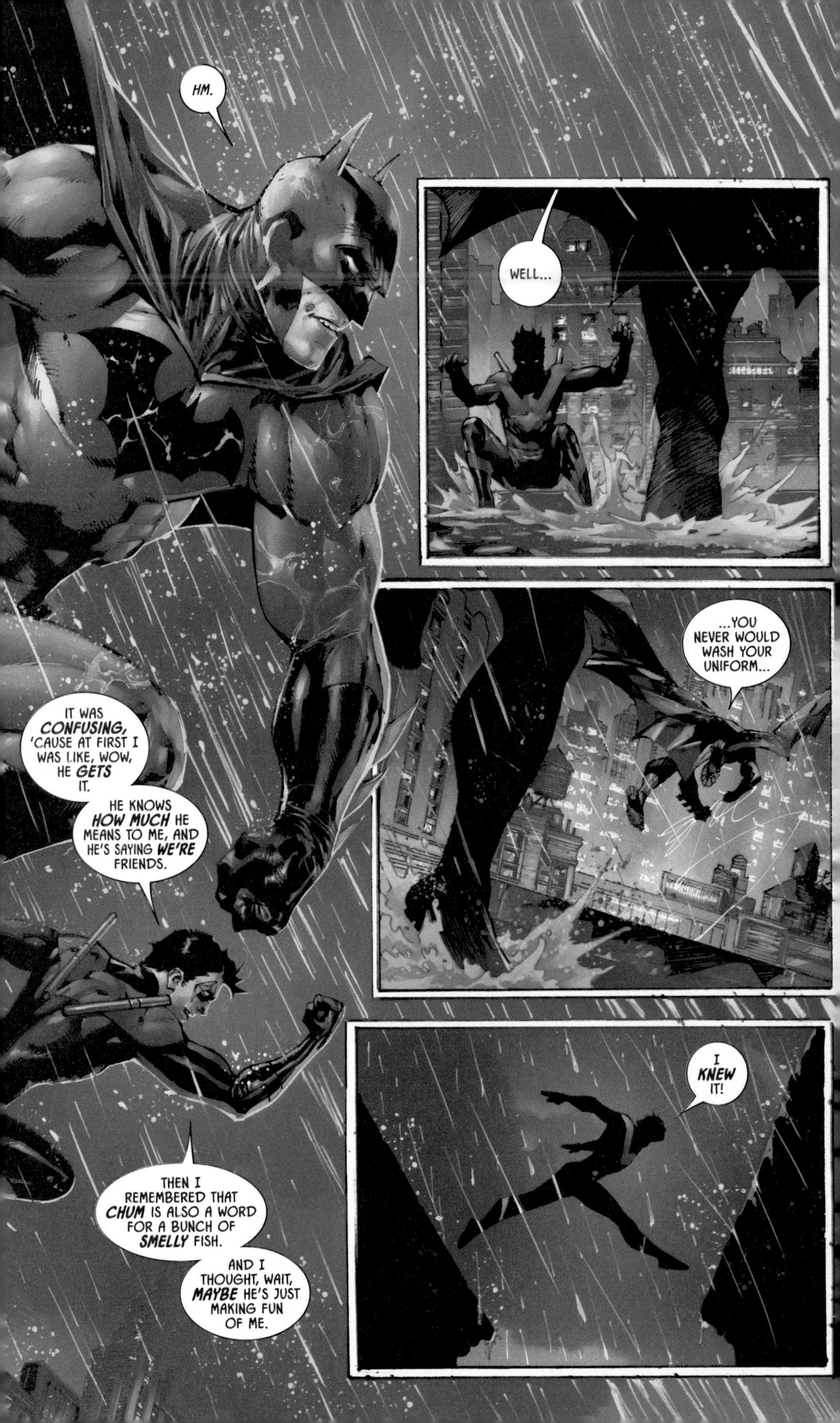
HM.
IT WAS CONFUSING, 'CAUSE AT FIRST I WAS LIKE, WOW, HE GETS IT.
HE KNOWS HOW MUCH HE MEANS TO ME, AND HE'S SAYING WE'RE FRIENDS.
THEN I REMEMBERED THAT CHUM IS ALSO A WORD FOR A BUNCH OF SMELLY FISH.
AND I THOUGHT, WAIT, MAYBE HE'S JUST MAKING FUN OF ME.
WELL...
...YOU NEVER WOULD WASH YOUR UNIFORM...
I KNEW IT!

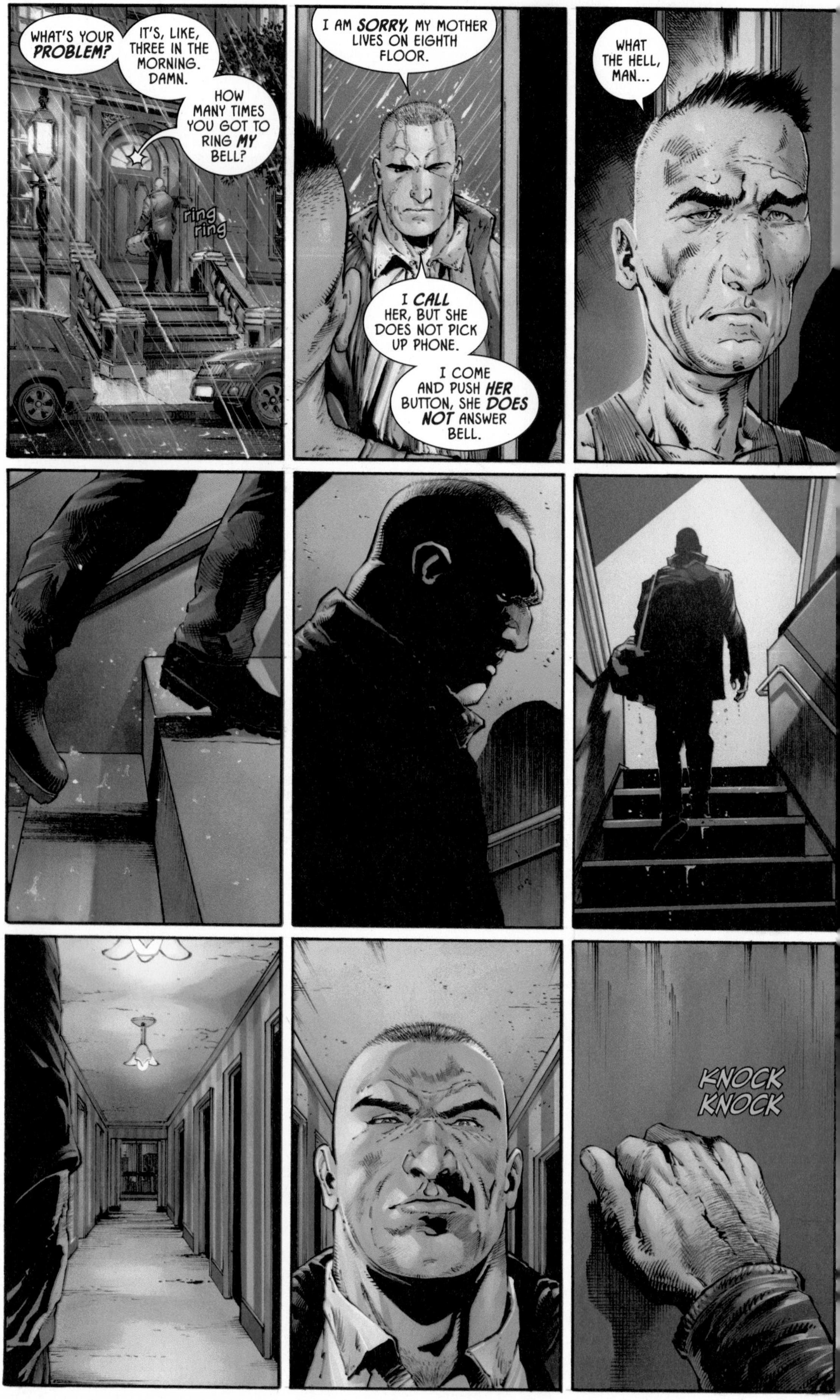
WHAT'S YOUR PROBLEM?
IT'S, LIKE, THREE IN THE MORNING. DAMN.
HOW MANY TIMES YOU GOT TO RING MY BELL?
ring ring
I AM SORRY, MY MOTHER LIVES ON EIGHTH FLOOR.
I CALL HER, BUT SHE DOES NOT PICK UP PHONE.
I COME AND PUSH HER BUTTON, SHE DOES NOT ANSWER BELL.
WHAT THE HELL, MAN...
KNOCK KNOCK

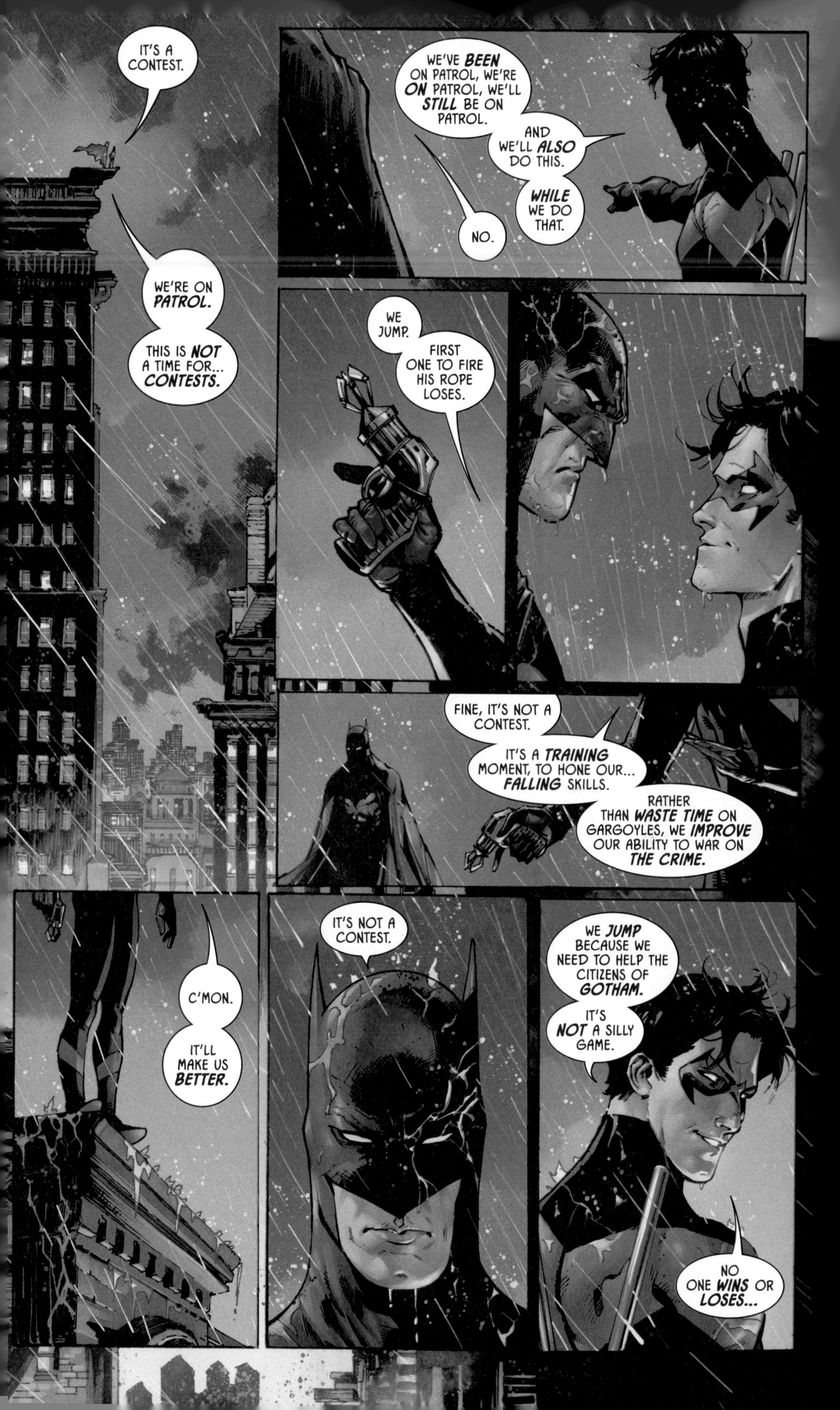
IT'S A CONTEST.
WE'RE ON PATROL.
THIS IS NOT A TIME FOR... CONTESTS.
WE'VE BEEN ON PATROL, WE'RE ON PATROL, WE'LL STILL BE ON PATROL.
AND WE'LL ALSO DO THIS.
WHILE WE DO THAT.
NO.
WE JUMP.
FIRST ONE TO FIRE HIS ROPE LOSES.
FINE, IT'S NOT A CONTEST.
IT'S A TRAINING MOMENT, TO HONE OUR... FALLING SKILLS.
RATHER THAN WASTE TIME ON GARGOYLES, WE IMPROVE OUR ABILITY TO WAR ON THE CRIME.
C'MON.
IT'LL MAKE US BETTER.
IT'S NOT A CONTEST.
WE JUMP BECAUSE WE NEED TO HELP THE CITIZENS OF GOTHAM.
IT'S NOT A SILLY GAME.
NO ONE WINS OR LOSES...

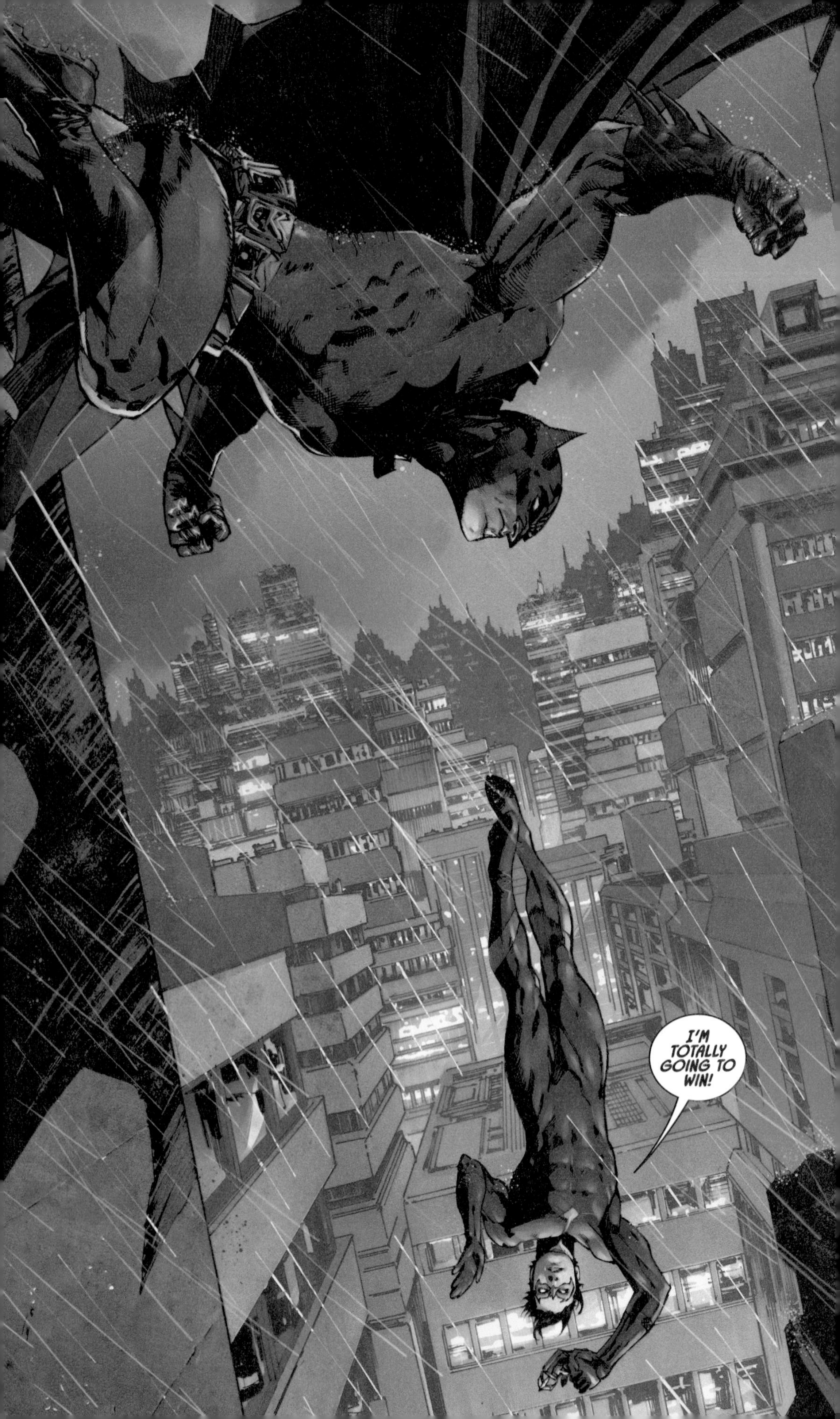
I'M TOTALLY GOING TO WIN!

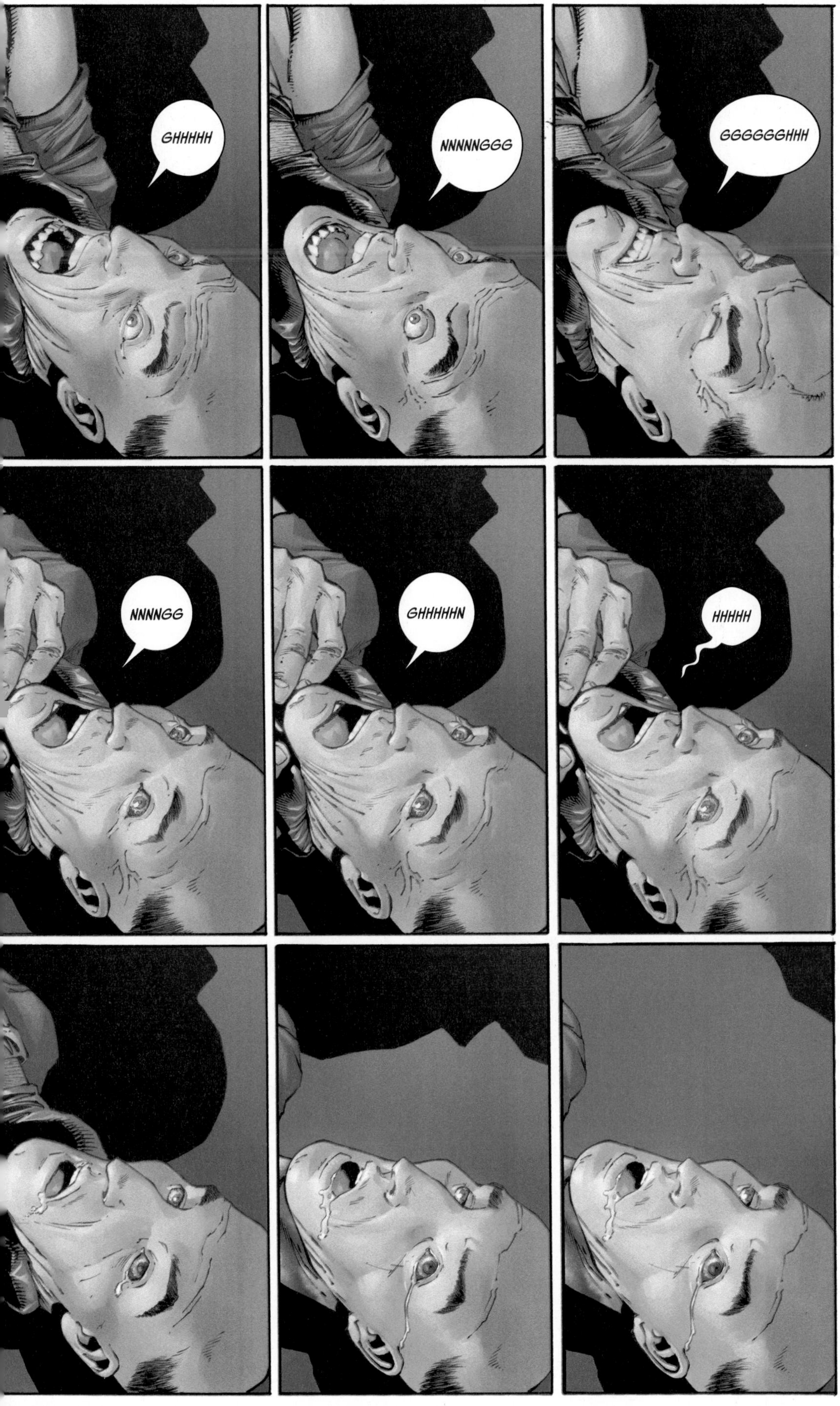
GHHHHH
NNNNNGGG
GGGGGGHHH
NNNNGG
GHHHHHN
HHHHH

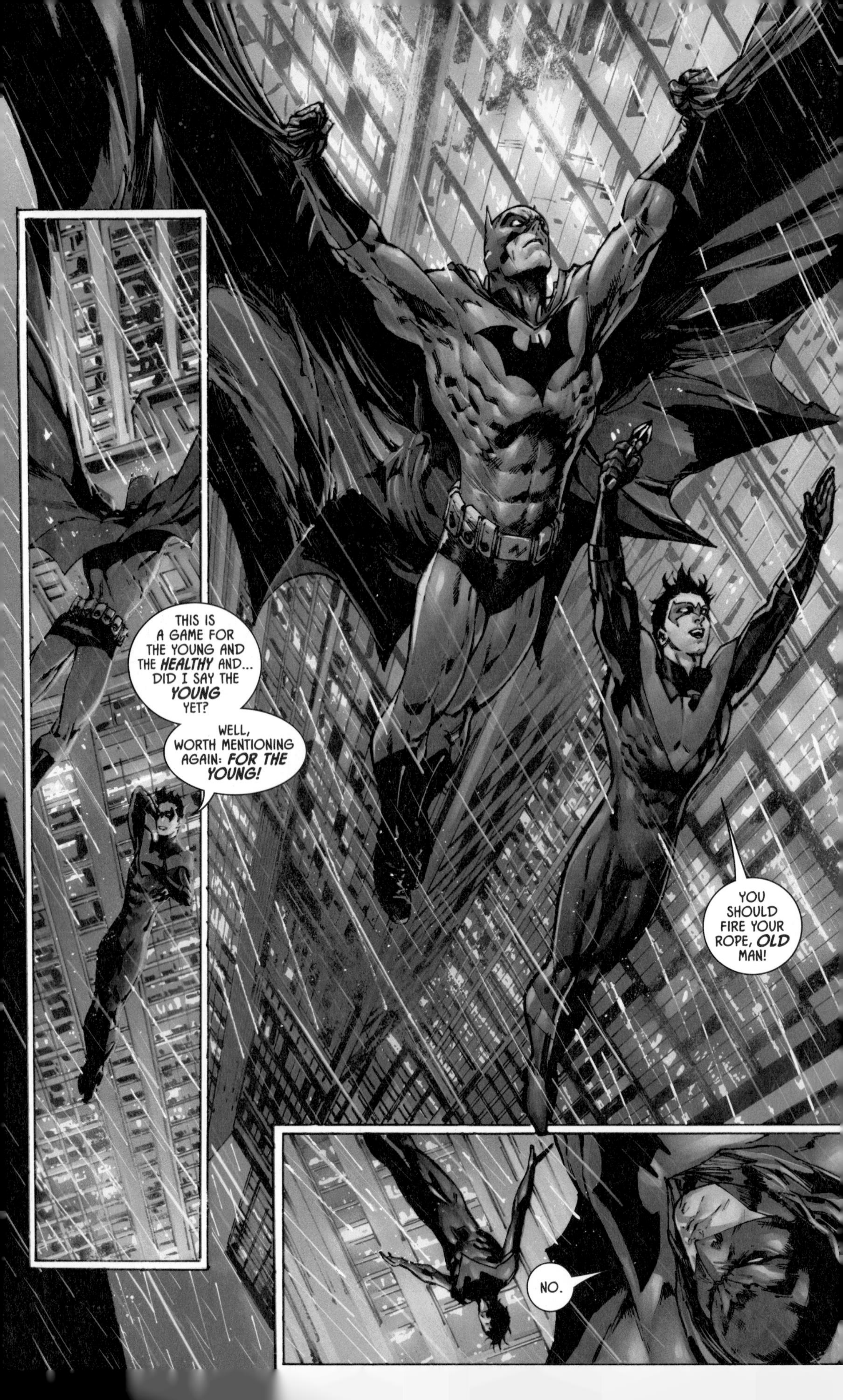
THIS IS A GAME FOR THE YOUNG AND THE HEALTHY AND... DID I SAY THE YOUNG YET?
WELL, WORTH MENTIONING AGAIN: FOR THE YOUNG!
YOU SHOULD FIRE YOUR ROPE, OLD MAN!
NO.

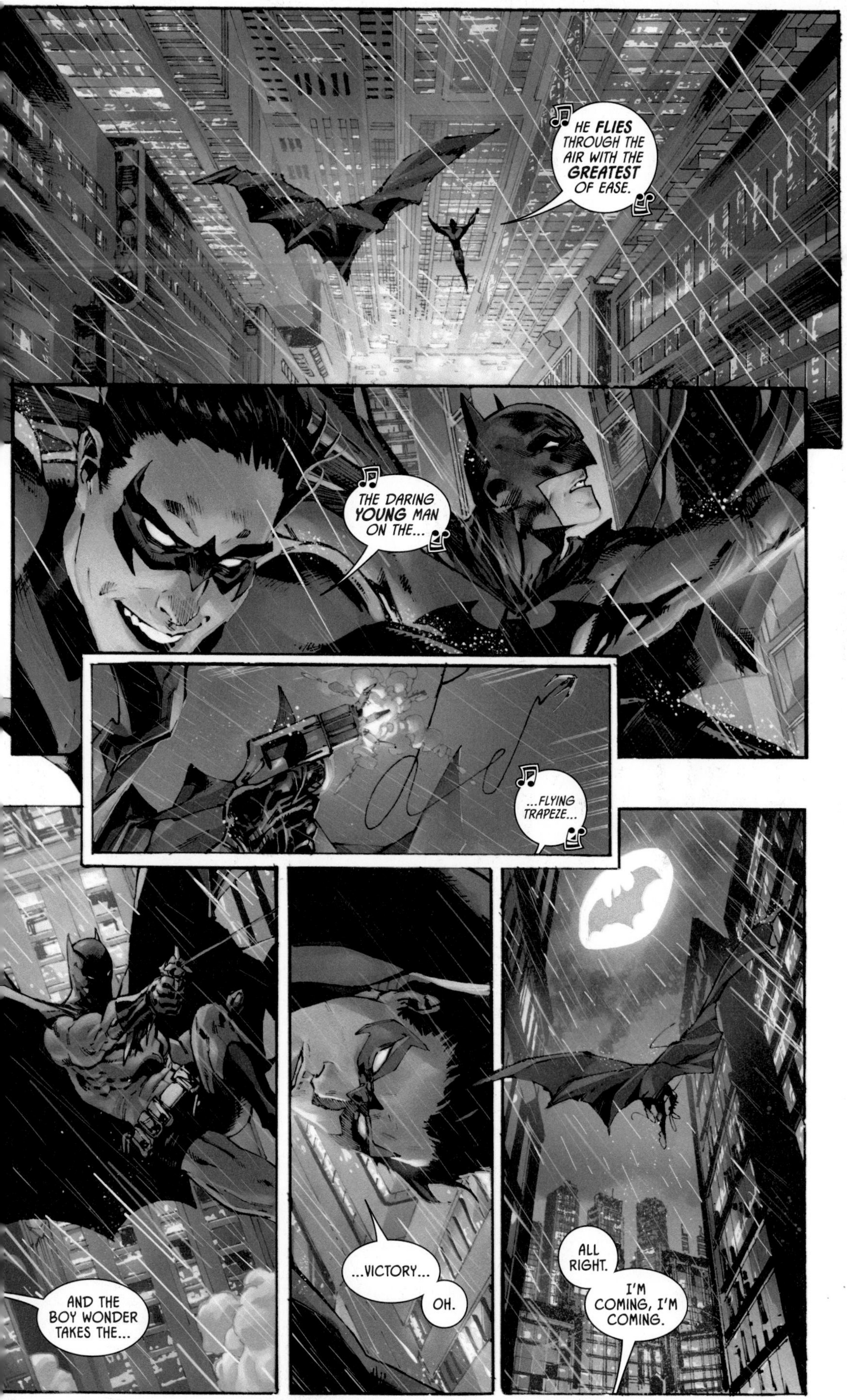
HE FLIES THROUGH THE AIR WITH THE GREATEST OF EASE.
THE DARING YOUNG MAN ON THE...
...FLYING TRAPEZE...
AND THE BOY WONDER TAKES THE...
...VICTORY...
OH.
ALL RIGHT.
I'M COMING, I'M COMING.

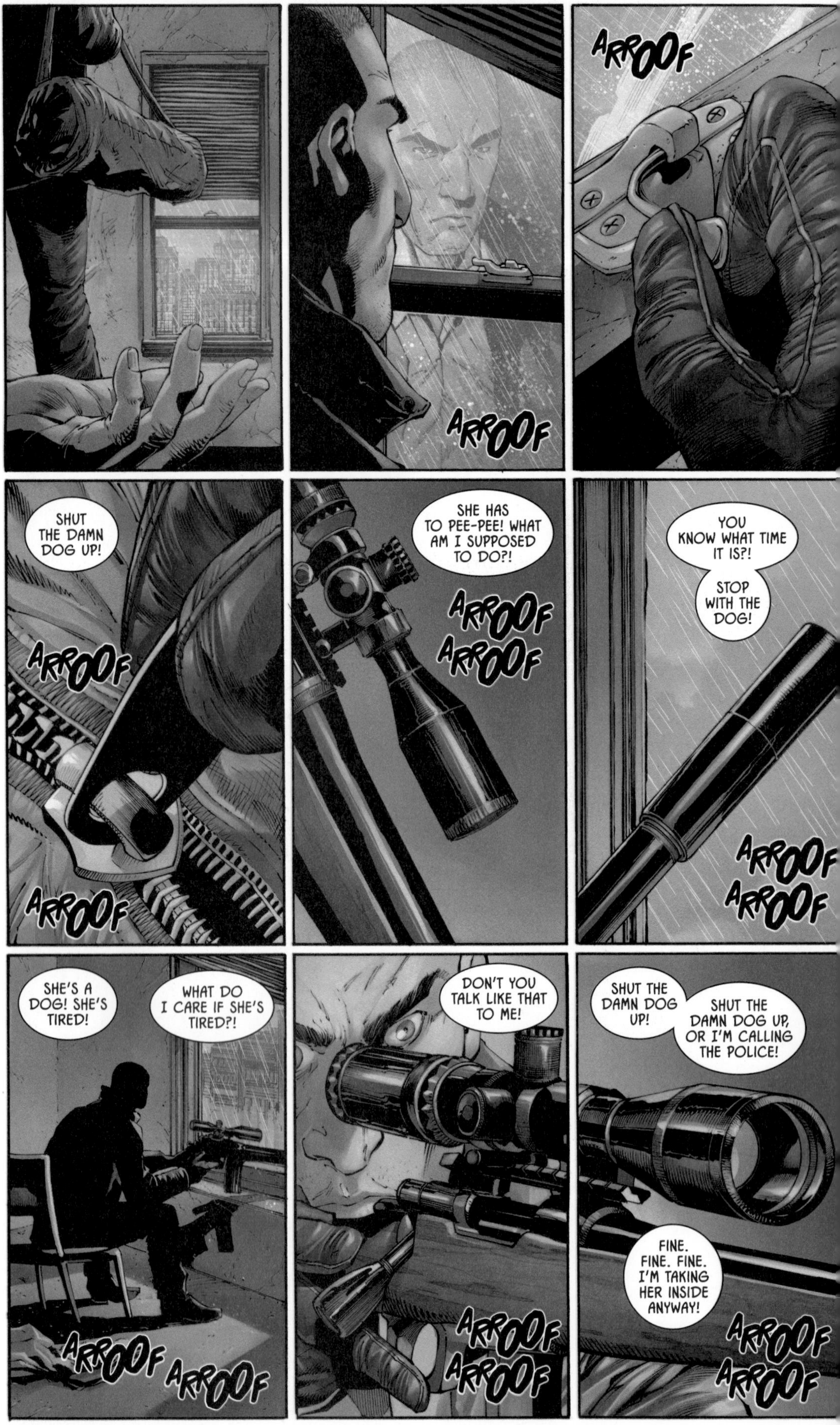
ARROOF
ARROOF
SHUT THE DAMN DOG UP!
ARROOF
ARROOF
SHE HAS TO PEE-PEE! WHAT AM I SUPPOSED TO DO?!
ARROOF
ARROOF
YOU KNOW WHAT TIME IT IS?!
STOP WITH THE DOG!
ARROOF
ARROOF
SHE'S A DOG! SHE'S TIRED!
WHAT DO I CARE IF SHE'S TIRED?!
ARROOF
ARROOF
DON'T YOU TALK LIKE THAT TO ME!
ARROOF
ARROOF
SHUT THE DAMN DOG UP!
SHUT THE DAMN DOG UP, OR I'M CALLING THE POLICE!
FINE. FINE. FINE. I'M TAKING HER INSIDE ANYWAY!
ARROOF
ARROOF

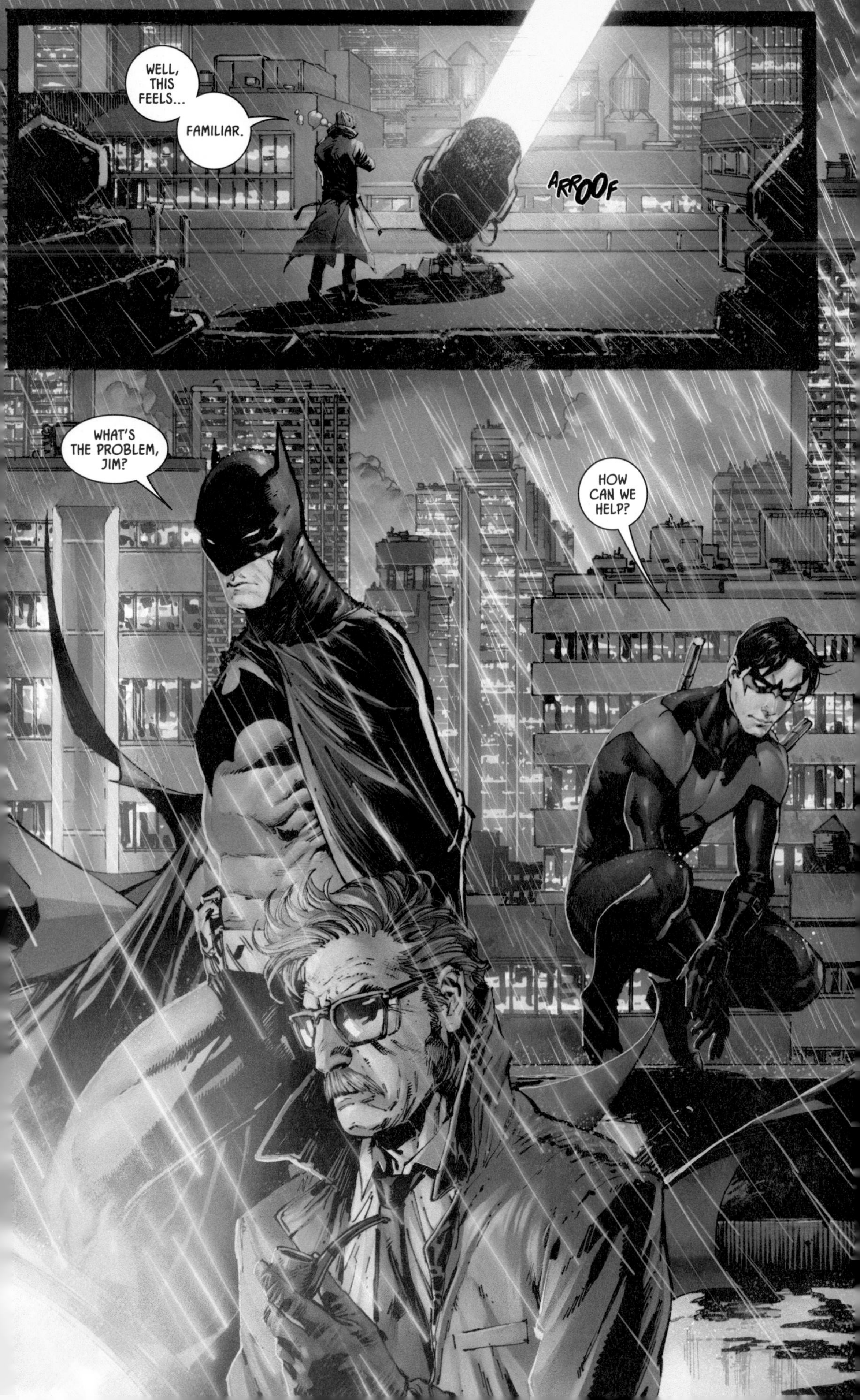
WELL, THIS FEELS...
FAMILIAR.
ARROOF
WHAT'S THE PROBLEM, JIM?
HOW CAN WE HELP?

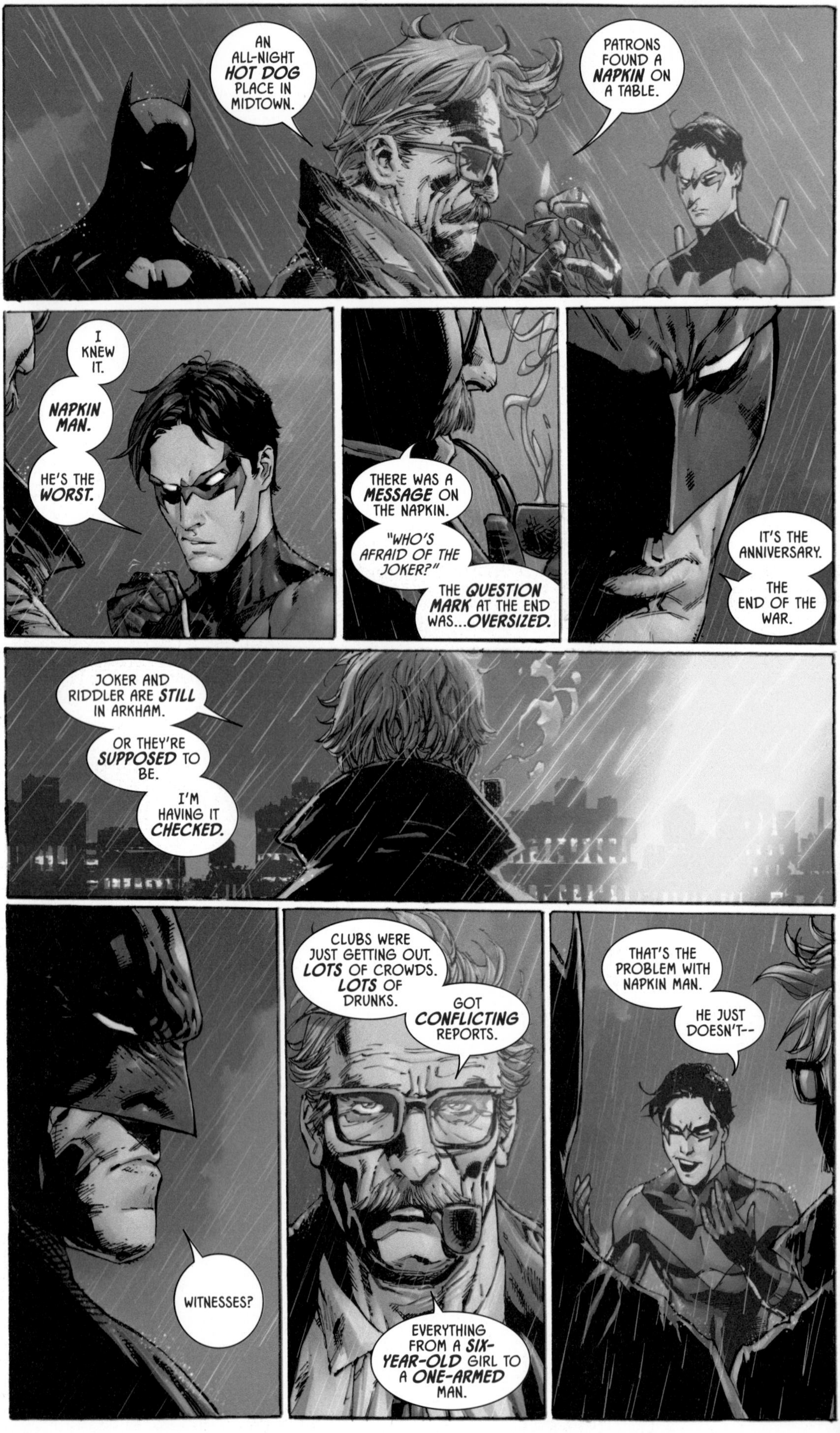
AN ALL-NIGHT HOT DOG PLACE IN MIDTOWN.
PATRONS FOUND A NAPKIN ON A TABLE.
I KNEW IT.
NAPKIN MAN.
HE'S THE WORST.
THERE WAS A MESSAGE ON THE NAPKIN.
"WHO'S AFRAID OF THE JOKER?"
THE QUESTION MARK AT THE END WAS...OVERSIZED.
IT'S THE ANNIVERSARY.
THE END OF THE WAR.
JOKER AND RIDDLER ARE STILL IN ARKHAM.
OR THEY'RE SUPPOSED TO BE.
I'M HAVING IT CHECKED.
WITNESSES?
CLUBS WERE JUST GETTING OUT. LOTS OF CROWDS. LOTS OF DRUNKS.
GOT CONFLICTING REPORTS.
EVERYTHING FROM A SIX-YEAR-OLD GIRL TO A ONE-ARMED MAN.
THAT'S THE PROBLEM WITH NAPKIN MAN.
HE JUST DOESN'T--

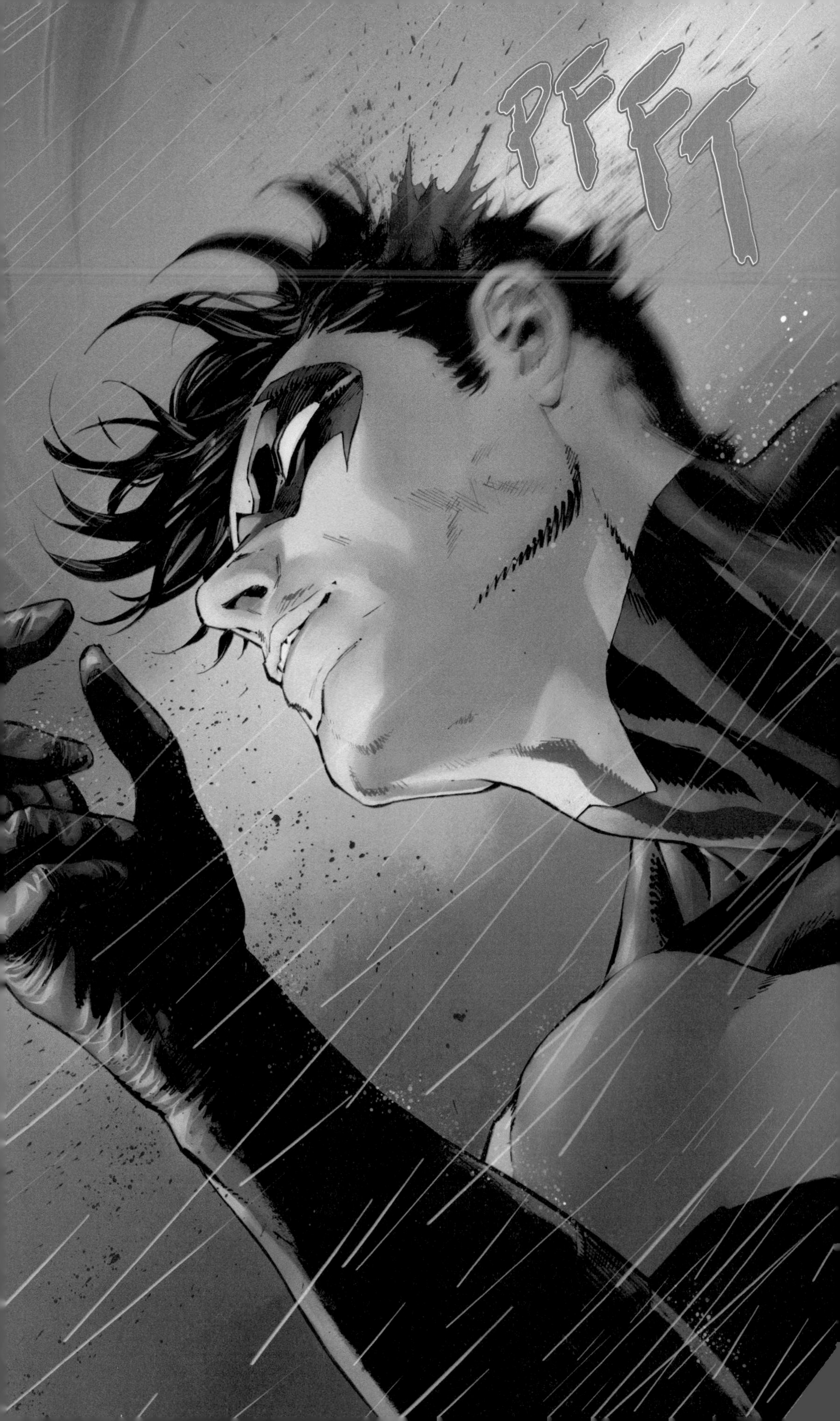
PFFT

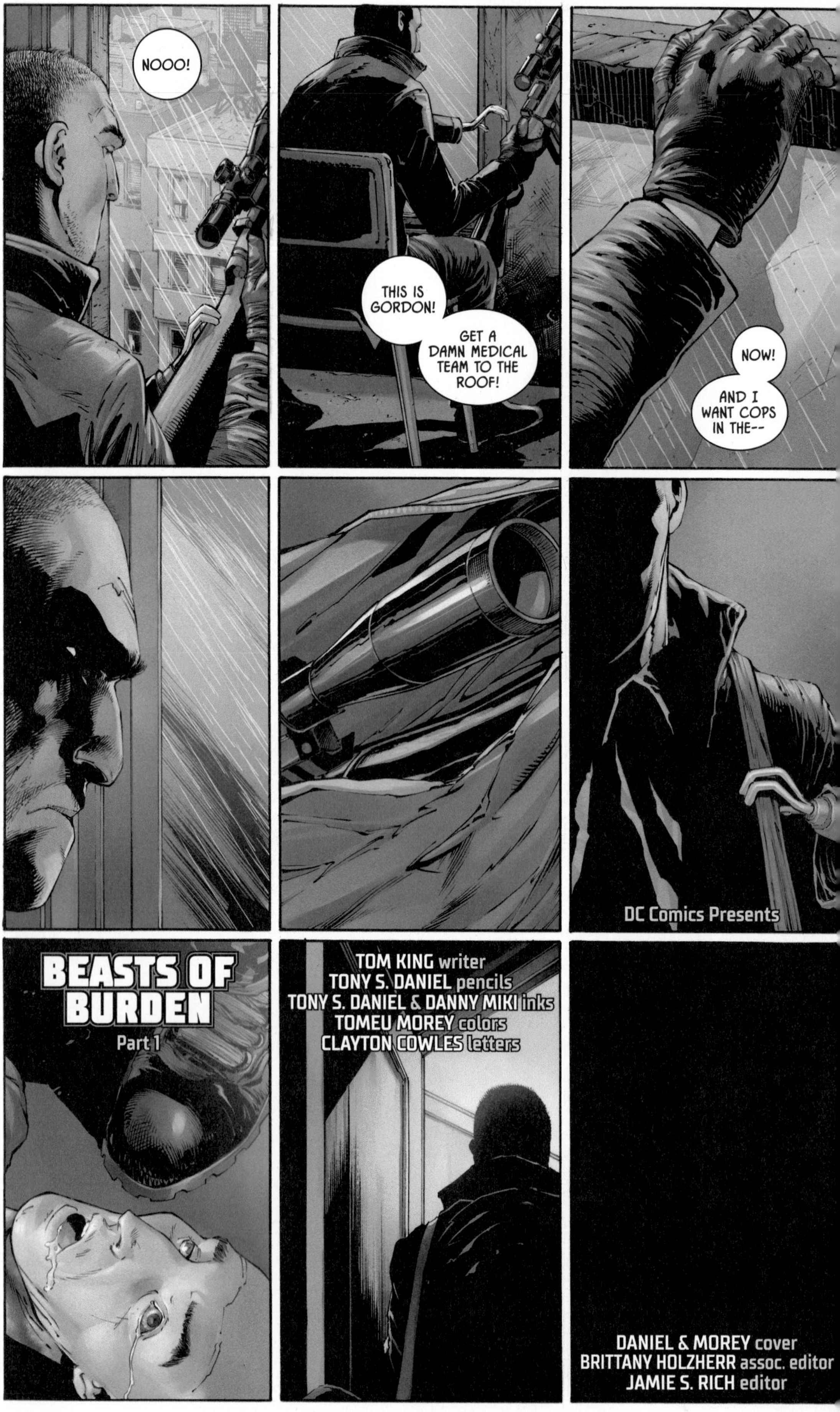
NOOO!
THIS IS GORDON!
GET A DAMN MEDICAL TEAM TO THE ROOF!
NOW!
AND I WANT COPS IN THE--
DC Comics Presents
BEASTS OF BURDEN
Part 1
TOM KING writer
TONY S. DANIEL pencils
TONY S. DANIEL & DANNY MIKI inks
TOMEU MOREY colors
CLAYTON COWLES letters
DANIEL & MOREY cover
BRITTANY HOLZHERR assoc. editor
JAMIE S. RICH editor

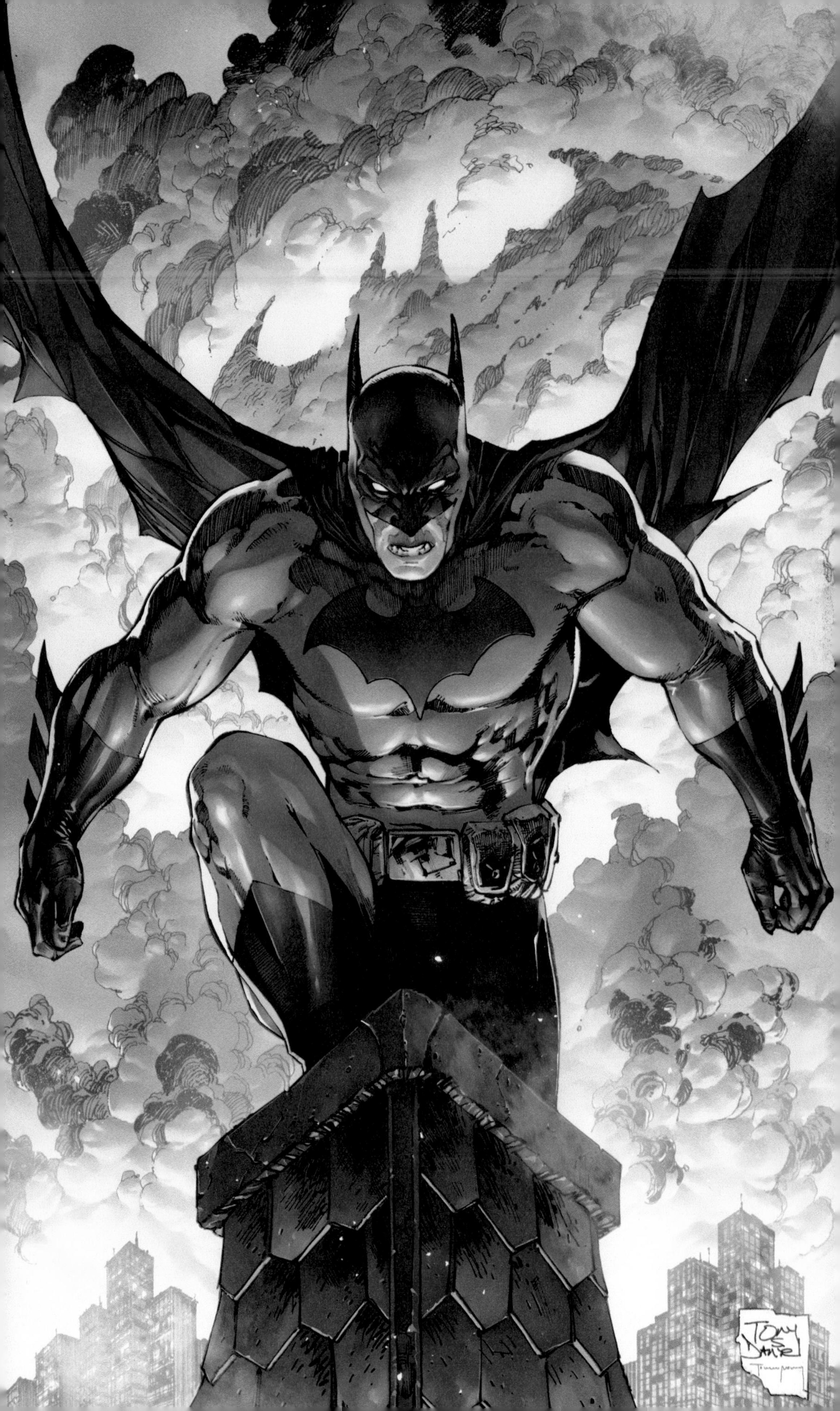
TONY S DANIEL

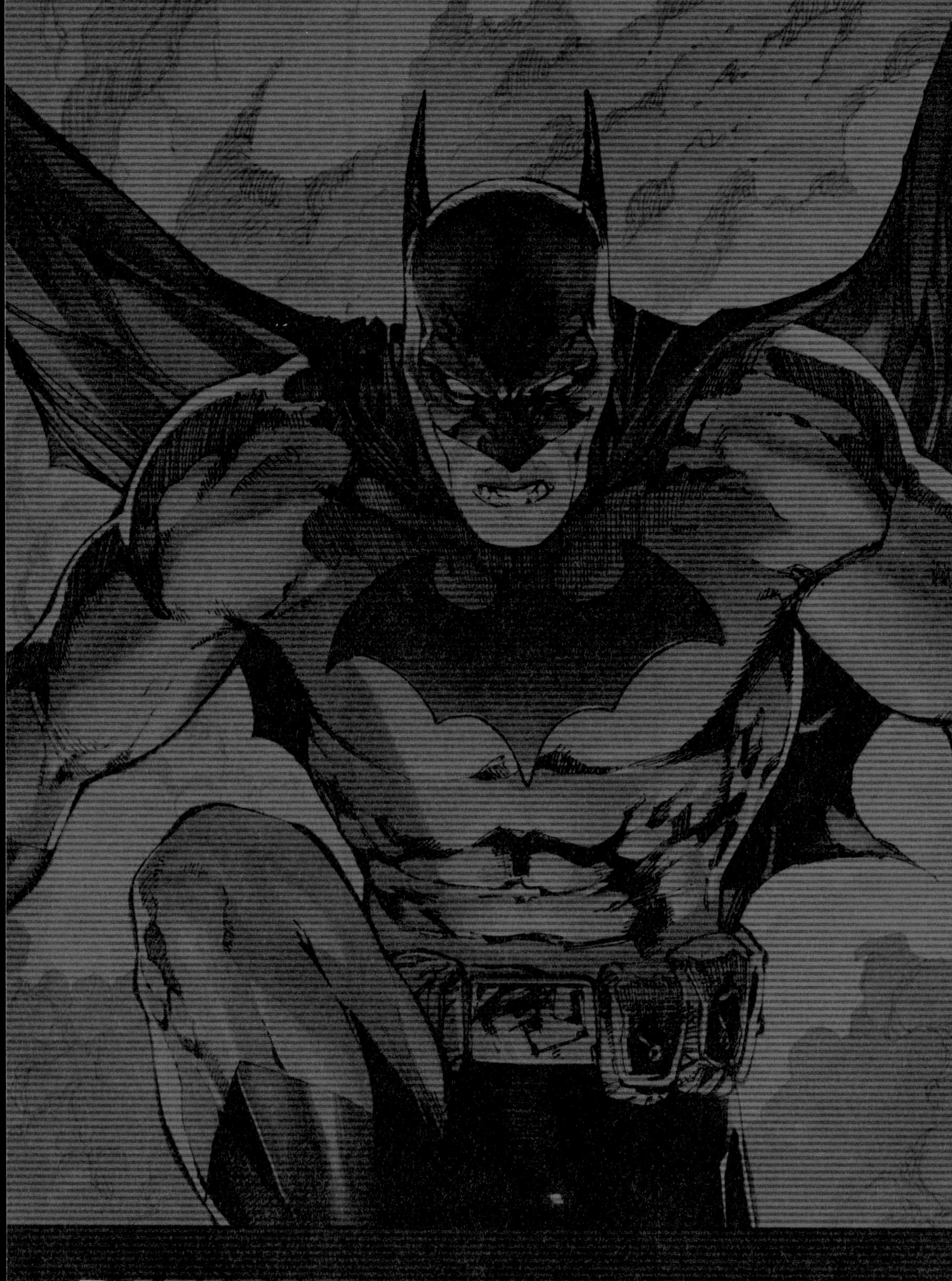

BATMAN
#56

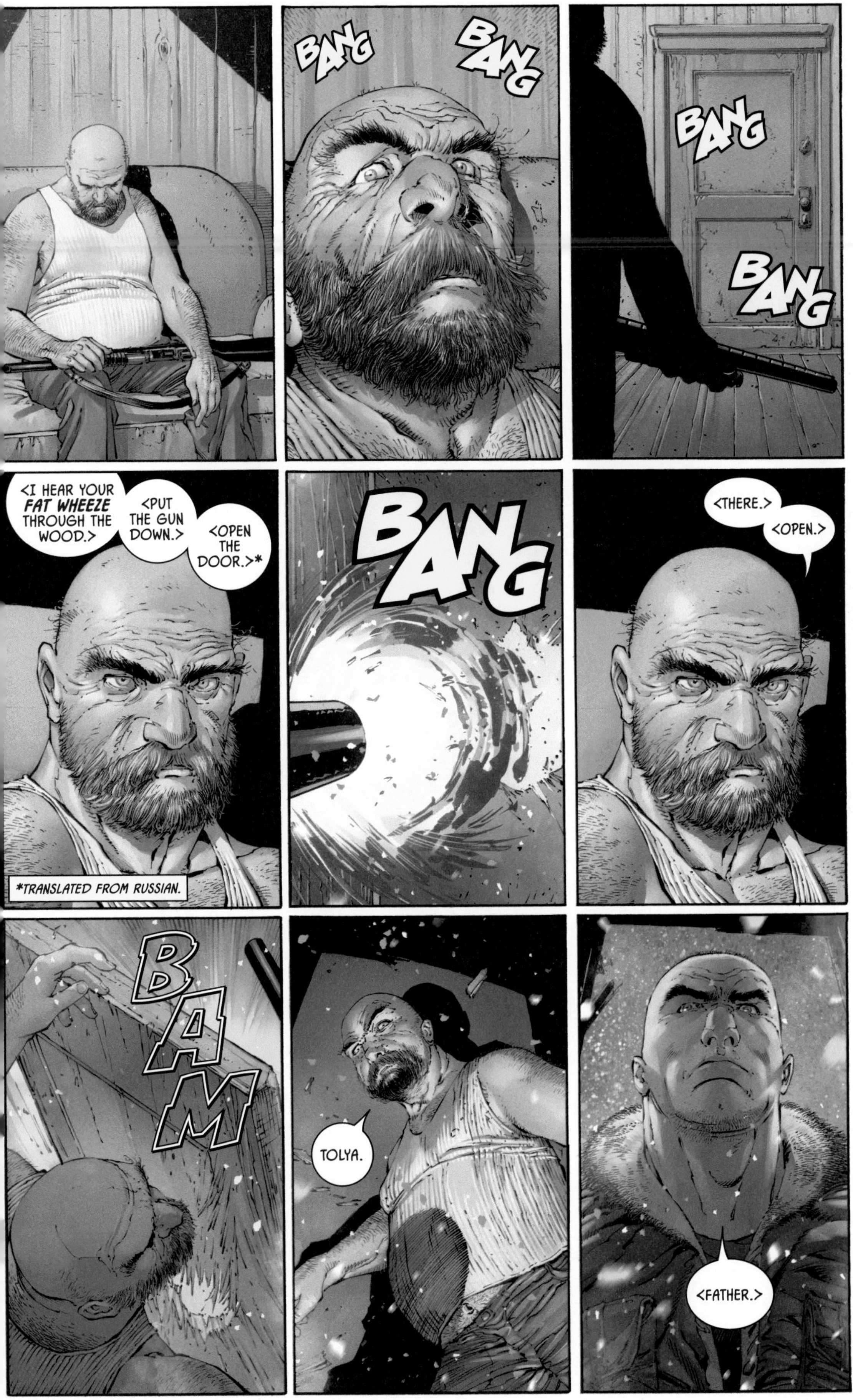
BANG
BANG
BANG
BANG
<I HEAR YOUR FAT WHEEZE THROUGH THE WOOD.>
<PUT THE GUN DOWN.>
<OPEN THE DOOR.>*
*TRANSLATED FROM RUSSIAN.
BANG
<THERE.>
<OPEN.>
BAM
TOLYA.
<FATHER.>

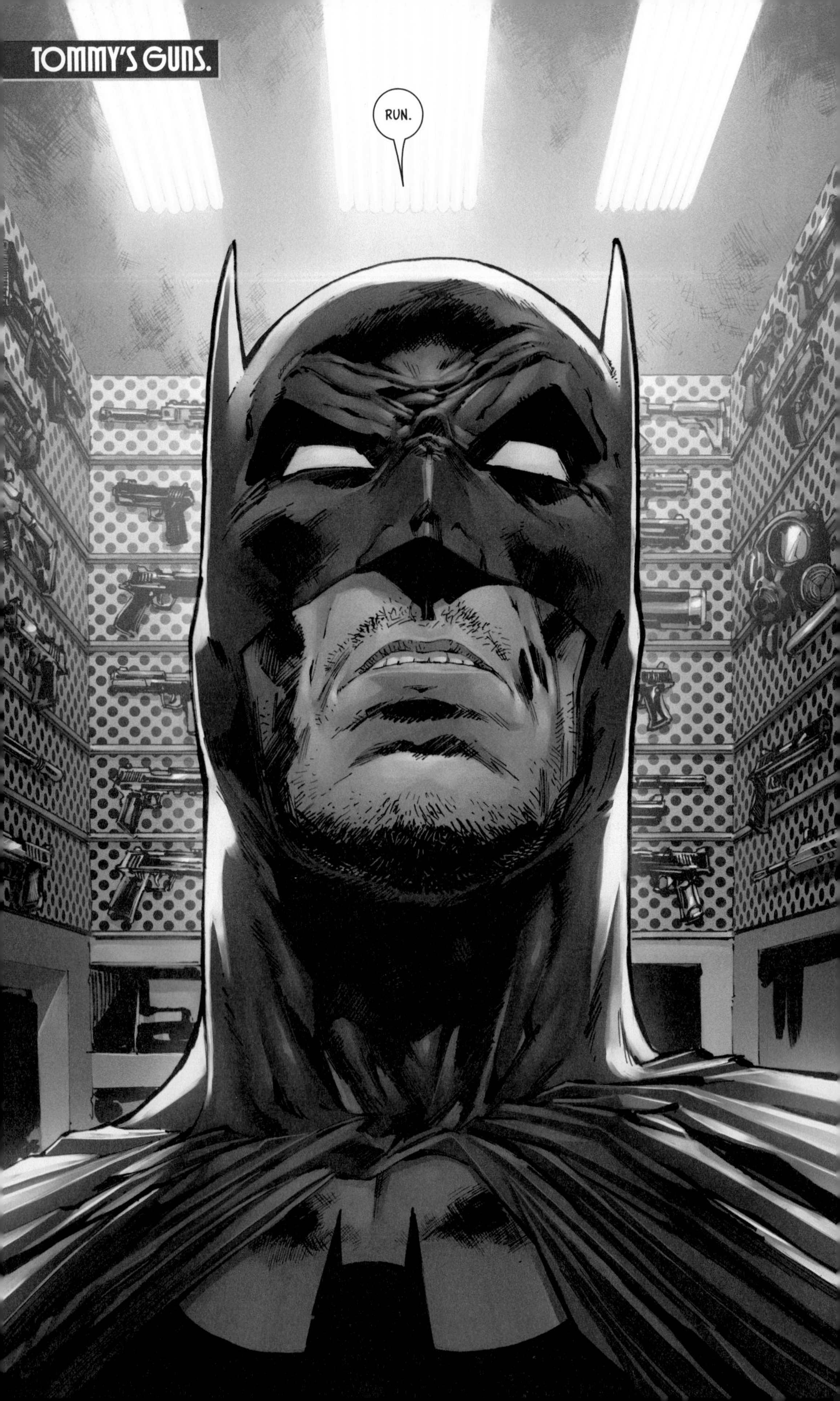
TOMMY'S GUNS.
RUN.

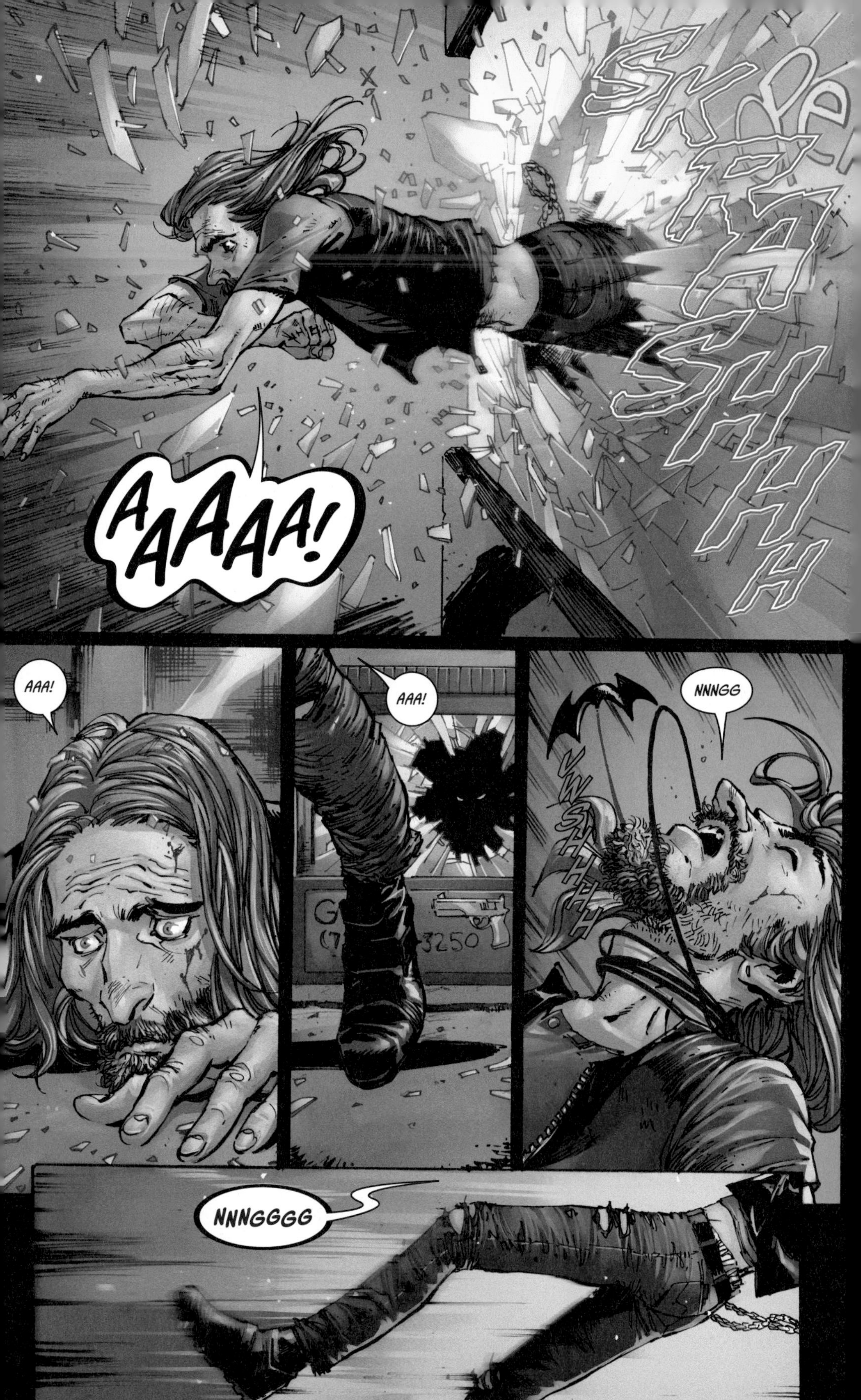
SKRAASHHHH
AAAAA!
AAA!
AAA!
NNNGG
VWSHHHH
NNNGGGG

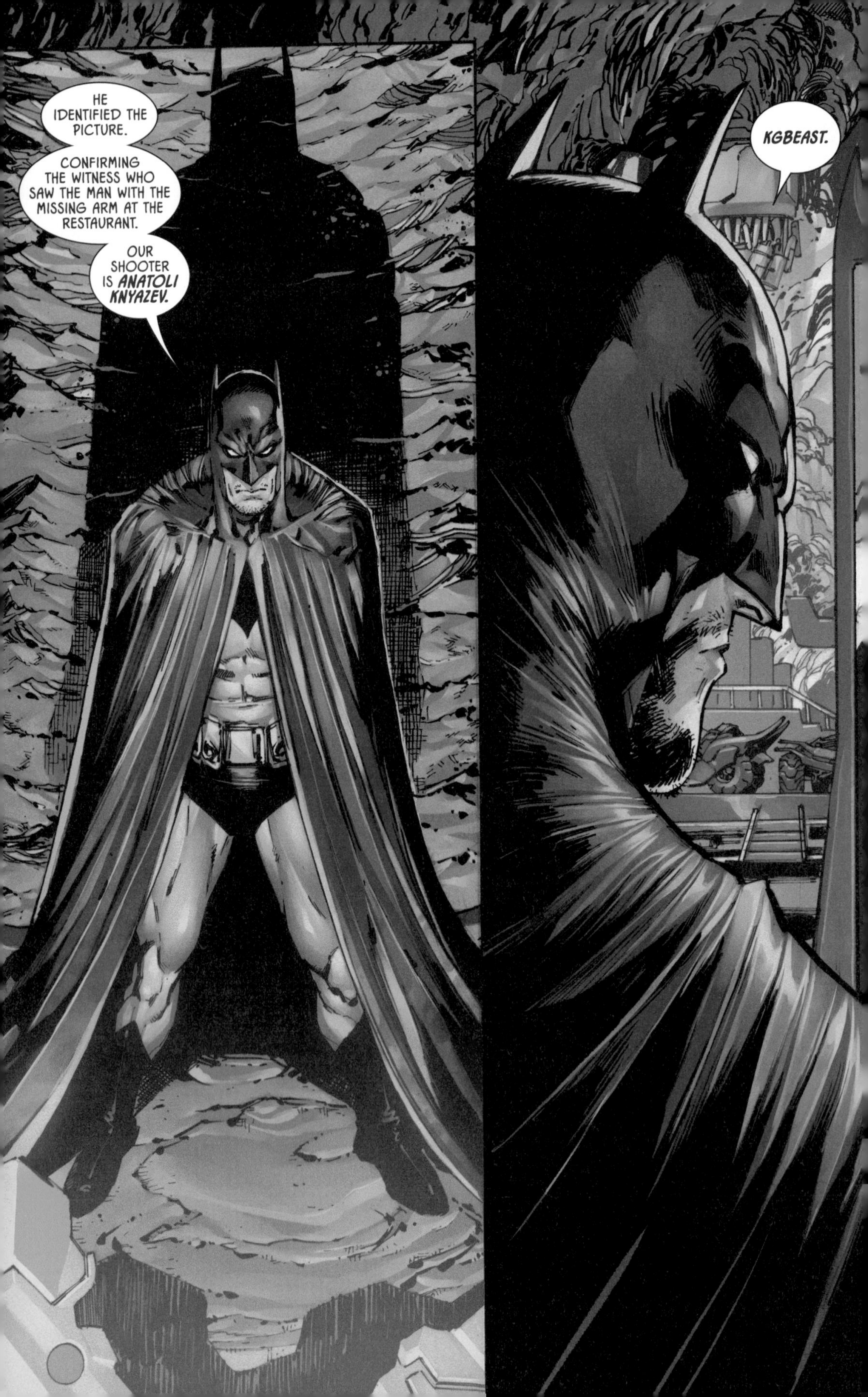
HE IDENTIFIED THE PICTURE.
CONFIRMING THE WITNESS WHO SAW THE MAN WITH THE MISSING ARM AT THE RESTAURANT.
OUR SHOOTER IS ANATOLI KNYAZEV.
KGBEAST.

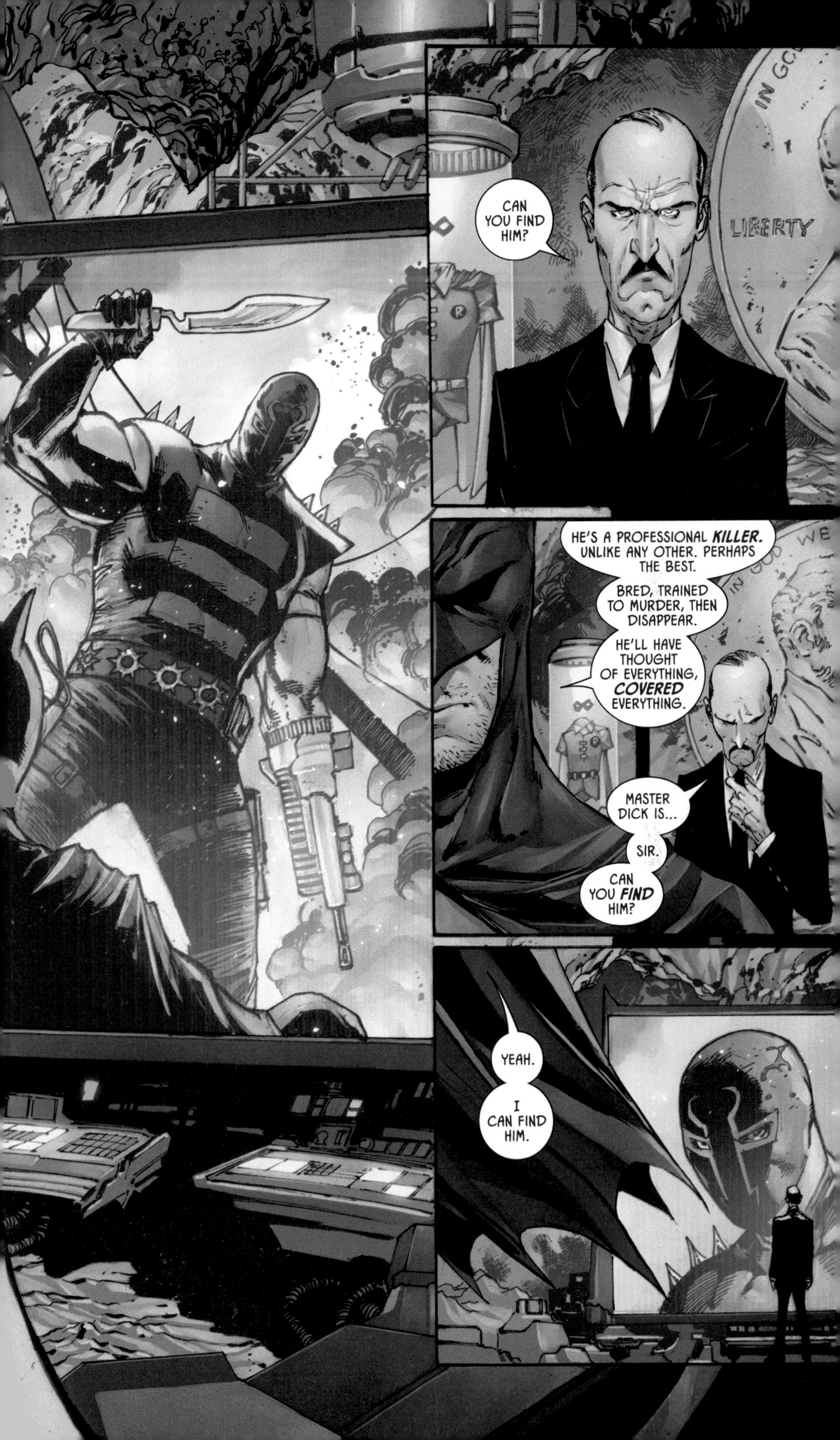
IN GOD
LIBERTY
CAN YOU FIND HIM?
HE'S A PROFESSIONAL **KILLER.** UNLIKE ANY OTHER. PERHAPS THE BEST.
BRED, TRAINED TO MURDER, THEN DISAPPEAR.
HE'LL HAVE THOUGHT OF EVERYTHING, ***COVERED*** EVERYTHING.
MASTER DICK IS...
SIR.
CAN YOU ***FIND*** HIM?
YEAH.
I CAN FIND HIM.

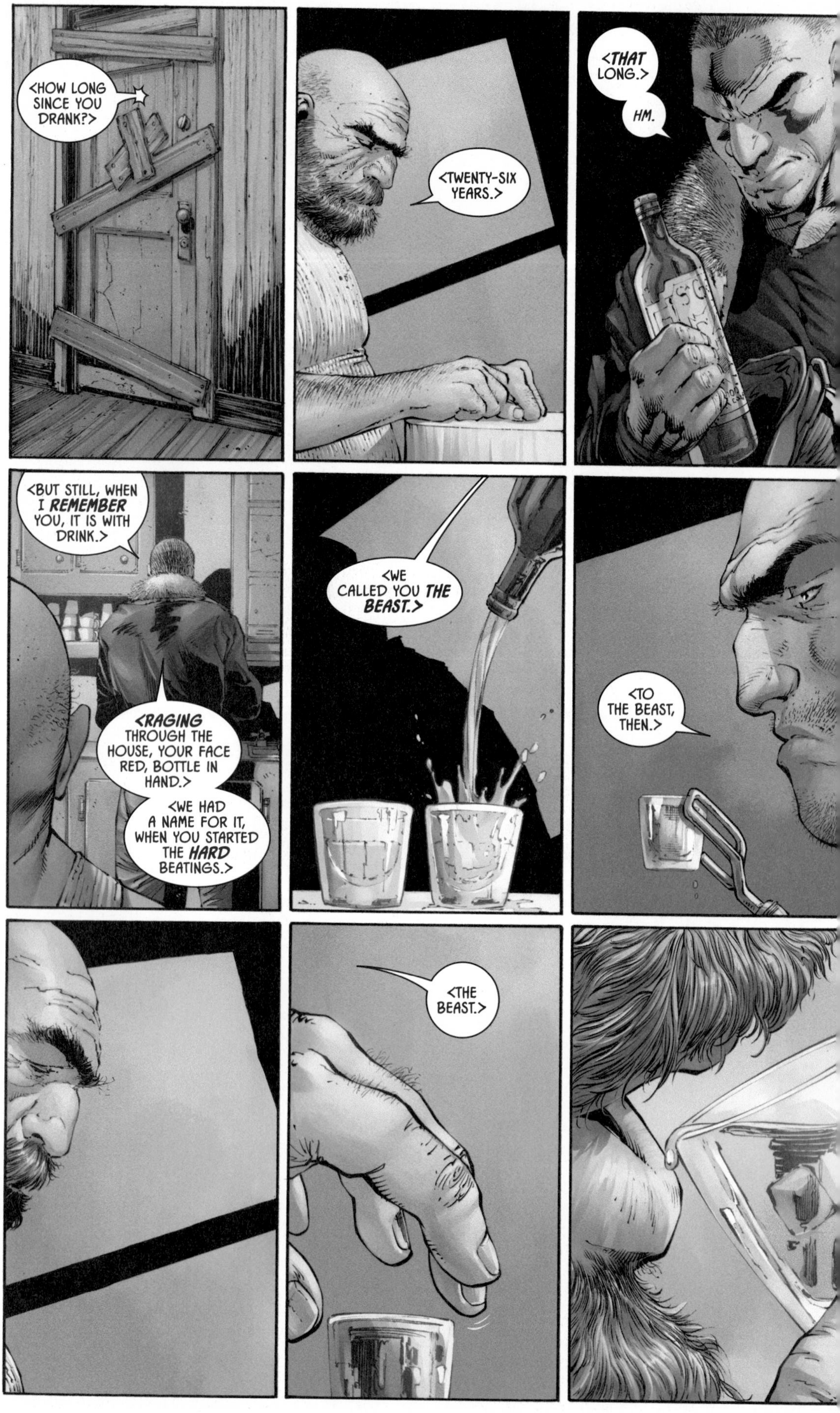
<HOW LONG SINCE YOU DRANK?>
<TWENTY-SIX YEARS.>
<THAT LONG.>
HM.
<BUT STILL, WHEN I REMEMBER YOU, IT IS WITH DRINK.>
<RAGING THROUGH THE HOUSE, YOUR FACE RED, BOTTLE IN HAND.>
<WE HAD A NAME FOR IT, WHEN YOU STARTED THE HARD BEATINGS.>
<WE CALLED YOU THE BEAST.>
<TO THE BEAST, THEN.>
<THE BEAST.>

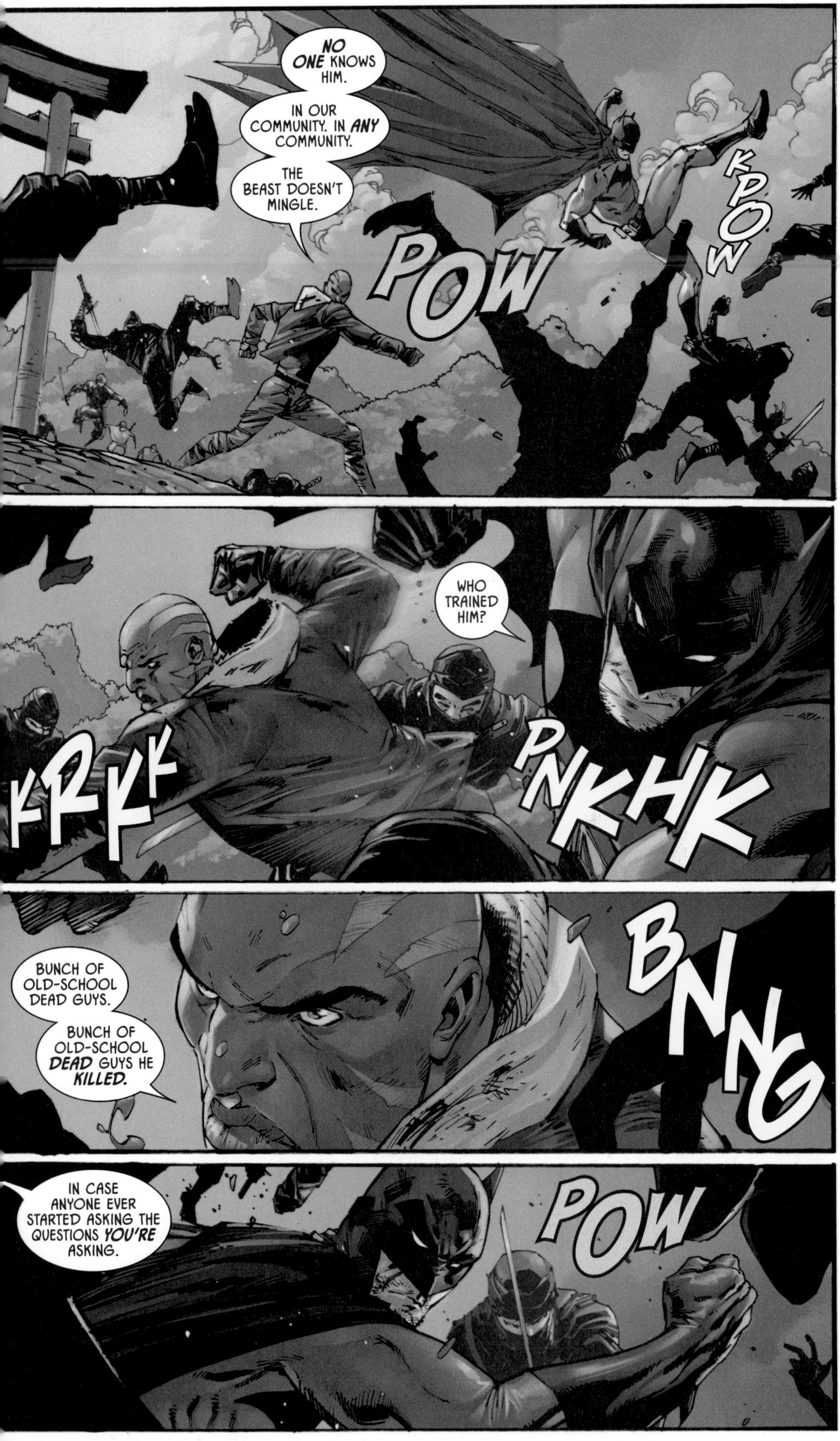
NO ONE KNOWS HIM.
IN OUR COMMUNITY. IN ANY COMMUNITY.
THE BEAST DOESN'T MINGLE.
POW
KPOW
WHO TRAINED HIM?
KRKK
PNKHK
BUNCH OF OLD-SCHOOL DEAD GUYS.
BUNCH OF OLD-SCHOOL DEAD GUYS HE KILLED.
BNNG
IN CASE ANYONE EVER STARTED ASKING THE QUESTIONS YOU'RE ASKING.
POW

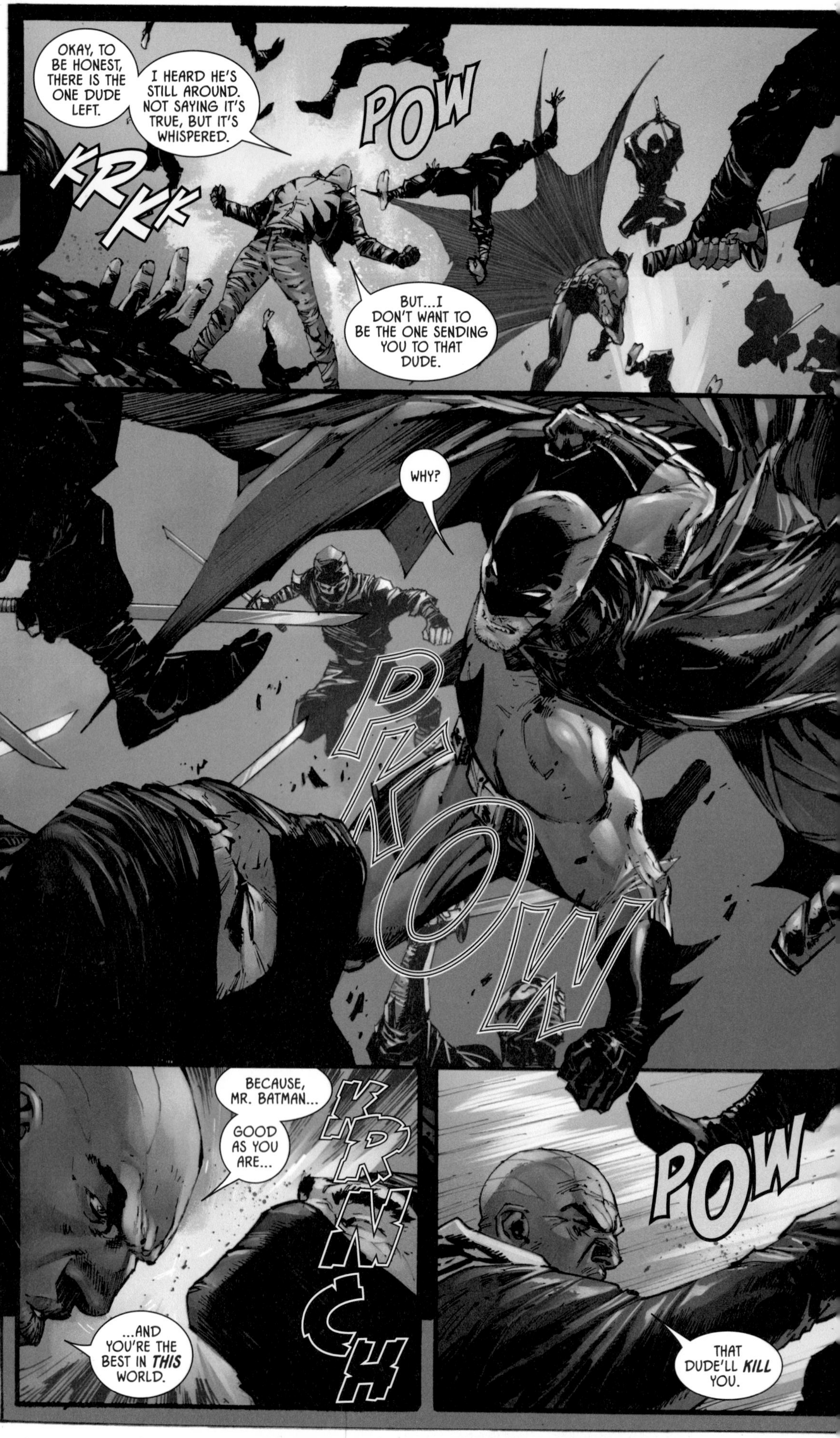
OKAY, TO BE HONEST, THERE IS THE ONE DUDE LEFT.
I HEARD HE'S STILL AROUND. NOT SAYING IT'S TRUE, BUT IT'S WHISPERED.
POW
KRKK
BUT...I DON'T WANT TO BE THE ONE SENDING YOU TO THAT DUDE.
WHY?
PKOW
BECAUSE, MR. BATMAN...
GOOD AS YOU ARE...
KRNCH
...AND YOU'RE THE BEST IN *THIS* WORLD.
POW
THAT DUDE'LL *KILL* YOU.

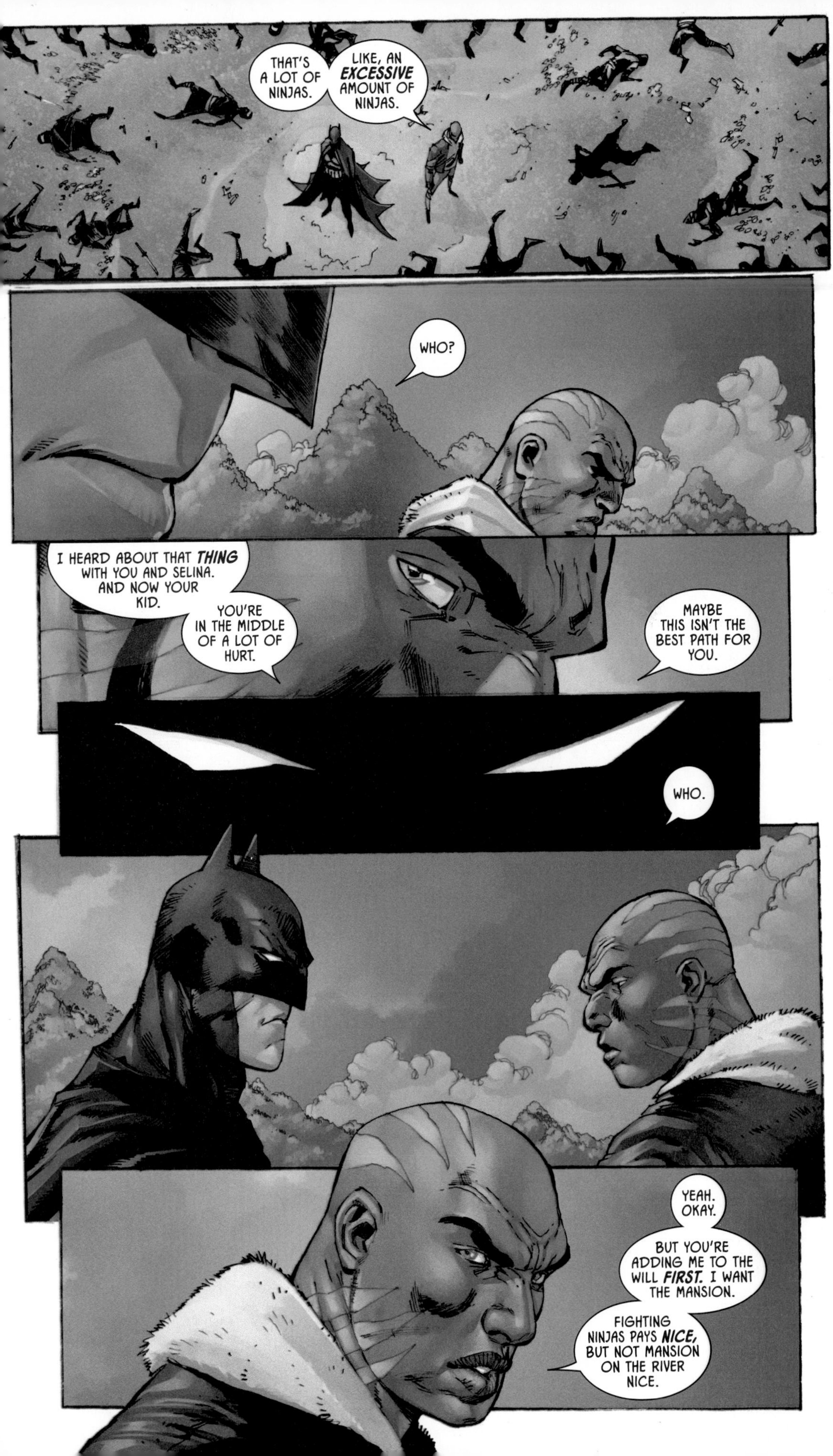
THAT'S A LOT OF NINJAS.
LIKE, AN *EXCESSIVE* AMOUNT OF NINJAS.
WHO?
I HEARD ABOUT THAT *THING* WITH YOU AND SELINA. AND NOW YOUR KID.
YOU'RE IN THE MIDDLE OF A LOT OF HURT.
MAYBE THIS ISN'T THE BEST PATH FOR YOU.
WHO.
YEAH. OKAY.
BUT YOU'RE ADDING ME TO THE WILL *FIRST.* I WANT THE MANSION.
FIGHTING NINJAS PAYS *NICE,* BUT NOT MANSION ON THE RIVER NICE.

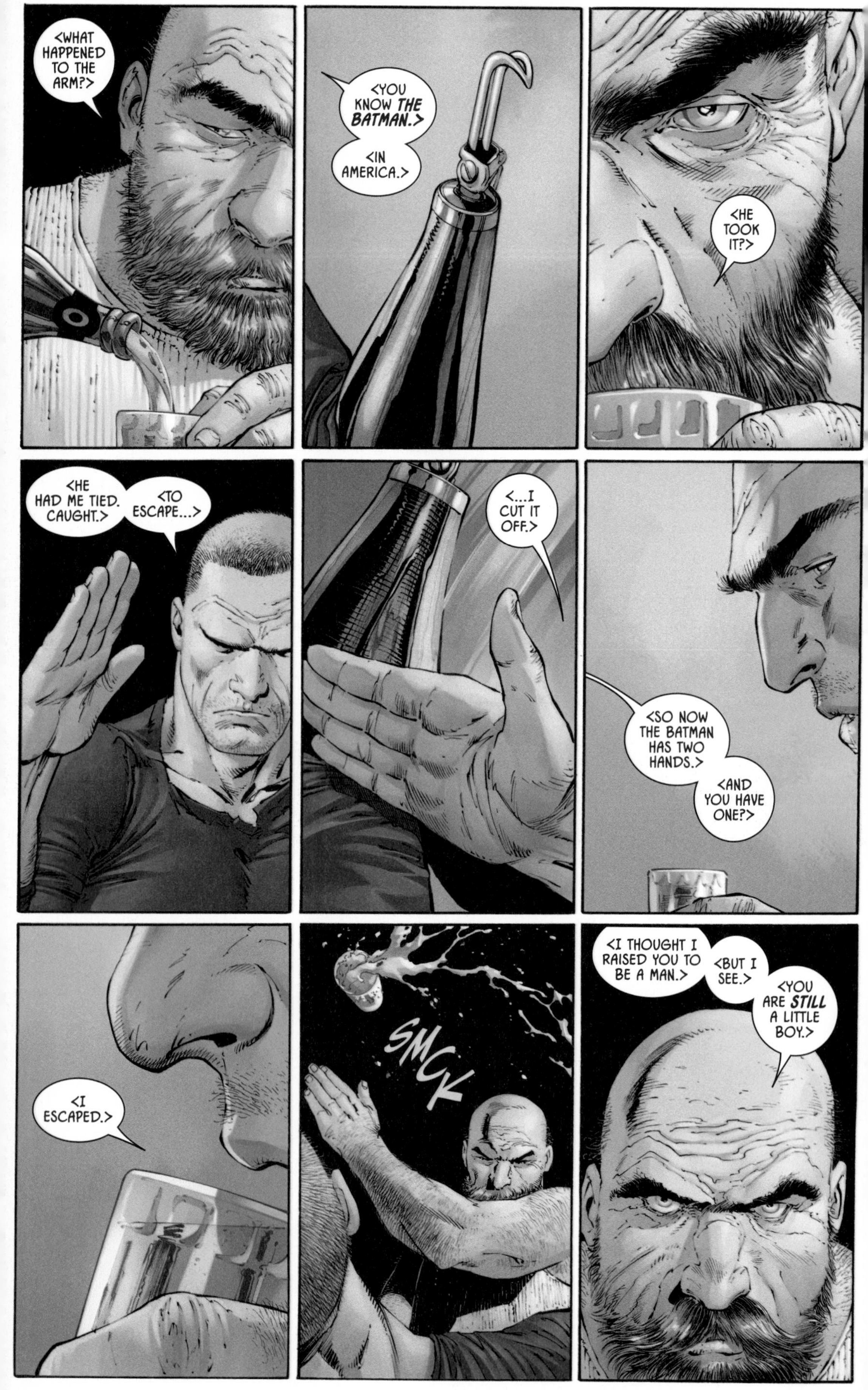
<WHAT HAPPENED TO THE ARM?>
<YOU KNOW *THE BATMAN.*>
<IN AMERICA.>
<HE TOOK IT?>
<HE HAD ME TIED. CAUGHT.>
<TO ESCAPE...>
<...I CUT IT OFF.>
<SO NOW THE BATMAN HAS TWO HANDS.>
<AND YOU HAVE ONE?>
<I ESCAPED.>
SMCK
<I THOUGHT I RAISED YOU TO BE A MAN.>
<BUT I SEE.>
<YOU ARE *STILL* A LITTLE BOY.>

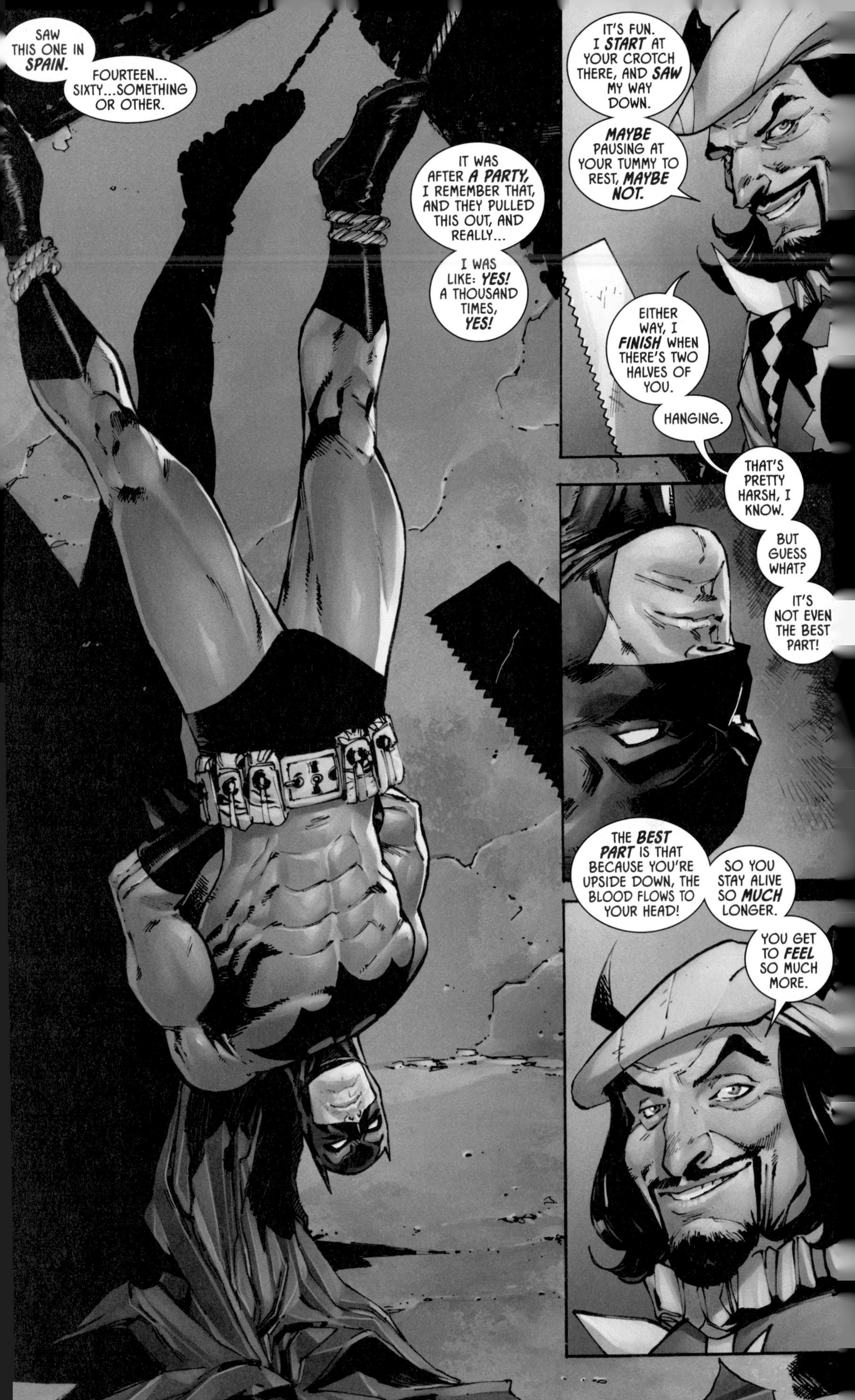

SAW THIS ONE IN SPAIN.
FOURTEEN... SIXTY...SOMETHING OR OTHER.
IT WAS AFTER A PARTY, I REMEMBER THAT, AND THEY PULLED THIS OUT, AND REALLY...
I WAS LIKE: YES! A THOUSAND TIMES, YES!
IT'S FUN. I START AT YOUR CROTCH THERE, AND SAW MY WAY DOWN.
MAYBE PAUSING AT YOUR TUMMY TO REST, MAYBE NOT.
EITHER WAY, I FINISH WHEN THERE'S TWO HALVES OF YOU.
HANGING.
THAT'S PRETTY HARSH, I KNOW.
BUT GUESS WHAT?
IT'S NOT EVEN THE BEST PART!
THE BEST PART IS THAT BECAUSE YOU'RE UPSIDE DOWN, THE BLOOD FLOWS TO YOUR HEAD!
SO YOU STAY ALIVE SO MUCH LONGER.
YOU GET TO FEEL SO MUCH MORE.

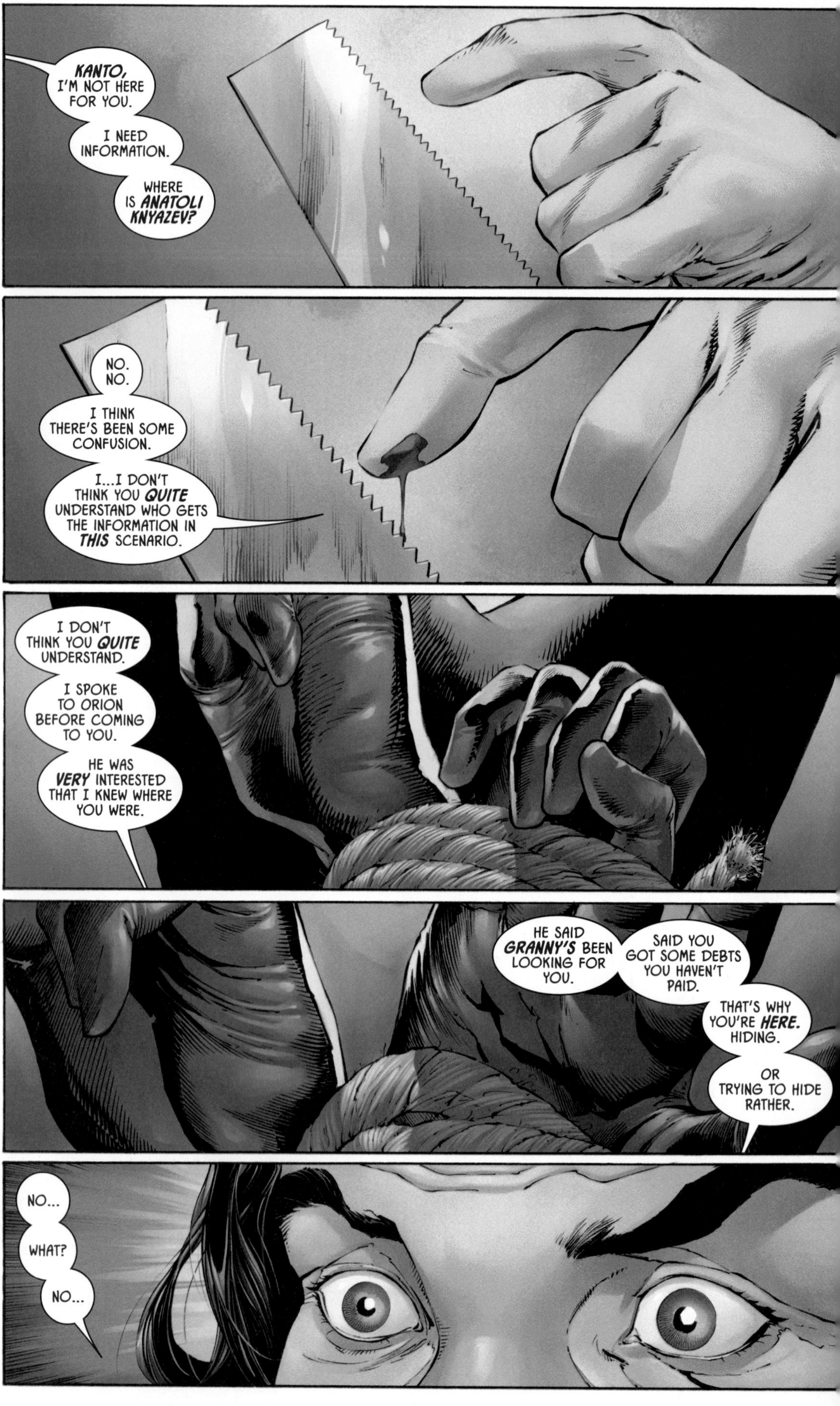
KANTO, I'M NOT HERE FOR YOU.
I NEED INFORMATION.
WHERE IS ANATOLI KNYAZEV?
NO. NO.
I THINK THERE'S BEEN SOME CONFUSION.
I...I DON'T THINK YOU QUITE UNDERSTAND WHO GETS THE INFORMATION IN THIS SCENARIO.
I DON'T THINK YOU QUITE UNDERSTAND.
I SPOKE TO ORION BEFORE COMING TO YOU.
HE WAS VERY INTERESTED THAT I KNEW WHERE YOU WERE.
HE SAID GRANNY'S BEEN LOOKING FOR YOU.
SAID YOU GOT SOME DEBTS YOU HAVEN'T PAID.
THAT'S WHY YOU'RE HERE. HIDING.
OR TRYING TO HIDE RATHER.
NO...
WHAT?
NO...

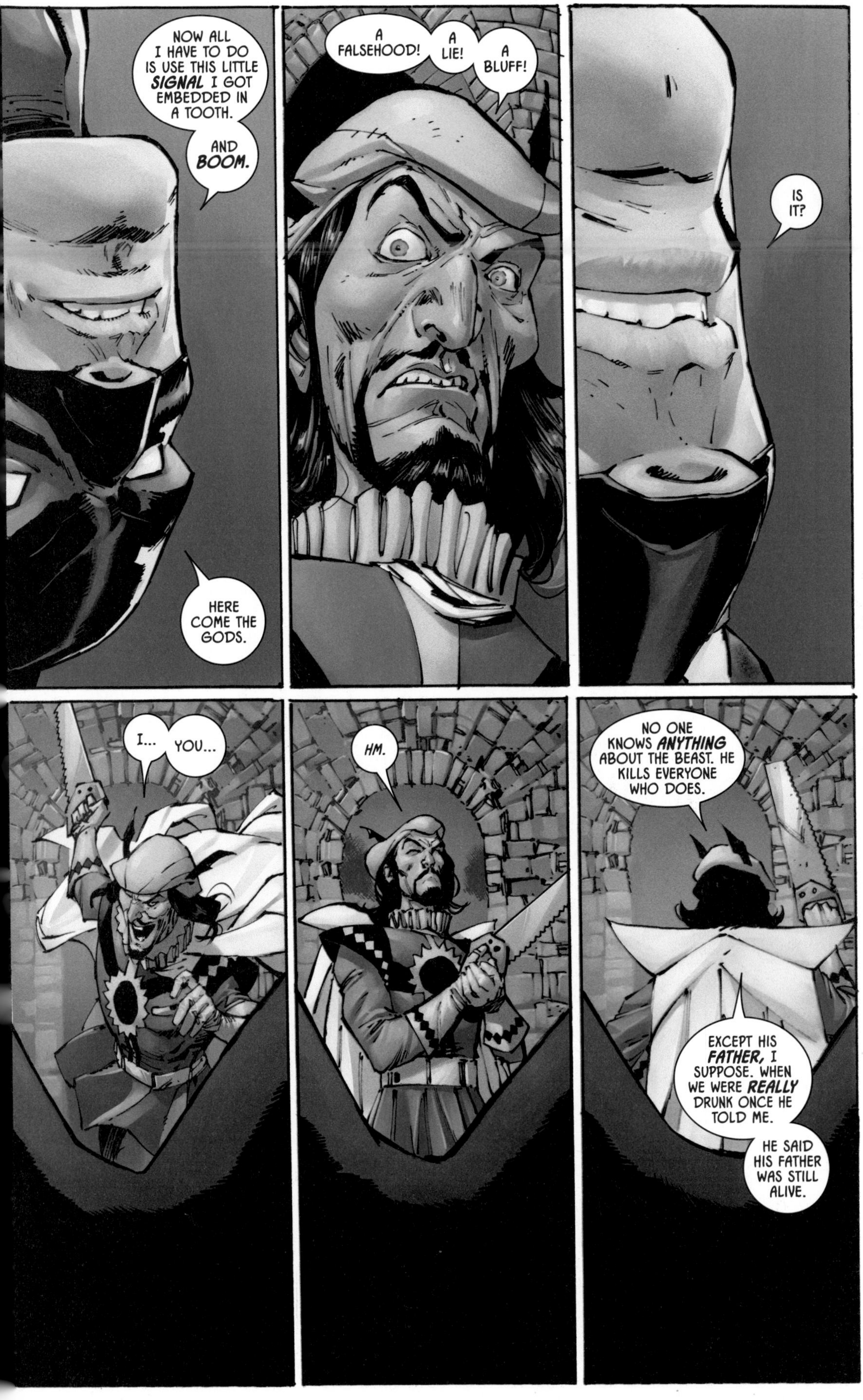
NOW ALL I HAVE TO DO IS USE THIS LITTLE SIGNAL I GOT EMBEDDED IN A TOOTH.
AND BOOM.
HERE COME THE GODS.
A FALSEHOOD!
A LIE!
A BLUFF!
IS IT?
I...
YOU...
HM.
NO ONE KNOWS ANYTHING ABOUT THE BEAST. HE KILLS EVERYONE WHO DOES.
EXCEPT HIS FATHER, I SUPPOSE. WHEN WE WERE REALLY DRUNK ONCE HE TOLD ME.
HE SAID HIS FATHER WAS STILL ALIVE.

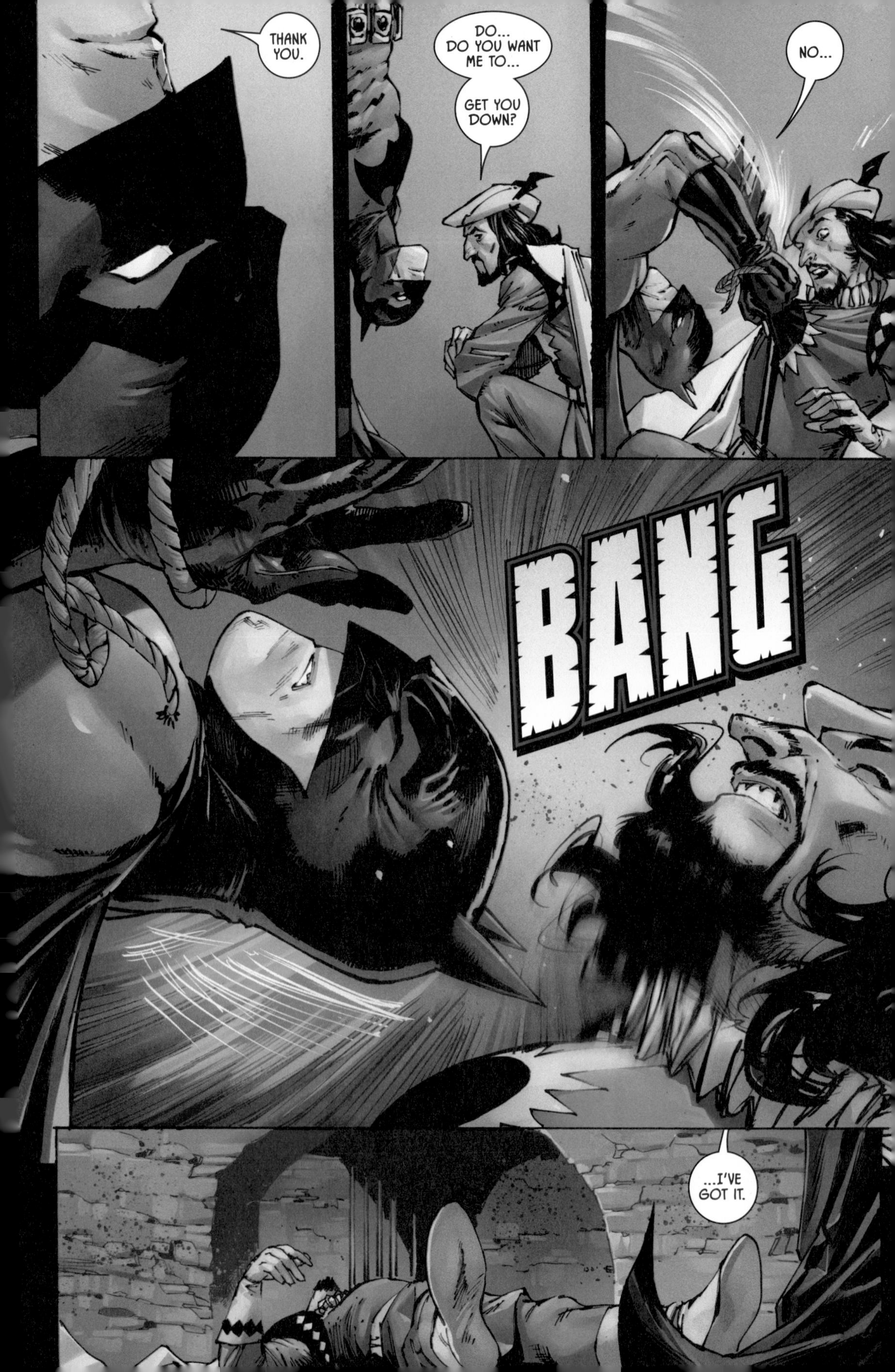
THANK YOU.
DO... DO YOU WANT ME TO...
GET YOU DOWN?
NO...
BANG
...I'VE GOT IT.

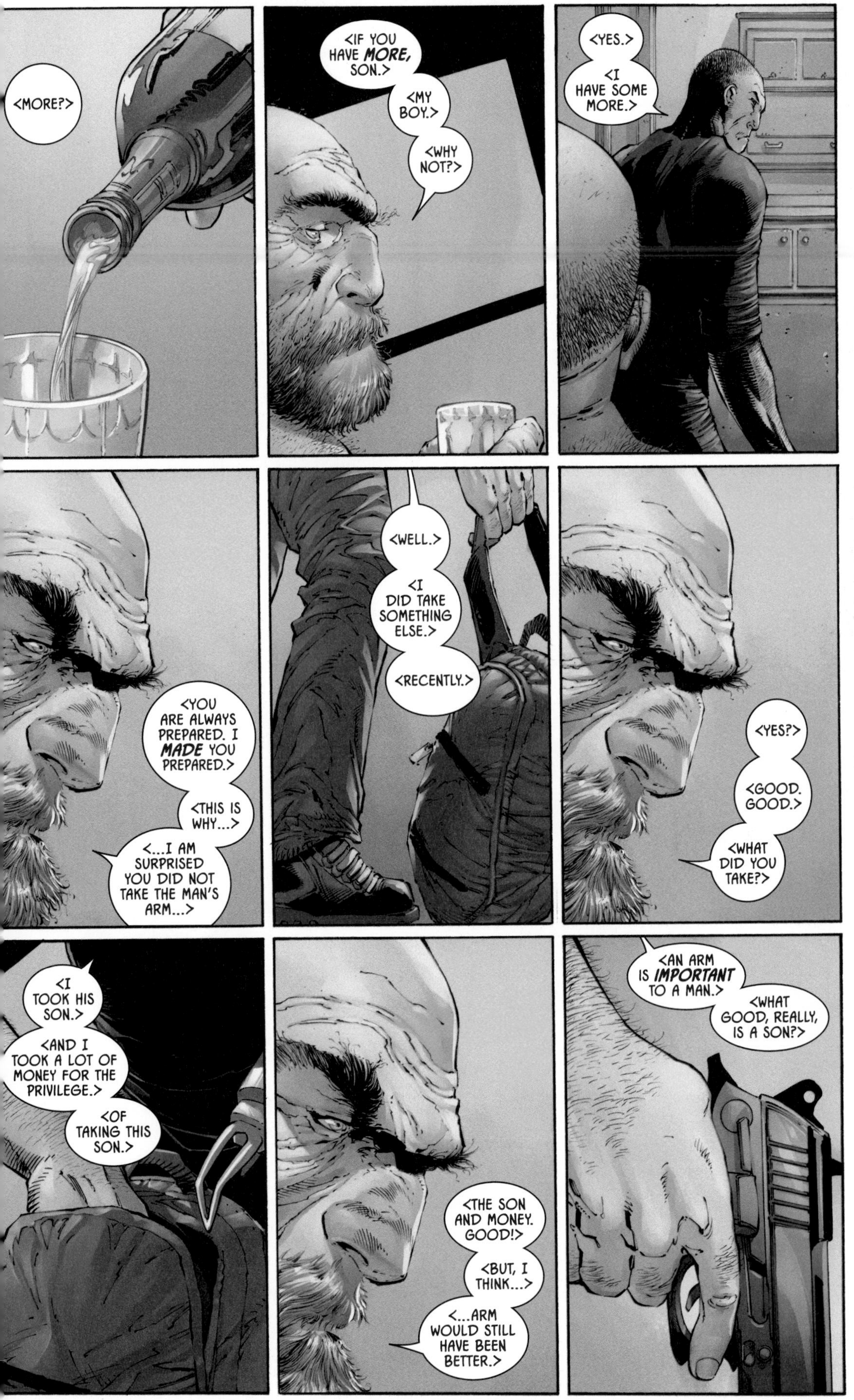
<MORE?>
<IF YOU HAVE MORE, SON.>
<MY BOY.>
<WHY NOT?>
<YES.>
<I HAVE SOME MORE.>
<YOU ARE ALWAYS PREPARED. I MADE YOU PREPARED.>
<THIS IS WHY...>
<...I AM SURPRISED YOU DID NOT TAKE THE MAN'S ARM...>
<WELL.>
<I DID TAKE SOMETHING ELSE.>
<RECENTLY.>
<YES?>
<GOOD. GOOD.>
<WHAT DID YOU TAKE?>
<I TOOK HIS SON.>
<AND I TOOK A LOT OF MONEY FOR THE PRIVILEGE.>
<OF TAKING THIS SON.>
<THE SON AND MONEY. GOOD!>
<BUT, I THINK...>
<...ARM WOULD STILL HAVE BEEN BETTER.>
<AN ARM IS IMPORTANT TO A MAN.>
<WHAT GOOD, REALLY, IS A SON?>

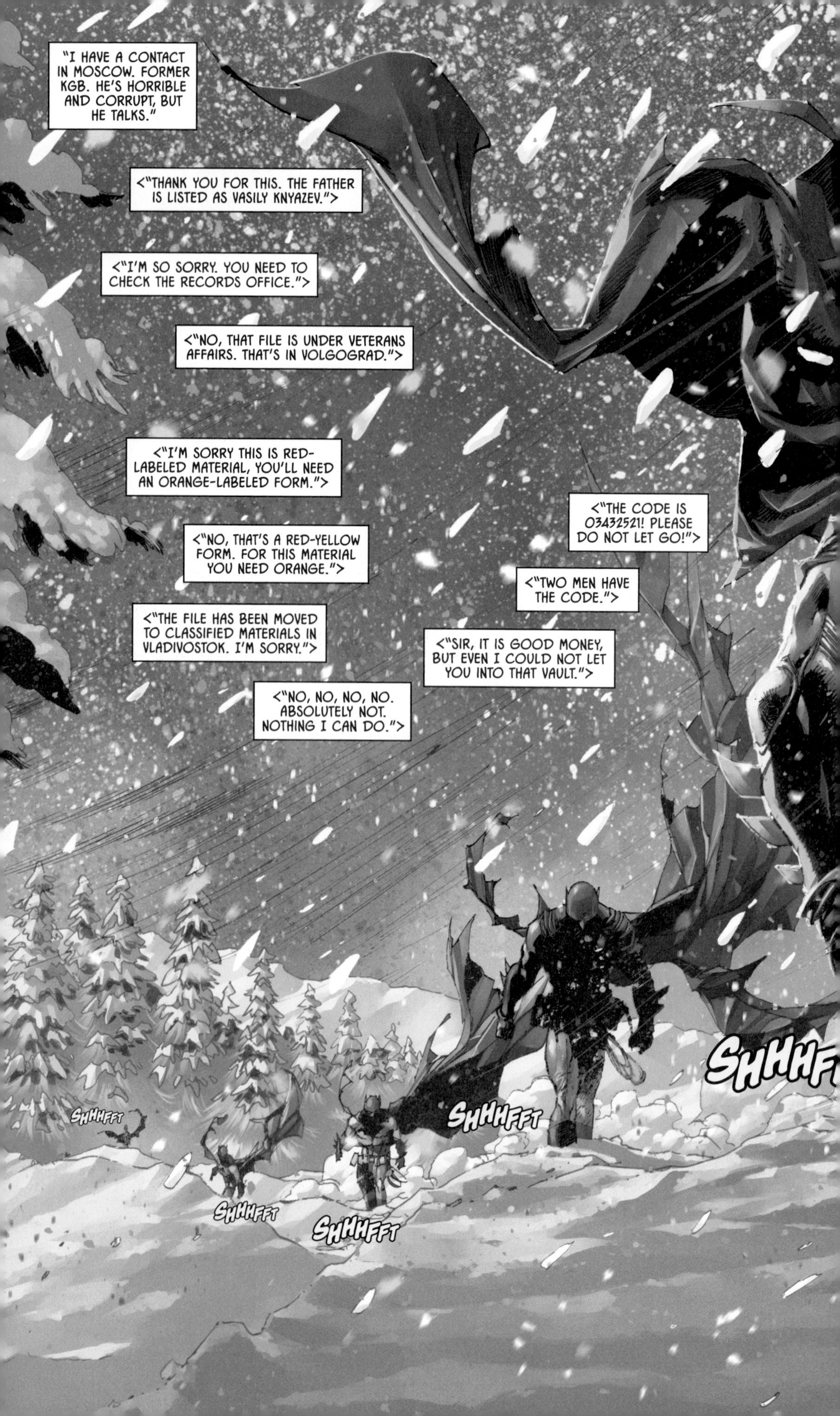
"I HAVE A CONTACT IN MOSCOW. FORMER KGB. HE'S HORRIBLE AND CORRUPT, BUT HE TALKS."
<"THANK YOU FOR THIS. THE FATHER IS LISTED AS VASILY KNYAZEV.">
<"I'M SO SORRY. YOU NEED TO CHECK THE RECORDS OFFICE.">
<"NO, THAT FILE IS UNDER VETERANS AFFAIRS. THAT'S IN VOLGOGRAD.">
<"I'M SORRY THIS IS RED-LABELED MATERIAL, YOU'LL NEED AN ORANGE-LABELED FORM.">
<"NO, THAT'S A RED-YELLOW FORM. FOR THIS MATERIAL YOU NEED ORANGE.">
<"THE FILE HAS BEEN MOVED TO CLASSIFIED MATERIALS IN VLADIVOSTOK. I'M SORRY.">
<"NO, NO, NO, NO. ABSOLUTELY NOT. NOTHING I CAN DO.">
<"SIR, IT IS GOOD MONEY, BUT EVEN I COULD NOT LET YOU INTO THAT VAULT.">
<"TWO MEN HAVE THE CODE.">
<"THE CODE IS 03432521! PLEASE DO NOT LET GO!">
SHHHF
SHHHFFT
SHHHFFT
SHHHFFT
SHHHFFT

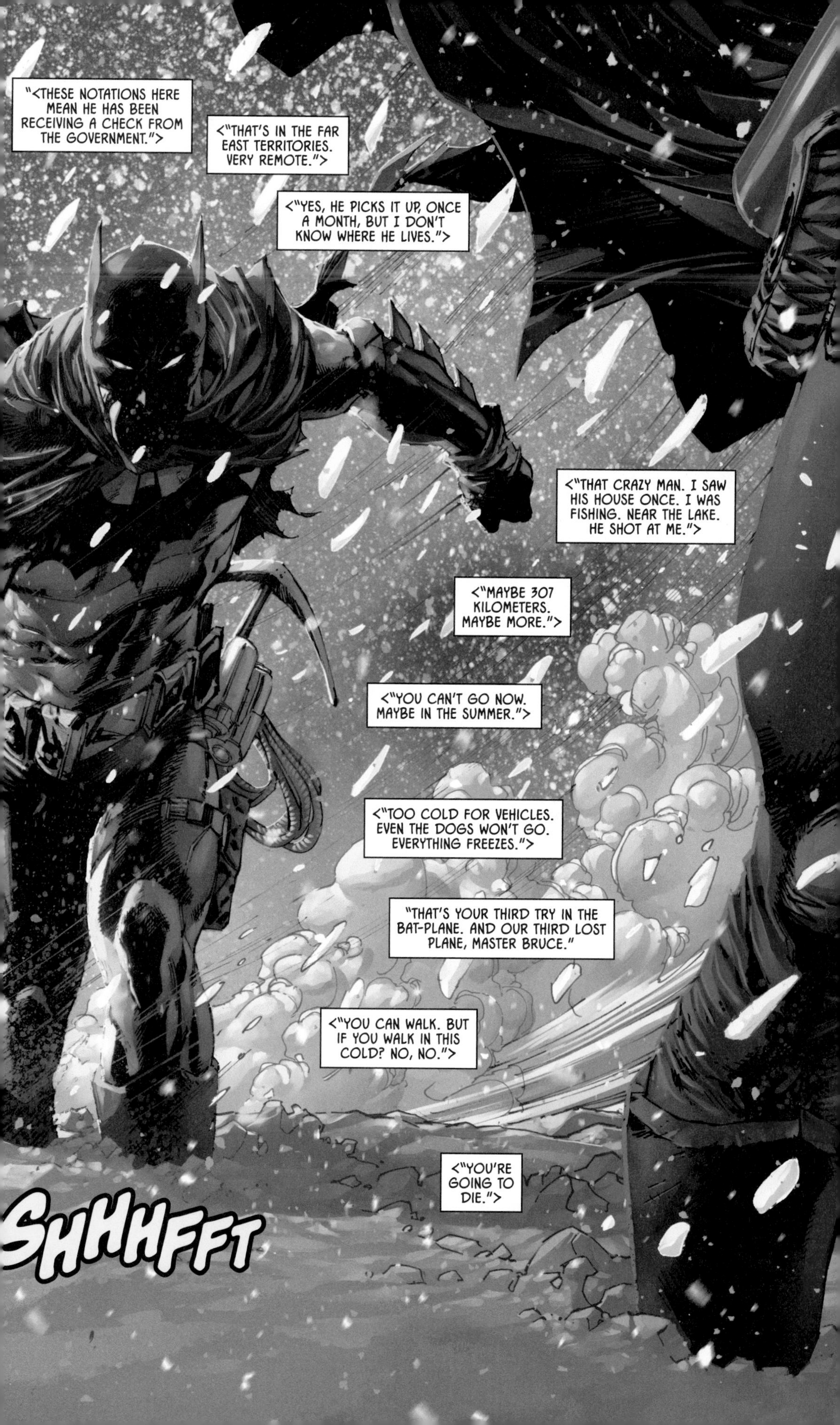
"<THESE NOTATIONS HERE MEAN HE HAS BEEN RECEIVING A CHECK FROM THE GOVERNMENT.">
<"THAT'S IN THE FAR EAST TERRITORIES. VERY REMOTE.">
<"YES, HE PICKS IT UP, ONCE A MONTH, BUT I DON'T KNOW WHERE HE LIVES.">
<"THAT CRAZY MAN. I SAW HIS HOUSE ONCE. I WAS FISHING. NEAR THE LAKE. HE SHOT AT ME.">
<"MAYBE 307 KILOMETERS. MAYBE MORE.">
<"YOU CAN'T GO NOW. MAYBE IN THE SUMMER.">
<"TOO COLD FOR VEHICLES. EVEN THE DOGS WON'T GO. EVERYTHING FREEZES.">
"THAT'S YOUR THIRD TRY IN THE BAT-PLANE. AND OUR THIRD LOST PLANE, MASTER BRUCE."
<"YOU CAN WALK. BUT IF YOU WALK IN THIS COLD? NO, NO.">
<"YOU'RE GOING TO DIE.">
SHHHFFT

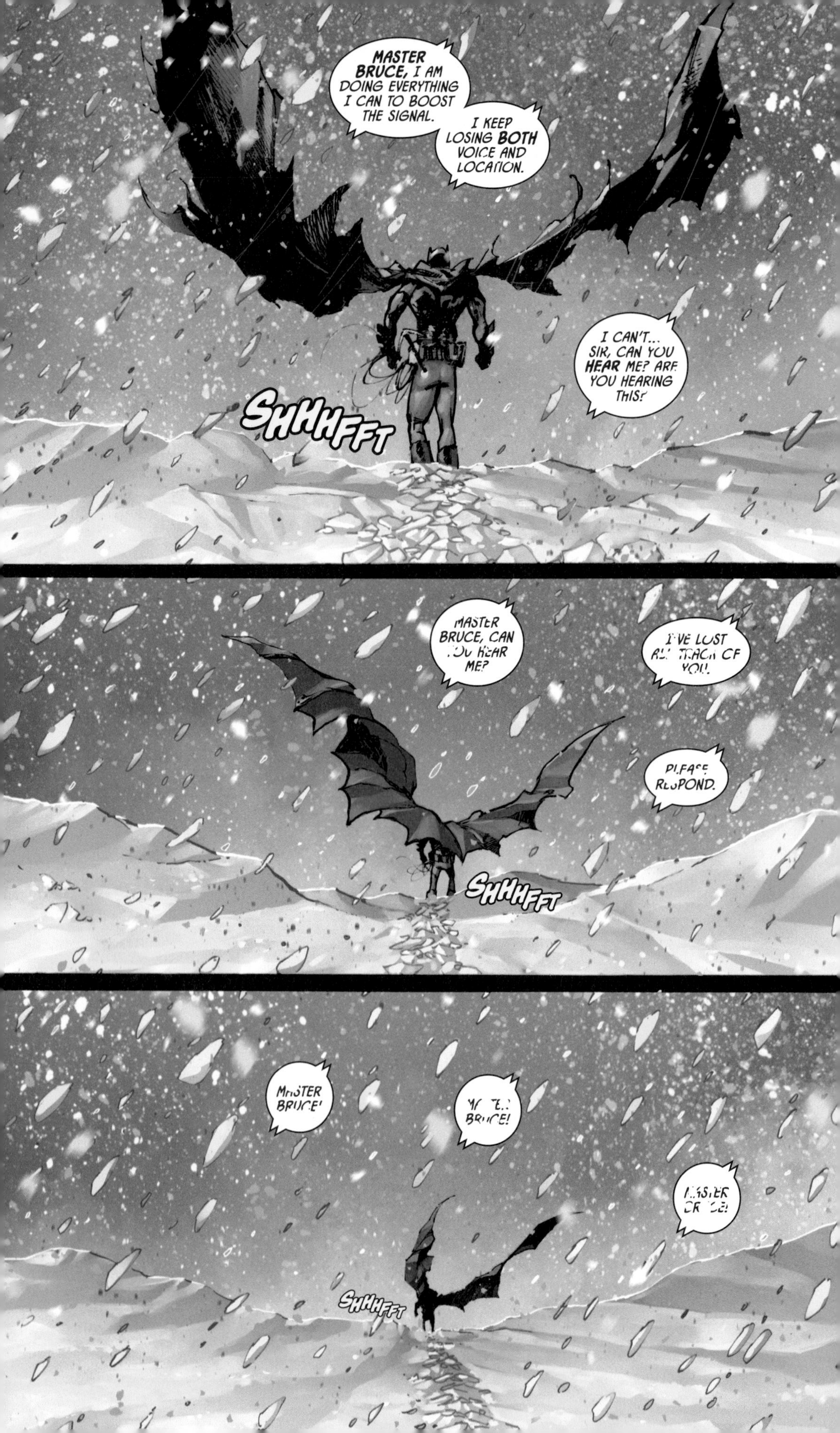
MASTER BRUCE, I AM DOING EVERYTHING I CAN TO BOOST THE SIGNAL.
I KEEP LOSING BOTH VOICE AND LOCATION.
I CAN'T... SIR, CAN YOU HEAR ME? ARE YOU HEARING THIS?
SHHHFFT
MASTER BRUCE, CAN YOU HEAR ME?
PLEASE RESPOND.
SHHHFFT
MASTER BRUCE!
SHHHFFT

<WHY DID YOU KEEP ME ALIVE?>

<YOU KILLED THE REST. YOUR BROTHERS. SISTERS. YOUR MOTHER.>

<BUT ME... WHY...>

<THEY WERE WEAK. YOU WERE STRONG.>

<SO I LOVED YOU.>

<I STILL LOVE YOU, FATHER.>

<HM. FOR THIS, YOU ARE WEAK.>

<BUT THAT IS MY FAULT. I LET YOU BE WEAK.>

<BECAUSE I LOVE YOU, TOO, SON.>

BANG

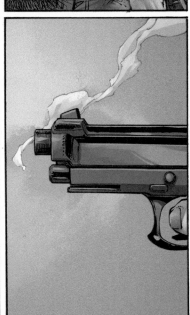

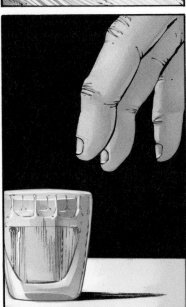

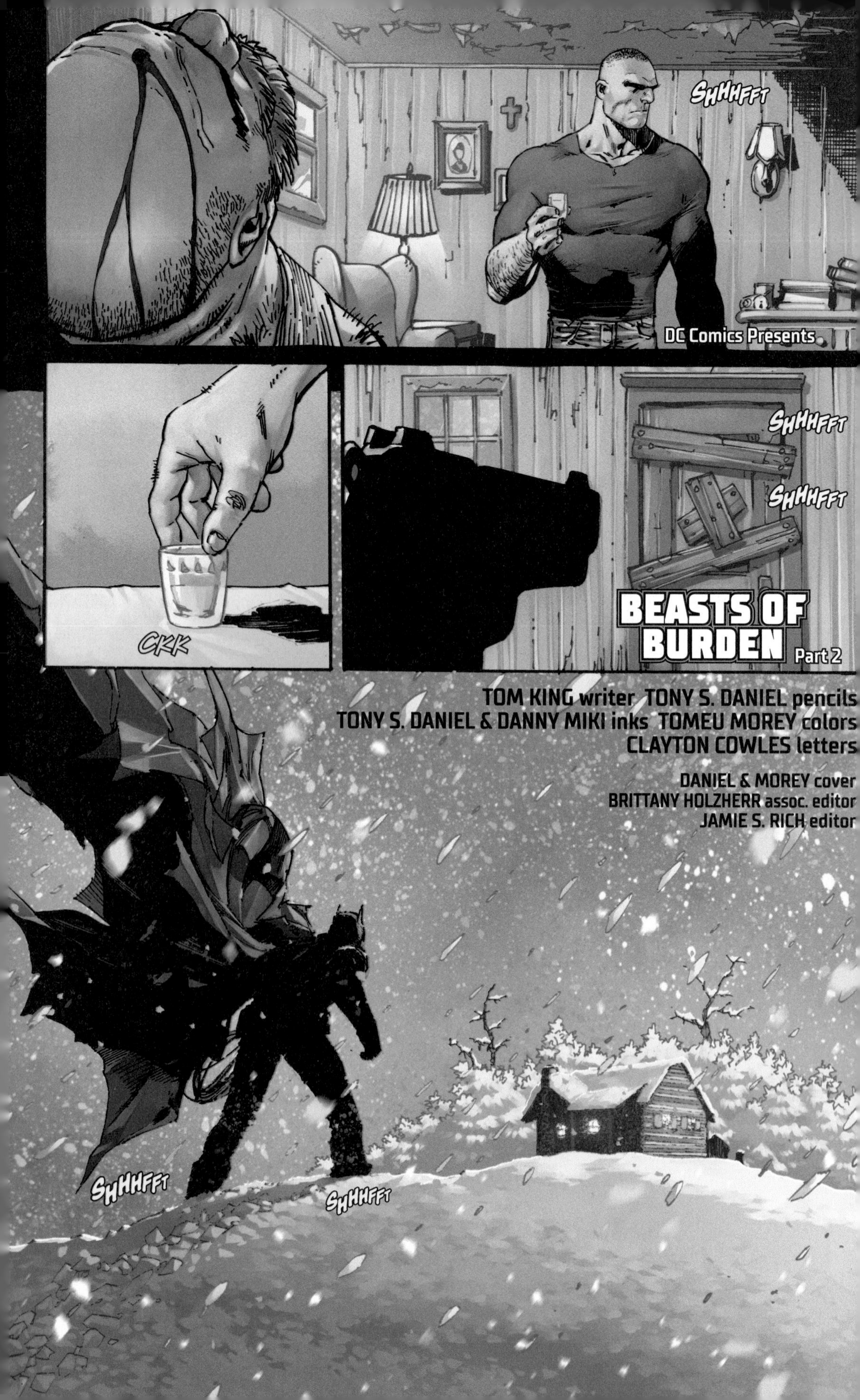
SHHHFFT
DC Comics Presents
CKK
SHHHFFT
SHHHFFT
BEASTS OF BURDEN Part 2
TOM KING writer TONY S. DANIEL pencils
TONY S. DANIEL & DANNY MIKI inks TOMEU MOREY colors
CLAYTON COWLES letters
DANIEL & MOREY cover
BRITTANY HOLZHERR assoc. editor
JAMIE S. RICH editor
SHHHFFT
SHHHFFT

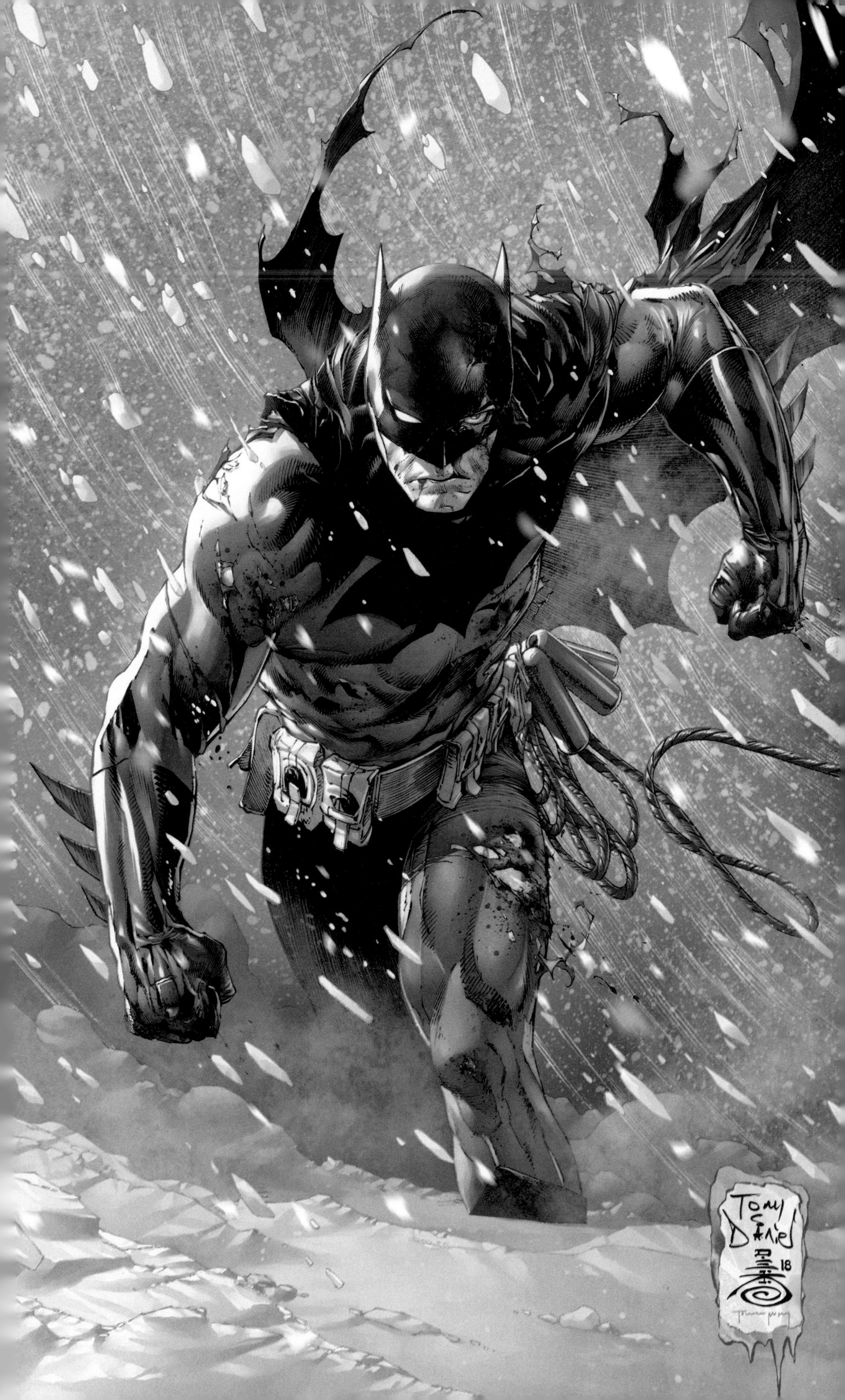
TONY S DANIEL
18

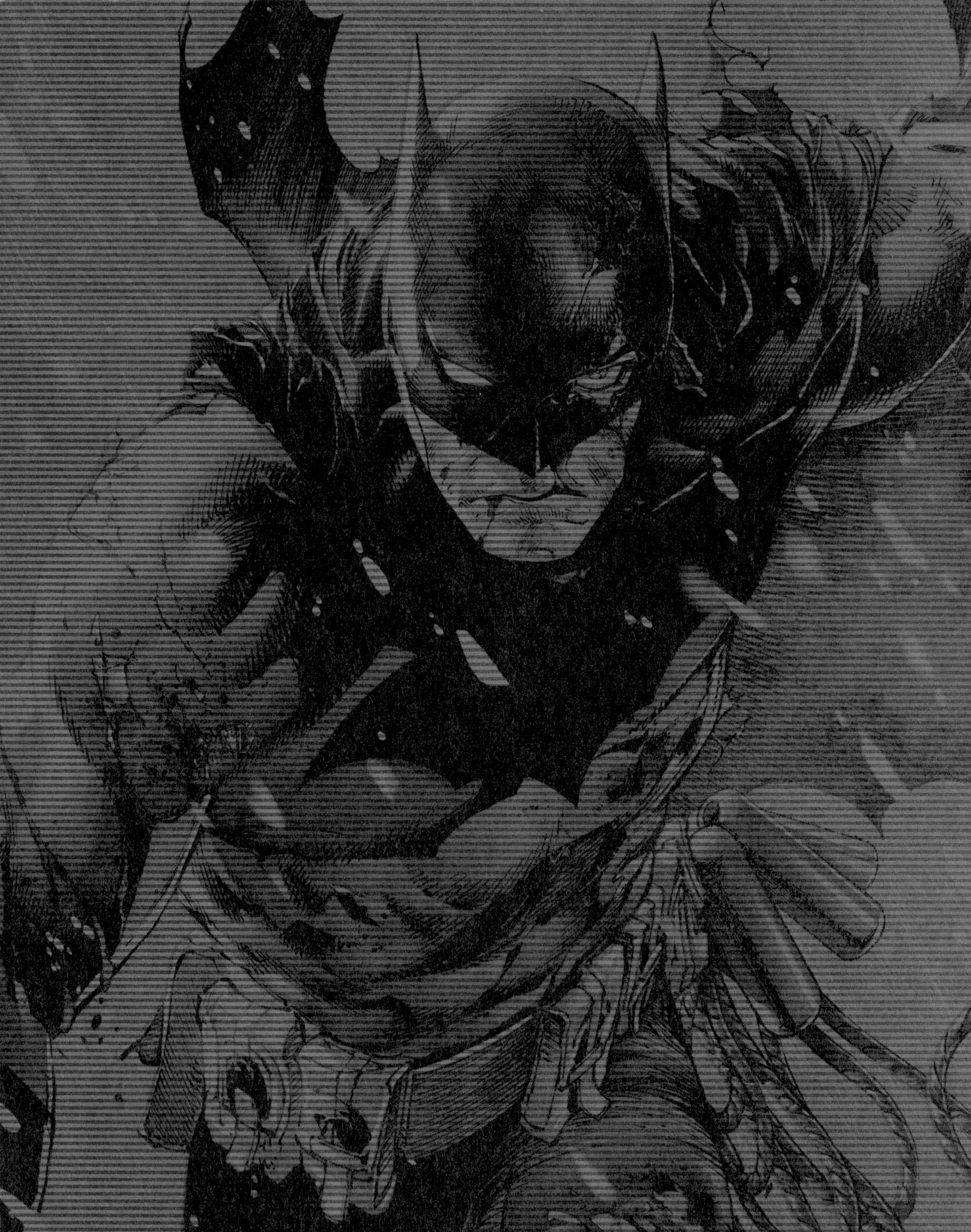

BATMAN
#57

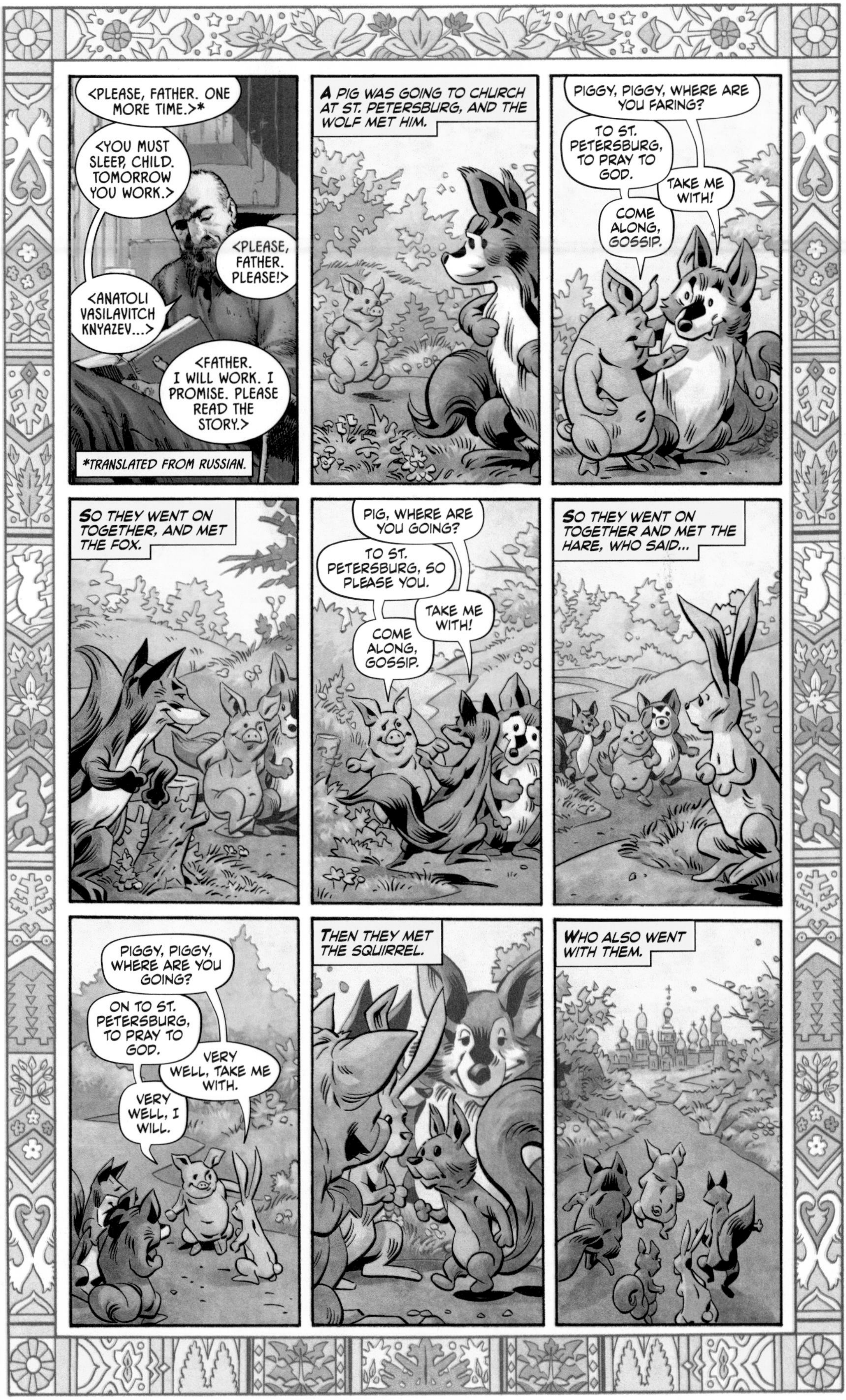
<PLEASE, FATHER. ONE MORE TIME.>*
<YOU MUST SLEEP, CHILD. TOMORROW YOU WORK.>
<PLEASE, FATHER. PLEASE!>
<ANATOLI VASILAVITCH KNYAZEV...>
<FATHER. I WILL WORK. I PROMISE. PLEASE READ THE STORY.>
*TRANSLATED FROM RUSSIAN.
A PIG WAS GOING TO CHURCH AT ST. PETERSBURG, AND THE WOLF MET HIM.
PIGGY, PIGGY, WHERE ARE YOU FARING?
TO ST. PETERSBURG, TO PRAY TO GOD.
TAKE ME WITH!
COME ALONG, GOSSIP.
SO THEY WENT ON TOGETHER, AND MET THE FOX.
PIG, WHERE ARE YOU GOING?
TO ST. PETERSBURG, SO PLEASE YOU.
TAKE ME WITH!
COME ALONG, GOSSIP.
SO THEY WENT ON TOGETHER AND MET THE HARE, WHO SAID...
PIGGY, PIGGY, WHERE ARE YOU GOING?
ON TO ST. PETERSBURG, TO PRAY TO GOD.
VERY WELL, TAKE ME WITH.
VERY WELL, I WILL.
THEN THEY MET THE SQUIRREL.
WHO ALSO WENT WITH THEM.

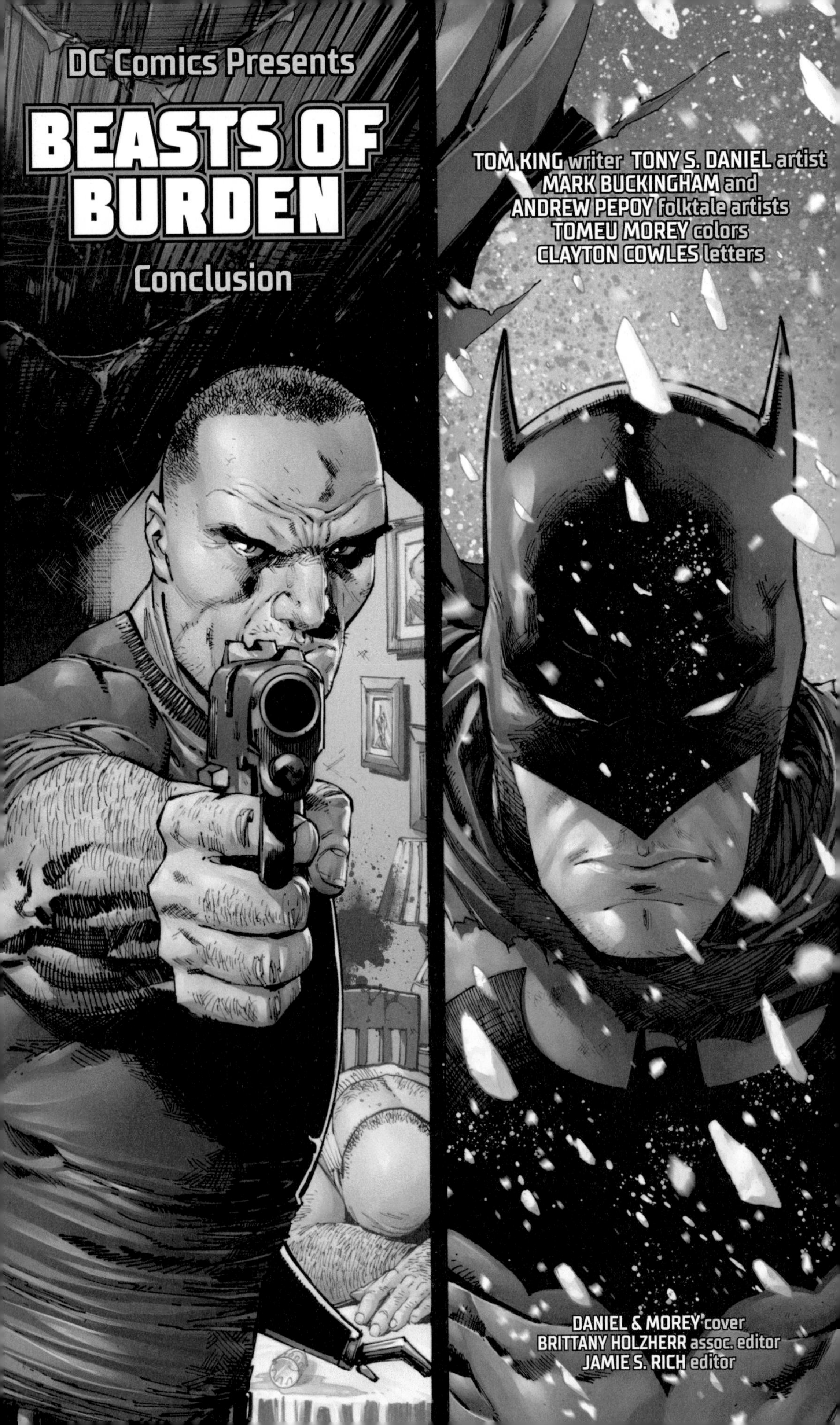
DC Comics Presents
BEASTS OF BURDEN
Conclusion
TOM KING writer TONY S. DANIEL artist
MARK BUCKINGHAM and
ANDREW PEPOY folktale artists
TOMEU MOREY colors
CLAYTON COWLES letters
DANIEL & MOREY cover
BRITTANY HOLZHERR assoc. editor
JAMIE S. RICH editor

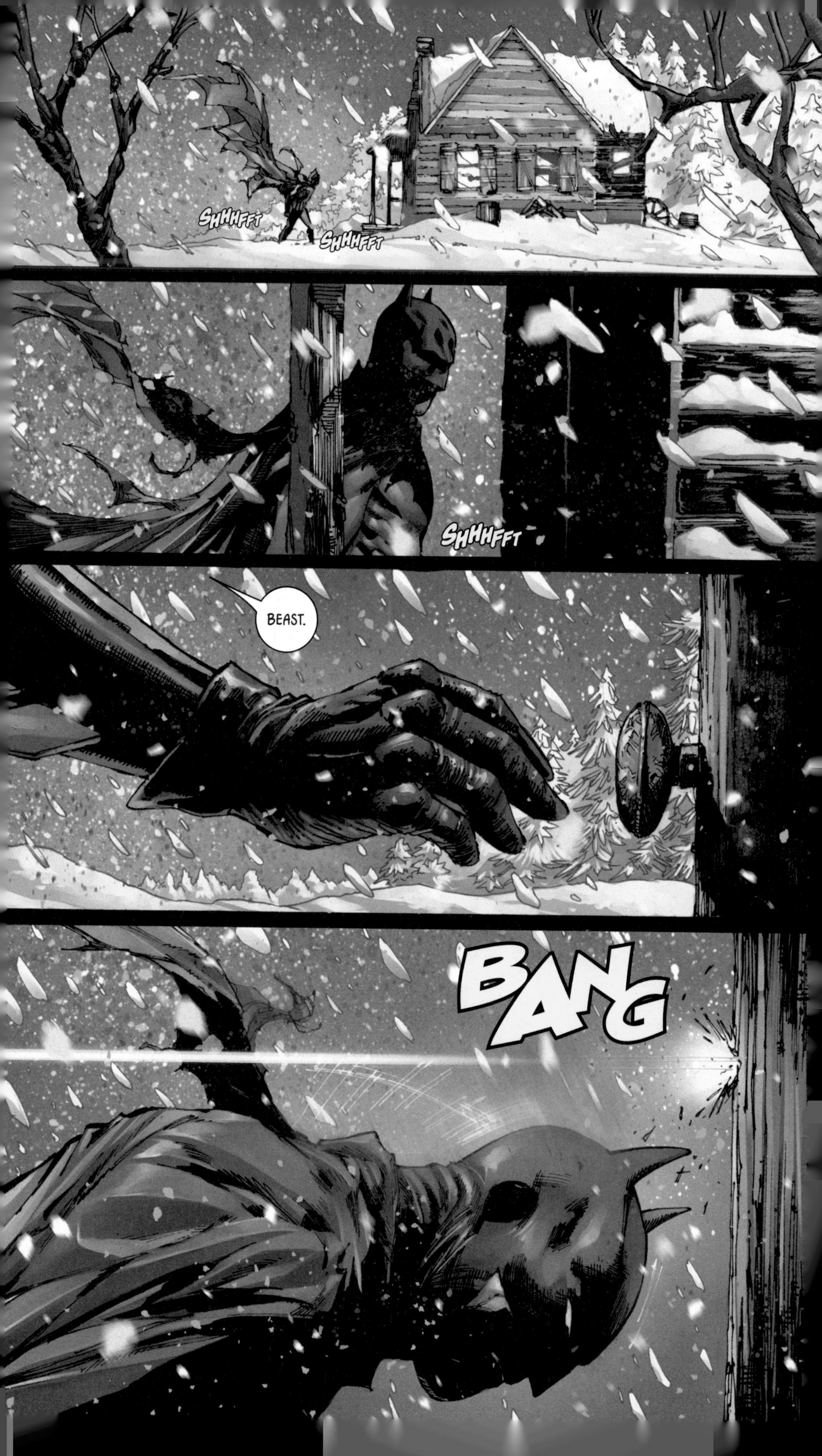
SHHHFFT
SHHHFFT
SHHHFFT
BEAST.
BANG

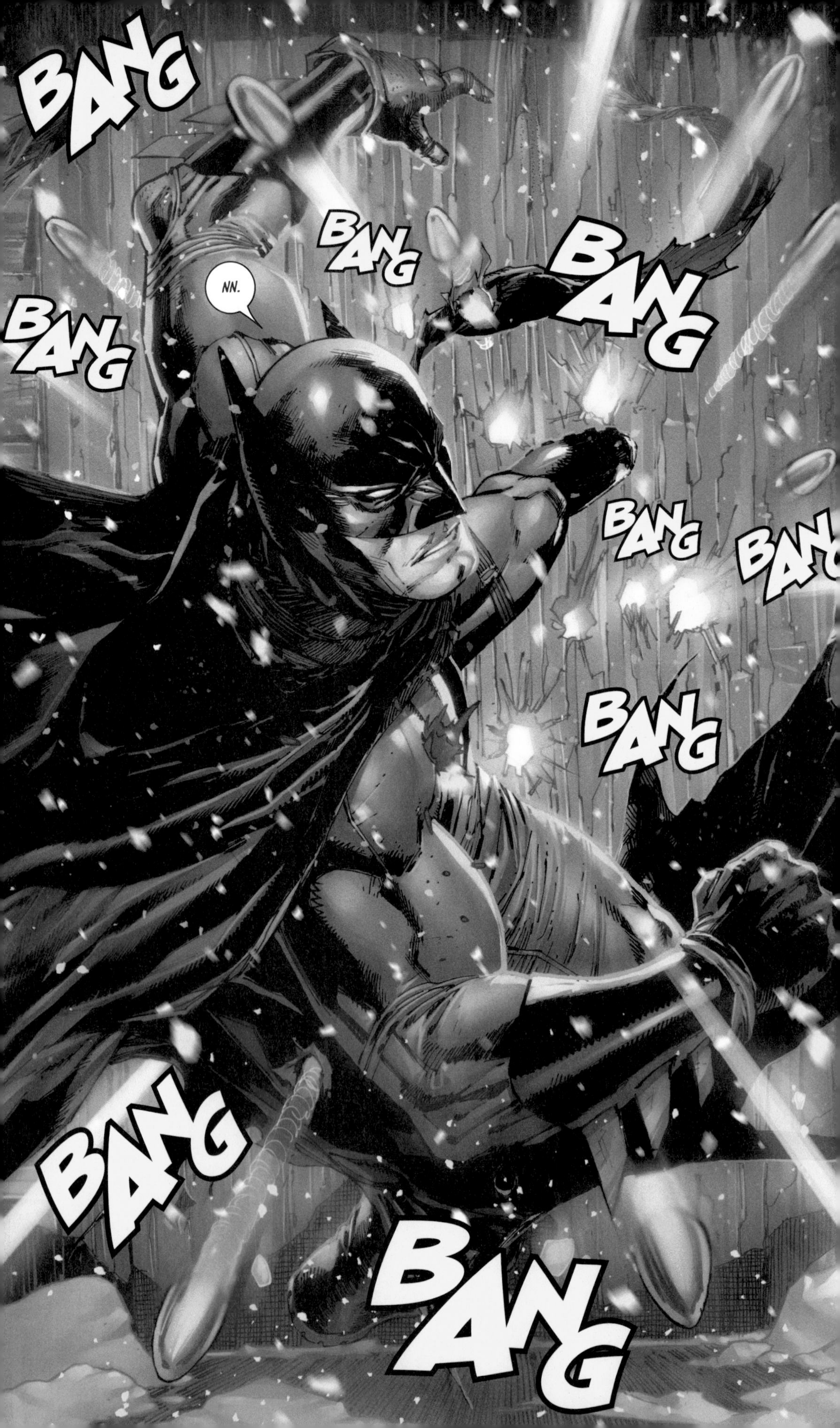
BANG
BANG
NN.
BANG
BANG
BANG
BAN
BANG
BANG
BANG

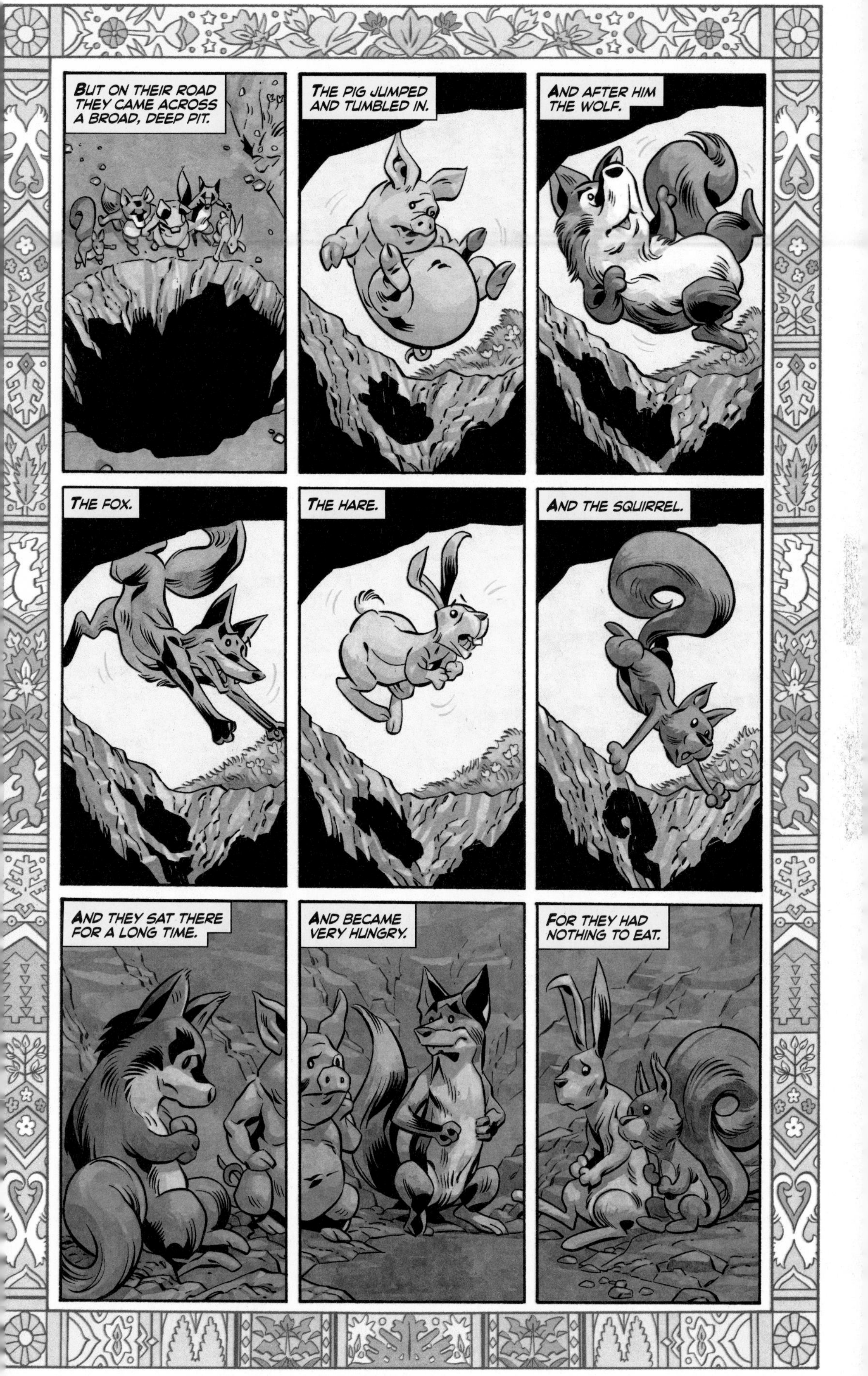

BUT ON THEIR ROAD THEY CAME ACROSS A BROAD, DEEP PIT.
THE PIG JUMPED AND TUMBLED IN.
AND AFTER HIM THE WOLF.
THE FOX.
THE HARE.
AND THE SQUIRREL.
AND THEY SAT THERE FOR A LONG TIME.
AND BECAME VERY HUNGRY.
FOR THEY HAD NOTHING TO EAT.

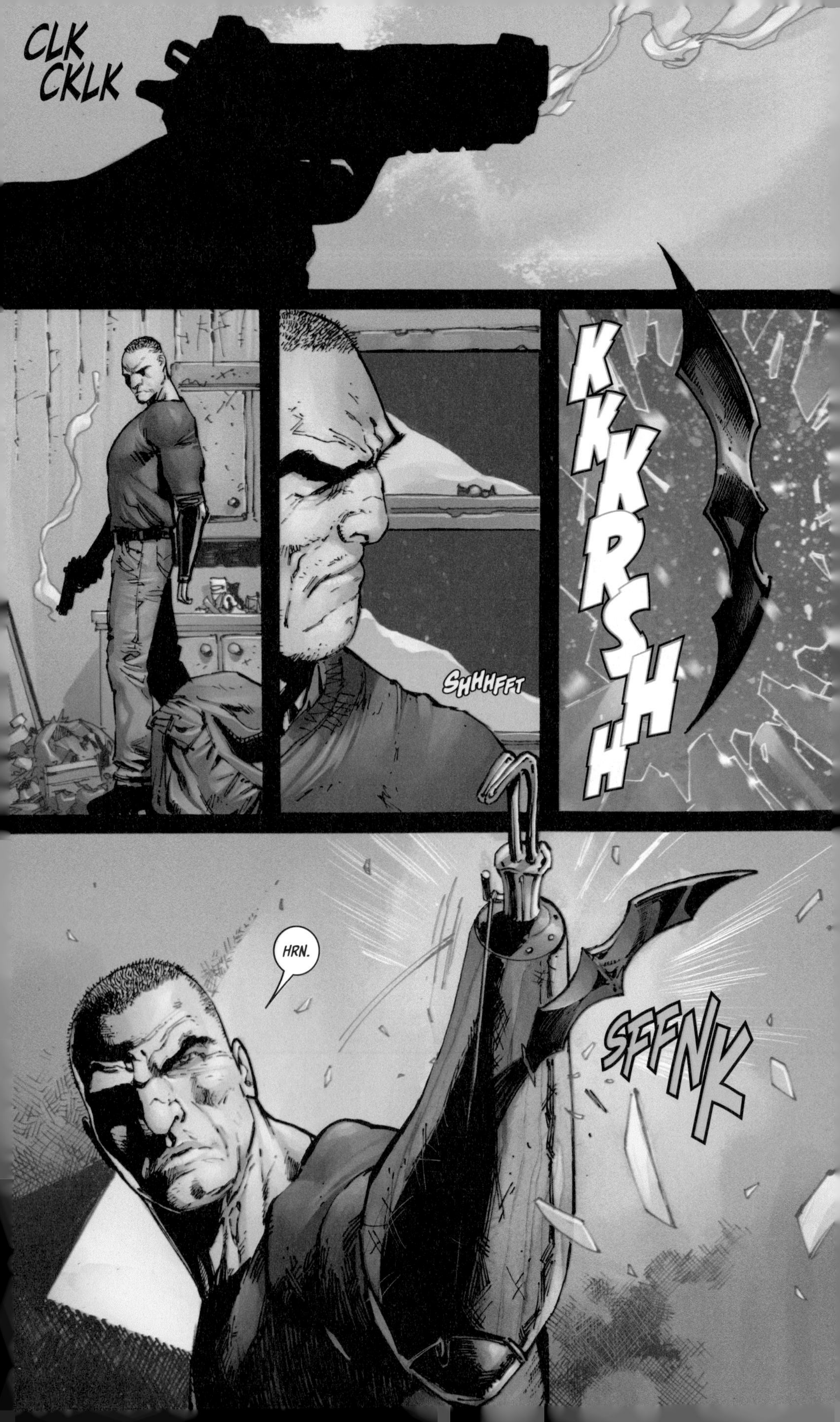
CLK CKLK
SHHHFFT
KKKRSHHH
HRN.
SFFNK

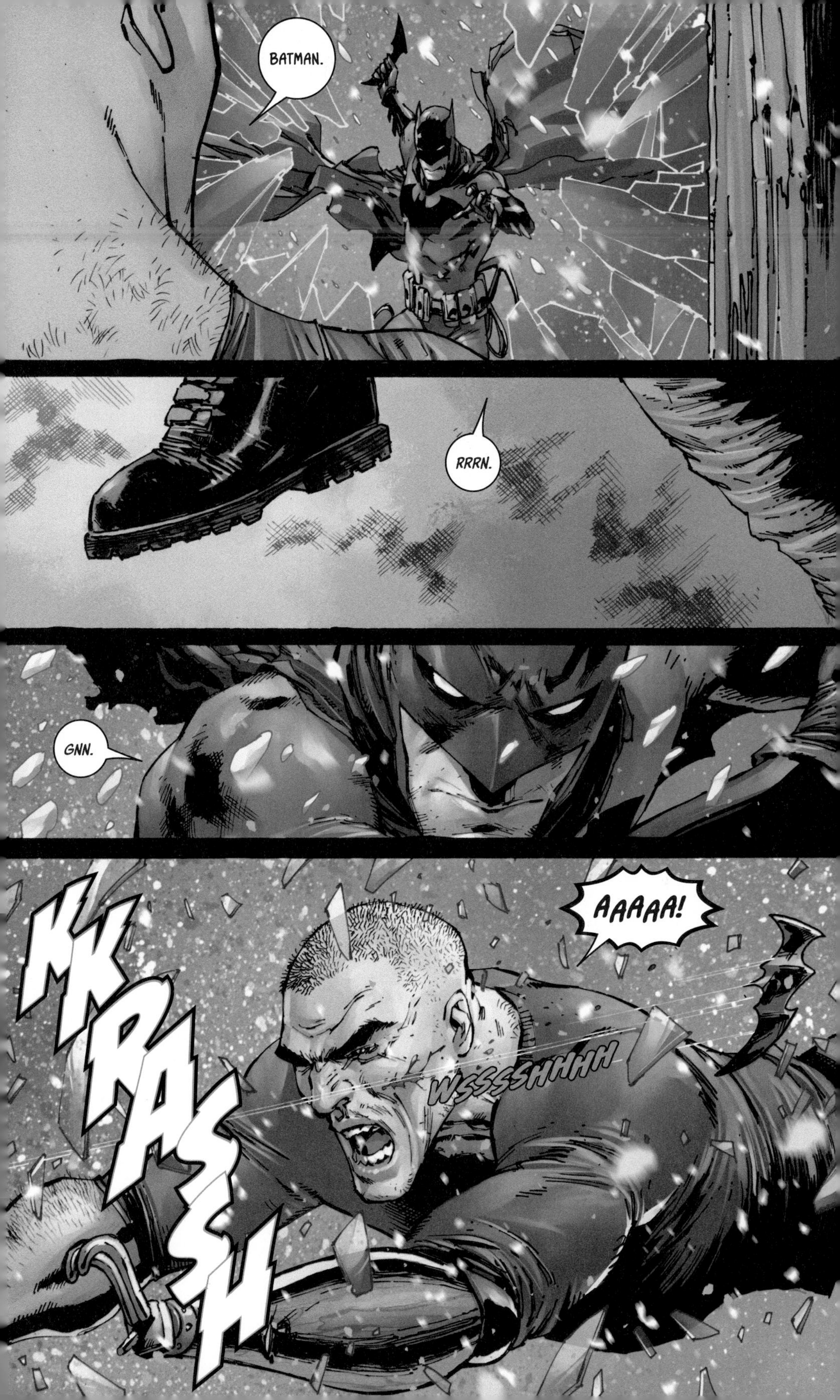
BATMAN.
RRRN.
GNN.
KKRASH
AAAAA!
WSSSSHHHH

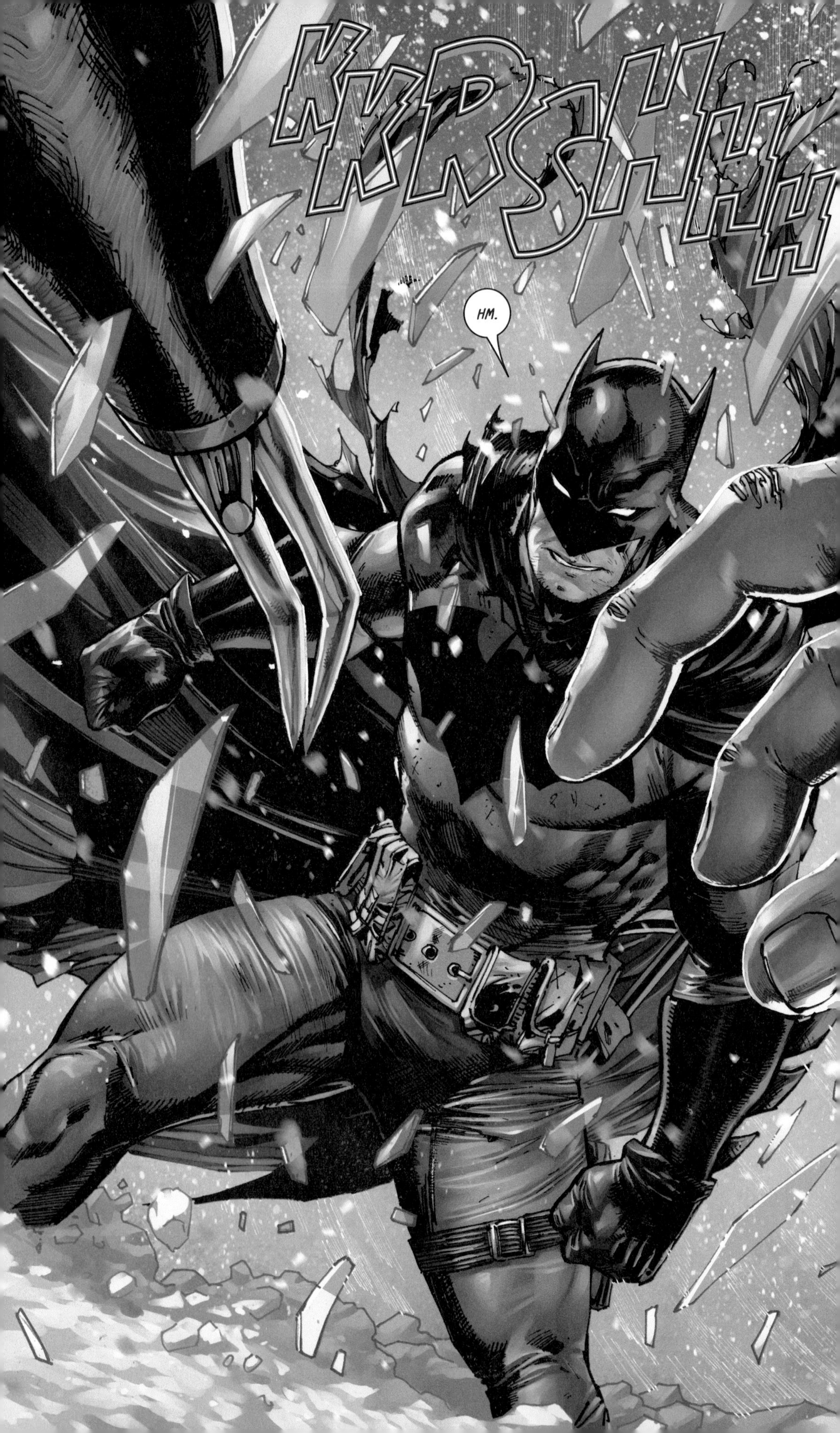
KKRSHHH
HM.

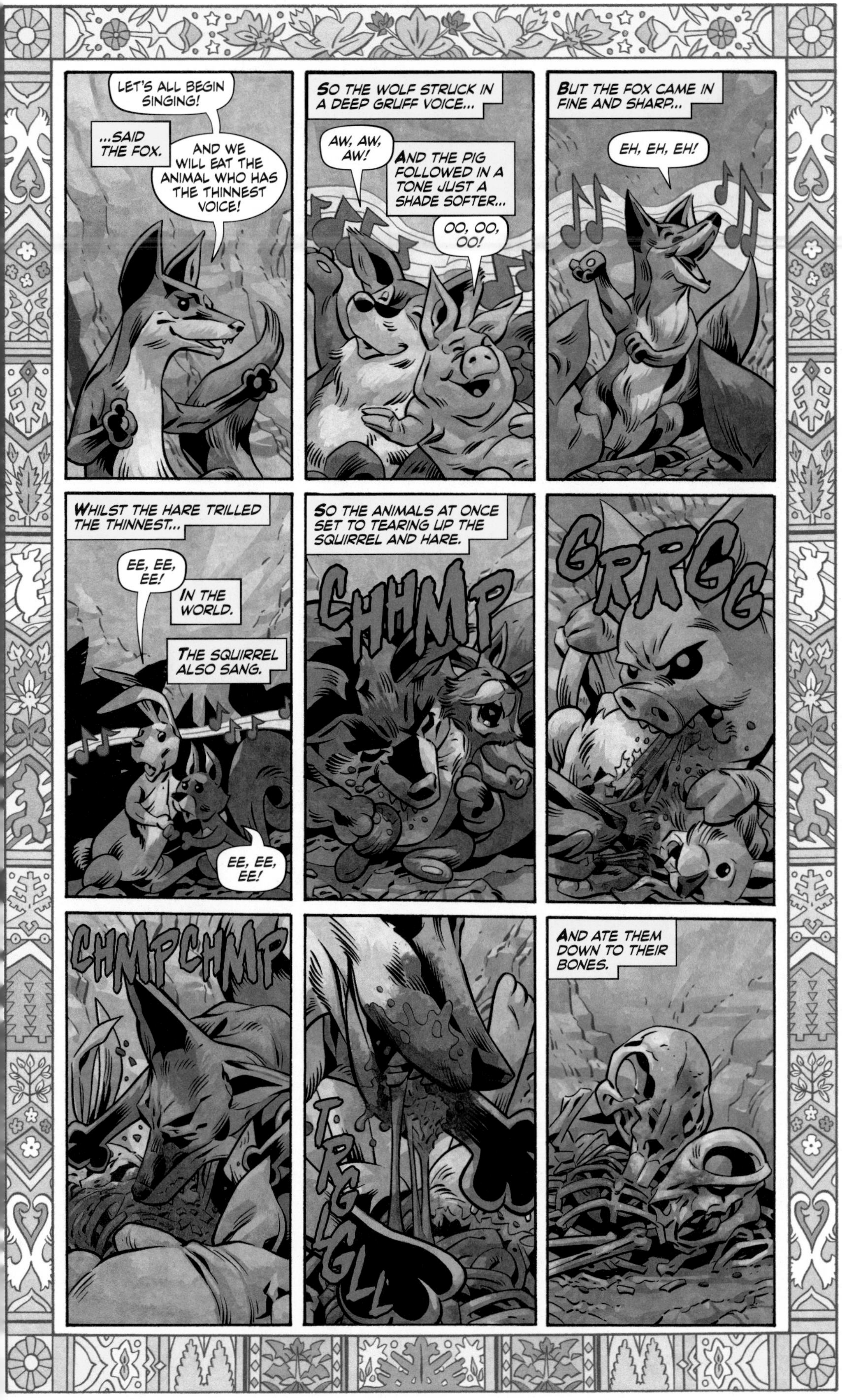
LET'S ALL BEGIN SINGING!
...SAID THE FOX.
AND WE WILL EAT THE ANIMAL WHO HAS THE THINNEST VOICE!
SO THE WOLF STRUCK IN A DEEP GRUFF VOICE...
AW, AW, AW!
AND THE PIG FOLLOWED IN A TONE JUST A SHADE SOFTER...
OO, OO, OO!
BUT THE FOX CAME IN FINE AND SHARP...
EH, EH, EH!
WHILST THE HARE TRILLED THE THINNEST...
EE, EE, EE!
IN THE WORLD.
THE SQUIRREL ALSO SANG.
EE, EE, EE!
SO THE ANIMALS AT ONCE SET TO TEARING UP THE SQUIRREL AND HARE.
CHHMP
GRRGG
CHMPCHMP
TRGLGLL
AND ATE THEM DOWN TO THEIR BONES.

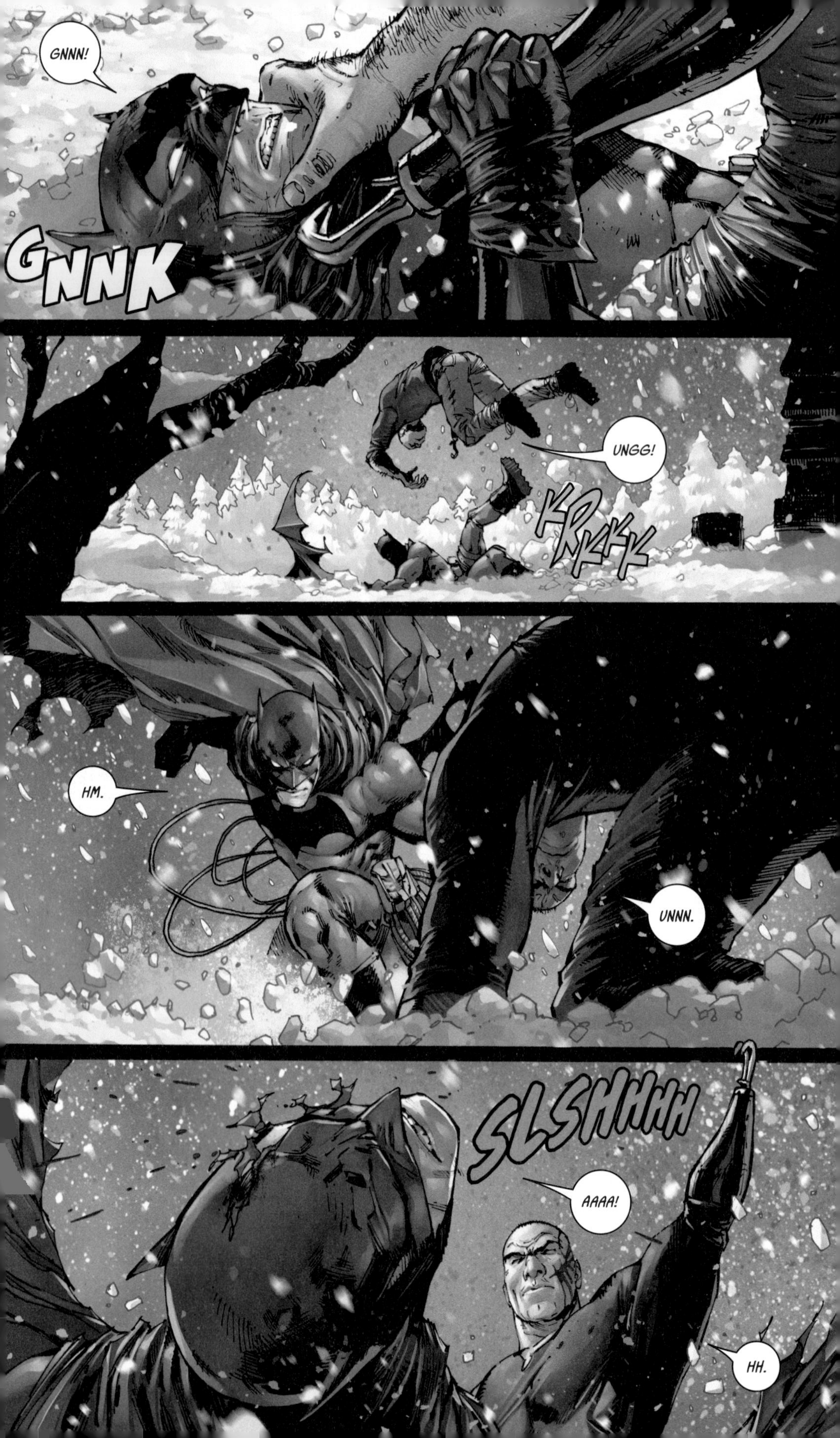
GNNN!
GNNK
UNGG!
KRKKK
HM.
UNNN.
SLSHHHH
AAAA!
HH.

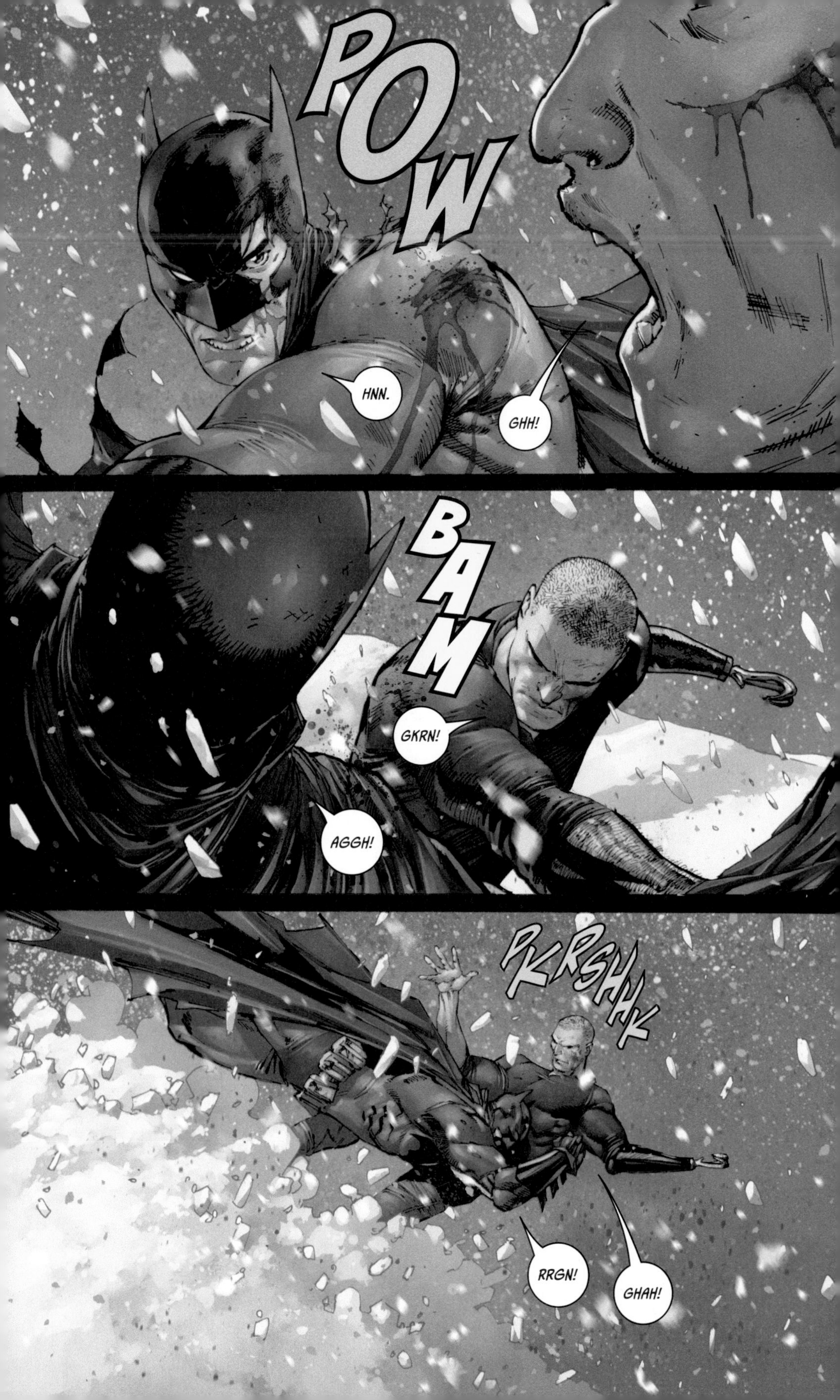
POW
HNN.
GHH!
BAM
GKRN!
AGGH!
PKRSHHK
RRGN!
GHAH!

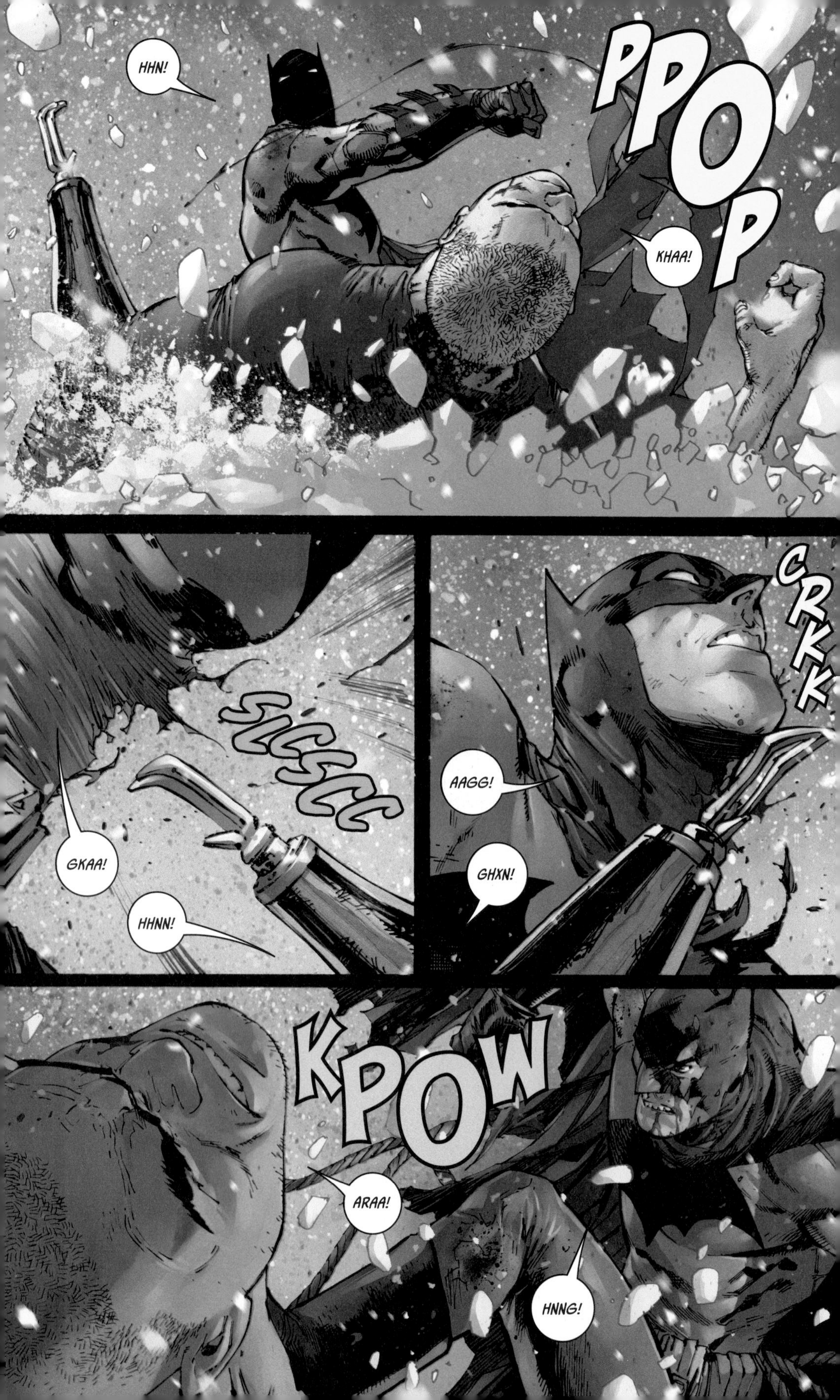
HHN!
PPOP
KHAA!
SLSCC
GKAA!
HHNN!
CRKK
AAGG!
GHXN!
KPOW
ARAA!
HNNG!

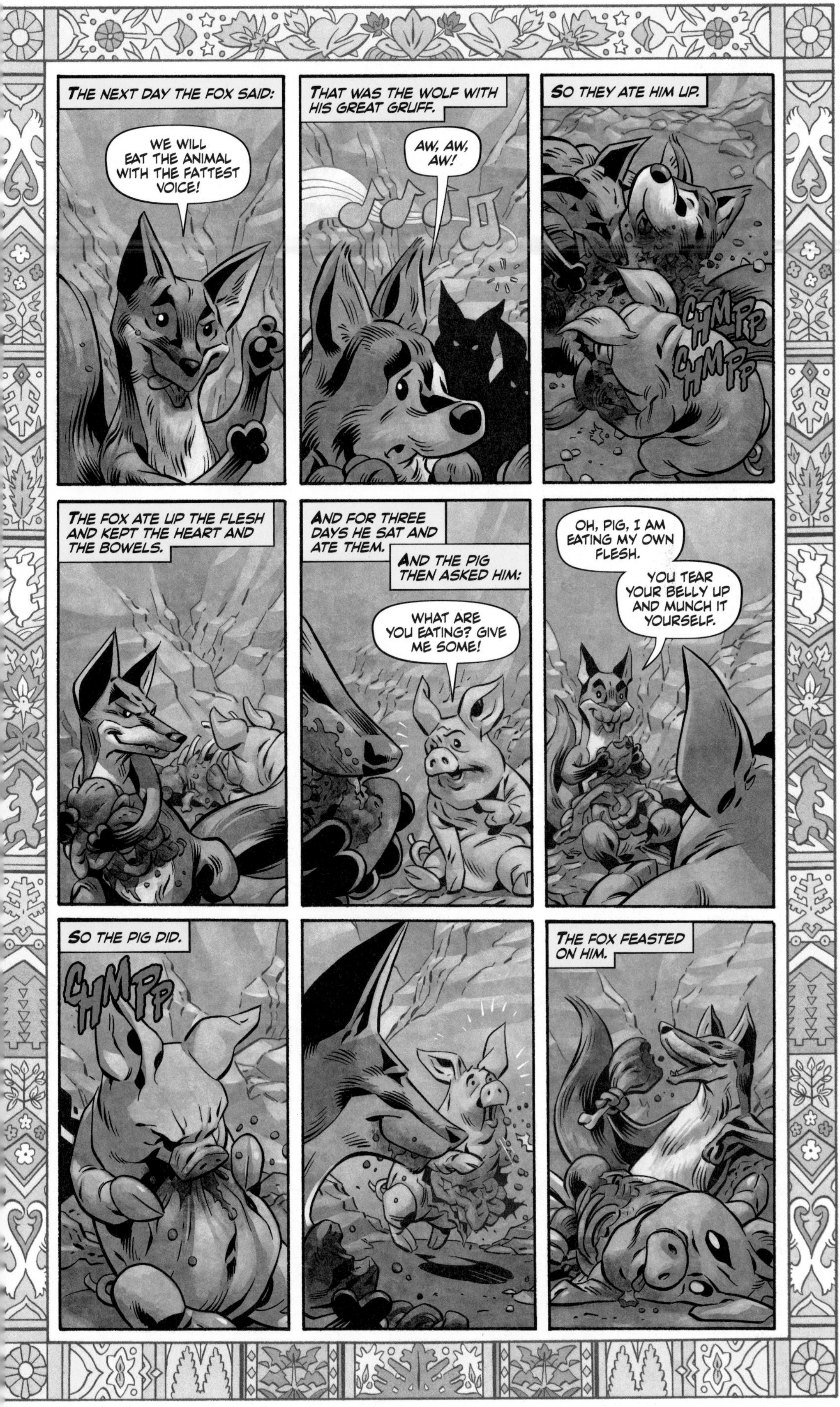
THE NEXT DAY THE FOX SAID:
WE WILL EAT THE ANIMAL WITH THE FATTEST VOICE!
THAT WAS THE WOLF WITH HIS GREAT GRUFF.
AW, AW, AW!
SO THEY ATE HIM UP.
CHMPP CHMPP
THE FOX ATE UP THE FLESH AND KEPT THE HEART AND THE BOWELS.
AND FOR THREE DAYS HE SAT AND ATE THEM.
AND THE PIG THEN ASKED HIM:
WHAT ARE YOU EATING? GIVE ME SOME!
OH, PIG, I AM EATING MY OWN FLESH.
YOU TEAR YOUR BELLY UP AND MUNCH IT YOURSELF.
SO THE PIG DID.
CHMPP
THE FOX FEASTED ON HIM.

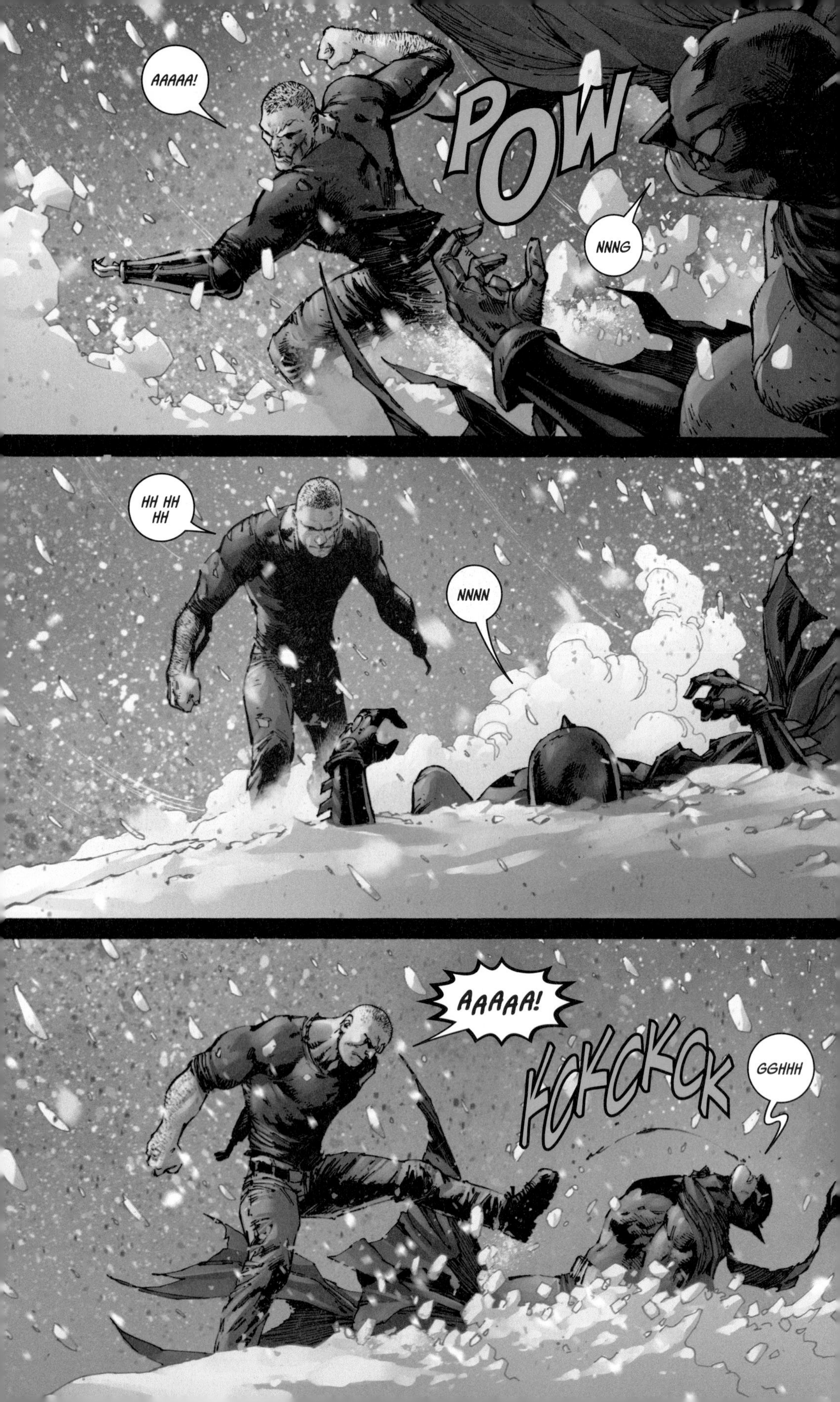
AAAAA!
POW
NNNG
HH HH HH
NNNN
AAAAA!
KCKCKCK
GGHHH

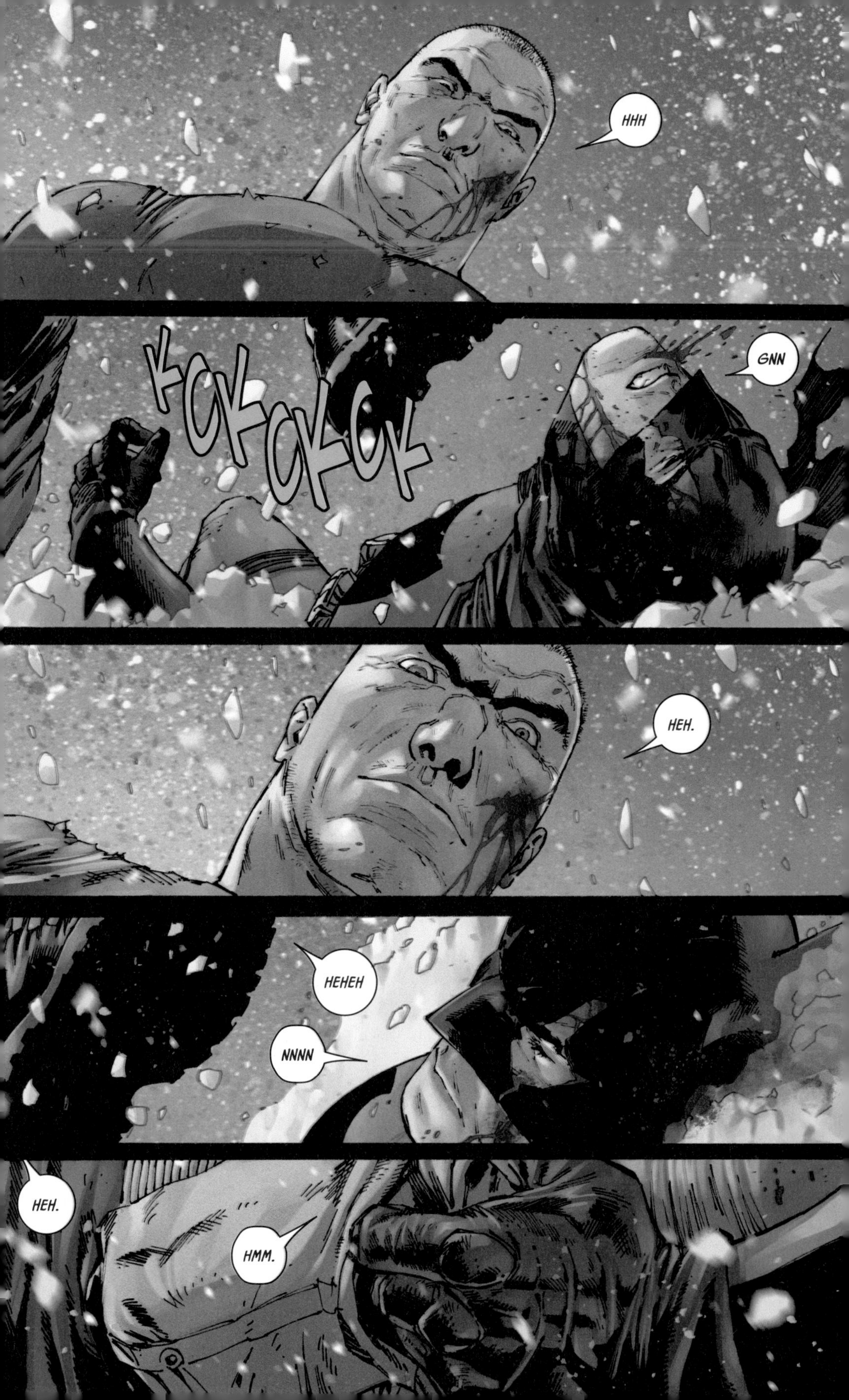
HHH
KCKCKCK
GNN
HEH.
HEHEH
NNNN
HEH.
HMM.

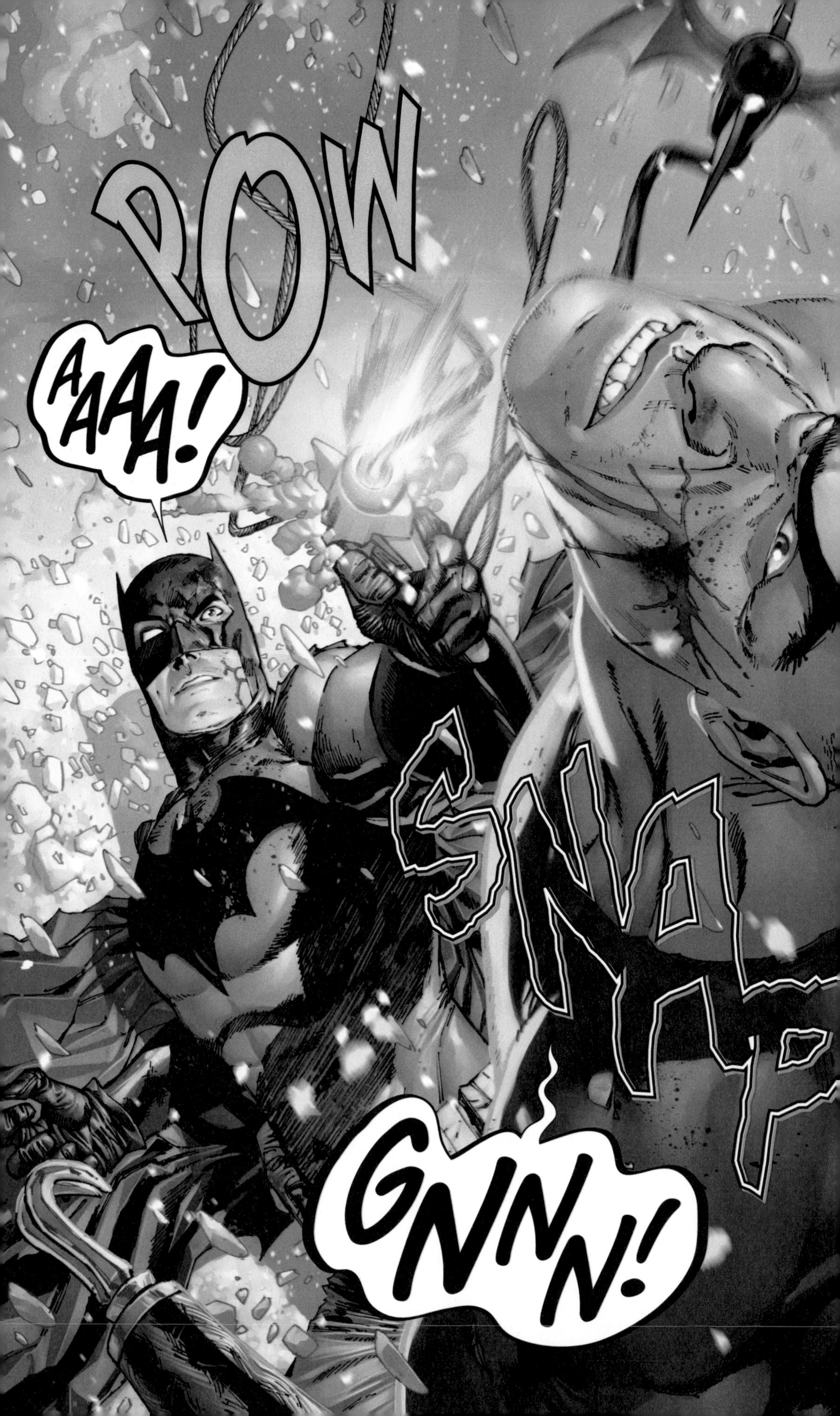
POW
AAAA!
SNAP
GNNN!

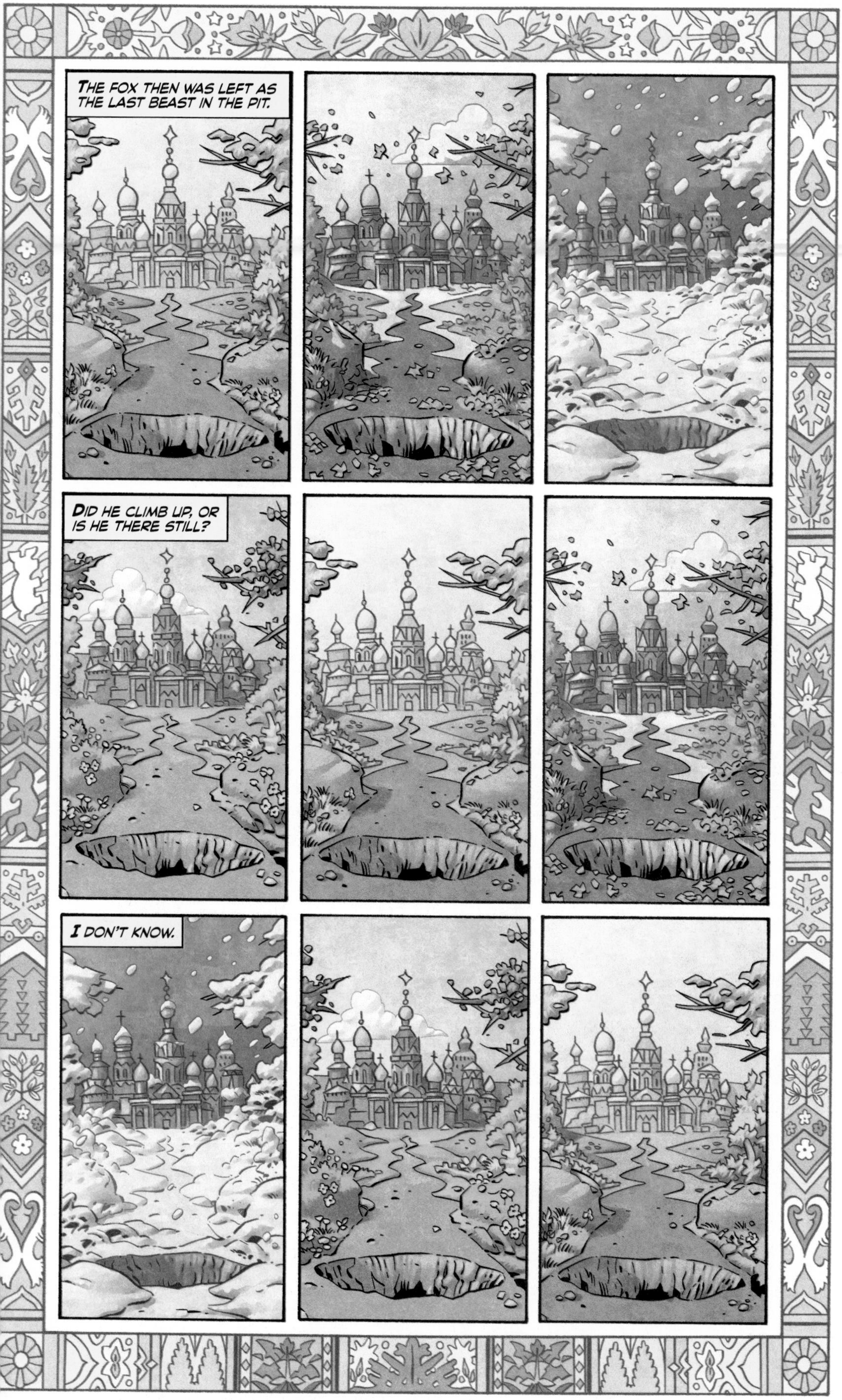
THE FOX THEN WAS LEFT AS THE LAST BEAST IN THE PIT.
DID HE CLIMB UP, OR IS HE THERE STILL?
I DON'T KNOW.

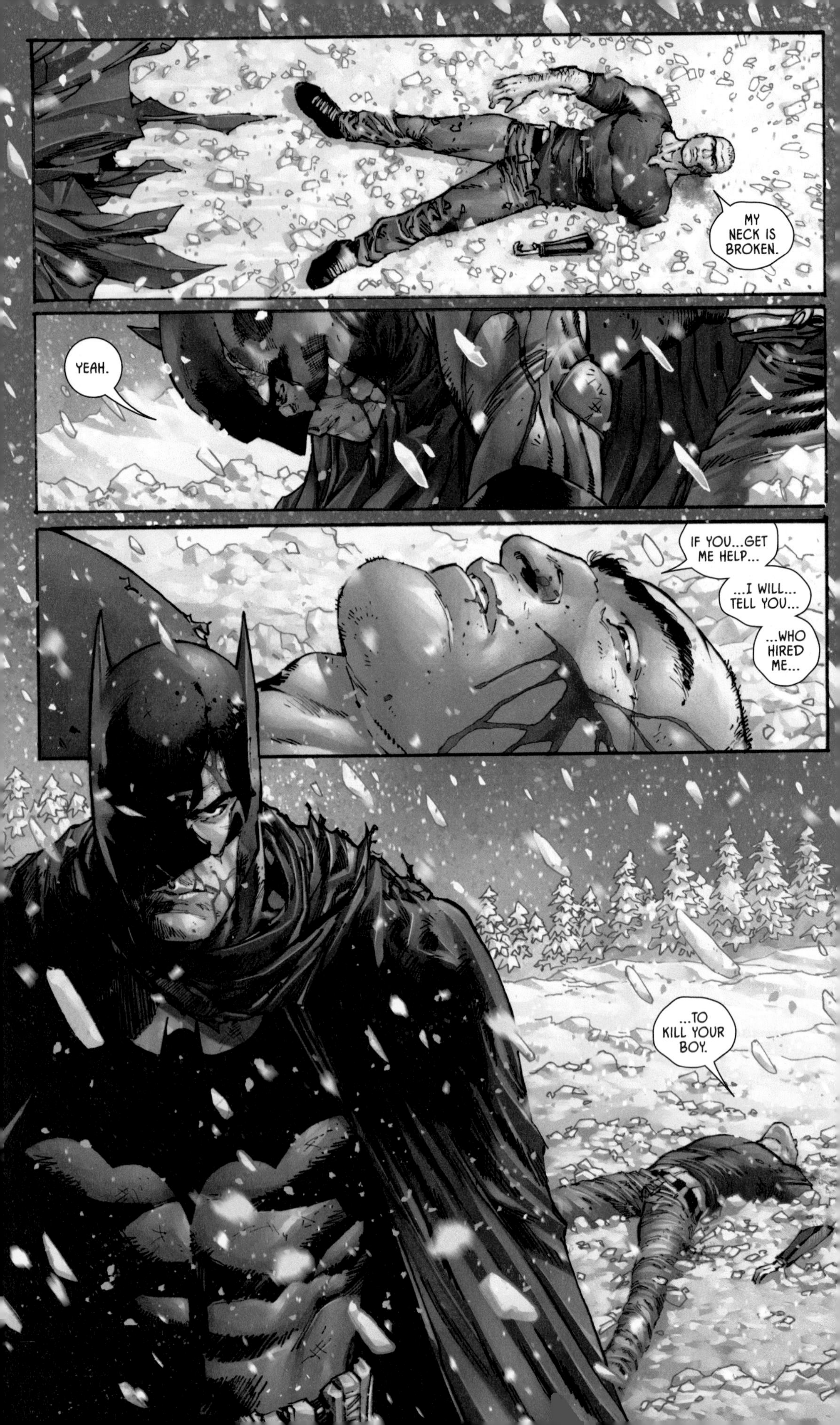
MY NECK IS BROKEN.
YEAH.
IF YOU...GET ME HELP...
...I WILL... TELL YOU...
...WHO HIRED ME...
...TO KILL YOUR BOY.

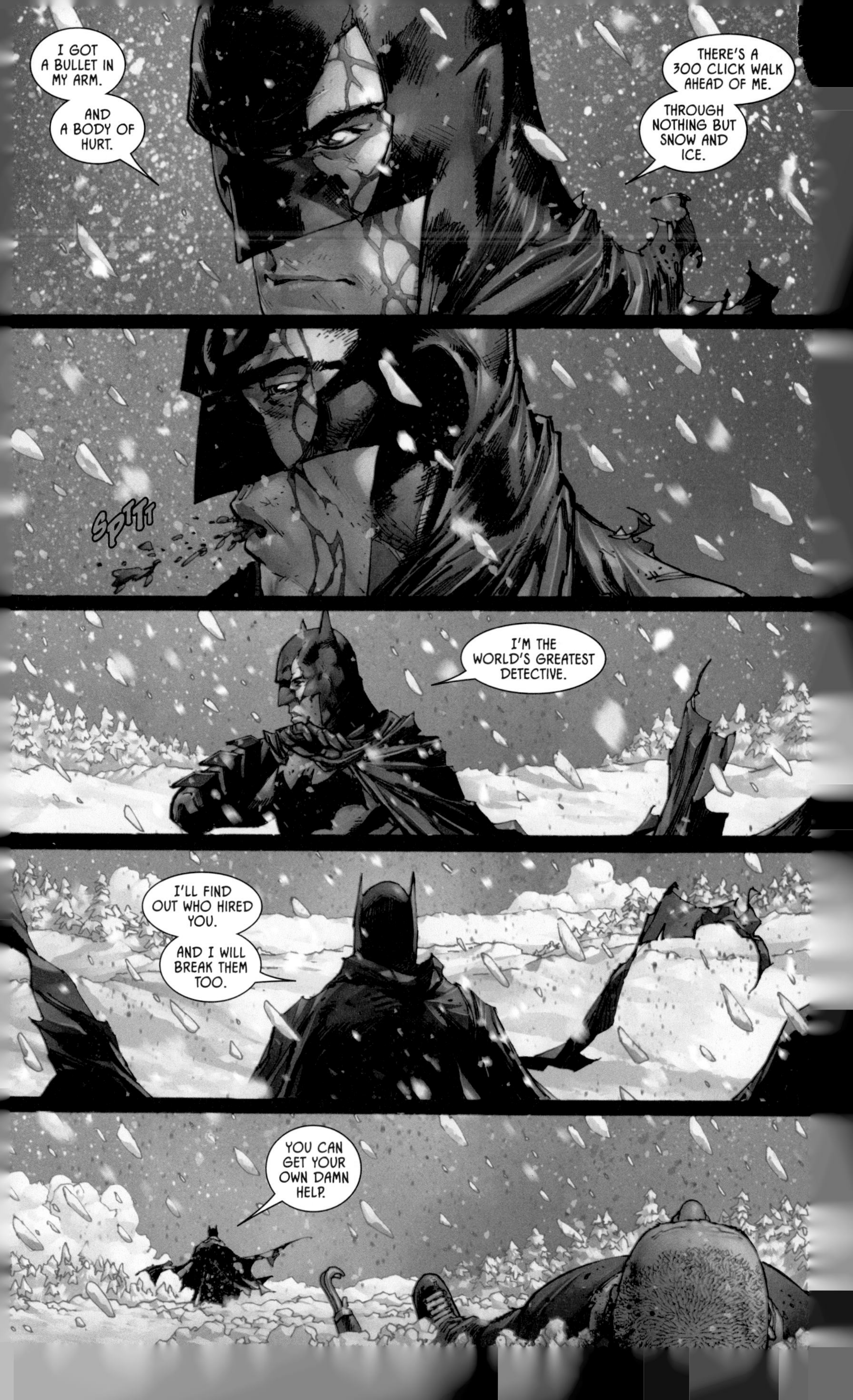
I GOT A BULLET IN MY ARM.
AND A BODY OF HURT.
THERE'S A 300 CLICK WALK AHEAD OF ME.
THROUGH NOTHING BUT SNOW AND ICE.
SPTTT
I'M THE WORLD'S GREATEST DETECTIVE.
I'LL FIND OUT WHO HIRED YOU.
AND I WILL BREAK THEM TOO.
YOU CAN GET YOUR OWN DAMN HELP.

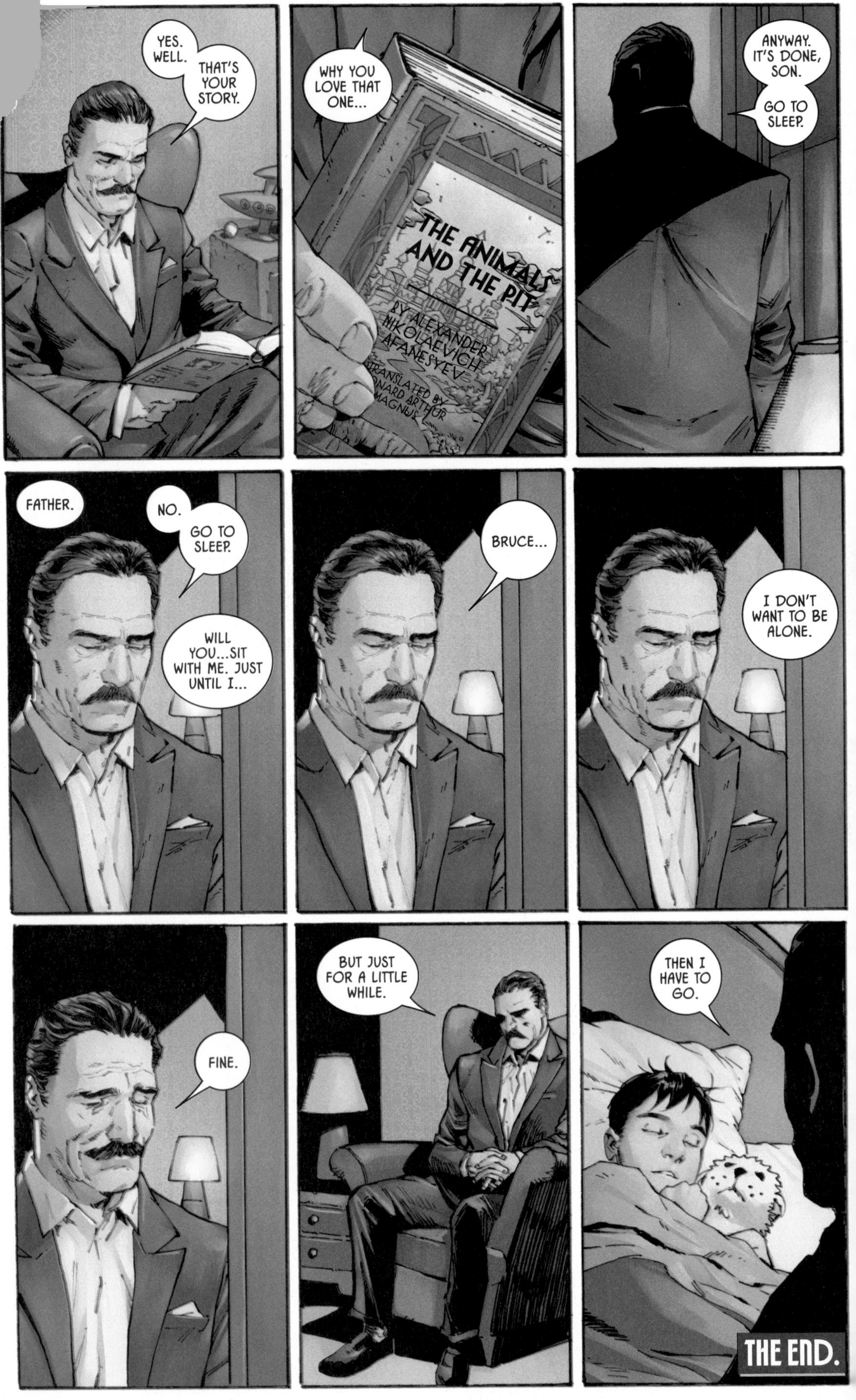
YES. WELL.
THAT'S YOUR STORY.
WHY YOU LOVE THAT ONE...
THE ANIMALS AND THE PIT
BY ALEXANDER NIKOLAEVICH AFANESYEV
ANYWAY. IT'S DONE, SON.
GO TO SLEEP.
FATHER.
NO.
GO TO SLEEP.
WILL YOU...SIT WITH ME. JUST UNTIL I...
BRUCE...
I DON'T WANT TO BE ALONE.
FINE.
BUT JUST FOR A LITTLE WHILE.
THEN I HAVE TO GO.
THE END.

VARIANT COVER GALLERY

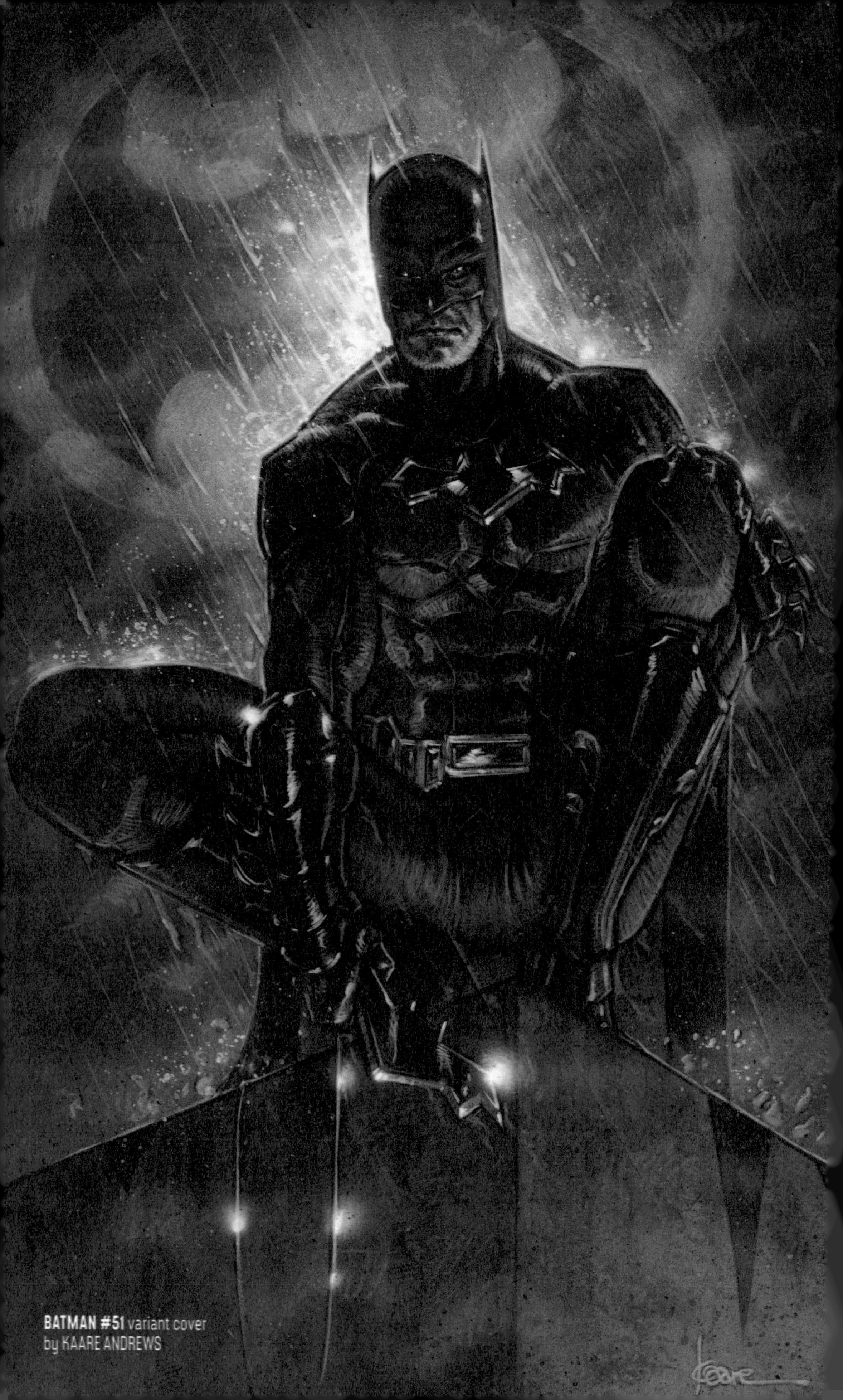

BATMAN #51 variant cover
by KAARE ANDREWS

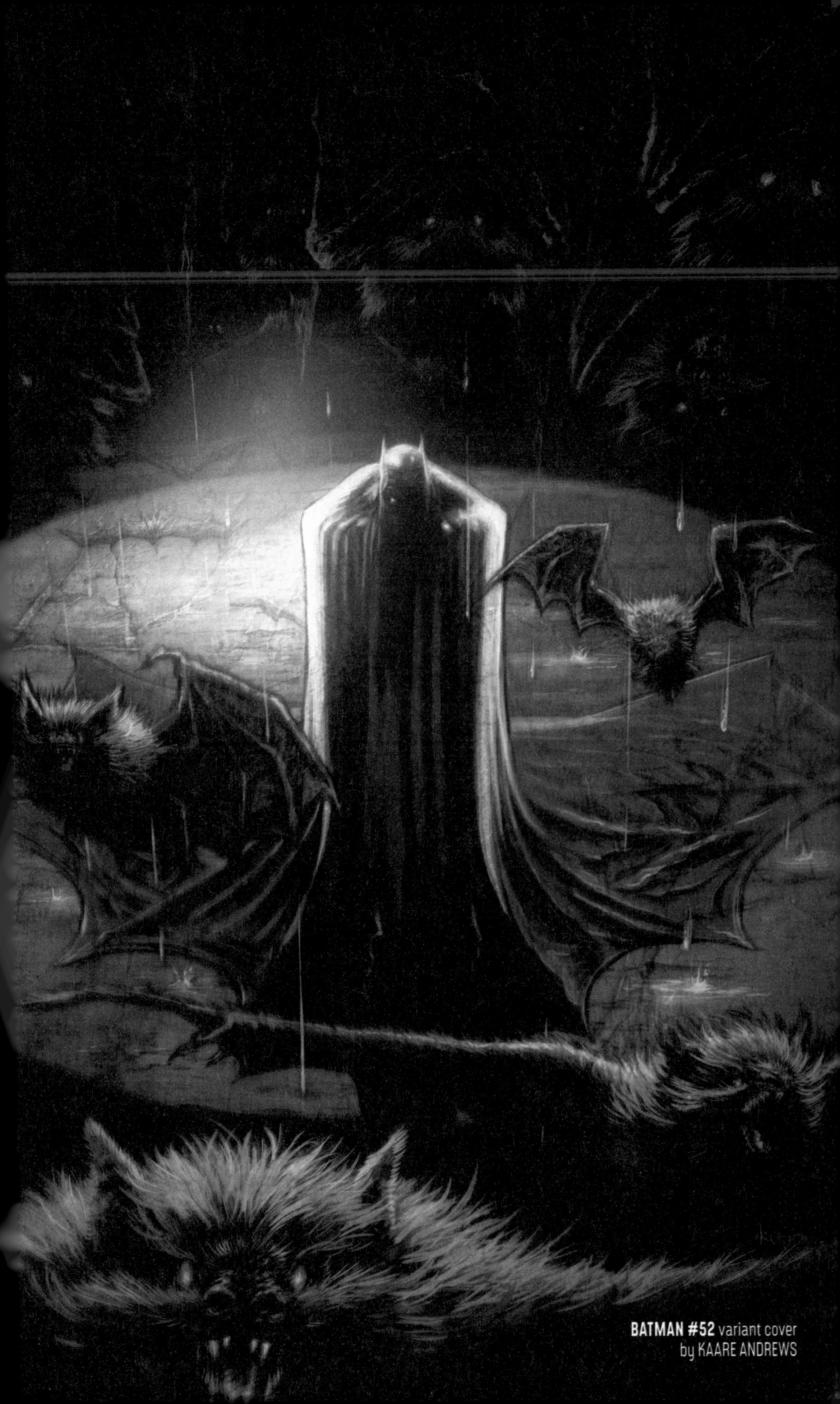

BATMAN #52 variant cover
by KAARE ANDREWS

BATMAN #53 variant cover
by KAARE ANDREWS

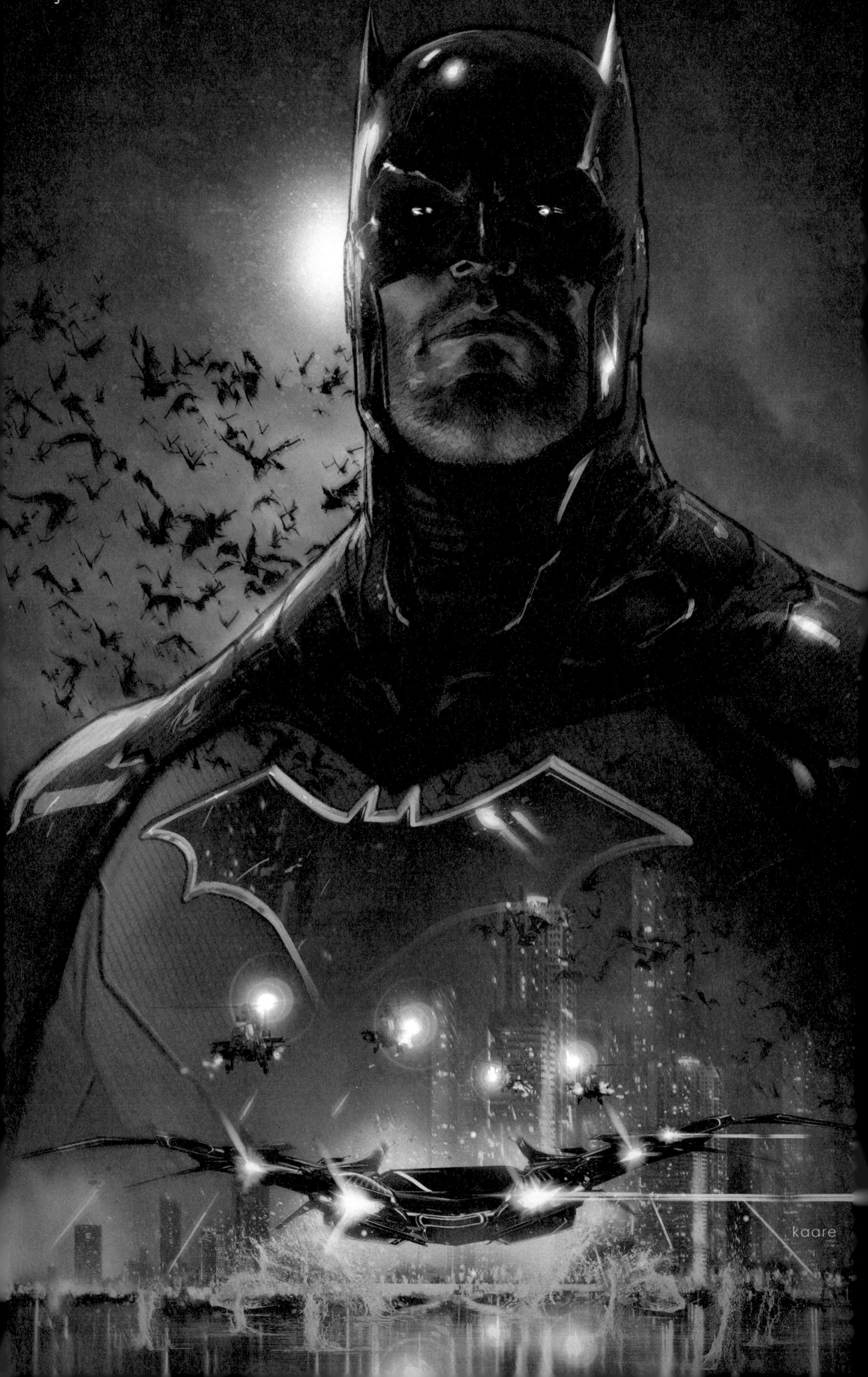
kaare

BATMAN #54 variant cover
by TIM SALE and BRENNAN WAGNER

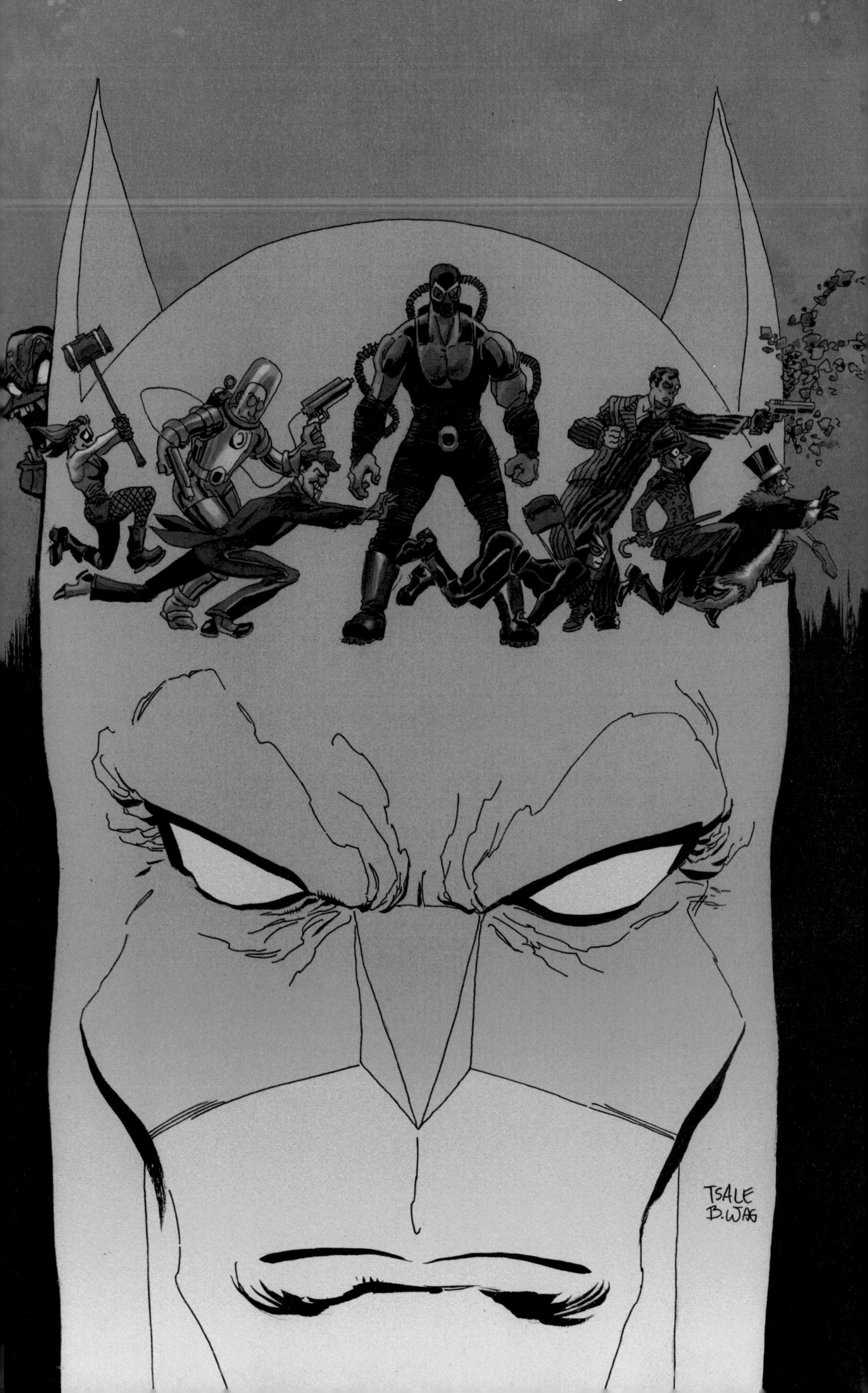
TSALE
B.WAG

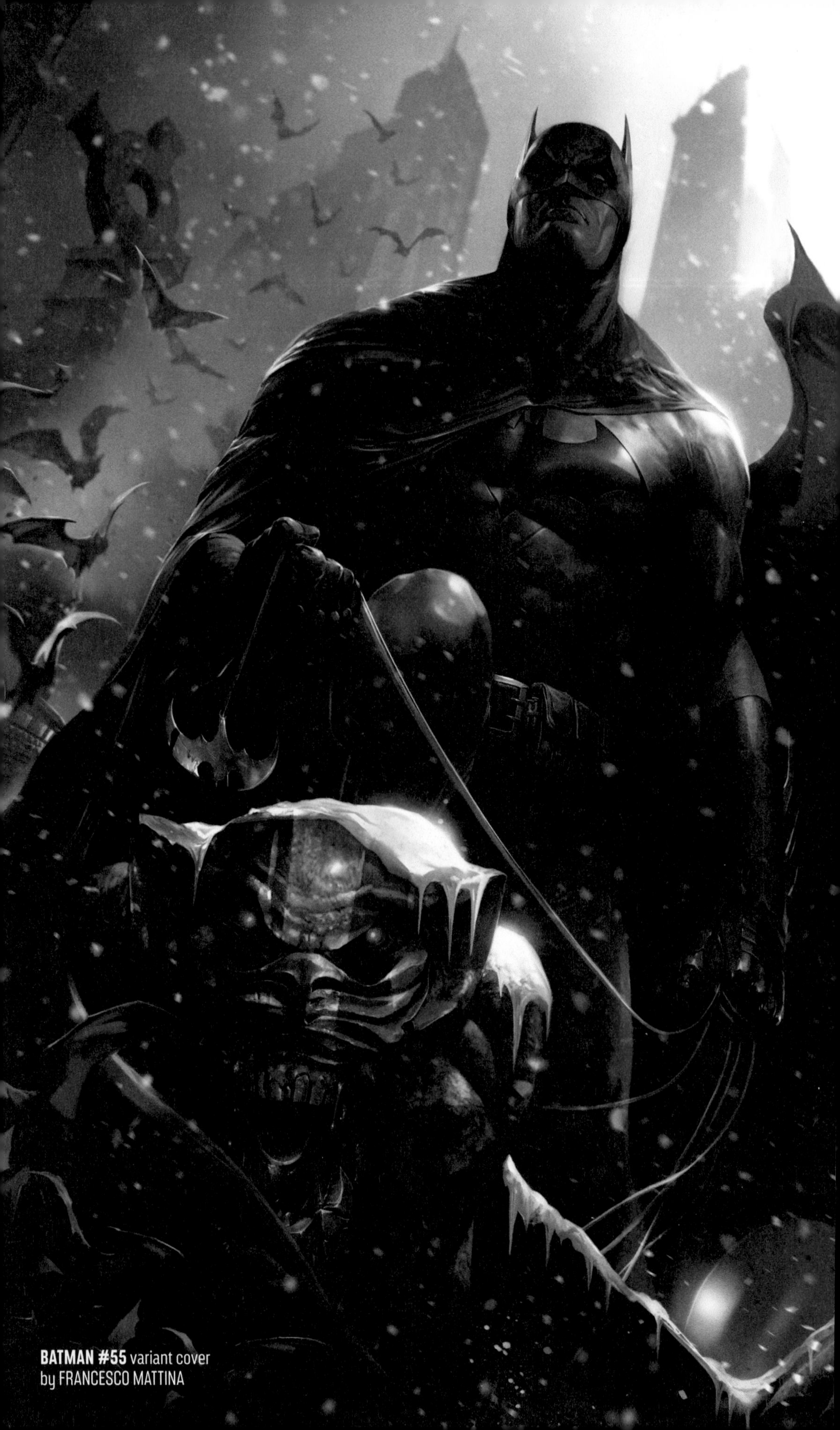

BATMAN #55 variant cover
by FRANCESCO MATTINA

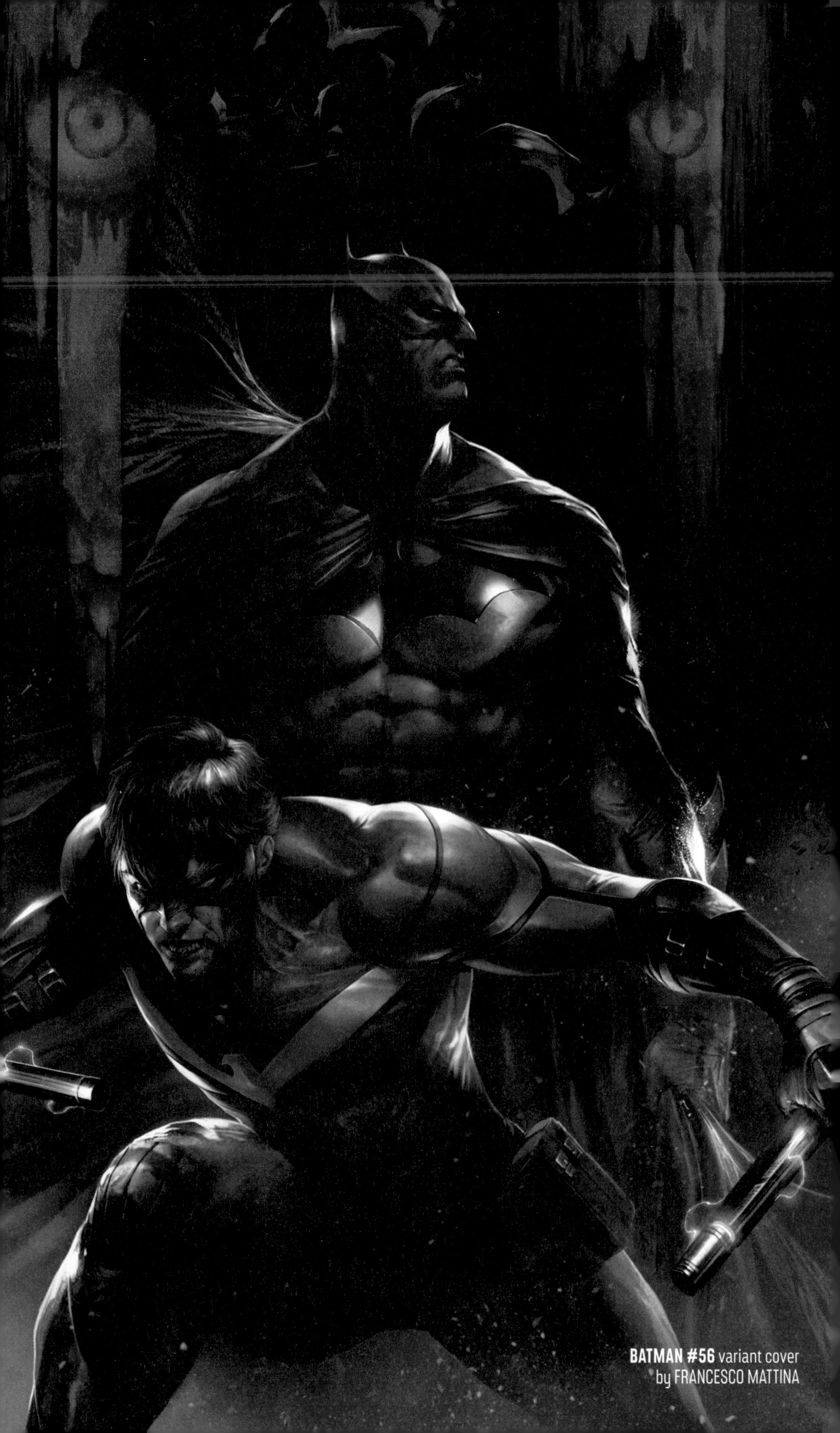

BATMAN #56 variant cover
by FRANCESCO MATTINA

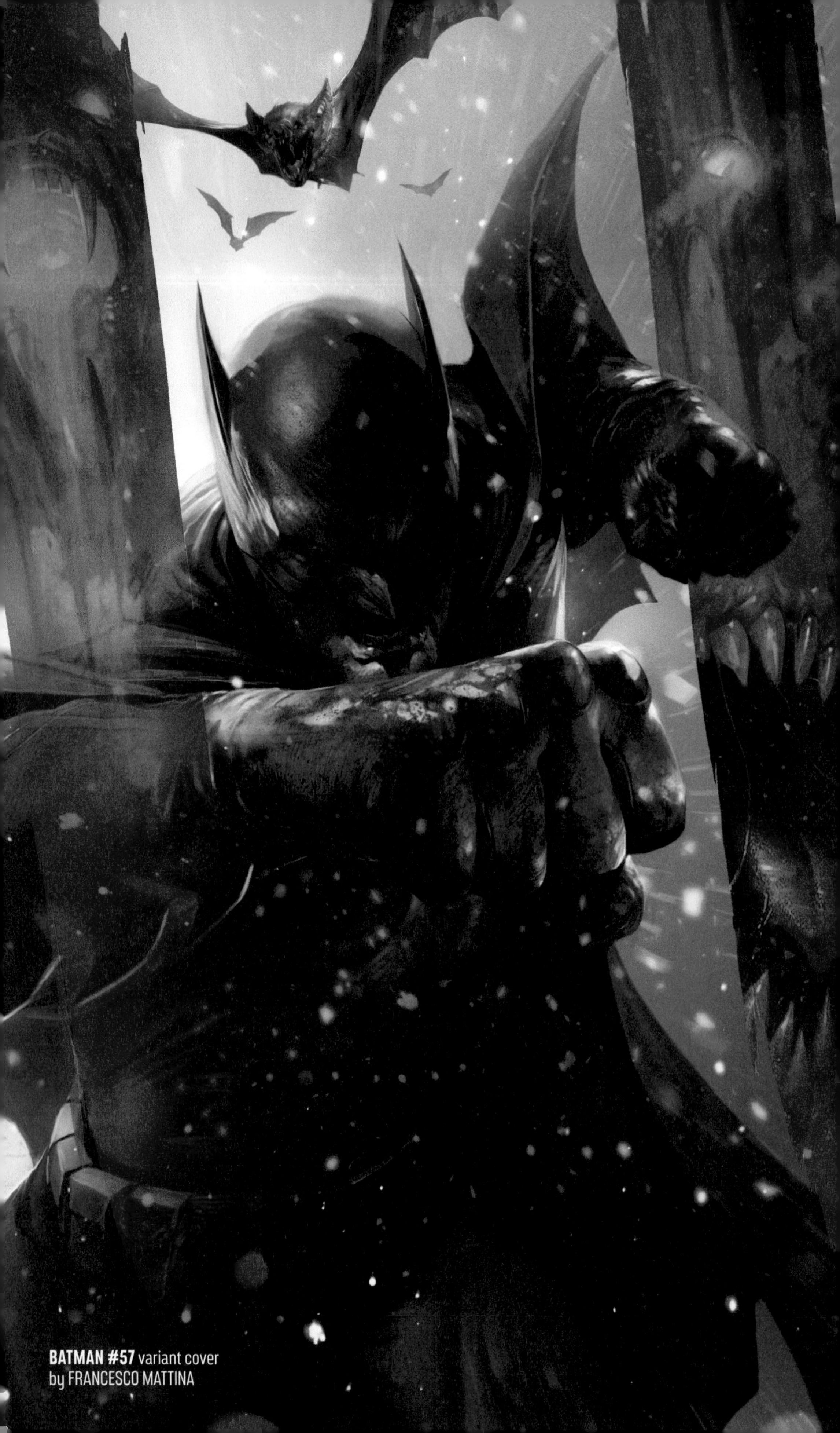

BATMAN #57 variant cover
by FRANCESCO MATTINA

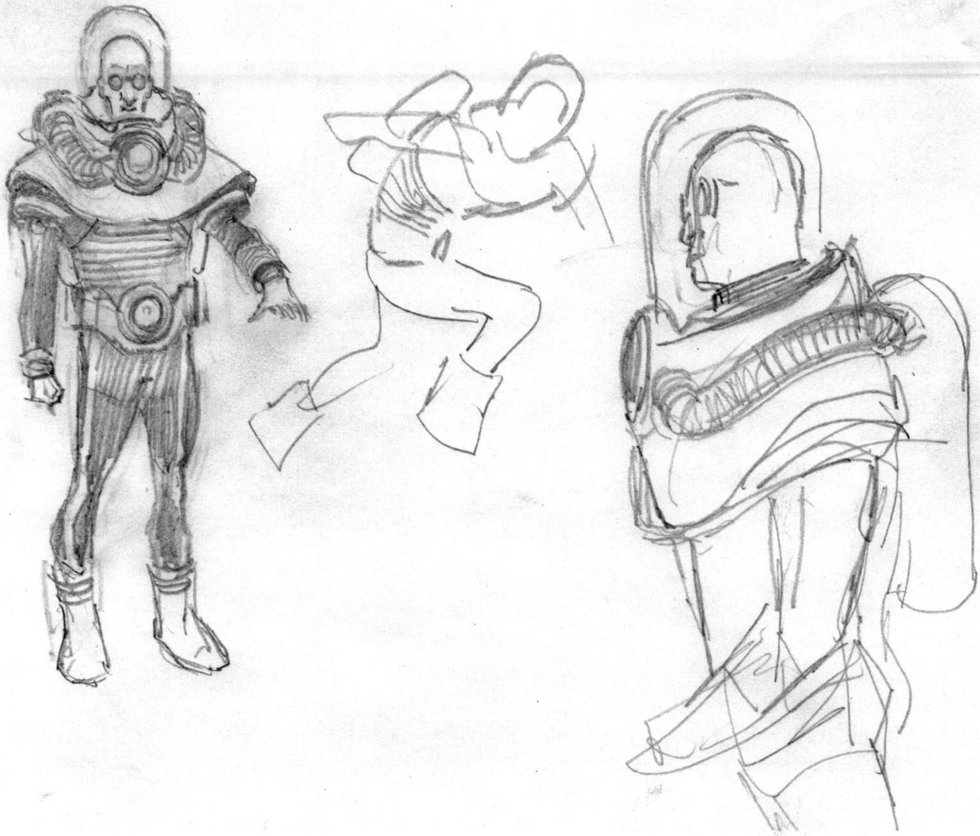

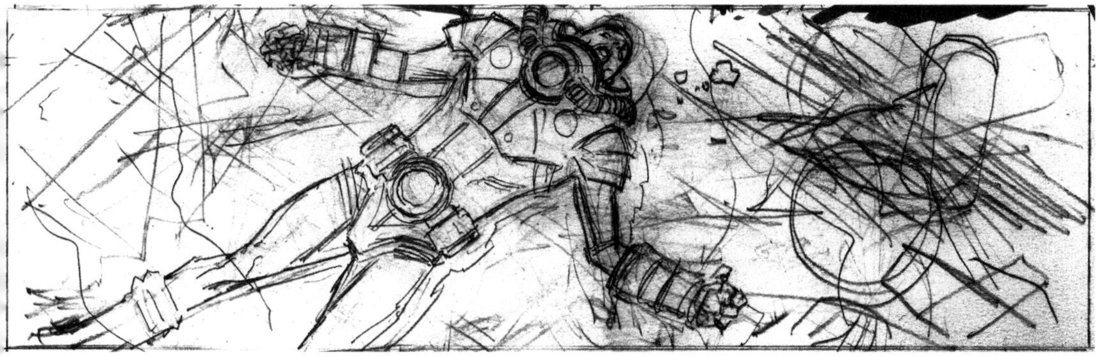

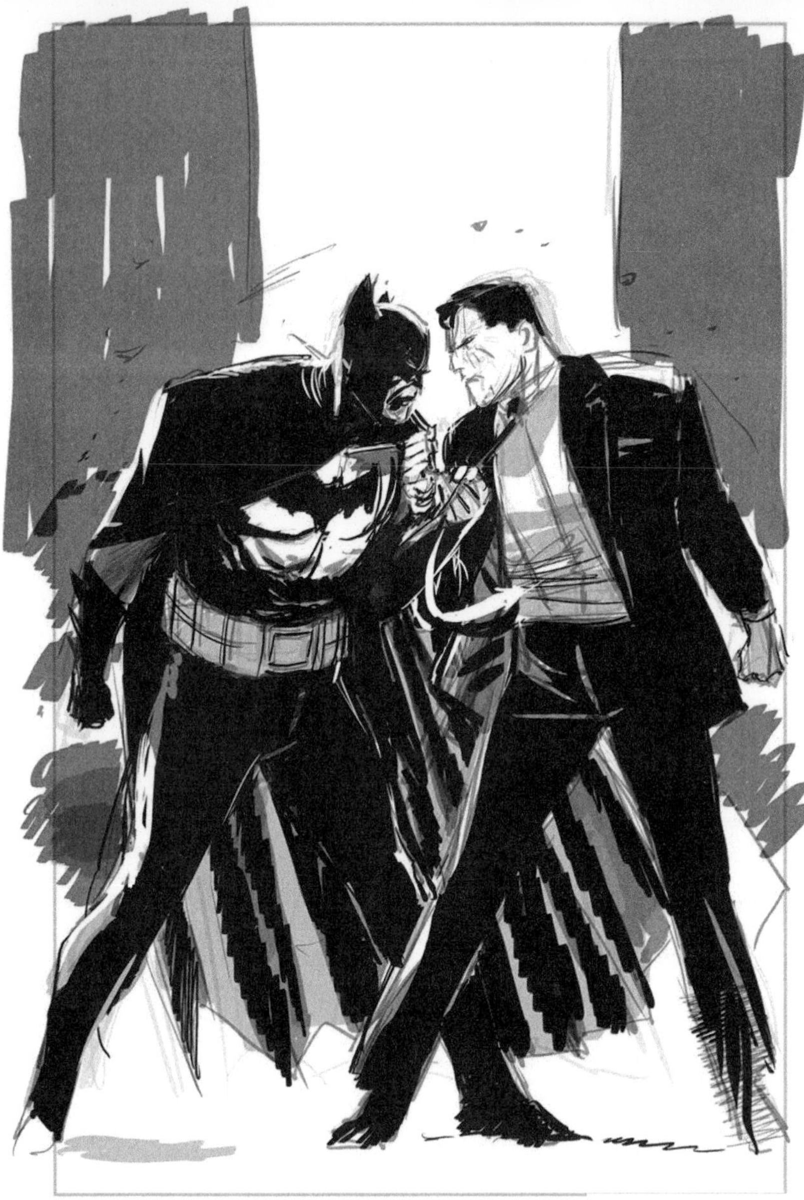

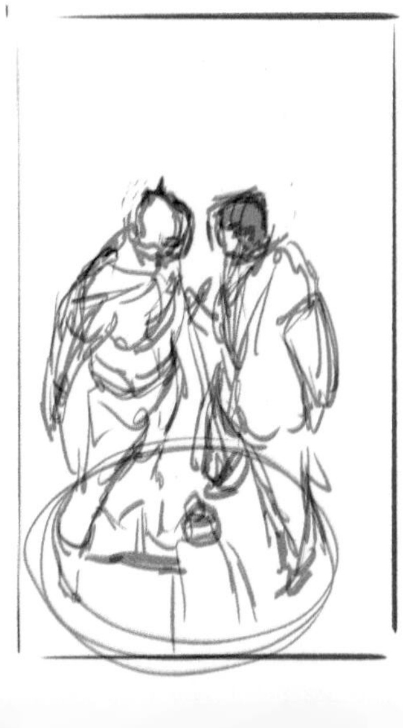

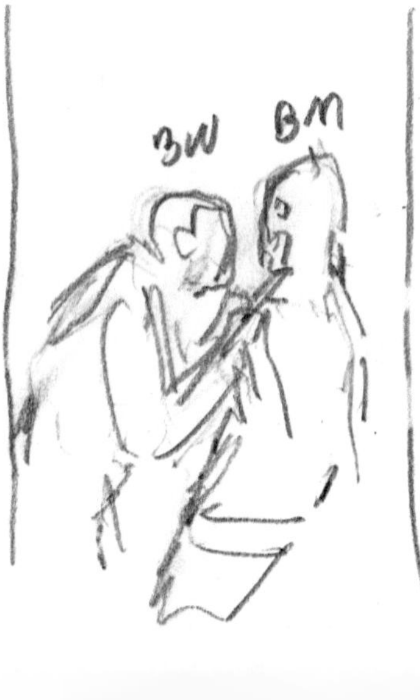
BW BM

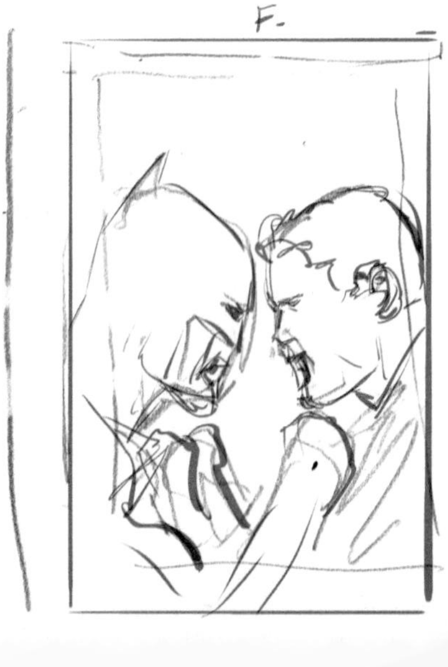
F.

A.

JUST LETTING
SETTING

B

GARGOYLE

B-2

GARGOYLE

B-3

GARGOYLE

E.

CW

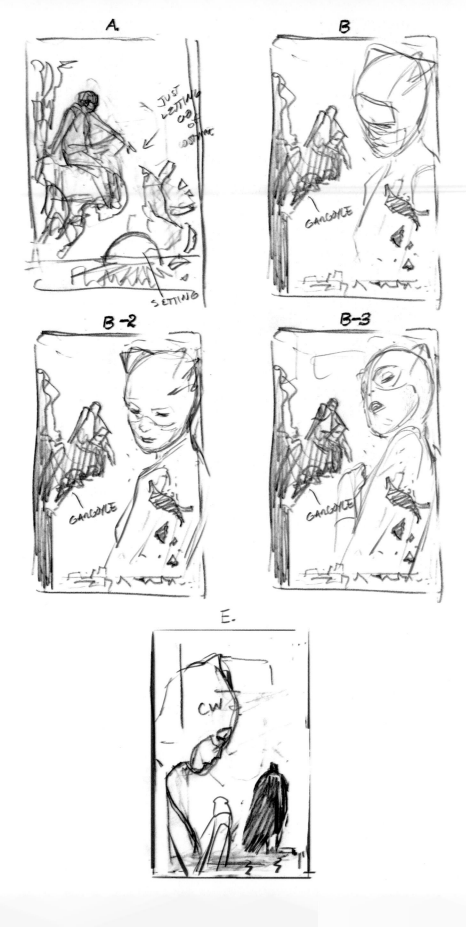

"Batman is getting a brand-new voice."
– USA TODAY

"A great showcase for the new team as well as offering a taste of the new flavor they'll be bringing to Gotham City." **– IGN**

DC UNIVERSE REBIRTH

BATMAN

VOL. 1: I AM GOTHAM

TOM KING
with DAVID FINCH

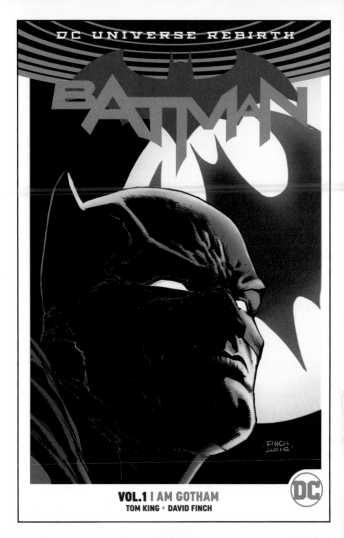

VOL.1 I AM GOTHAM
TOM KING * DAVID FINCH

**ALL-STAR BATMAN VOL. 1:
MY OWN WORST ENEMY**

**NIGHTWING VOL. 1:
BETTER THAN BATMAN**

**DETECTIVE COMICS VOL. 1:
RISE OF THE BATMEN**

Get more DC graphic novels wherever comics and books are sold!

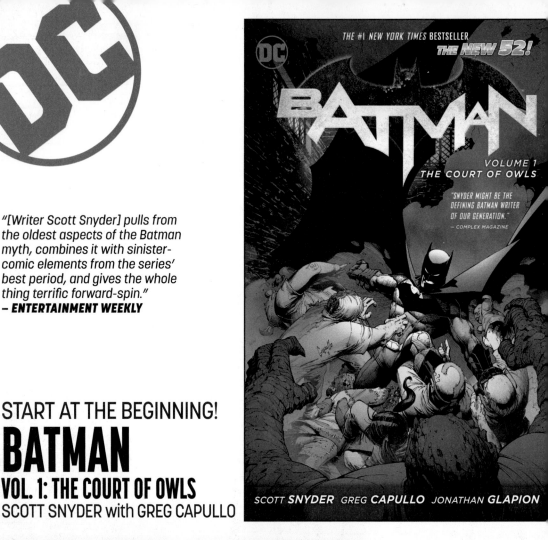
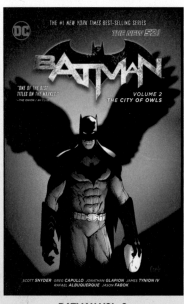
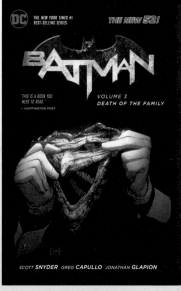